D1198884

The Complete

Cat

Encyclopedia

Forewords by Ivor Raleigh and Richard Gebhardt

Associate Editors in America
Blanche V. Smith and Raymond D. Smith

Special photographs by Anne Cumbers

The Complete Cat Encyclopedia

edited by Grace Pond

Crown Publishers, Inc.
New York

Library of Congress Catalog Card No: 72-77778
ISBN 517 500 175

First published in the U.S.A., 1972
by Crown Publishers, Inc.

Third Printing

Grace Pond
Author of
Warne's Observer's Book of Cats
Cats
Long-haired Cats
Pet Library's Complete Cat Guide
Batsford's Book of Cats
Cats — Pet and Fancy Series
The Perfect Cat Owner
Persian Cats
Editor of
Collins Cat Diary — annual
Contributor to
Chambers Encyclopaedia
Fur and Feather
Champion Cats of the World

Created by Walter Parrish International Limited, London, England

Designed by Alan Rice

Printed and bound in Yugoslavia by Mladinska Knjiga, Ljubljana

Forewords

All men, unless they be wholly evil, feel within them the need to express affection towards those creatures whom nature has endowed with beauty; and of all animals the domestic cat most abundantly possesses those qualities which are generally considered to be worthy of admiration. Like all true beauty, that of the cat is immanent as well as external. The splendid symmetry, the proud and graceful carriage, the natural fastidiousness and the admirable independence of the cat make him in every way an object supremely deserving of respect and even of love; and his persistent and widespread popularity throughout the ages bears witness to the fact that he inherently merits the fond attention which has always been bestowed upon him by all but the most base and insensitive of men.

Any creature that is worthy of love is also worthy of study; and in this respect the cat has proved no exception. Hundreds of books have been written about every aspect of his being in the tongue of every civilized land; many thousands of people throughout the wide world have grouped together in clubs and societies devoted to the task of classifying the lore of the cat, and of refining his natural beauty by the standard process of selective breeding, evaluated by expert judges at well-organised shows against the background of carefully and thoughtfully established Standards of Points. At the same time, the organisation of such clubs and societies, and participation in their numerous activities, has provided a very interesting and socially satisfying hobby for countless people.

At this point the writer of a foreword must ruthlessly thrust aside the intellectual opportunities which this subject offers, and confine himself to the task in hand, which is to introduce the cat lover to a work compiled by a large number of exceptionally experienced people who possess collectively a formidable body of knowledge, not only of the cat, but of the relationship between the cat and man. Many of the contributors to this excellent work are well-known to the writer; and gladly and confidently he enjoins the reader to profit by what they and their colleagues have to say.

Dr Ivor Raleigh
Chairman, Governing Council of the Cat Fancy.

A century of organized interest in cats has just passed. The leading cat associations in America have growr up. We in America have not celebrated a hundred years as our English counterparts have, but we have enjoyed and benefited from their years of breeding fine cats. My twenty-five years in cats has enabled me to witness a dramatic growth in the feline world. I have had the honour and pleasure of working with many of the great leaders throughout the world.

The governing associations of the American cat fancy, including the largest, the Cat Fanciers Association, have been a strong force in the organization of the fancy. American breeders take pride in themselves in their efforts to protect the pure breeding of many of the sacred breeds of long existence. We have made great contributions along with the Governing Council of the Cat Fancy, in Great Britain, and the Fédération Internationale Féline de l'Europe on the European continent, in developing new breeds, new colours, and new mutations, which have done so much to broaden the interest in cats.

The American fanciers are indebted to the outstanding breeders of England, whose stock has given us the very foundations from which our great cats descend. Today, the C.F.A. and the other American associations have initiated programmes which are aimed at bringing unity and uniformity to the cat fancy throughout the world. Our constant effort to exchange judges, to encourage the importing and exporting of bloodlines as well as the exchange of knowledge in scientific research, has played an important role in our desire to unite our interest in cats.

The C.F.A. is the largest cat organisation in America, and the C.F.A.'s international committee has created a council to bring better understanding of the efforts of all foreign societies. The C.F.A. Judges Association had added professionalism to our highly skilled judges and the C.F.A. Year Book has become one of the most valued books of reference in recording the history of the American feline. Today the American cat fancier has the benefit of the finest up-to-date computer service possible. Twenty-seven thousand cats were registered in 1971 by the C.F.A. alone for a total income of over $162,000.

This book is evidence of the spreading interest in cats. In addition, as breeders and fanciers, we have to dedicate ourselves not only for the development of the animal but also for the welfare and the protection of all cats. Then and only then can we take pride in the awards we receive.

Richard H. Gebhardt
President, Cat Fanciers Association Inc.

Contents

The terms "Long-hairs" and "Short-hairs" are used here purely descriptively. The long-hairs, other than Angora, Balinese, Birman, Himalayan, Maine Coon and Turkish, are often grouped together in America as colour varieties of "Persian". In Britain there is a quite separate Standard for each long-hair recognized—the term "Persian" is no longer used officially.

Other Matters Relating to Cats

Colour Plates

Editor's Introduction

The history of the domestic cat is long and varied, going back thousands of years, and rich in legendary and magical associations. By the time of the Ancient Egyptians, several thousand years ago, the cat was firmly established as one of the most prominent domestic animals and, indeed, was elevated to the level of a god by the civilisation of that time. Over the centuries, however, the cat has had an important part to play, too, as a working animal – even in ancient times it was trained for hunting, and has always been used to keep down rats and mice on farms and in the home.

Perhaps it is just because the cat has always been so familiar to us and to our ancestors, that comparatively little has ever been written down about its beginnings and early history. It is only within the last century or so that there have been "fancy" or pedigree cats, and we know relatively little about the origins of the individual breeds and varieties before that. In 1971, the National Cat Club held its 75th Championship Cat Show at Olympia, London – this was a special occasion, celebrating as it did the centenary of cat shows as we know them, for it was a hundred years before then that the world's first official cat show was held – in 1871 at the Crystal Palace in London. This was, in itself, a relatively small affair, but it was from this event that directly or indirectly, all the cat fancies of the world today sprang. It was not until the first cat shows had been held, both in Great Britain and the United States of America, that it was realised that people were interested in cats with specific coat colours and patterns; and fanciers began to plan breeding in the hope of obtaining more certain results.

In comparison with, say, dogs, differences in the sizes and shapes of cats are relatively small; but the early days of the cat fancy saw the gradual introduction of many new varieties into Great Britain and North America from other parts of the world, notably the East, and clear variations in type and coat began to emerge. Eventually, through selected or unplanned matings, three main types were established. Most members of the general public know the main differences between the long-hairs or Persians (in Great Britain the term "long-hair" has officially replaced "Persian" in breed names, although the latter is used officially elsewhere in the world, and still commonly by fanciers in Britain); the British, American and Exotic Short-hairs; and the "foreign" varieties, such as the Siamese. Several varieties do not quite fit into these categories, but the differences are relatively small. Breeding today is becoming a more and more sophisticated business, and the possible permutations of fur colourings and coat patterns more and more numerous, with coat lengths varying from the very long to the comparatively hairless Sphynx.

Governing bodies and cat clubs have come into being in practically all countries, with more and more shows being held, and the numbers of entries increasing annually. The biggest show in Britain can expect entries literally in thousands, and the numbers are not so very far behind elsewhere in the world. Registrations are ever increasing, as is the sale of pedigree stock, and the world's cat fancies will have to follow the lead of the Americans in modernising methods and procedures to cope with an ever-increasing volume of work.

Against this background, the need for a book such as *The Complete Cat Encyclopaedia* is all the more apparent. There has never before been an attempt to present the reader with such a detailed and comprehensive picture of the cat world within a single volume. The fancier will find no lack of small handbooks on cats, or books dealing in greater detail with a particular breed, but cat lovers will agree that the pedigree cat deserves a more serious and comprehensive approach. The articles in this book have been specially written by people with first-hand knowledge of their subject, who have set down in great detail their knowledge and experience concerning the breeds in which they are interested. Without doubt, this authoritative information will be of great value to all interested in cats. Unfortunately. space does not permit the inclusion of contributions from all the famous British and American breeders whose stock appears consistently among the winners; but those included are an impressive cross-section of the cat world's leading authorities.

The part of the book dealing with the breeds themselves is divided into two sections – long-hairs and short-hairs. The reader will find therein articles on all the breeds recognized in Britain or America or both, plus articles on breeds which are being experimentally bred, but which are not yet recognized – part of the fascination of the breeders' work is the establishment of new breed characteristics on a scientifically sound basis. Each variety is dealt with in much the same way, beginning with a full account of its origins and subsequent history. In many cases the names of famous cats of the past are mentioned, whose names appear many generations back in the pedigrees of some of today's winners. Special points of character, care and show grooming are fully dealt with. For reasons of space it would obviously have been impracticable to include, in full, the G.C.C.F. Standards for each breed, plus all the different descriptions accepted officially by the nine different North American registering authorities, and so a general description is given, setting out the salient points in the Standards, and highlighting any significant differences between the Standards of different authorities for the same breed. Of course, anyone contemplating taking up breeding or exhibiting in a serious way should obtain a copy of the breed Standards from the appropriate body.

After the breed articles there are a number dealing with the many more general aspects of cats and their welfare, ranging over nutrition, breeding, boarding, showing, evolution and history, and so on – making in all a most comprehensive and informative book. Particular attention has been paid to the photographs, both black and white and in colour, many specially taken by the eminent animal photographer, Anne Cumbers. From the point of view of the serious enthusiast, one of the most novel aspects of the book is the way in which a series of photographs of a male and female cat from different vantage points are included in many of the articles for comparison, and Anne Cumbers and I are most grateful to all the owners of the many cats shown, for their patience and co-operation. Several photographs are included to show bad points as well as good; there are photographs of numerous champions from many parts of the world, and from the recent and more distant past.

The notes on the contributors give a brief resumé of their careers and achievements in the cat world, and the bibliography lists many books on cats, both old and new. Some of the old, alas, are difficult to obtain, but may be picked up from time to time in second-hand book shops, but the majority mentioned may probably be obtained from local libraries or from book shops.

I am particularly grateful to my co-editor, Mrs Blanche Smith, who has worked hard to ensure that the book presents a true picture of the American cat fancy; to Mrs Edna Field for her contribution on the Canadian cat scene; to Mrs M. Batten, for writing on the cat fancy in Australia and New Zealand; and to Mrs L. Emery, who wrote on South Africa. I would like to thank, for their forewords, Dr Ivor Raleigh, Chairman of the Governing Council of the Cat Fancy, and Mr Richard Gebhardt, President of the Cat Fanciers Association, and I am grateful to the Governing Council of the Cat Fancy and the American governing authorities for the official Standards given throughout the book. Generally, I would like to thank anyone who has helped in any way towards the writing and production of this book.

Grace Pond F.Z.S.

Acknowledgments

Photograph Credits

The photographs in this book have been obtained from various sources in Britain and America, some of them selected by the contributors themselves. The publishers express their gratitude for the photographs and for the information and advice on individual subjects during the preparation of the book.

So many photographs are included that there is not sufficient space for us to credit each individual picture to the photographer whose work it is, and we have therefore listed them, initially in the order of magnitude of each photographer's contribution, and subsequently in alphabetical order.

The majority of the black and white and colour photographs were specially taken for this book by Anne Cumbers of Reigate, Surrey, England, including both pictures on the cover design. Serge Serafino of Paris, France, provided 18 photographs; Sonia Halliday of Weston Turville, Bucks, 8; and Creszentia and Albert Allen, of West Orange, New Jersey, U.S.A., 7. Photographs were also contributed by Victor Baldwin of California, U.S.A.; Bamsen's International Press Service Limited, London; Bill Beck of Towson Md, U.S.A.; Beckett Newspapers, Littlehampton, England; Hans Bomskow of Glendale, U.S.A.; The British Museum, London; *Cats Magazine*, U.S.A.; Jan Claire, U.S.A.; Curtis, U.S.A.; Davis and Davis, U.S.A.; George W. F. Ellis of Bodmin, Cornwall, England; Hal Fisher of San Diego, Texas, U.S.A.; Adam Frecowski of Chicago Heights, Illinois, U.S.A.; S. & A. Frith of Sheffield, England; Raymond Garnett of London; Terence A. Gili, U.S.A.; The Globe & Mail, Toronto, Canada; Holland's Farm, Tarzana, California, U.S.A.; Gordon Jarvis, California, U.S.A.; Johnny Johnston of California; Ellen P. Laflin of New York; Donald A. Larson, U.S.A.; Daphne Negus of California; Allen Nield of Stockport, England; Jim Shinkle of San Francisco, U.S.A.; Hugh Smith of Sevenoaks, Kent, England; Joseph R. Spies of Arlington 1, Va, U.S.A.; John Thorne of Sheffield, England; I. Vincent of Australia; The Zoological Society, London.

The drawing for the endpaper design was by Janet Fairman, of London, England; those for the article on Anatomy, by Frank Jackson, of Crawley, Sussex, England.

Opposite: Pathfinders Stormflash (male),
a Bi-Coloured Long-hair bred and owned
by Miss N. Woodifield.

Above: Ch Deebank Gay Cavalier (male), a Black Long-hair bred by Miss M. Bull and owned by Mrs L. Shepard.

Dixiecrest Dreamtime, an American blue and white Bi-Coloured Persian owned by Mrs Barbara Prendergast and Mrs Joyce Miller.

Opposite: An American Black Persian male; Gr Ch J.B.'s Mr Moor, bred and owned by Richard Gebhardt.

Ch Honeymist Tiamaria, a female Blue-cream Long-hair, bred and owned by Mrs M. Howes.

Below: Simbelair Meisha, a female Blue-cream Persian, or Long-hair, bred and owned in Canada by Mrs Lois Weston.

A male Shaded Cameo, Gowlaren Orpheus,
owned by Miss E. Sellar.

Above: Six Peachy Pink Cameo kittens, owned by Mrs Ellis and Mr and Mrs Britton.

Below: Nevern Una, a Blue Long-hair bred by Miss P. Broadwater and owned by Mrs Grace Pond.

Above: Three of Mrs R. Gowdy's Jemari Chinchilla kittens.

Below: A female Chinchilla, Mrs F. Roden's Chicquot Milady.

Above: Mrs S. Harding's male seal-pointed Colourpoint Long-hair, Ch Mingchiu Mudoba. The Colourpoint Long-hair is known in America as the Himalayan.

Opposite: Quadruple Gr Ch Ren Sim's Shai, a Himalayan male bred and owned by Mary L. Misner of New Jersey.

Right: Ch Mingchiu Chirk (male), blue-pointed Colourpoint Long-hair, bred and owned by Mrs Harding.

Honeymist Cream Tiara, a female Cream Long-hair bred and owned by Mrs M. Howes.

The Maine Coon, one of the oldest North American breeds.

Mr R. Chapman's Long-haired Brown Tabby male, Ch Karnak Brochfael.

Below: Ch Plantagenet Vetta, a Long-haired Silver Tabby female owned by Mr Chapman.

Ch Bruton Angelo, a male Red Tabby Long-hair, bred and owned by Mrs Ṅ. Rosell.

*Above: Mrs L. Russell's Turkish female,
Van Fethiye.*

*Two Tortoiseshell Long-hair females:
Mrs V. Ford's Bruton Bronze Maid and
Beach Girl.*

Two "Plantagenet" Silver Tabby Long-hair kittens at eight weeks.

Long-hairs

A fine Chinchilla from America—three-year-old Gr Ch Gray-Ivy Bouffant of Fayron, a female owned by Mr and Mrs Ronnie Acosta of California.

Angora

An adult female Angora, with a fine, silky coat.

For many years, the terms "Angora" and "Persian" were used almost synonymously, and most people outside the cat fancy used them to mean "long-haired cat".

The name of the breed, Angora, is an earlier form of the name of Ankara, the Turkish capital. An ancient breed in that country, these cats were also mentioned in some of the early cat books. In *Our Cats and All About Them*, published in 1889, Harrison Weir writes: "The best are of high value, a pure white with blue eyes, being thought the perfection of cats, all other points being good, and its hearing by no means defective. . . . The colours are varied, but the black which should have orange eyes, as should also the slate colours, and blues, and the white are the most esteemed. . . ." In England, during this period, there were also reports of Smokes.

The Ankara Zoo now protects its famous breed of cats by supervizing and maintaining a strict breeding programme. Only white Angoras are raised and accurate records are kept on all the offspring. It is extremely difficult to secure these cats from the Zoo, but in 1963 an American couple, Colonel and Mrs Walter Grant, were finally given special permission from the Governor of Ankara to take an unrelated pair to the United States. The female, Yildizçek, was amber-eyed, and the male, Yildiz, odd-eyed, with one eye brilliant blue and the other amber. Although there are, no doubt, other Angoras in North America, taken there by various means, these two cats were the first "official" ones to arrive, complete with all their records. In 1966, Col. and Mrs

This adult male Angora, from Thornton's Desert Cattery in Arizona, U.S.A., shows the tapering jaw and long ears described in the provisional Standard for the breed.

The Angora is finer-boned than the "Persian" varieties—this is an adult male; as with many breeds, females tend to be a little smaller than the males.

Grant returned to Turkey and, as previously arranged, bought another unrelated pair, only this time reversing the eye colours, with the female, Mavis, being odd-eyed and the male, Yaman, having amber eyes.

Possibly because the Zoo raised only the white Angoras, this is the only colour accepted in North America at the present time, although the three different eye colours are allowed – amber, blue and odd-eyed. While white is reported as being dominant in cats, absorbing all other colours over a period of time, it can, apparently, carry other colours as a recessive and it is possible that another colour could appear in a litter.

Unfortunately, as in most breeds of white-coated cats, deafness can occur, especially in the blue-eyed and odd-eyed cats, and breeders must be especially careful to place the deaf or partly deaf cats in homes where the owners will understand and allow for the partial handicap.

The Angora differs considerably in body-type and coat texture from the Persian. Compared to the short, cobby body, round massive head and short nose and tail of the Persian, the Angora has a longer body, head, legs and tapering tail. But although structurally so different from the Persian, the Angora is still solid and firm, yet lithe and graceful. The medium-length coat is silky and fine, with a tendency to wave, especially on the stomach. Not nearly as heavy as that of the Persian, the soft coat improves with age and as the Angora does not mature until approximately two years of age, the coat continues to improve each year.

The Angora is extremely intelligent, affectionate and quick to learn simple tricks, and eager to "show off" to company. Breeders and owners of these delightful cats are always emphatic about the wonderful temperament and personality of this breed, which no doubt will soon be taking its place in the championship classes of North American cat shows, although, at present, included in the non-championship "Provisional Breed" class. It is not recognized in Great Britain.

The provisional Standard for the Angora calls for a small-to-medium-sized head, wide at the top, and with a definite taper towards the gently-rounded chin. The jaw should be tapered, and the nose of medium length with a gentle slope and no break. The ears should be wide at the base, long, pointed and tufted. The Angora's eyes should be large, almond to round in shape, and with a slight slant upwards. The body of the female Angora is small to medium in size, while the male is slightly larger. A long and graceful torso is combined with a light-framed chest. The Angora is fine-boned; Persian type is a disqualification fault on the show bench. The legs are long, the hind legs slightly more so than the front, so that the rump is carried slightly higher than the front of the cat. The paws are dainty, small and round, with tufts between the toes.

The tail should be long and tapering, with a wide base, and narrow at the end. It is a full tail, carried lower than the body but not so as to trail along the ground. In movement, the cat carries its relaxed tail horizontally over the body, sometimes almost touching the head.

The Angora must have a pure white coat – no other colouring is acceptable. Paw pads, lips and nose leather should be pink. Mottling on pads or nose leather is to be considered a fault on the show bench.

Balinese

Long-hair

The Balinese shows the same type and coat-pattern as the Siamese, but carries long, silky fur. This young blue-pointed male comes from Holland's Farm Cattery in California.

In the early 1950's, several Siamese breeders in the U.S.A. were amazed to find "fuzzy" kittens appearing among litters of "normal" Siamese kittens, especially as both parents were pure-bred and from good pedigrees, with no possible faults in the background. Most of these kittens were destroyed as undesirable and their appearances kept secret, or they were placed in homes as hybrid pets. However, two breeders, Mrs Helen Smith of New York and Mrs Marion Dorsey of California, decided that they should not be so treated. They were treasured, raised and bred and it was discovered that the "long-haired" Siamese bred true and produced litters of all-long-haired kittens.

Interest soon spread and before long, kittens were placed with other breeders who were determined to establish the new breed. At this time, another name was sought, as breeders of normal-coated Siamese objected to the term "Long-haired Siamese" and, in addition, the lovely new cats deserved a more exotic name. The Eastern-sounding name "Balinese" was readily accepted. In 1968 a club, the Balinese Breeders and Fans of America, was formed.

Many people still ask "What is the difference between a Balinese and a Himalayan?" There is a very great difference; the Balinese has the same type as the Siamese – the only difference is the fur, which should be two inches or more in length and silky in texture. The Himalayan breed has the Persian type (short, cobby body, round massive head, short nose and tail) with Siamese colouring. The temperament of the Balinese cat is – naturally enough – very much like that of the Siamese although the voice is usually not as loud. The daily grooming chore of the Persian cat is not necessary for the Balinese, for the latter's coat is soft, silky and seldom mats. Depending on the climatic conditions, the Balinese seldom sheds heavily and the daily care is extremely simple – usually no more attention is needed than that given most short-hairs.

Combining a gentle, affectionate nature with exotic grace the Balinese is steadily gaining popularity in North America. Before being accepted for championship status, the Balinese breeders kept lengthy careful and accurate records. After many years of showing, in non-championship A.O.V. classes, the Balinese were finally accepted by one of the American associations – C.F.F. – in 1963. They are now accepted by all the American and by the Canadian registering Associations for full championship competition and are recognized in four colours – seal-point, chocolate-point, blue-point and lilac-point.

According to the Standard, the ideal Balinese is a svelte, dainty cat with long tapering lines, very lithe but muscular in build. The head is a long, tapering wedge, medium-sized and in good proportion to the body; the wedge starts at the nose and flares out in straight lines to the tips of the ears, to form a triangle, with no break at the whiskers.

The skull is flat in profile, forming a long straight line from the top of the head to the tip of the nose. There should be no bulge over the eyes, or dip in the nose, which should be long and straight. The Balinese has strikingly large ears, pointed and wide at the base, continuing the lines of the wedge-shaped head. The eyes are medium-sized, almond-shaped, and slant towards the nose. They should be uncrossed, and placed well within the frontal plane of the face.

The neck is long and slender, as are the legs; the hind legs should be higher than the front. Paws are dainty, small and oval, and the tail long and thin, tapering to a fine point.

The coat of the Balinese should be long, fine and silky, and even in colour, with subtle shading where this is allowed. You have to make allowance for darker colour in older cats, as Balinese generally darken with age – but there must be definite contrast between body colour and points. Points colour should be dense, and clearly defined, and all the points should be of the same shade without white hairs. The mask should cover the entire face including the whisker pads, and is connected to the ears by tracings. It should not extend over the top of the head.

In the seal-point variety the body colour is an even pale fawn to cream, warm in tone, shading gradually into a lighter colour on the stomach and chest; points a deep seal-brown, nose leather and paw pads the same colour as the points. Partial or total lack of pigment in the nose leather of any variety of Balinese is considered a fault. The chocolate-point has an ivory body with no shading; points milk-chocolate in colour and warm in tone, nose leather and paw pads cinnamon pink. The bluish-white body of the blue-point is cold in tone, shading gradually to white on the stomach and chest; points colour deep blue, nose leather and paw pads slate-coloured. In the lilac-point the body is glacial white with no shading; points a frosty grey with a pinkish tone, nose leather and paw pads lavender-pink.

All varieties of Balinese have deep vivid blue eyes.

Holland's Farm Bali-Katuk and Saba of Chen Ye, male and female seal-pointed Balinese.

Bi-Coloured   *Long-hair*

At eighteen months, this red and white
Bi-Coloured female, Miss N. Woodifield's
Pathfinders Wild Poppy, shows a pleasing
expression, good eyes and long-hair type.

Cats of two colours are among the oldest varieties and have been
exhibited in "Any other Colour" classes ever since the first cat shows
were held. They were known as "Magpie" cats, and as the name
implies, were mostly black and white, but blue and white, orange and
white, and cream and white were the other colour variations. The
Standard then was very exact and was set to resemble the markings of
a Dutch rabbit. The self-colour, i.e. black, blue, orange or cream had
to start immediately behind the shoulder around the barrel of the body,
and to include the tail and hind legs, leaving the hind feet white. The
ears and mask of the face were also self-coloured. White shoulders,
neck, forelegs and feet, chin and lips were white; as also the blaze up
face and over the top of the head, joining or running into the white at
the back of the skull, thus dividing the mask exactly in halves.

This pattern has been bred to a high degree of excellence in the
Dutch rabbit, but for obvious reasons, it has not been possible to do
this with cats, and for some time it has been realised that the Standard
for Bi-Colours was impractical. The distribution of self colour and
white is not strictly patterned, and for the Dutch rabbit coloration to

From America, Dixiecrest Joy of Olde-
Calico, a cream and white Bi-Coloured
female Persian, owned by Mrs Barbara
Prendergast and Miss Joyce Miller.

Mrs R. Knight's female Greenwood Goldilocks.

Pathfinders Wild Poppy, showing a beautifully groomed coat.

Above: Pathfinders Tangle, an outstanding black and white male. He was exported to America, but lost in a fire after making a great contribution to the breed there.

Below: Greenwood Trudi, dam of Greenwood Goldilocks.

be reproduced consistently it would be necessary for a new gene to appear.

At the time of writing, the Bi-Colours in Britain do not possess a specialist club of their own, and the Colourpoint, Rex-Coated and A.O.V. Club caters for their needs. In 1971, the committee of this club, in consultation with other informed people, submitted an amended Standard for Bi-Coloured Long-hairs and Short-hairs, which was accepted by the Governing Council of the Cat Fancy. This revised Standard, which came into operation in June 1971, allows much more latitude in the distribution of colour and markings. Any colour and white, with not more than two-thirds of the cat's coat to be coloured and not more than a half to be white, is the new requirement. In America, this colour of Persian is now recognised by C.F.A., but has made little headway in the independent registering bodies. It is known, however, that many of the long-haired cats first registered in the U.S.A. were Bi-Colours. There is a National Bi-Color Club with some thirty members.

The proposed American Standards call for same type and coat features as all other Persians; colour patterns are similar to those of the British Standard.

As with the Tortoiseshell and White, the charm of Bi-Colours lies in their individuality – alike, in having two colours in the coat, yet each possessing a different beauty; this is their fascination. In the days when the Dutch rabbit pattern was strictly required, many fine exhibits, conforming in all but small detail to the exact markings, had Challenge Certificates withheld, and it was rare for a Bi-Colour to become a Champion. Now the amended Standard opens the way for new interest in the breeding and showing of these lovely, striking cats.

In 1966, Bi-Coloured Long-hairs and Short-hairs were granted recognition with championship status. Miss Norah Woodifield, breeder of the well-known Pathfinders prefix, bred the first Bi-Colour champion in England, Ch Pathfinders Sunray (red and white), now in Sweden. Ch Pathfinders Goldstrike (male) and Ch Pathfinders Brightstone (female), both red and white; and two fine black and white males, Ch Pathfinders Pacemaker and the late Pathfinders Tangle, went to the U.S.A.

It is necessary to use sires of top quality to up-grade breeding stock. Outstanding males of solid colour can be used for the purpose of improving type, but this should be done with discretion and not too often, or too many self-coloured kittens may appear in future litters. A Red Self stud or a Cream (the dilute form of red) can be mated to a red-and-white or a cream-and-white queen in the hope of obtaining red-and-white or cream-and-white bi-coloured kittens. Similarly, a Black stud can be used for a black-and-white queen, a Blue for a blue-and-white, etc. If the colours are crossed, e.g. black to red-and-white, blue to cream-and-white, etc., kittens of three colours may result, e.g. Tortoiseshell, Tortoiseshell-and-White or their dilute varieties.

I have found Bi-Colours to be hardy, long-lived cats, resistant to disease and easy, straightforward breeders. Perhaps their mixed ancestry of solid and broken colour may have something to do with this. They also grow to a large size. Their care and management is the

same as for any other breed of cat, plenty of good, varied food, fresh
air and space for exercise. Fresh water should always be available, day
and night. It is surprising how this can be overlooked, but it is very
important.

The grooming and show preparation of Bi-Colours is similar to that
for other long-hairs, but I do not use powder on the coat, as this dulls
the contrast between the self-colour and white. The appearance of the
cat should be immaculate and sparkling, with the colour clearly defined. An off-white coat completely spoils the effect. In Britain, the
Standard of Points describing the long-haired Bi-Colours since June
1971 calls for a combination of any solid colour and white. The patches
of colour must be clear, even, and well-distributed. Not more than
two-thirds of the cat's coat should be coloured, and not more than a
half white. The cat's face should be patched with colour and white.
Tabby markings are a fault. The coat should have a silky texture, and
it should be long and flowing, extra-long on the frill and tail. The body
of the cat should be cobby and massive in build, with short, thick legs,
and a short, full tail. If the tail is long it is a fault.

Our Bi-Colour should have a round and broad head – there should be
a good width between the ears, which should themselves be small, well-
placed and tufted. The cat's face is characterised by a short, broad
nose, full cheeks, wide muzzle and firm chin. The large round eyes
should be set well apart, and coloured deep orange or copper – yellow
or green eyes are a fault.

Birman

Ch Praha Hu-Tsung, Mrs E. Fisher's seal-point Birman male. The characteristic coat pattern is clearly visible—the Birman has seal-brown or blue points, but the paws themselves are white.

The Birman is an exotic cat, majestic in its demeanour but, at the same time, very friendly and intelligent by nature. Although it originated in Burma, this breed should not be confused with the Burmese, to which it is quite unrelated.

One of the most striking features of the Birman is its colour – its body fur is of a creamy-gold shade, while for the points – that is, the mask, ears, tail and eyes – the British Standard recognises either seal-brown or blue. The colouring of the legs is particularly characteristic; the paws themselves are white and, on the hind legs, the white area reaches to the first joint, coming to a point on the heel, like a gauntlet.

The unusual colouring of the Birman is the subject of a charming legend. Centuries ago, the Khmer people of Asia built the Temple of Lao-Tsun in which to worship a golden goddess with sapphire-blue eyes, Tsun-Kyan-Kse. Mun-Ha, a much-loved priest, often knelt in meditation before the goddess with Sinh, a beautiful white temple cat, beside him gazing at the golden figure. One night raiders attacked the temple and Mun-Ha was killed. As he died, Sinh placed his feet upon his fallen master and faced the golden goddess. As he did so, the hairs of his white body turned golden, and his yellow eyes to sapphire-blue, like hers; his four white legs turned earthy brown – but where his paws rested gently on his dead master, they remained white as a symbol of purity. Next morning, the hundred white cats of the temple were as golden as Sinh, who did not leave the sacred throne until, seven days later, he died, and carried his master's soul into paradise. Since that time, whenever a sacred cat died in the Temple of Lao-Tsun, the soul of a priest was said to accompany it on its journey to the hereafter.

At this point legend ends, and history begins. The temple was left in peace until it was raided at the beginning of this century. Two westerners, Auguste Pavie and Major Gordon Russell, came to the aid of the priests; as a gesture of gratitude the priests later sent to the two men, then living in France, a pair of Birman; this was in 1919. Unfortunately, the male did not survive the ocean trip; but the female by then was pregnant, and the survival of the breed in the West was ensured. The earliest pedigrees were lost; the breed as we know it, and which was recognised in France in 1925, stems from one pair, Orloff and Xenia de Kaabaa. But the Birmans were to suffer further setbacks in Europe – after a relatively prosperous period in France in the 1930's, by the end of the Second World War, there was once again only a single surviving pair, and it took many years for the variety to recover.

In the early 1960's, Mrs E. Fisher, whose main interest had been the breeding of Siamese, became fascinated with the Birman, also known as the Sacred Cats of Burma, with their distinctive white-gloved paws, after seeing them at the shows in Europe. Together with Mrs M. Richards, she imported the first Birmans to be seen in Britain. These included Ch Nouky de Mon Reve, a male seal-point, bred in France in 1964 by Madame Poirier (owner Mrs M. Richards), a

This fine seal-point Birman, bred in America by Rolph Griswold, is owned by Mr and Mrs G. L. Soper.

Pipo Duclos Fleuri, a seal-point male with good head and frill.

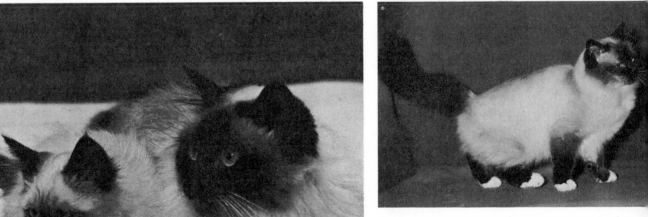

Above: Merlika, female, a seal-point International Champion from France.

Left: Mrs M. Richard's Paranjoti Isolde, a fine queen, showing distinctive points colouring and white gloves, with one of her promising young kittens.

Paranjoti Kathmandu, a blue-point female with good type.

female, Orlamonde de Khlaramour, a blue-point (owner Mrs E. Fisher), bred in France in 1965 by Madame A. Moulin, and the Champion Osaka de Lugh, another blue-point female bred in France in 1966 by Madame Y. Broissier, owned by Mrs Fisher.

These imports and others which followed have become the foundation for Birman breeding in Britain, and Praha (Mrs Fisher) and Paranjoti (Mrs Fisher and Mrs Richards) kittens have been exported all over the world. Other British fanciers have entered the Birman scene and the variety is at least as popular in Britain as it is in France. As well as the original blue- and seal-points, lilac-points are now appearing.

Recognised as a breed in Britain in 1966, the Birman was not recognised in the United States until 1967, when the C.F.A. approved the Standard. They had, however, been shown in "experimental" classes for several years before this, and appeared in championship competition in 1965. Mrs G. Griswold owned two, Phass and Klaa Khmer, sent to her from Cambodia, and others were imported from Britain, but the Birman is, nevertheless, a relatively rare cat in America.

The Birman is a majestic cat with a wonderful temperament; it is very intelligent, loving and gentle. Because of its sweet nature it is very easy to handle, shows well, and makes an ideal companion, with its small voice and tiger-like gait. Birmans do require routine daily grooming – I use powder, a bristle brush and a steel comb. They mate easily, and produce their kittens without strain or problems, in litters generally

Above: Ch Praha Hu-Tsung in profile—the blue eyes complement the Siamese colouring.

Right: International Champion "Hamlet", a fine French male example of the breed.

Two blue-pointed kittens of great promise: the points and mask are just beginning to show, but the feet will remain white. Breeder: Mrs E. Fisher.

of four to six. In rare cases litters of eight have been known.

The British Standard for the Birman, which is much the same as the original French Standard, calls for fur, long and silky in texture, slightly curled on the belly. This cat has stocky legs and a good bushy tail.

The head should be round, with full cheeks, and slightly flat above the eyes. There should be a good ruff around the neck. The front paws carry five toes, the hind paws, four. Eyes should be round, deep-blue on the seal-pointed variety, and bright china-blue on the blue-point.

The U.S. and Canadian Standards are based on the British, but go into greater detail e.g. saying that the head should be strong, broad and rounded, and that the nose should be Roman in shape, medium in length, with nostrils set low. These Standards point out that the front paws should have white gloves ending in an even line across the paw at the third joint, and that each back paw should have a white glove covering the entire paw and ending in a point, called the laces, going up the back of the hock.

Four colours are recognised in North America, the Seal, the Blue, the Chocolate and the Lilac, the eye colour being blue, the deeper and more violet the better. The paw pads are all to be pink, but the nose leather varies with the point colour: Seal-point same colour as points; Blue-point, slate colour; Chocolate-point, cinnamon pink; Lilac-point, lavender pink.

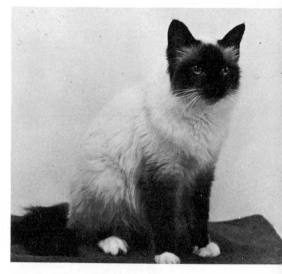

Ch Praha Shawnee shows a beautiful pale body colour, dark points and well-gloved paws.

Left: A seal-point Birman queen, Praha Trulka, and her two-week-old kittens, one of which is shown above in more aggressive mood. The kittens' eyes are now open, but the contrasting points have not yet developed.

A happy trio of Miss R. Brown's seal-point Birman kittens, showing well-defined gloved paws.

Black

Mrs Shepard's Willowglen Gaiety Girl, with big eyes, good type, and a full black coat.

Gr Ch Vel-Vene Voo Doo of Silver Wyte; this outstanding American male was bred by Mr and Mrs Green and owned by Mr Richard Gebhardt.

Of some twenty varieties of long-haired cat recognized in Britain, the Black is one of the oldest, and one of the most outstanding in its appearance and character. Writing on the Persian cats in 1889, Harrison Weir described the Black as "the most sought after and the most difficult to obtain. A good rich, deep black, with orange-coloured eyes and long flowing hair, grand in mane, large and with graceful carriage, with a mild expression, is truly a very beautiful object, and one very rare." This description still holds good.

One noted breeder at the turn of the century, Mr R. Little, evidently believed in titles for his cats–Lord Albemarle, Sir Robert, Lady Bruin. The last-named was so called because, as with many Blacks, her coat was brown when young, turning to deepest black as she grew to adulthood–she was a constant winner, and mated to Johnny Fawe, a noted stud of the time, produced many prize-winning kittens.

Blacks were still very rare, and the next decade saw little increase in numbers, although Mrs Benest's Ch Dirty Dick is still spoken of as one of the greatest Blacks known. The breed became rather more numerous between the two World Wars, however, with Miss M. Rodda's "Chadhurst" prefix, Mrs Askew's "Takeley", and Miss I. Sherlock's "Bircotte" always appearing among the winners. Ch Hillingdon Jackdaw was a stud who made a notable contribution to the improvement of the breed. The present general high standard of the breed has not always been so evident. There was a time when Blacks

Above: Ch Shaareen Christobel. Breeder: Mrs Trickett.

Left: Ch Petravian Black Panther—male. Breeder: Mrs Reynolds.

Deebank Magnus, son of Ch Deebank Mascot, at nine months.

did not excel in type, inclined as they were to be too long and narrow in the muzzle, with a narrow skull and pricked ears. Careful planned breeding has brought about the great improvement that we see today.

The novice breeder might well assume that Black should be mated to Black to obtain the best results. In practice, this is not the case, and an out-cross is often used, to improve type. That this policy is effective is evidenced by the number of the outstanding Blacks today who have one Blue parent. Ch Treales Candy Velvet, Ch Petravian Black Panther, Ch Deebank Mascot, Ch Petravian Virginia, Ch Bourneside Black Orchid and Ch Shaareen Christobel are just a few—all these winning cats had a Blue sire or a Blue dam. Whites too can be used in out-crosses, as can Tortoiseshells, Creams, and Red and Silver Tabbies.

There was a time after World War II when, to some extent, Blacks seemed briefly to lose their popularity. It is hard to understand why, for they are usually noted for having a particularly nice nature. They make gentle studs, very good mothers and delightful pets. Perhaps one reason is that as kittens they are usually very shady in colour and, therefore, not always easy to sell to any one other than an experienced breeder, who will know that the more shady a Black kitten is up to six months of age, the better and sounder its coat will be as an adult. Over the last ten years, however, show entries have increased considerably.

Black Persians have always been more popular in the U.S.A. than in

Miss M. Bull's fine long-haired Black male, Ch Deebank Mascot, with one of his many trophies.

Below: Willowglen Gaiety Girl in full face.

Showing a good wealth of coat, Ch Evendine Georgie Boy (male), owned by Mrs P. Haines.

Britain, and several were sent from Britain at the beginning of the century, to do well at the American shows. The first great Black cat of modern days was perhaps Gr Ch Pied Piper of Barbe Bleue, owned by Mrs F. S. Campbell and Mrs B. H. Morse, and All-American Cat of the Year in 1951. He appears in almost every outstanding Black pedigree since then. More recently, Gr Ch Vel-Vene Voo Doo of Silva-Wyte bred by Mr R. A. Greens of New Jersey and owned by Mr R. Gebhardt was 1959 All-American Cat of the Year. Voo Doo's death at the age of ten in 1966 was a great loss, as not only was he Best in Show many times, but his progeny included over two hundred Champions and International Champions. Voo Doo's daughter, Gr Ch Silva-Wyte Trafari of J-B, bred by Richard Gebhardt and owned by John Bannon of New Jersey, was C.F.A.'s 1967 Cat of the Year and All-American Second Best Cat and O.S. Cat of the Year.

An outstanding mother and daughter won All-American high honours in the three following years: Gr Ch Conalon's Miss Prettee of Walhall, owned by Theodore Napolski of California, and bred by Commander and Mrs Alan Bath; and Walhall's Isolde, bred and owned by Mr Napolski.

The Black's coat requires plenty of care. Both sunshine and damp weather can tend to give it a rather rusty appearance. Regular grooming is of the greatest importance, and this should be started at an early age so that the kitten becomes used to handling, and grooming becomes a daily pleasure. With most cats powder can be used as a dry

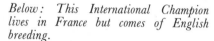

Left: Peachy Parody, a promising kitten at about four weeks. When young, blacks often have rusty or greyish coats. Owners: Mrs Britton and Mrs Ellis.

Below: This International Champion lives in France but comes of English breeding.

shampoo on the coat, but no powder should ever be applied to a black coat. Instead the coat may be treated with a grooming spray specially formulated for cats. As a final touch, the coat may be polished with a soft chamois leather or velvet glove.

A week before a show, the Black may be bathed (*see* The Cat in the Home) to remove dirt and grease from the coat, always making sure that the soap or shampoo used does not contain bleach. By the time show day arrives, the coat should be looking in the peak of condition. Special attention should also be given to ears and eyes and the tufts between the toes.

At the show, the long-haired Black will be judged in Britain according to a Standard which demands a lustrous coat, raven black to the roots, and free from rustiness, shading, white hairs or markings of any kind. The coat should be long and flowing on the body, with a full frill and a short, broad brush.

The body should be cobby and massive in build without being coarse. The head should be round and broad, with small, neat and well-covered ears, short nose, full cheeks and a broad muzzle. The eyes should be large, and round, copper or deep orange in colour with no green rim.

In Britain the interests of the long-haired Black are catered for by one of the oldest cat clubs, the Black and White Cat Club, founded in 1902. It caters entirely for Blacks and Whites, both long-haired and short-haired.

Ch Deebank Gay Cavalier in profile (above) and full face (below). Bred by Miss M. Bull and owned by Mrs L. Shepard, Gay Cavalier is a good sire and has produced Torties and Red Selfs of high quality.

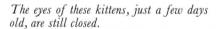

The eyes of these kittens, just a few days old, are still closed.

Blue Long-hair

Ch Lecreme Arcturus, bred by Mrs M. Bishop, already a full Champion at only eighteen months. He is a fine example with well-shaped head, short nose, good width between the ears, lovely eyes and firm chin.

Peela Genevieve, owned by Mrs M. Bishop and bred by Mrs B. Metcalf, shows a wonderful wealth of coat and full tail.

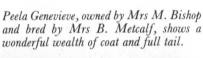

The Blue Long-hair (formerly known as the Blue Persian in Britain, and still known as such in the United States, Canada and elsewhere) is one of the most popular of all the varieties with long fur, and, apart from the prolific Siamese, is the pedigree cat that appears in greatest numbers at the shows.

The first long-haired cats are thought to have been taken to Europe by travellers from Angora, or Ankara, in Turkey. Referred to at first as French cats, as they came via France, they were later called Angoras, after their place of origin. They were mostly white, although some were said to be of a smoky hue. The heads were small, noses long and the ears big. Other cats with long fur, but broader heads, shorter noses and smaller ears came from Persia (now Iran), and so were called Persians. The colours were various; the most valuable being the black with orange eyes, and then the slate or light blue colour.

It was not until the first official cat show was organised in Britain in 1871 by Harrison Weir that fanciers began to be interested in the

possibilities of breeding for various colours, but found it very difficult
to produce cats with pure self-colouring, as little was known of their
genetic background.

The early Blues had tabby markings, white patches and lockets and
were every shade of blue to a light black, and invariably the eyes were
bright green. Gordon Stables writing in *The Domestic Cat* in 1876 said
of the Blue cat: "Although she is called a blue cat, don't fancy for a
moment that ultramarine is anywhere near her colour, or himmel
blue, or honest navy serge itself. Her colour is a sad slate colour; I
cannot get any nearer to it than that".

Harrison Weir who, in addition to organising the cat show, was also
the author of *Our Cats and All About Them* (1889), considered that blue
was merely a "weakened" black, being an uneven mixture of black and
white. He wrote of the blue colouring that "this beautiful tint is very
different in its shades. In some it verges towards a light purplish or
lilac hue, and is very lovely; in others it tends to a much bluer tone,

Profile of Peela Genevieve showing a short snub nose, good brow, and a magnificent set of whiskers.

These Perivale kittens, bred by Miss Collins, make a charming study.

Below: Kim, showing head shape and type very close to the set Standard. But as a monorchid, he cannot be exhibited in Britain and should not be used in breeding.

having a colder and harder appearance, still beautiful by way of contrast; in all, the colour should be pure, even and bright, not in any way mottled, which is a defect".

There had been cat shows of sorts before the first official one held at the Crystal Palace in London, but these frequently took the form of side shows at agricultural and county shows and even at circuses. At the first Crystal Palace show, naturally none of the cats had pedigrees, as they were not then considered of sufficient importance to have records kept of their parentage. The Blues appeared first in the "Any Other Variety" classes, and it was not until 1889 at the Crystal Palace show organised by the National Cat Club, that they had their own class "Blue–Self-coloured, without white". They were called Self Blue for some years to distinguish them from the many Blues with tabby markings. The entries were so good that in 1890 the class was divided into male and female, with Miss Frances Simpson's Beauty Boy taking first prize in the male class and Mrs H. B. Thomson's Winks winning the female. Blue kittens were still entered in the same class as black and white kittens, and it was several years before they, too, were given their own class.

By 1899, there were more Blues exhibited than any other variety, probably because Queen Victoria had a Blue, and high society followed her lead, with H.H. The Princess Victoria of Schleswig Holstein, the Lady Decies, the Countess of Aberdeen, the Countess of Strafford and others owning and exhibiting cats. Even the Prince of Wales (later Edward VII) visited the shows with the Queen, and gave his own personally signed photograph as a prize to winning Blues. Soon, the numbers increased rapidly, and it was possible for early fanciers to breed only from the best, with the result that of all pedigree varieties, the Blues came closest to their Standard.

This was drawn up by the Blue Persian Society formed in 1901 by Miss Frances Simpson, a Blue Persian breeder and author of *The Book of the Cat*, one of the first comprehensive books on cats to be published. The Blue Persian Society was the first specialist club to run a show for one particular breed, and is still the only long-haired club to do so in Britain.

In the United States, following the importation by Mrs Clinton Locke of the prize-winning male, Bumble Bee, renamed The Beadle, Blues rapidly became popular, and other importations followed until the numbers rivalled those in Britain. Breeding was conducted on carefully planned lines and pure-colour breeding was strictly adhered to in many cases. (In America today, however, the Blue no longer holds the dominant position it once did–of the first eleven Cats of the Year in the *Cats Magazine* All-American competition from 1947 to 1957, six were Blues, including the first four; but since then there have been no Blue Persian Cats of the Year.)

Although the Persian type was preferred to that of the Angoras, with the consequence that the latter subsequently disappeared completely, early photographs of winning Blues show that the heads were small and narrow and the ears big. Many years of selective breeding have been necessary to produce the broad heads, the small neat ears, the wide-apart, large, round, deep-orange eyes, the strong firm chins, the cobby bodies, short full tails, and wonderful full, long coats of pale blue

An early prize-winning Blue; Miss Frances Simpson's kitten, Bonnie Boy, with old-fashioned type—narrow head and big ears.

Starlight of Dunesk—a young male now in America.

seen in many of today's Champions. Through cross-mating, the Blues have been responsible for the high quality of many of the present day Blacks, Whites and Creams, and they were also used in early matings in attempts to combine the coat pattern of the Siamese and the type of the long-hairs in the Colourpoints, or Himalayans.

Blues play a vital part in the production of Blue-creams and, mated to a Cream female, a Blue male will sire Blue-cream females and Cream males, but if a Cream male is mated to a Blue female, Blue-cream females and Blue males result. A Blue male mated to a Blue-cream female may produce Blue females, Blue-cream females, Blue males and Cream males. Cross-matings are necessary, as Blue-creams are normally female, any males born proving sterile. Although the majority of the Blues are good, there are still faults, with jaws undershot or overshot, the eyes small and deep set, the frills paler than the rest of the coat, and noses on the long side.

In endeavouring to breed kittens of high standard, the pedigree of both the male and the female should be considered. Unless line breeding is fully understood, i.e. the mating of father to daughter or mother to son in the hope of perpetuating a distinguishing feature, such as a very beautiful pale blue coat, too close a relationship should be avoided.

The kittens, when first born, may have shadow tabby markings, but these rapidly disappear as the fur grows, and the most marked kitten at birth frequently has the best coat when adult. At a very early age, it is possible to judge the future potentialities of the kittens. Such early

Above: Gay, bred from elderly parents with old-fashioned type—hence the long nose and very open ears—both bad faults.

Below: Mrs Ford's year-old Winterbourne Nichlaus, a very promising stud with good head type and magnificent mane.

A female kitten—Dulce of Dunesk, now in Germany.

Myowne Gallant-Homme—an International Champion from France, bred in England.

Milord O'Mendip, born 8th May 1919 and owned by Mrs Frank Stevens; note the long ears and head, undesirable in the Blues of today.

A promising three-weeks-old Blue kitten.

judgments are not infallible, but the width of the head, the position of the ears, the length of the tail, which should be short, give good indications of quality.

Blue Persian kittens are by no means delicate and need no extra special care and attention. Grooming should start when the kitten is about three weeks old, but at this age only two or three minutes a day is necessary. A baby's soft hair brush could be used and a small toothed comb, with the fur around the little face being gently brushed up to encourage the full frill to grow and stand up around the head, and the rest of the coat being brushed up away from the skin. The grooming period gets the kitten used to being handled and also gives the breeder an opportunity to make sure all is well.

Very few of the Blue breeders believe in bathing their cats, even prior to the show, preferring to use talcum powder to remove the grease from the coat. This should be sprinkled well down into the roots and then brushed out completely. Any very bad patches of grease in the coat may be rubbed away gently with cotton wool dampened with a little surgical spirit. Blues that are stroked a lot do tend to get a dark greasy mark along their back and this could be treated in that way. Some are inclined to be over-typed, that is the nose is flatter and shorter than really liked, and frequently this causes brownish matter to collect in the corner of the eyes, which, if unattended, may form rivulets down the side of the nose. This must be wiped away daily if the appearance is not to be spoiled, particularly if the cat is being shown.

Myowne Gallant-Homme in repose.

An outstanding American cat, Gr Ch Ol-Ray Blue Mist, owned by Mrs Raymond Klotz.

The Blues are noted for their intelligence and strength of character. They love to be the centre of attraction and should another cat be petted, will push in to get their share of attention. The males have delightful personalities and it is a great pity that because of their habit of spraying around in the house, they are forced to spend so much of their time in their shed and run. If possible, they should be allowed out for exercise under supervision in the garden, and also played with and talked to as much as possible. They make good studs and, when the introduction to the queen is made, will talk and croon to her through the wire, until allowed to meet face to face. The females make good mothers, loving their kittens, and chirping to them with almost bird-like sounds. House-training of the kittens can start at about the age of three weeks.

They make very good pets, adoring their owners and remaining kittenish to the end of their days which, on average, is about fifteen years. The Canadian and American Standards are far more explicit than the British, but there are a few vital differences. The former require a short, snub, broad nose with "break". It does seem that America prefers a more typy cat than Britain, but strangely enough there is still a constant flow of outstanding Blue kittens from Britain to the United States, and not infrequently they win very high awards. The British Standard says "Any shade of blue allowable", while the American states definitely "lighter shade preferred", although it does go on to say that the colour should be "sound to the roots. A sound darker shade is more acceptable than an unsound lighter shade". The Canadian Standard also says "lighter shades preferred", but it goes on "type must not be sacrificed for lightness of colour".

The fur, according to the British Standard, should be long, thick and soft in texture, sound and even in colour, and free of markings or white hairs. The full frill is one of the most outstanding features of the Blue Long-hairs.

The head should be broad and round, with good width between the ears, which should be small and tufted. The face and nose should be short, with well-developed cheeks. The large, round eyes should be deep orange or copper in colour, without a trace of green.

Cobby in build, this cat stands low on its legs, with a short, full tail. The tail should not taper towards the end, and a kink is a fault.

Esmeralda of Dunesk was Best Blue Kitten in Show at Hanover in 1971.

Blue-cream *Long-hair*

The Blue-cream Long-hair was not formally recognized as a breed in Britain until about 1929, but had been known for some years as "Blue and Cream mixed". Judy of Cardonald, bred by Miss Darlington-Manley won her first Championship certificate in 1929, and was the first Blue-cream to do so. In 1932 she was joined in the Champions' ranks by Captain Powell's Daphne of Hanley, Mrs Crooke's Ch Rani of Brux, and Mrs E. Soame's Mist of Boreham.

Some years before this, in her book *Cats for Pleasure and Profit*, published about 1920, Miss Frances Simpson did not specifically mention Blue-creams as such, for the name they later bore had not gained universal currency at that time. She wrote "A Blue may be mated to a Tortoiseshell if Creams are desired, and again, a Blue may be mated to a Cream for the same purpose. You must run the risk however of getting an *oddity* of half Blue and half Cream commonly called a Blue Tortoiseshell".

The naming of this so-called oddity was apparently the subject of great controversy. Some well-known Cream and Blue breeders advocated the name Blue Tortoiseshell, and indeed this is no doubt what the breed is genetically. In the early 1900's the first "Blue

Tortoiseshell" appeared in Championship competition in America, but by 1931 its designation had been changed to Blue-cream. As with the Tortoiseshell, the Blue-cream is almost always female. Very occasionally a male is born, but there has never been a known Blue-cream stud.

Until their recognition as a definite breed, Blue-creams were entered in the British Stud Books as "Any Other Colour". In Stud Book Vol. 3, 1923-27, under the heading "Any Other Colour Long-hairs", there is entered one Blue-cream, Josephine Jinks, born on 27th July 1921, bred by Miss Harmer. The sire was a Blue, the dam a Tortoiseshell and White. In the subsequent volume covering the years 1927-30 there are seven of the breed listed; these few years mark their establishment in Britain. The show popularity of the breed today seems to vary from year to year; indeed part of the attraction of this variety is probably that the breeder can never gauge the competition in advance–there is always room for the unexpected. The breed has certainly had its moments of glory in recent years: in 1963 a Blue-cream had the distinction of being not only Best Long-hair, but also Best Exhibit at the National Cat Club Show at Olympia, London. This was Ch Barwell Athene, bred and owned by Mrs Phyllis Fawell. Athene won her open class again the following year, and although she is now ten years old only the fading colour of her eyes betrays her age.

The Blue-cream was it would seem the by-product of an attempt to improve the Creams, not remarkable for their good type, by out-crossing to Blues. Today, Blue-creams still usually come from Blue/Cream matings although sometimes a Blue-cream is born to a Tortoiseshell mother; but as the red colouring in the Tortoiseshell is to be avoided, this is certainly not the best way to set about breeding a pale Blue-cream with the intermingled colouring called for by the British Standard. Because of this cross-breeding of two varieties now with good type, Blue-cream type is frequently excellent.

The breed's increasing popularity in Britain today can probably be attributed in part to their companionable characters, for they seem to attach themselves very strongly to one person; they are most devoted and possessive. Usually very energetic, they are not content to curl themselves into a bundle and stay that way for hours. Coddling is unnecessary–they enjoy playing out-of-doors, but will come back inside when called by name. As they are so gentle and affectionate they make excellent mothers.

The interests of the Blue-cream Long-hair are catered for in Britain firstly by the Red, Cream, Tortoiseshell, Tortoiseshell and White, Blue-Cream and Brown Tabby Society, and secondly by the Long-Hair Cream and Blue-Cream Association, formed later.

The American and British Standards for this breed differ, particularly with respect to disposition of colour. In the United Kingdom the blue and cream colours in the coat should be intermingled, particularly on the face, the cream being as pale as possible without any trace of red. The effect should be rather like shot silk. There must be no definite patching of colour; this is most difficult to achieve–so often there is a cream patch on the face or under the chin. Many judges look for "broken" colouring on the feet, but this is not essential to an otherwise top quality cat.

Mrs P. Fawell's Ch Barwell Athene on show.

Above: Profile of Ch Honeymist Tiamaria, showing her beautiful snub nose and broad head.

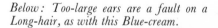

Below: Too-large ears are a fault on a Long-hair, as with this Blue-cream.

Above: Mrs A. Steven's Mystral Milovlee, a young female showing the blaze up the forehead, which, although not specified in the Standard, is liked by many breeders.

In North America, however, the disposition of colour is not the same. A good Blue-cream must be blue, with patches of solid cream clearly defined and well broken on both body and extremities. In practice, preference is given to cats with half-and-half cream and blue chins, noses and foreheads of alternating colour, and with cream on at least three feet.

No Blue-cream on either side of the Atlantic would be of first-class quality without good type. The head should be broad and round, with tiny ears well-placed and well-tufted. The nose should be broad and short, and the chin firm. The eyes should be deep copper or dark orange in colour. The body should be short, cobby and massive, with short thick legs; a dense coat is called for, soft and silky in quality.

Above: Mrs Wade's Zenith Estella; a female of eleven months.

Right: Ch Honeymist Tiamaria—an outstanding example of this all-female variety, with the intermingled colouring required by the British Standard.

Cameo *Long-hair*

For very many years Cameo cats have cropped up by accident in occasional mis-mated litters but, in the late fifties and early sixties, a few breeders in various countries decided to develop this lovely breed of pink-coated cat.

In 1962, these cats were being bred in Australia and New Zealand and, at about the same time, a Cameo was born by accident in the Netherlands. This occurred when a "silver with red spots" was mated to an Orange-eyed White, and the resulting litter contained a shaded Cameo male. In America, the 1901 Stud Book of the Beresford Cat Club listed a "Shaded Orange" cat, which may well have been similar to today's Cameos. All of today's Cameos, however, owe their origin and championship status to Dr Rachel Salisbury whose planned breedings brought about the first of these beautiful cats late in the 1950's. The colour was accepted first by the American Cat Fanciers Association in 1960, and other associations soon followed suit. The first All-American Cameos were listed in that year.

In Britain, there is no specialist club for Cameos, but in North America the breed is sponsored by the Cameo Cat Club of America. The foundation work to produce Cameos is very difficult, and can be heart-breaking. Many breeds have been introduced into Cameo breeding programmes with varying success, but basically the Cameo is a cross between a silver and a red. Silver Tabbies should not be used as tabby marks are a fault, although in the U.S.A. there is a class for Cameo Tabbies, requiring red tabby markings on an off-white ground.

Chinchillas, another silver breed, have been used in some cases with great success, but the Chinchilla's green eye colour can cause problems.

Profile of Peachy Pink Parfait, a Shaded Cameo male; bred by Mrs B. D. Ellis and Mrs G. R. Britton.

Above: Peachy Pink Beau (male); the Shaded Cameo is produced by selective breeding. Below: Three kittens showing the Cameo line of development: Ch Bamboo Betula (Tortoiseshell), Peachy Puzzle (Shaded Tortoiseshell) and Peachy Pink Porcelain (Cameo). Owners: Mrs Britton and Mrs Ellis.

Above: Gr Ch Montpellier Chanteuse— an American Cameo female, bred by Mrs Bertha Montpellier and owned by Vaughn Barber of Baton Rouge.

Right: Peachy Pink Parfait (male) showing off his beautiful thick coat.

The introduction of green eyes into a copper-eyed breed can be hazardous as it may bequeath to offspring an undesired green rim to the eye. The copper-eyed Smoke has been used with good results as a basic cat for Cameo breeding, although Smoke-bred Cameos tend to lack the lustrous coat of the Chinchilla-bred Cameo. For the other parent, a red must be found. In Britain, Red Tabby, like Silver Tabby, is ruled out, because of markings. Red Selfs of superb type are very few and far between, and therefore can be more-or-less discounted. The Cream (dilute of Red) is ideal but, unfortunately, very many Creams carry a great deal of blue in their pedigrees; while this is not a fault, the purer the cream in the animal's background, the better on the whole will be the results. Tortoiseshells also are very useful as the females carry red and invariably have excellent natures and constitutions, even if their type is generally not as good as the best Creams.

The kittens produced in the first litter of perhaps a Smoke male mated to a Cream female could consist of red, cream and/or Cameo males plus blue-cream, tortoiseshell, shaded blue-cream and/or shaded tortoiseshell females. There will never be a Cameo female in this first cross. Thus a two-year wait is necessary while one of the male Cameos is raised to maturity, before a female can be produced by mating this Cameo male to a suitable queen, perhaps a shaded blue-cream or shaded tortoiseshell from another litter. Though not Cameos themselves, these females are excellent stock for Cameo breeding as they carry genes for both silver and red. If no Cameo male is available, they can be mated to red or cream to produce Cameo females. These multi-coloured queens are most attractive in their own right, and are already recognised for championships in the U.S.A.

The Cameo cat is basically a red cat with a silver undercoat. This, however, can take six different forms. A Cameo cat can either be red-tipped or cream-tipped (in America only red tipping is allowed), cream being dilute of red, and each of these two colours can take one of three strengths of colour; first comes Shell, a very lightly red- (or cream-) tipped coat, giving at a distance the effect of a white cat. The second colour strength is the Shaded Cameo, a more heavily coloured cat. The darkest of the three shades is the red (or cream) Smoke Cameo, a cat of exceptional beauty appearing in repose to be pure red or cream; but if you blow gently into the coat you will see a white undercoat rather like that of the blue and black Smokes. During movement, the general effect is that of a rippling pink-coated cat.

Generally the Cameo cat should be given the same care as any other light-coloured long-haired cat, but to preserve a sparkle in the coat, especially for shows, a bath a week beforehand is important. Very great care must be taken to rinse out all shampoo and to dry the fur most carefully, preferably with a hair dryer to save chills, combing all the while. When the coat is very nearly dry, baby powder should be worked into the coat to bring back the body and, for three days following the bath, the coat should be well powdered and brushed daily. Then relax a little, giving just enough grooming to keep the coat tidy, using a little powder every day. Then every hair should stand alone and the tail should be a bush.

Of necessity in the development of a new breed, a certain amount of in-breeding has to be done, and problems of temperament and weak litters can arise. The best way to avoid excessive in-breeding and produce high quality Cameos is to have many breeders producing them, in order that an exchange of blood-lines can be made. Temperament, particularly, must be watched carefully, and ill-natured or weak kittens should be rejected for further breeding. They should be neutered and sold as pets, as should kittens with any sign of green eye colour. It is most important that a new breed should be furthered with only the best and healthiest stock, and all unneeded stock should be

Above: Cameo male—Barrose Honey Bear, bred by Mrs Ellis.

Below: Ten-week-old Peachy Pink Poppet is a male Shaded Cream Cameo and litter brother of Peachy Pink Porcelain.

A Cameo kitten, very true to type. Peachy Pink Porcelain (male) at about ten weeks.

61

Below: A Shaded Cameo only a few days old. The eyes have not yet opened. Bred by Miss Sellar.

Six Cameo kittens, Shaded and Smoke, from two litters, at about six weeks old. Bred by Mrs Ellis and Mrs Britton.

neutered. Most Cameos have beautiful natures, a trait common in long-hairs and, especially as neutered pets, they are the most friendly and loving of cats.

In type, the Cameo is similar to most other long-hairs. It is in the colour that the breed's main interest lies. In the Shell Cameo in Britain, the undercoat should be off-white to very light cream in colour; in America, the undercoat is described as "ivory white". The face and legs may be slightly shaded, but the chin, ear tufts, stomach and chest should be white without ticking. Nose leather and eye rims should be rose-coloured, and eye colour should be copper. Barring is a fault.

The coat of the Shaded Cameo should be pure in colour and un-marked – the proposed British Standard is red or cream shading down the sides, face and legs to whitish cream on the belly, chest and chin and under the tail. The American requirement is for a white (C.F.A.) or an ivory-white undercoat (A.C.F.A.) and white or ivory-white on chin, chest, stomach and under tail. The general colour effect should be much deeper than that of the Shell Cameo. Eyes should be copper, nose leather and eye rims rose-coloured. Barring or heavy patching are faults.

In the Smoke Cameo, in America called the Red Smoke (C.F.A.) or Cameo Smoke (A.C.F.A.), the undercoat should be ivory to light cream in colour, ticked (not shaded) with red or rich cream; the American Standard calls for white (C.F.A.) or ivory-white (A.C.F.A.) ground colour. Again, only red ticking is allowed. The mask, too, should be red or rich cream. Frill and ear tufts should be light cream, and nose and eye rims rose-coloured. Here, too, eye colour should be copper. Barring is a fault.

The A.C.F.A. in America also recognises for championship competition the Cameo Tortoiseshell, as do many other associations except the C.F.A. The Standard calls for a silvery white undercoat with black or blue ticking, or tipping (silver) and red or cream ticking (cameo), the pattern resembling the standard Tortoiseshell.

Chinchilla
(Silver)

The Chinchilla is one of the most beautiful of the long-haired breeds. A really good specimen, well-prepared, never fails to attract attention at the shows. The origin of the breed is generally accredited to a Mrs Vallence who, in the early 1880's, mated a smoke-coloured cat to a Silver Tabby, and one of the females from the resulting litter gave birth to the first "Chinchilla" male. This cat, named Silver Lambkin, became quite famous, sweeping the board at the Crystal Palace show in London in 1888, and when he died at the age of seventeen, his body was preserved – it can still be seen at the Natural History Museum, South Kensington, London.

H.R.H. Princess Victoria, a grand-daughter of Queen Victoria, herself a great cat-lover, was the only member of the British Royal Family to take up cat breeding seriously; she became the Patron of the National Cat Club, and exhibited on many occasions, her specialities being Blue Persians and Chinchillas. Her stud Chinchilla, Puck III, was advertised at stud at the beginning of the century, for a fee of one guinea (about $2.50). In 1894, a Chinchilla appeared at the Crystal Palace show, but would not be recognised as the Chinchilla we know today, for it was a much darker-coated cat, with very apparent bars on the legs. Today, this barring is considered the worst fault, and has been eliminated from the breed, which, in Britain, is catered for by the Chinchilla, Silver Tabby and Smoke Cat Society.

In America, the Chinchilla (called Silver in many of the associations)

Jemari l'Innocence is the daughter of two worthy champions and has a beautiful, flowing, lightly-ticked coat. Bred and owned by Mrs R. Gowdy.

Ch Jemari Rebecca, with lovely, wide sea-green eyes.

*Gr Ch Gray-Ivy Keepsake of Silver Paws
—a splendid female owned by Mrs Ivan
Over of California, U.S.A.*

Below: A Jemari female profile.

*Below: Ch Bonavia Flute—a well-known
stud bred by Mrs M. Turney and owned
by Mrs Gowdy. His progeny has been
exported all over the world.*

became one of the most popular of the long-hairs in the early 1900's,
and has maintained that popularity over the years. The American
associations also have a classification for the Shaded Silver (*q.v.*) a
darker cat than the Silver/Chinchilla.

From the showing point of view, the Silvers are handicapped in
America by having to meet the same Standard for type as the other
Persians, whereas traditionally, their type is not the same. A few
breeders have attempted to introduce Blues into Silver breeding in
order to change the Silver's naturally dainty, fine-boned type, but
such practice is anathema to most American Silver breeders who, whatever the Standards may say, prefer the typical Silver characteristics.

Though thus handicapped, the Chinchillas or Silvers do take top
fancywide awards in America – but somewhat less frequently than
other equally popular colours and breeds. Mrs Merald Hoag's Grand
Champion Arlington Sensation II was All-American Cat of the Year
in 1953, and Dr and Mrs V. Von Zele's Grand Ch Kerry-Lu Ramon
of Casa Contenta gained that honour in 1954 and 1955.

Although delicate in colouring and fairy-like in appearance, the
Chinchilla is a very hardy cat. No special care is needed and, apart
from the daily grooming that any long-haired cat requires, no coddling
is necessary. My cats are all born and bred in an outside cattery and
infra-red heating is installed for use only in really severe weather. I am

Ch Bonavia Flute showing the required cobby body and short, thick legs.

Profile of Ch Sonata Sovranino (male). For a Chinchilla his type is quite exceptional and at only eighteen months he became a Champion. Owned by Mrs F. Roden.

a great believer in fresh air, and the kittens come and go all day and night, thus building up a natural immunity to cold and disease. Also, without heat, the cat grows a much denser coat; nature provides the means to combat cold.

I cannot advocate too strongly to novice breeders the advantages of owning their own stud cats. Naturally, suitable accommodation must be provided, with a large house and exercising run, but owning a stud will save much of the inconvenience of sending your queens away. I let my studs live with a permanent mate – it is dreadful to keep a male cat in solitary confinement, as they are the most affectionate of creatures.

Mine lives quite happily with a queen, accept being taken to another house when visiting queens arrive, and then after serving the visitor return to their own queen; thus they lead a normal life, remain with the queens after kittening and take their turn at washing the kittens – perhaps I have been lucky but, living under such conditions, I find the males never "spray", which, after all, is their way of attracting the queens. If it is not practical to keep a stud, then select a mate for your queen that will correct any fault which is apparent; do not be blinded by the latest champion's array of winning cards – he may only accentuate some undesirable trait in your own queen.

Chinchillas do not, as a rule, produce large litters, the average being three or four, though I believe the first Chinchilla I owned

Study of Ch Sonata Sovranino's immaculately groomed head, with snub nose and small well-tufted ears.

65

Right: Now in Germany, Jemari Valentino, bred by Mrs R. Gowdy, photographed here at about eight weeks. He shows a fine ticked coat. Far right: Ch Bonavia Contenta—a sire of champions in twelve countries. Bred by Mrs M. Turney.

Above: Ch Bonavia Loretta, sired by Ch Bonavia Contenta. Owner and breeder: Mrs Turney.

claims the record – a litter of ten. House-training is no problem, provided patience and scrupulous cleanliness are the rule.

When showing a Chinchilla for the first time, shampoo at least seven days prior to the show as this gives the coat a chance to recover some of its "body". Each day fill the coat with a good talcum powder – I use baby powder – parting the coat all over and also filling the tail. Brush it all out afterwards. The night before the show brush the coat vigorously to remove absolutely all traces of powder.

To the novice breeder the sight of the first litter may come as quite a shock. Tabby markings are often seen on the back and sides and the tail shows distinct rings. These markings indicate that the breed originated through a striped cat, but, with maturity, they resolve into the ticking which makes Chinchillas so attractive. In young kittens, a yellow tinge can be caused by the acid in the queen's saliva when she

Ch Sonata Sovrano, sire of Ch Sonata Sovranino, bred by Mrs Roden.

A lovely trio of Jemari kittens. A good feature on all kittens is the dark rims to the eyes, giving a "spectacle" effect. The nose leather is brick-red.

washes them, more so if the kittens are in direct sunlight, and this must be taken into consideration when young kittens are being judged at shows. It is generally accepted that the Chinchilla, of all the long-haired varieties, is the hardest to judge.

According to the British and American Standards, the undercoat of the Chinchilla should be pure white. The characteristic sparkling, silver appearance is imparted by the fact that the fur on the back, flanks, head, ears and tail is tipped with black or silver. This tipping must be evenly distributed. The legs may be very slightly shaded with the tipping, but the chin, ear tufts, feet, stomach and chest must be pure white. Any tabby markings or brown or cream tinge are a drawback. The tip of the nose should be brick-red, and the visible skin on eyelids and pads should be black or dark brown.

The head should be broad and round in shape, with good breadth between the ears and at the muzzle. The Chinchilla has a snub nose and small well-tufted ears. Eyes should be large, round and most expressive, emerald or blue-green in colour.

According to the Standard, the body should be cobby, with short, thick legs. Nevertheless, the Chinchilla stands apart from all the other Persians inasmuch as it should present a low, stocky appearance but, according to the British Standard, should never be as heavily boned as a Blue Persian, for example. As we have seen, the position is different in America.

The Chinchilla coat is silky and fine in texture, long and dense, and extra long on the frill. The tail is short and bushy.

Above: Chinchilla kittens even show markings when born. These, bred by Mrs Derby, are two days old. The eyes are still closed and they can hardly crawl.

Below: A Chinchilla male from France.

Int Ch Bonavia Statesman, bred by Mrs Turney. Best in Show in France, Germany, Italy, Holland, Belgium and Switzerland. Owned by the Hon. Mrs Haden Guest.

Calico
see page 108

67

Colourpoint (Himalayan) *Long-hair*

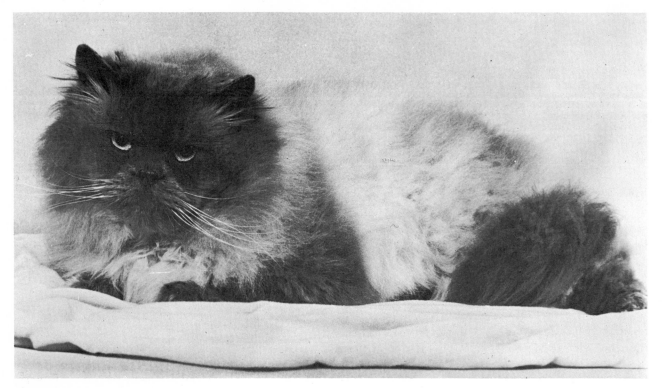

Mrs S. M. Harding's chocolate-point male, Ch Mingchiu Ptan.

Kala Yasmeen at five months; this female blue-point is bred in a direct line from Kala Dawn by Miss D. M. Collins.

The Colourpoint Long-hair (known as the Himalayan in America) was first recognized in Britain in 1955. Some eight years of planned breeding before this time led to their recognition, the initial spade-work being largely done by Mr B. A. Stirling-Webb in the Briarry Cattery. There had been isolated examples in previous years and in many parts of the world of cats with long hair and the Siamese colour pattern turning up, or being bred, but none of these led to any stable lineage and none had the full Persian type; the very first Himalayans were produced in America in the early 1930's by breeders such as Mrs Goforth, Virginia Cobb and Dr Clyde Keeler. The English breeder, Mrs Barton-Wright, inaugurated in 1935 after a visit to the U.S.A. the Experimental Breeders Club in Great Britain; she produced the first F1 Himalayans in England from a Siamese male named Moza and an unregistered Blue Long-hair female. One of the F1 females was acquired by Miss Dorothy Collins who registered her as Kala Dawn. Breed recognition was not granted to the Colourpoints at this stage; the Second World War put a stop to Colourpoint development, but in 1948 Miss Collins sold Kala Sabu, son of Kala Dawn, to Mr Stirling-Webb as an addition to the programme of Colourpoint breeding which he was then establishing.

The project leading immediately to the Championship recognition of the Himalayan in America began in 1950 with the work of Marguerita Goforth in California whose Goforth's LaChiquita became the first U.S. Champion–in A.C.F.A., which had accepted Himalayans in the mid-1950's. By the early 1960's the Himalayans had been accepted in all the American associations and have become among the most popular breeds.

At the same time that Mrs Goforth was working on her line, Ann and Ben Borrett of Alberta, Canada, were working on the Chestermere Himalayans in the origins of which some of Mr Stirling-Webb's Briarry stock, imported from England, played a vital part. From these two lines, and from Mingchiu stock imported from England, have developed the many American lines of today, with Chestermere cats predominating in numbers in the shows at the present time.

The ultimate aim of Colourpoint breeding in Britain has always been the combination of full long-hair type with the Siamese coat pattern, and since no other variety shows this coat pattern, it was necessary as the first step to mate long-hair with Siamese. The resulting kittens are quite different from either of their parents, for the gene for self-colour of any sort is dominant to that for the Siamese coat pattern; these kittens are therefore self-coloured in appearance, but invisibly carry the gene for the Siamese pattern. Similarly, they will have short hair, while invisibly carrying the gene for long hair, which they will pass on to their own progeny.

Thus, if two of these self-coloured, short-haired cats are mated, on average one in sixteen of the resulting progeny will show long hair and the Siamese coat pattern, both characteristics inherited from both parents. We can call this kitten a "primitive Colourpoint". There is nothing specially "man-made" about the primitive Colourpoint. Matings between domestic long-hairs and Siamese occur often enough in the cat populations of the world, particularly where cats enjoy their freedom. Colourpoints have turned up in the wild in England, Scotland, Kenya and so on, but the type is not good. Chance matings rarely produce potential champions. But even the type of deliberately-produced primitive Colourpoints is poor–the nose is too short for a good Siamese, and too long for a good long-hair, and so on.

Above: This seal-point male shows a long nose and pointed ears. A poor specimen of the breed.

Below: Beaumist Genevieve—a fine blue-point female bred and owned by Mrs B. Nicholas.

Above: Head study of Ch Merryn Ptolemy, a young male seal-point, bred and owned by Mrs D. Cunis.

Left: Mrs Nicholas's Beaumist Candida (female), a seal-point shown here at five months and now in Sweden.

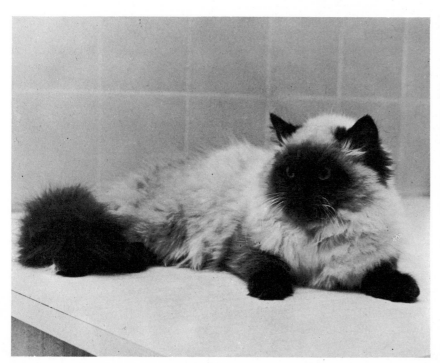

Colourpoints as we see them today are the result of years of planned and selective breeding. If two primitive Colourpoints are mated together their kittens will show some variation in characteristics. Those with the more Persian appearance can be used for further breeding and repeated selection can slowly shift the type of the breed towards that of good Persians. This method has, in the past, been favoured particularly by Americans because of their preference for many successive generations of like-to-like breeding.

But greater progress was made in a few years in the Briarry and Mingchiu Catteries in Britain by, in addition, making suitable out-crosses of Colourpoints to self-coloured long-hairs with the finest type, or even mating two fine carriers together. Only a known proportion of the offspring will be Colourpoints. Such out-crossing must be done with discretion and not too frequently or too much of the Colourpoint's blue eye colour may be lost; but by this means, Colourpoints have been produced which regularly win the very highest awards in our largest shows.

Long-haired, self-coloured cats carrying the genes invisibly for the Colourpoint coat pattern are often themselves of exceptional quality – for example, a champion Black Long-hair carrying Colourpoint pattern has never been beaten, whether as kitten or adult, on the show bench.

Since the self-coloured cats first used in the foundation of the Colourpoints were Blacks and Blues, at the time of their British recognition in 1955 Colourpoints existed in either seal-pointed or blue-pointed form. The next step was the formation of a club to take care of the welfare of the Colourpoint; it has since expanded to embrace a number of new colour-varieties, and is now known as the Colourpoint, Rex-coated and A.O.V. Cat Club. To produce the chocolate- and lilac-pointed varieties of Colourpoint, out-crosses were made to both Chocolate-pointed Siamese and to Chestnut Brown Short-hairs (Havanas), in order to introduce the chocolate-brown gene. In due time, the first chocolate-pointed Colourpoints emerged from the Mingchiu Cattery, and at once were in demand the world over. Lilac-points followed from this, as lilac colour is due to the combination of chocolate with the genes for blue-dilution passed on by both parents. Lilac-pointed Colourpoints were, like the chocolate-points, well received by the world's cat fanciers – cats have passed from the Mingchiu Cattery to many other parts of the world, and both the lilacs and the chocolates have achieved championship status both in Britain and abroad.

More recently, tortie-, red-, and cream-pointed Colourpoints have been produced in Britain and America. These varieties can be produced directly with no loss of long-hair type, because the necessary orange (red) gene is already present in the Red and Tortoiseshell Long-hairs and in the dilutes, Cream and Blue-cream.

The body colour is generally uniformly pale in young Colourpoints of all points colours, but sometimes a darkish coat in early kittenhood may change to a normal pale coat by the age of five months or less. The pale body colour contrasting well with the points is much sought after. In seal- and blue-points, slight shading or darkening of the body colour usually occurs after the second adult moult, although the colour con-

Above: Head and shoulders of Beaumist Genevieve.

Above: Mrs Nicholas's blue-point Beaumist Felicia (female) showing promise at eight months old.

Below: Beaumist Genevieve in profile.

Opposite page: Mrs Nicholas's Ch Mingchiu Shan, a six-year-old seal-point male, bred by Mrs S. Harding.

Above: An imposing male, Ch Merryn Ptolemy.

Below: A tortie-point kitten, bred by Mrs Amphlett.

Quad Gr Ch Ren-Sim's Shai, a male blue-point Himalayan with his seal-point male kitten, Ren-Sim's Little Man; bred and owned by Mary L. Misner, New Jersey.

trast with the points remains. In the chocolate and lilac-points the pale body colour remains for life. The pale coat colour so typical of Colour-points in Britain is one of the primary aims of Colourpoint breeding, but the coat can be darkened unduly by faulty housing conditions, such as an excess of dry heat. Coats thrive best on plenty of out-door life.

The temperament of Colourpoints is such as to make them the most attractive of pets. Their devotion to humans is almost dog-like. They are decidedly not "the cats that walk by themselves" and each indivi-dual demands its own particular form of daily attention, be it a repeated tummy rub, or a display of rolling that must be attentively watched by the owner. A female close to her owner will ask to have her paw held when her kittens are due, will tell the owner if her kittening box is too hot or too cold, too this or too that; she will ask for help if she has not enough milk and so on. But a happy, contented female usually rears her young with no difficulty, although she likes the fact to be appreciated.

The care of Colourpoints is no different from that of other long-hairs. They should have plenty of liberty, and should not be caged or shut away from all activity. As with all long-hairs, some grooming is essential, particularly during the spring moult. Nail-clipping is not required if the animals lead happy, healthy lives with plenty to do.

The British and American Standards call for similar cats; in Britain the Standard requires a coat which is long, thick and soft in texture, with a full frill. The colours are:

i.   Seal-points with cream body colour.
ii. Blue-points with glacial white body colour.
iii. Chocolate-points with ivory body colour.
iv. Lilac-points with magnolia body colour.
v.   Red-points with off-white body colour.
vi. Tortie-points with cream body colour.

The points should be of solid colour in each case, and the body shading, if any, should tone with the points.

The head is broad and round, wide between the ears. The face is short, with a short nose with a distinct break or stop. The ears are small and well-tufted, and the cheeks are well-developed. The eyes are large, round and full, of a clear, bright blue. The body is cobby and low on the leg, and the tail short without taper. There should be no similarity in type to the Siamese.

Above: A charming group of four seal-pointed kittens bred by Mrs Stringer.

Right: Beaumist Sacha—Mrs Nicholas's blue-point male kitten at two-and-a-half months.

Cream

Long-hair

The Long-haired Cream is one of the most attractive of the long-haired varieties, its coat pale, clear and uniform in colour, and showing up in contrast to the deep copper eyes. The creams of the early 1900's were somewhat different from those we know today. The breed was known as the Cream or Fawn Persian (it is still known as the Cream Persian in North America and elsewhere), and the cats then appearing on the show bench were much darker than is implied by the name "cream", and many were quite fawn in colour; often they also showed a darkened spine line with barring on legs, head and tail. From photographs it is clear that the type left much to be desired; ears were big and high and noses long and straight.

The Cream or Fawn Persians were first looked upon as sports and, when appearing in a litter bred from orange parents, were considered as spoilt "oranges", given away or sold very cheaply as household pets. In due course, however, they began to come into favour, appearing at the shows where classes were provided for both males and females. One of the pioneer breeders of the long-haired Cream was Miss Beal, whose two studs, Romaldkirk Admiral and Romaldkirk Midshipmite, were well known. From Midshipmite, Mrs D'Arcy Hildyard bred Matthew of the Durhams who later became the property of Mr Western, the celebrated breeder and fine judge of all breeds. Mr F. Norris was the breeder of many fine Creams, although he came up against many of the faults then common – fawn coats, the markings and barrings, and

Mrs M. Howes's female Honeymist Cream Tiara, showing a full coat and tail and good sturdy legs.

Miss Winifred Beale's historic Cream, Ch Romaldkirk Admiral, a famous winner from the early years of the century; note the old-fashioned type—long nose and large ears, undesirable today.

Holdenhurst Amber Star, a young male owned by Mrs Weaver, showing a fine even coat and full brush.

Above: This neutered male has a good coat, but would fail on his too-long nose.

Below: A Cream kitten bred by Mrs E. Aitken.

the long, snipy faces with curious slit-eyes instead of the correct large, round, orange eyes.

Ch John Barleycorn was a well-known cat in the 1920's; he was owned by Mrs Clive Behrens. His pedigree was unknown, but this did not prevent his making a very considerable contribution to the breed's progress. From this point the Cream Long-hairs moved steadily forward. Miss Sylvia Langhorne's prefix "O' the Combe" became well known, and for Mrs Stevenson, breeder of many fine Creams, perhaps the most famous was Ch Buff of Hanley, sire of many Cream and Blue-cream champions. In the early days of the breed, Cream males were mated to Tortoiseshell females; it was not until comparatively recently that mating to a long-haired Blue proved to be a much better out-cross–the coat became paler and sounder and–very important–there was a great improvement in type. It was Mrs Stevenson who introduced this blue blood, preferring to accept neither tortoiseshell nor red queens to her studs. At about this time Capt St. Barbe's Culloden prefix began to appear on many winning Creams.

Due to the care and foresight of Miss Kathleen Yorke, who prepared the cats in the Culloden Cattery for show and breeding, Creams were able to survive the Second World War, for she placed that fine male Sweetaboy with Mrs. E. G. Aitken at Banstead and he was kept there at stud throughout the war. Queens visited him from all parts of England and the cat fancy benefited from his progeny when shows again started. This cat was a grand fellow. His coat was pale and sound and had no bars or markings, and he had exceptional type which he passed on to his children. He was only shown once and that was at the last show before war started; after the war he was past his best and so never appeared again. There perhaps is hardly a Cream today which has not Sweetaboy among its forebears.

Honeymist Cream Ricardo—a well-developed female at seven months. Owned by Mrs M. Howes.

Left: Gr Ch Castilia Pekoe of Nor-Mont, a male bred by Marcena Myers and owned by Mrs Myers and Maurine Hoag of Pennsylvania. Below: Mrs M. Howes's female Honeymist Cream Tiara shows a good short nose, big, round eyes and neat well-feathered ears.

Below: Bourneside Cream Puff, a young male bred by Mrs Aitken.

Another wonderful Cream stud during those war years was Widdington Warden, who became a Champion in the shows immediately after the war, and he was never beaten. As a stud he was also among the best, and his is another name constantly appearing in pedigrees. It is the owners of such studs as these, and the breeders who continued breeding with their Cream and Blue-cream queens during and after the Second World War, that we have to thank for avoiding the near-extinction that threatened some other breeds in Britain at that time. In the breeding fraternity of today, there is still a tremendous interest in the Cream. As a matter of fact females are scarcer than males, because females can only be produced by mating cream males to cream or blue-cream females. Mating Cream males to Blue females produces only male Creams and Blues, and female Blues and Blue-creams; mating Blue males to Blue-cream females produces only Blues, male and female, and female Blue-creams.

In 1900 the Orange, Cream, Fawn and Tortie Society was formed, which was responsible for introducing classes for Creams at the shows, and for the growth of interest in the breed–today Creams are one of the most popular of the long-haired varieties. Over the years the society became interested in other varieties, which were added to the name, and eventually it also amalgamated with the Brown Tabby Club, becoming known as the Red, Cream, Tortoiseshell, Tortoiseshell and White, Blue Cream and Brown Tabby Society. The other specialist club particularly interested in the Cream is the Long-Hair Cream and Blue-Cream Association founded by Miss Kathleen Yorke, late Chairman of the G.C.C.F., in 1961.

In the U.S.A. there were only five Creams listed in the first A.C.A. Stud Book of 1907 (compared with seventy Whites and fifty-seven Blues); however, today they are one of the more popular Persian

Above: A beautiful head study of Mrs M. Wade's Ch Wivlingham Jubilee, showing good all-round type.

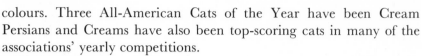

colours. Three All-American Cats of the Year have been Cream Persians and Creams have also been top-scoring cats in many of the associations' yearly competitions.

If there is a fault to be found in the specimens on the show bench in Britain today, it is that the coat colour tends, with a few exceptions, to be too "hot". In the breeders' scale of priorities type seems in some cases to have taken precedence over colour. With careful selection of breeding stock this can be overcome.

The correct type is quite clear from the G.C.C.F. Standard, which requires a cobby, solid body with short, thick legs. The head should be broad and round, with small ears well set and well tufted, a short broad nose, and full, round cheeks. The coat should be long, dense and silky with a short, flowing tail. The colour should be pure and sound throughout, without shading or markings. Eyes should be large and round, deep copper in colour. Although not mentioned in the Standard, a white tip to the tail is regarded on the British show bench as a very serious fault.

For type and coat North American Standards call for the same features as in other Persians. Eye and coat colour are the same as in the British Standard.

Above: A good male profile—Holdenhurst Amber Star. Right: Gr and Quad Ch Glad-Low's Teddi in a typically decorated cage at an American cat show.

Two eight-weeks-old females, Zenith Polly Flinders and Zenith Francine, owned by Mrs M. Wade, showing good, pale coats, free from markings.

Maine Coon   *Long-hair*

The Maine Coon Cat is one of the oldest of North American breeds, although it was originally confined to the north-eastern area that gave it the name.

The origin of the cat is uncertain, as there are many old wives' tales surrounding its early history. These range from the story that the breed is the offspring of domestic cats mating with the wild American bob-tail (this is unlikely) to the more probable tale that the sea-faring captains from New England brought back long-haired cats–possibly Angoras or long-haired Russians–from their Eastern travels and that these cats interbred with the local cats. Thus in time they would establish their own line; long hair being recessive, the

The nose of the Maine Coon is not as snub as that of the Persians.

Himalayan
see page 68

77

characteristics of a new breed would be founded. Originally, these cats were limited to the New England area, but were soon shipped to other parts of the country as the demand for long-haired pets increased.

Back in 1861, Mr F. R. Pierce stated in his book *The Book of the Cat* the fact that he and his brother owned a large black Maine Coon cat called Captain Jenks of the Horse Marines. Eighty years ago, the Maine Coon cat dominated cat shows in the East and Mr Pierce's book notes that Leo, a tabby Maine Coon, was given the Best Cat award in a show in New York City in 1895 and was also a consistent winner at the Boston shows in 1897, 1898, and 1899, being defeated by his son in 1900. However, the interest in these cats gradually decreased for some unknown reason and by 1904, they had just about disappeared from shows. Fortunately, a few people from Maine did not forget them and established the Central Maine Cat Club in 1953, which has held shows exclusively for Maine Coons. By the mid-sixties, other people from outside the Maine area had joined them and helped the breed make a successful come-back. In 1968, they formed the Maine Coon Breeders and Fanciers Association for the advancement of the breed and helped spread the word about the qualities of this old and well-loved cat, accepted now for Championship classes by some of the registering associations; this dedicated group of people is now working towards re-recognition by all associations. Although there were no cat registers in the days of Captain Jenks, the first volume of C.F.A.'s registry included twenty-eight cats identified as Maine Coons!

One of the attractive qualities of this breed is its large size; some weigh upwards of thirty pounds. The temperament is usually shy, quiet and intelligent. These cats appeal to many people who like long-haired cats but who do not like the short snub noses of the Persian breed. The coat varies in length, depending on the part of the body, being short at the shoulders and long on the stomach. The hair on the ears and feet should be tufted. The coat is silky and flows rather than stands out from the body as in the Persian. There is very little undercoat and thus it is easy to groom, a simple combing every few days will usually suffice. Not noted as a very prolific breed, the Maine Coon will usually produce just one litter a year, although they are excellent mothers and will not hesitate to take over other kittens.

The cat stands high on the legs, with a muscular, long and powerful body, yet walks with dignity and grace. It is gentle with children, quiet and intelligent, and owners of Maine Coon cats are emphatic that they make ideal pets and, as they appear in any colour or combination of colours, there is one to please everyone!

The type of the Maine Coon is brought out well in the Standard put out by the Maine Coon Breeders' and Fanciers' Association, which calls for a medium-width head, with high cheek bones–although in older, more developed studs, the head should be quite broad. The nose and face should be medium long, with an appearance of squareness to the muzzle, and little or no break in the nose. Ears large, tufted, pointed and wide at the base. Eyes should be large, round and wide-set; the setting should be slightly oblique. The firm chin should be in line with the upper lip and nose. Undesirable features, according to the Standard. are a short, flat face, or long, pointed nose. An undershot chin should be avoided, as should short, rounded, narrow-set ears, or narrow, slanting eyes.

The neck is of medium length – in older, more mature cats, especially studs, the neck should be thick and muscular, giving the appearance of power and strength.

The body itself should be muscular, powerful and long. A full chest is called for, medium to large in size. Although the body should be level, in stance the hind legs should hold the body slightly lower than the front. Where the hind legs join the body at the rump, there should be a definite squareness. A rounded rump is a bad feature. All the physical aspects of the cat should be in proportion to one another. A short cobby body and short neck are undesirable in the Maine Coon – on the other hand, a delicate, dainty bone structure should be avoided. The Maine Coon has a long full tail, wide at the base and tapering to the end with no kinks. Its legs are substantial and muscular, wide-set and of medium height. All the paws should be large, round and well tufted, with five toes in front and four behind. Short legs and untufted feet are faults.

The coat of this cat should be fine, heavy and lustrous, and should fall smoothly. The fur is short on the front shoulders and should become gradually longer along the back towards the tail, ending in a shaggy, heavy coat on the "britches". On the sides it gets gradually longer until the stomach, where it should be long and full. Although a full ruff is not expected, there should be a slight frontal ruff beginning at the base of the ears. The Maine Coon may carry a slight undercoat. The coat described here is the optimum – in actual fact you do find some variation with climate, and the Standard acknowledges this.

The coat may be any colour or combination of colours – awards are not to be withheld for "buttons", "lockets", or spots. Eye colour may be green, or complementary to the coat colour concerned; in any case clarity of eye colour is desirable.

Peke-face *Long-hair*

Ch Smithway Juliet, a Peke-face Red Tabby female owned by Mrs Helen Smith, California; was Best Opposite Sex Tabby, C.F.A. Southwest Region, in 1971.

The first appearance of Peke-faced Reds and Red Tabbies in North American championship classes was in the early 1930's. They have appeared consistently since then and are accepted in all nine American associations.

Prominent in the early history of the Peke-faces were Mabel Davidson of Lafayette Cattery, Mrs Earl Posey of Polychrome, Mrs W. R. More of Kootenai, Ella Conroy of Elco and Mrs Eugene Fouque of McKinley Park. Today Mrs Joseph Udinsky, of Tab-B-Town, Mrs Leonard Smithway, and the Aristocat and Hedgerow catteries are carrying on their tradition.

While not among the most popular breeds, the Pekes are shown continent-wide, and in 1971 earned awards in four of the five All-American sections. There are no American speciality clubs.

The Peke-face Persian is recognized in two colours only, red and red-tabby. These cats should conform in colour/markings and general type to the Standards set forth for the Red and Red Tabby Persian cat, except that the head should resemble as much as possible that of the Pekinese dog from which it gets its name. The nose should be very short and depressed, or indented between the eyes. There should be a decidedly wrinkled muzzle, and there is a wrinkle running from the inside corner of the eye to the outside of the mouth. Eyes are round, large and full, set wide apart, prominent and brilliant.

Breeding Peke to Peke is no guarantee that there will be Pekes in the litter. Most best Pekes are bred from a standard Red Tabby with good type, and a good Peke, or one who throws Pekes. Very careful selective breeding should be used as, with the extremely short nose and the deep nose break, breeders often run into problems with malocclusion, i.e. a faulty closure of the upper and lower teeth. Care should be taken to discourage the breeding of cats with protruding teeth or deformities that cause chronic "sniffles" and breathing difficulties.

Some kittens will take up to six months before they get the "break" in their noses; others will show it within twenty-four hours of birth. Pekes have been occurring spontaneously for many years in litters of Red and Red Tabby Long-hairs.

Although at one time quite popular, the Peke-face is rarely seen in shows today, and this is a variety unrecognized in Britain.

Red Self
(Solid Red)

Mrs L. Shepard's neutered male, Premier Willowglen Tiger Tim. The lack of facial markings is a good point.

Mrs W. Vidal's Orange Persian male, Torrington Sunnysides.

In the early days of pedigree breeding the Red Self in Britain was known as the Orange, popular as long ago as 1894. The early breeders found it very difficult to produce the Orange without markings and tried a number of crosses, including Blues, Blacks and Tortoiseshells. Invariably it was found that Orange to Orange produced the best self-coloured cats; orange females were rare, as it was not realized that it was necessary for both the male and the female to be of pure orange breeding.

Classified in the first cat shows with the Creams, and then in the first Club Standard of 1900 with the tabbies, in the G.C.C.F. Stud Book for 1900–1905 these cats were called Orange Long-hairs. In the Stud Book for 1910, they were referred to as Red or Orange, with a separate classification being given for the Red and Orange Tabbies. By 1915 the classes were for Red Self or Shaded, and for Red Tabbies, the name "Orange" completely vanishing. Mrs Western's Wynnstay Ruddiman was winning constantly at the shows at that time, eventually becoming a Champion.

After this, for some years interest seemed to wane in this variety probably because in attempting to improve the colour, cross-breeding with Red Tabbies was tried, which resulted in the introduction of

undesirable markings.

There is today still some way to go before the Red Self becomes as well established in Great Britain as some of the more popular long-haired pedigree breeds; nevertheless, the last two decades have seen several Reds of exceptional quality. Two of the most striking were a father and daughter, which appeared in the 1950's, Ch Syke Ruddy Glow and Syke Amber, both bred by Mrs M. Newbigging. The former was bred from a black male, Ch Chadhurst Sambo, and a Tortoiseshell female, Crazipatch of Carne; while the latter was sired by Ruddy Glow out of Ch Hillgarth Adele. These cats were a beautiful dark red, the colour was quite sound to the roots of the hair, and there were no tabby markings to mar the effect. Unfortunately this promising strain died out at this point. A contemporary of these cats was Gracefield Montbretia, owned by Miss M. Grace and bred by Mrs Harriott, a well known early Red Self enthusiast. Montbretia was sired by a Red Tabby, Barwell Derry, out of a Tortoiseshell, Ch Penchar Hope. Penchar Hope was herself the daughter of a Red Self female, Noxa Fenolla.

Of the Selfs at present appearing on the show bench one of the most beautiful is Premier Deebank Tahzib, sired by a Black, Ch Deebank Mascot, out of a Tortoiseshell, Deebank Tabitha. Miss N. Woodifield has made her contribution to the breed's progress in the form of Ch Pathfinders Rose Red, and with her male, Ch Pathfinders Golden Dawn who took prizes all over the country in the early 1960's, although unfortunately this breed is not her speciality.

One of the most prominent of the specialist breeders is Mrs L. Shepard, whose Willowglen prefix is associated with self-reds and Tortoiseshells. Ch Willowglen Rouge Soleil excels in type and richness of colouring. The efforts of these and other breeders are resulting in a steady improvement of Red Self type and depth of colour, although today's breeding programmes have a long way to go before all markings and bars are consistently eliminated.

In North America the Solid Red, or Red Persian, as it is known, has been bred since the last century; but as in Britain it was known as "Orange" in the early days. One of the most important contributions to the breed in more recent times was made by Mrs Horace Reed, whose Spoon River Cattery produced some excellent cats in the 1940's; her Ch Spoon River Cock of the Rock was acquired by Mrs Nikki Slobodian (now Horner), and from Mrs Horner's Shawnee Cattery have come many of today's finest Solid Reds, including her Shawnee Painting the Town Red II, today's outstanding Solid Red.

The genetic basis of Red Self breeding is still somewhat complicated, since the breed is not at the point where like-to-like mating is possible, due to the lack of self-red females, but it is hoped that the position may soon improve. Meanwhile, a start can be made with a really good tortoiseshell bred from a black; mated to another black, this tortie will produce red male and female, black male and female, and of course tortoiseshells. The mating can also produce creams and blue-creams, neither of which should be sold as breeding-stock. Stage two consists in mating one of the resulting red females, if of sufficiently good quality, to a black. At the same time, a red male should be mated to a black female – from this mating red females should result, in this way

Opposite page: Ch Willowglen Rouge Soleil; living proof that Red females can be produced from pure Red breeding. Bred and owned by Mrs Shepard.

Above: Premier Deebank Tahzib, bred by Miss M. Bull and owned by Mr F. Greenlees. Below: Miss N. Woodifield's Pathfinders Rose Red, a demure young female with good type and round eyes.

Profile of Miss E. Sellar's Coylum Ruby—good female type, showing few markings and a pleasing expression.

Above: The full male face has not yet developed in this young five-month-old, Mrs Shepard's Willowglen Rouge Etoile, later to become a champion.

Below: A three-weeks-old Red Self kitten bred by Mrs Shepard, with its mother, a Tortoiseshell.

Below: Ch Willowglen Rouge Etoile in profile.

Above: Ten-days-old kitten with eyes just opening.

Right: Premier Tiger Tim has an unusually good coat showing no sign of tabby markings. Owned by Mrs Shepard.

both red males and females should be produced in either litter. Using the blacks as an out-cross for the production of reds, it should be possible to establish the basis for Red Self to Red Self breeding. Cats being what they are, it may be a long time before unexpected and unwanted colours cease to appear in the litters.

When you are looking for a kitten likely to grow into a first-rate Red Self show specimen, bear in mind that it may be marked at birth, and that it takes a good eighteen months to two years for the coat to reach full maturity. At this point the owner's work really begins. To remove any grease on the coat, warm bran should be well rubbed in and equally well brushed out; next give the coat a good rub with a little bay rum (of the non-poisonous variety) and finally a polish with a chamois leather until your arms ache and the cat's fur is gleaming. To finish off use a rubber-pronged hand-brush, which takes out dead hair without pulling the undercoat. All this grooming should be done with the lie of the coat.

At a British show your Red Self will be judged on a Standard of Points which calls for a deep, rich red coat without markings; it should be long, dense and silky, and the tail should be short and flowing. The body of the cat should be cobby and solid, standing on thick, short legs. Its head should be broad and round, with small ears well-set and well tufted, a short, broad nose and full round cheeks. The eyes should be large and round, and deep copper in colour.

The breed is catered for in Britain by the Red, Cream, Tortoiseshell, Tortoiseshell and White, Blue-Cream and Brown Tabby Society.

Shaded Silver *Long-hair*

In North America the Silvers are subdivided into two separate colour classes – Chinchilla and Shaded Silver.

Whereas the overall general effect of a good Chinchilla is a pure white undercoat with a light black tipping on the back, flanks, head and tail, giving the characteristic sparkling silver appearance, the Shaded Silver, on the other hand, has considerably more tipping and shading across the shoulders, back, sides, face and tail – referred to in the Standard as a "mantle". Many judges prefer to stand back to view the Shaded class as the overall colour effect should be one of pewter rather than the silver of the Chinchilla class. The type and eye colour in the two classes is identical; the only difference is in the colouring.

Some breeders have problems in determining which kittens are Chinchillas and which are Shaded, as both colours can appear in the same litter. Both colours of kittens are striped at birth, and if the breeder knows the blood-lines well he can often predict the colour immediately.

85

However, it is not always that easy as sometimes the darkest kittens can develop into the Chinchilla kittens. Other breeders feel that the kittens born with the lighter mackerel tabby markings will eventually be Chinchillas and the ones with the darker classic markings will be Shaded Silvers.

For this reason, breeders often delay in registering their kittens and do not show young cats until the colour has "set", for if a cat completes a championship as a Chinchilla and later the coat darkens and stays as a Shaded, the cat cannot be transferred to the Shaded class, and can never be shown again, for certainly it would be heavily penalized for wrong colour, or even be disqualified.

In the early days of the cat fancy both Chinchillas and Shaded Silvers were recognized in Britain; but in 1902 the Silver and Smoke Persian Cat Society dropped the Shaded Silver classification as judges often could not distinguish between the two varieties. Indeed at one show a cat was judged under both classifications, winning prizes for both. The present Standards in America for the Shaded Silver are more specific!

Like Chinchillas, Shaded Silvers are recognized in North America in short-haired as well as long-haired form, although the problems of colour classification arise mainly in relation to long-hairs. Shaded Silver colour classes come also within the American Short-hair, Exotic Short-hair, Manx and Rex breeds in North America.

The Standard in America for the Shaded Silver calls for a white undercoat, with a mantle of black tipping shading down from the sides, face and tail, from dark on the ridge to white on the chin, chest and stomach, and under the tail. The legs should be of the same tone as the face. The general effect is much darker than that of the Chinchilla.

Eye colour should be green or blue-green; nose leather should be brick red; and paw pads should be black. The rims of the eyes, the lips and the nose should be outlined with black.

A thoughtful expression: Gr Ch Candy of Mary Crary, female, owned by Mrs W. Velman.

Silver
see page 63

Smoke

Long-hair

Often called "the cat of contrasts", the Smoke has a full silver ruff framing a black face, with silver ear-tufts, an undercoat as nearly white as possible, and black top-coat, which shades to silver on the sides and flanks. When the cat is in motion the undercoat should show strikingly through the black. The Blue Smoke is also recognized on both sides of the Atlantic—the only difference is blue coloration in place of black.

Smokes have been known since the earliest days of the fancy, as early as 1860, said to have been produced by chance matings between Blacks, Whites and Blues, and were known as "Smokies" or "Blue Smokies". One was shown in Brighton in 1872, perhaps that described by Harrison Weir when he wrote in *Our Cats* "a beauty was shown at Brighton, which was white with black tips to the hair, the white being scarcely visible, unless the hair was parted; this tinting had a marvellous effect".

It was not until 1893 that Smokes had their own show classes in Britain; the Silver and Smoke Persian Cat Society came into being in 1900, later to become the Chinchilla, Silver Tabby and Smoke Cat Society, and thanks to their efforts numbers increased rapidly. Probably the most famous early Smoke was Mrs H. V. James's Ch Backwell Jogram who, according to the National Cat Club Stud Book and Register for 1900–1905, took many firsts in the first years of the century. He sired several outstanding kittens. This stud book lists the amazing number of sixteen males and fourteen females—comparable to today's figures. From that time on, however, numbers tended to drop, and it is only comparatively recently that Smokes have regained their former popularity.

In North America Black Smokes (known in Britain simply as Smokes) have always been moderately popular. In the early days, lighter-coloured Smokes were preferred; as the reverse was the case in Britain,

Ch Backwell Jogram, owned by Mrs H. V. James, was the first Smoke Champion in the late 1890's. He sired many noted winners and was in demand as a stud.

A study of a fine male profile—Ch Fishermore Nabucco, a Blue Smoke, owned by Mrs Ellis and Mrs Britton.
Below: Mrs Roden's Premier Treetops Zero.

Above: Sonata Concerto (male), bred by Mrs Roden.
Below: Miss D. M. Collins's Kala Kavalier (male)

Opposite page: Mrs F. Roden's six-month-old male kitten, Sonata Virtuoso has a magnificent ruff contrasting well, which is unusual for his age, with his darker mask; a promising future Champion.

a British cat, Watership Caesar, was bought by Mrs Thurston in the States and did very well in American shows, as did Lady Marcus Beresford's Cossey. Over the years, there have been a number of dedicated American breeders, such as Mr and Mrs R. Green of Ja Bob fame, and Mrs T. O'Hara, whose Black Smoke female Gr Ch Araho's Moonmist has done very well.

As with the other "silvers", the traditional Persian type required has presented a challenge to breeders. Blue Smokes dropped out of the American picture for many years, but, due largely to the efforts of Katherine Beswick of California, interest in them revived in the early 1950's, and by 1957 they were recognized in most of the American registries and won All-American awards. More recently, however, interest in the variety has again declined, and almost all Blue Smokes appearing in the American shows are inferior to those of fifteen years or so ago.

Breeders in Britain have been comparatively few up to recent times. Miss D. Collins has done well with her Kala strain; mating her black female, Kala Satara, to Mrs Alexander's outstanding Smoke, Ch Suffolk Dumpling, she produced Ch Kala Moonflower, and she has since bred a number of other worthy champions. Miss I. Sherlock's Bircotte cats have done well, as have Mrs P. Dyer's Slaptons.

A name to be recalled in the post-war history of the Smoke in Britain is that of Mrs D. Fletcher, who founded the Treetops strain. Mr Leving bought one of Mrs Fletcher's females, which became Ch Treetops Zephyr, which he used to breed the well known male of his day Ch Beauvale Conquest, sire of many lovely cats. One was Mrs Hoyle's Beauvale Conchita, founder of the Hardendale Smokes, which have made such good progress in recent years. The Wildfell, Fishermore and Bianca prefixes have all been doing well recently. I, myself, bought a kitten from Mrs Fletcher as a neutered pet – he became Pr Treetops Zero. Through owning him I learned a great deal about Smokes, and ultimately began breeding the "Sonata" strain which has produced champions overseas as well as at home.

From time to time, there will be some Black or Blue selfs in a Smoke litter, and the Blues should be sold as neutered pets, for other colours should never be introduced into Blue breeding. Using a Silver Tabby brings with it the risk of introducing tabby markings – one writer on Smokes at the beginning of the century said: "Above all things shun, as you would sin, tabbies of any colour, and let your choice fall on a heavily coated sire".

When the cat is in full coat, the undercoat should show quite strikingly as the cat moves – this is in addition to the obvious pale silver frill and chest. This contrast must be preserved at all costs, as the Standard in Britain specifies an undercoat "as nearly white as possible".

Kitten coats undergo many changes, and are at their best at about seven months, on the approach to young adulthood. They then follow the adult pattern, losing some of the pigmentation as moulting approaches. There is often at the same time a darkening at the roots of the hairs, preparatory to the coat change, which is quite alarming to the novice breeder – there are actually three colours on the one hair! With the new coat this clears, and the top-coat and mask lose the paleness, or rustiness, which they often have in the summer. The Smoke

Above: A promising young Smoke stud, Mrs Roden's Sonata Riguardo, showing a fine, contrasting coat. Below: A fine male head—Ch Fishermore Nabucco.

Above: Mrs Shepard's female Sonata Sonorita. Below: A typical female profile —Ch Sonata Toccata.

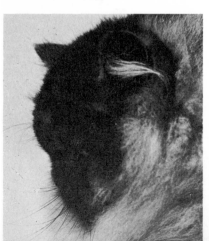

must be kept well-groomed, and the old coat must be combed out as it dies, keeping the roots free so that the new one will come in well. The second adult coat is usually better than the young adult coat, and it should be emphasized that three colours should be present in a full coat – black top-coat, mask and legs, silver frill, eartufts and bib, and undercoat as white as possible.

Eyes, according to the British Standard, should be orange or copper in colour. The earliest Standard specified orange eyes, but several fanciers at that time thought that amber or green should also have been allowed. One well known judge said at that time that she considered a good Smoke with green eyes should always win over a poor specimen with pale yellow eyes. Nowadays, however, green eyes or even a green rim to the eye would be faulted when being judged.

The Blue Smoke is exactly similar in appearance to the Smoke except for the substitution of "blue" in place of "black" in the above description.

American Standards for the Smoke differ little from the British – Smokes are recognized in America also as colour varieties of Exotic Short-hair, American Short-hair, Manx and Rex. Although one or two short-haired Smokes have been seen in Britain, they are not recognized by the G.C.C.F.

Above and below: Smoke kittens—Kala Kasomir (four-and-a-half months), Kala Kavalier (four weeks) and Kala Kamelot (two weeks), all bred by Miss Collins. Left: Head study of Ch Sonata Toccata, showing excellent long-hair type.

Tabby, Blue *Long-hair*

Male long-haired Blue-tabby owned by Mrs Thomas Martinke of Delaware.

This charming tabby variety has appeared naturally for many years in litters of Brown Tabbies, but it was not officially recognized for championship status in the U.S.A. until 1962. Recognition was largely due to the efforts of Mrs Jane Martinke of Delaware. It is still one of the rarer Persian colours in the United States, and is not officially recognized in Great Britain.

Contrary to some beliefs, the colouring of the Blue Tabby is not dark blue on a lighter blue background. The contrast is far more dramatic, for, as the Standard makes clear, the ground colouring, including the lips and chin, is a pale, bluish ivory, while the markings are a very deep blue, affording a good contrast. The colouring throughout shows a warm fawn overtone or patina. The nose leather is described as "old rose" in colour, paw pads are rose-coloured, and the eyes are brilliant copper. The colouring of the Blue Tabby is so distinctive that judges never hesitate over them as they sometimes have to in trying to distinguish a Red Tabby from a Solid Red.

Although Blue Tabby kittens can appear in litters from two Brown Tabby parents, they can also be produced by mating Brown Tabbies with Solid Blues – some breeders use this practice to improve Brown Tabby type. The resulting Blue Tabby coat is not generally outstanding; however Blue Tabbies bred in this way can, when mated to a good Brown Tabby, produce some of the best and most beautifully marked Brown Tabby kittens.

In North America, the Blue Tabby is an accepted variety not only of Persian, but of American Short-hair, Exotic Short-hair, Manx and Rex. Both classic and mackerel tabby patterns are acceptable.

Solid Red
see page 81

Tabby, Brown *Long-hair*

Mrs B. Chapman's Ch Karnak Brochfael. This male is a good example of a comparatively rare variety, with clear face markings, as required by the Standard.

The Tabby is undoubtedly one of our oldest breeds, although originally very different from the beautiful animals that can be bred today. In the closing years of the nineteenth century and the early years of the twentieth, Brown Tabby long-hairs were comparatively popular, though few were the lovely sable colour we admire today. They even had their own club in Great Britain, the Brown Tabby Persian Cat Society, which catered, as its name implied, for this one breed. The Society also had a Delegate elected by members to represent them at Governing Body meetings; but as this was before the formation of the Governing Council of the Cat Fancy in 1910, one can only surmise how Delegates' meetings were convened.

Miss Southam was the first to introduce the sable ground colour in the breed, in her famous Birkdale Ruffie. In 1896 at the Crystal Palace Show in London, England, this beautiful, clear, bright colour came into its own: Ruffie swept the board – Championship, firsts and Specials galore, including one award which must have been greatly prized by the winner, that for the best "rough-coated" (long-haired) cat in the show. This took the form of a handsome, framed and autographed photograph of King Edward VII (then Prince of Wales), presented by himself.

My own first interest in Brown Tabbies was aroused in 1916, when I visited my first Championship Show at Lambeth Baths in London. There were only two exhibits, both beautiful and belonging to that great authority on the breed, Mrs Slingsby. This was during the First World War; by the time the war was over, British breeders of this striking breed could be counted on the fingers of one hand. This is still unfortunately the case today. The breed's specialist club was amalgamated with the Orange, Cream and Tortoiseshell Society, and became the Red, Cream, Tortoiseshell, Tortoiseshell and White, Blue-Cream and Brown Tabby Society.

In North America, Brown Tabby Persians, as they are still called, have been recognized since the very beginnings of the American cat fancy in the 1890's. While this is not one of the most popular breeds, it does have a devoted following and is always placed in the All-American listings.

The Brown Tabby is far from "ordinary" as the uninitiated often think. It is very affectionate, hardy, intelligent and long-lived, and seems to have a particular appeal to men. The lovely contrast between the sable and the black makes for a cat of dignified beauty, full of character–a miniature tiger in the home. From pansy-faced kittenhood, through maturity to old age, no cat "wears" so well. In Miss Frances Simpson's classic *Book of the Cat* she described the Brown Tabby as comfortable and homely, with a more expressive countenance than any other cat. She believed no other Persian cat to be as healthy and strong as the Brown Tabby.

For anyone about to start out in the cat fancy for pure love and not financial gain, Brown Tabbies afford greater opportunities on the show bench than the more fashionable varieties. Unfortunately few breeders specialize in these cats, but good specimens are occasionally available from reliable sources. Brown Tabby parentage and ancestry are desirable on at least one side–always check the pedigree before buying.

Miss Frances Simpson's Champion Persimmon—died in 1902; he has an outstanding record as a show cat and a stud.

Gr Ch Owen's Tango (male), an American Brown Tabby bred by Mr and Mrs K. D. Owen and owned by Mrs C. A. Coughlin.

There are certain principles that the breeder should follow – generally I would advise mating like to like to keep the pedigree as pure as possible. This was easier between the two World Wars than it is today, as there existed then seven or eight different strains, and several excellent studs; however only two strains survived the Second World War – Miss Fisher's Hadleys and my own Trelystans. Interested breeders have been relatively few in recent years, and today long-haired Brown Tabbies do not figure prominently in British shows – perhaps seventy-five per cent or more are neutered and sold as pets. This situation may force the breeder to try mating a Brown Tabby female to the best available Black male; this should enhance type and eye colour without harm to markings or the production of white lips. A dark Blue male might also be used, although black is preferable. A Brown Tabby male could be mated to a Tortie female of the best possible head type, to a dark Blue, a Black, or even a Blue-Cream. Throughout, ensure that bad points in one parent are balanced by good points in the others. There is nothing to gain by crossing with a Red Tabby; we already have the sable colour, and the Reds will not improve type. A Silver Tabby should never ever be used, for the true sable colour of the Brown Tabby will be diffused into browny-grey, and the orange eyes diluted with green to become an indefinite yellow-green. Confine out-crosses to orange or copper-eyed stock.

Mrs J. F. Paddon's Ch and Premier Trelystan Fire Opal, a well-known cat from the fifties (above) and, now in Canada, Mrs C. Oliver's male, Int Ch Trelystan Felspar (below).

Profile of Ch Karnak Brochfael, showing his well-developed male head with good whisker-pads and good bold eyes.

Brown Tabby kittens are easy to rear, and are naturally disposed to be clean, invariably following their mother to the sanitary tray. There are no special feeding problems. It is important for kittens to become used to being groomed early in life. Grooming in preparation for a show demands a rather special technique, so that the markings on the fur are well defined. Really hot, dry bran rubbed into the coat removes grease: rub it in gradually, a little at a time, and then brush it out completely, using the brush in both directions. Then comb the back and sides carefully with a fine tooth comb, and give the cat a final smoothing down with a silk stocking or handkerchief. As with all long-hairs, the frill should from the start be brushed upwards towards the ears to form a halo, and brushing the tail upwards helps to promote the growth of hair. In the absence of hot bran, natural fuller's earth could be used – but never use the refined kind, or any other white powder, on a Brown Tabby.

Ch Trelystan Garnet (male), bred and owned by Mrs Paddon, was the pre-war foundation of the Trelystan line.

The ground colour of the Brown Tabby is a rich, vivid sable, the tabby markings a dense black, and rather narrower than the ground colour between. There should be delicate black pencilling running down the face. The cheeks should be crossed with two or three distinct swirls, and the chest by two unbroken narrow lines. There should be butterfly markings on the shoulders. The front of the legs should be striped regularly from the toes upwards. The saddle should have deep

Ch Karnak Brochfael—such distinct markings are difficult to achieve on a long coat.

95

Miss V. Roll's good cobby female kitten Zimalus Chocolate Fudge has a wealth of coat for her age.

bands running down, and the tail should be regularly ringed. The British Standard of Points makes no reference to the oval whorls on the sides, known as the "oyster". If these are missing and the sides merely have downward stripes, the cat is "mackerel-marked". In the U.S.A. there are separate show classes for "classic" and "mackerel" tabbies. The hardest fault to breed out is the white lip and chin, but it can be done. Even though they may not be as deep in colour as the rest, they should not be white.

According to the British Standard of Points the coat should be long and flowing, with a short, full tail. The body of the cat should be cobby and massive in build, with short legs. The head should be round and broad, with small, well-placed and well-tufted ears, a short broad nose, and full round cheeks. Eyes should be large and round, and hazel or copper in colour.

Mrs Paddon's Trelystan Coral and Trelystan Pearl (females), born in 1956.

Tabby, Cream *Long-hair*

Of all the tabby coats, the Cream Tabby is one of the most difficult for the breeder to perfect, because, as a dilute, there is very little contrast in colour–this may be one reason why there are very few good specimens in evidence at today's shows.

This variety has been recognized in America only in the last decade and appears only rarely in the cat shows.

The Standard requires a ground colour, including lips and chin, of very pale cream. The tabby markings, buff or cream in colour, should be sufficiently darker than the background to afford a contrast with it, but remaining at the same time within the dilute colour range. Nose leather and paw pads should be pink, while eye colour should be brilliant copper.

The Cream Tabby is recognized in the U.S.A. in "classic" or "mackerel" form, and is catered for within championship classes not only for Persians (long-hairs), but also for Exotic Short-hairs, American Short-hairs, Manx and Rex cats. This tabby variety is not known in the British Isles, although many of the Cream British Short-hairs, which should be self-coloured, do have ringed tails and some shadow markings.

Later to become successful show cats, Ch Trelystan Spinel (female) and Int Ch Trelystan Felspar as kittens.

97

Tabby, Red

Long-hair

Ch Bruton Angelo—a good stud with full, long, silky coat, bred and owned by Mrs N. Rosell.

The red long-hairs (self-coloured and tabby) originated from what, in the very early days of cat breeding, were known as Oranges. The original Standard of Points, drawn up in 1900, called for a long, silky, fluffy coat, massive shape with plenty of bone, and short legs, a round head with short, broad nose, small, well-opened ears and large eyes of bright orange or hazel. There was no separate Standard for selfs, which were distinguished only by their absence of markings and a sound, even colour. This first Standard was established in Britain by the Orange, Cream and Tortoiseshell Society, now called the Red, Cream, Tortoiseshell, Tortoiseshell and White, Blue Cream and Brown Tabby Society, which was founded in 1901 and which, together with the Tabby Cat Club, established in 1969, represents the Red Tabby in the cat fancy today. An early source (1912) states that the desired colour in reds was a rich, bright, golden red, not a chestnut shade, which was considered to be too dark.

One of the earliest Red Tabby breeders in Britain was Mrs Vidal, whose orange Persian male Torrington Sunnysides, born in 1889, was shown in London in 1900. At that time many of the registered orange cats had no known pedigree, and where the parentage was known they appear to have been closely connected with the Creams. Other early breeders were Mrs Darcy Hildyard (Durham prefix), Mrs Slingsby (Thorpe), and Miss Beal (Romaldkirk), and they were followed by Mrs Behrens (Swinton), Mrs Neate, who bred the celebrated Champion Red Leader, Mrs Tod (Hail) and Mrs Fosbery (Eastbury) whose Champions figure in almost every Red Tabby pedigree, if traced back far enough.

The two World Wars took their toll of the breed which only survived in Britain through the efforts of the late Mrs Campbell Fraser and her daughter, who maintained Red Tabbies throughout the Second World War, breeding such Champions as Hendon Sir Roderic and Hendon Puck, one of the finest Red Tabbies for colour and stripes the breed has seen; Puck was bred from stock imported from America.

Since 1950 Red Tabbies have enjoyed something of a return to favour; Mrs Fawell (Barwell), breeding in the 1950's, produced some beautiful cats, among them Ch Barwell Pedro, who had an outstanding show career and figures in many a Red Tabby pedigree today. Since then the breed has been consistently supported by two breeders in Britain, Mrs Rosell (Bruton) and Miss Vine (Comari). Champions Bruton Paisano and Comari Clover are among the products of these two catteries, while Mrs J. M. Newton has bred some beautiful Red Tabbies out of her Tortoiseshells, mated to Blacks, Ch Cherry of Carne and Ch Sherry of Carne, who were litter brothers, among them. Ch Redmire Red Rumba, bred by Mr Rush out of Ch Bruton Perdita (Tortoise-shell) and Ch Deebank Mascot (Black), excels in massive type and rich colour. Unfortunately Mr Rush is no longer breeding Red Tabbies.

Persian cats called "Orange Tabbies" appeared in North America in the 1890's or earlier. About 1916 their official names were changed to Red Tabby Persians. Such breeders as Mabel Davidson of Ovid Cattery and Mrs Ella Conroy of Elco did much to keep alive interest in the Reds from the 1920's right though to the 1960's. Today there is no lack of Red Tabby breeders in North America.

Ch Bruton Angelo has a good head, showing typical tabby markings and a good frill.

Mrs Helen Smith's Gr Ch Smithway Rusty Nail was Best Tabby and Third Best Long-hair male at C.F.A.'s Southwest Region show, U.S.A. in 1970.

The care of the Red Tabby involves no special procedures, other than the attentions required by most other long-haired varieties, except that the use of powder should be avoided because it deadens the gloss of the coat and dulls the colour. The coat should be brushed so as to enhance the markings, which rules out brushing up the wrong way, as one would do with a Blue or a Cream. Frill and furnishings, however, may be brushed forwards. Male cats should have their tails shampooed to eliminate stud grease, which is very disfiguring and increases with age. The Red Tabby coat does not have the body of that of the Blue or Cream Persian, and it is this very silky quality which makes it a difficult animal to prepare for a show; the darkest and best specimens have a tendency to develop a greasy coat. The condition can be produced by

A Red Tabby International Champion from France.

100

excitement or stress, and even travelling to a show and being handled throughout the day can make an inpeccably prepared Red Tabby look tatty. Fuller's earth and warm bran baths help to counter the condition and special care should be given to general fitness. I have found that a greasy coat can be associated with intestinal worms, and its general appearance can improve marvellously when the worms are eliminated (*see* Diseases).

Owing to their comparative scarcity it is not always possible to breed red to red in order to obtain the required coloration, even if this were always desirable. Other colours must therefore be used, particularly black and tortoiseshell. Some breeders recommend a cream out-cross to improve type, but this practice may lead to loss of the desired silky coat texture and possibly also to a light-coloured tail tip, which is a bad fault. Blacks are traditionally recommended if improvement in definition of stripes is sought, and it is a fact that if Red Tabby is bred back to Red Tabby over too many generations, a tendency develops for the stripes to become blurred, particularly the important three dorsal stripes—a solid back is a fault in a Red Tabby. The traditional red, black, tortoiseshell formula, therefore, remains one of the most reliable.

It is a commonly held belief that all Red Tabbies are males. But Red Tabby females are not uncommon, and even occur among "mongrels" Red Tabby mated to Red Tabby will as a rule produce all red offspring, and some of these may well be near Red Selfs. Red Tabby to Tortoiseshell produces Reds, Blacks, Tortoiseshells, and other variants, depending upon the pedigree of the Tortoiseshell dam. Black to red produces Reds, Blacks, and Tortoiseshells, also Creams and possibly Blues if the black sire has cream or blue in *his* pedigree. Such Creams and Blues are valueless except possibly for a Tortoiseshell or Self-Red breeding programme and should *never* be introduced into a Cream or Blue pedigree. It seems that Reds are less frequently produced from Black/Tortoiseshell crosses.

As a breed the Red Tabby is a late developer; a male will often take as long as two years before he is ready to sire. From about the age of nine months the Red Tabbies go through a very gawky rather ugly stage, which can last for several months, but the ugly duckling does at last turn into a lovely shining swan.

The British Standard calls for the coat to be a deep, rich red with markings clearly and boldly defined, continuing down the chest, legs and tail. The coat should be long, dense and silky, the tail short and flowing without white at the tip.

The American Standard gives a much more complete description of the markings desired in a "classic", or "marbled" tabby coat, requiring, for instance, that the marks on the face, between the ears and down the neck should meet the "butterfly" on the shoulders, which divides the head lines from the spine lines; back markings to consist of a distinct stripe down the middle of the back with stripes of the ground colour on either side of it, and lines on either side of them. In America there are separate classes for classic and mackerel-marked tabbies.

The body is cobby and solid, with short, thick legs. Otherwise, apart from the fact that the large, round eyes should be deep copper in colour, the Standard for Red Tabbies is the same as for selfs.

This attractive kitten bred by Miss G. Sellar, has good round feet and the makings of a good male.

Ch Bruton Angelo, showing a dignified, lion-like profile, very good type for a Red Tabby.

Tabby, Silver *Long-hair*

Mrs M. Greenwood's Ch Dorstan Darius, a well-known male of a variety comparatively rare in Britain.

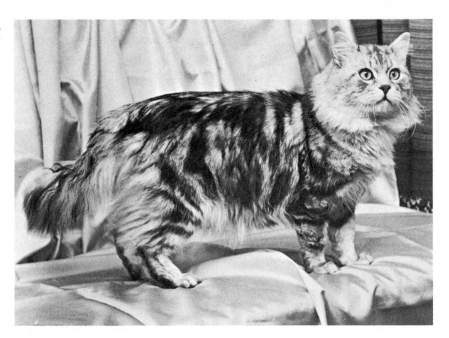

Above: Your Pets' Meese, owned and bred in America by Mrs Dorothy Baker.

A good long-haired Silver Tabby is a beautiful creature with its long silky coat bearing dense black markings on a pure silver ground. There are unfortunately few of them about and the lack of interest among breeders that this reflects is a matter for regret. At the beginning of the century the long-haired Silver Tabby classes at the shows were large; but, except for a few, the cats were not up to the standard of those of recent years.

One of the best Silver Tabbies of sixty years ago was the well-known Ch Don Pedro of Thorpe, and the pedigrees of many of our cats today can be traced back to him. For some years there were seldom more than one or two specimens at the shows, but during the last few years the numbers have increased slightly, and several good examples have been shown, the best of these being Ch Dorstan Darrall, Ch Dorstan Darius, and Ch Wilmar Wade. However, there is still a lot of work to be done by breeders in improving the general standard – this is the breeders' challenge.

When they are shown, Silver Tabbies attract much attention, and there is no doubt that they would become more popular if they were in the public eye more often. Silver Tabbies are said to have been used to help in the establishment of the Chinchilla breed, and this has been advanced as one reason for their decline, as it was said that the fairy-like appearance of the Chinchilla was preferred. There is however little evidence to support this theory.

In 1900 a Silver Society was founded by Mrs Chambers, establishing three classes for the Silvers, the collective name given to the Chinchillas, Shaded Silvers and the Silver Tabbies. The Society proved to be short-lived, with the departure of its founder for America. In the same year a new Society came into being, the Silver and Smoke Persian Cat Society. At first it recognized the same three varieties, with the

Winner of many awards in the early days of the fancy, Ch Don Pedro of Thorpe was owned by Mrs Slingsby.

Below: Head study of Ch Karnak Mailoc.

addition of the Smoke, but in 1902, the Shaded Silver classification was dropped.

In 1908 the Chinchilla, Silver and Smoke Cat Society was formed and took the place of the Silver and Smoke Persian Cat Society; it is still in existence with a much increased membership. The late Miss Langston, who bred the famous Allington Chinchillas, was the Honorary Secretary from 1921 until her death in 1971. In 1969 the Tabby Cat Club was formed by a few Tabby Cat lovers to cover all tabby cats – long-haired, short-haired, brown, red and silver. Membership has grown rapidly, proving that many people in Britain really are interested in tabby cats.

Silver Tabbies had been bred in America long before the beginning of the fancy there in the 1890's. However, the difficulty of maintaining good markings while trying for the desired Persian type still challenges American breeders and has been successfully overcome only rarely. Thus Silver Tabbies do not often win Best Cat honours in the shows, but when one does, it is a great tribute to the cat and to the owner.

Long-haired Silver Tabbies are very active and intelligent creatures, and quite quick-tempered, although they are affectionate and devoted pets. The females make good mothers who love their kittens and look after them without creating any problems. They are proud of their kittens and willing to show them off to visitors when they are a few weeks old. My queens make it very clear that they want some one near by when they are having the kittens. Silver Tabbies are not difficult to breed; the average litter is three to four, but I do know of one litter of eight sired by my stud Ch Dorstan Darius; this is unusual. My own studs are very affectionate and they do not enjoy living isolated in a cat-house away from everyone. They need human company and if left alone too long will complain bitterly. Even with kittens they are very

Above and right: Enjoying the sunshine, Ch Plantagenet Vetta, with her beautiful short nose, as required by the Standard and the pencilled marking "M" clearly visible on her forehead.

Ch Plantagenet Vetta (female), bred and owned by Mrs R. C. Chapman.

trustworthy and gentle–Darius is quite happy to "baby sit" if given the chance, washing the kittens and later playing games with them.

As soon as kittens become mobile they are very inquisitive and adventurous, exploring everywhere–a closed door seems to present a challenge to them, be it a room or cupboard! Nothing is more enchanting than a litter of Silver Tabby kittens playing, with the mother cat keeping a watchful eye on them, and often joining in the fun. Silver Tabbies do not need a lot of special care and attention; they are strong and hardy, and many live to an old age. The kittens are not difficult with feeding or house training.

There are many mongrel tabbies about, but it is not always realized that the markings of a pedigree tabby must conform to a specified pattern. The best Silver Tabbies are black at birth, except on the legs and sides, but as the coat grows the markings begin to show, with the true pattern developing at 4–6 months. Kittens well marked at birth are usually poorly marked when adult. A good marbled specimen should have a long silky coat with dense black markings on a pale silver ground. Stripes and bars around the shoulders form a pattern like a butterfly on the back and two stripes reach from the shoulders along the back to the base of the tail. The hindquarters and forelegs should be evenly barred and the tail ringed. There should be two black lines round the chest known as "necklaces" or "Lord Mayor's chains". There are pencilled markings forming an "M" on the forehead, and swirls on the cheeks. Any brown tinge is a definite fault, as is brindling. The main faults in Silver Tabbies on the show bench today are a too-white ground colour, and lack of definite markings when in full coat.

Brown Tabbies should not be used in the breeding of Silver Tabbies as brown is a dominant factor. Many years ago a Brown Tabby was used and even now, many, many generations later, a Brown Tabby will appear in a litter from a parentage where for many generations there has been pure Silver Tabby. Black and Blue have been suggested as an out-cross but the orange and copper eyes of these breeds are very difficult to breed out. A Chinchilla was used a few years ago with success. I have used a short-haired Silver Tabby as an out-cross and found that it has improved the density of the markings and not in any way affected coat length or eye colour.

Like all Persians, the Silver Tabby has a cobby body with short thick legs. Its broad round head is wide at the muzzle, with good breadth between the ears, which are small and well tufted.

The Standard calls for a small nose, green or hazel eyes. It carries a beautiful coat, long, dense and silky, and extra long on the frill, and the tail is short and bushy.

This little kitten is two weeks old.

Mrs Chapman's queen, Ch Wilmar Whimsy, and her kittens.

A litter of "Plantagenet" kittens.

105

Tortoiseshell *Long-hair*

Two imposing females of an all-female variety, Ch Bamboo Betula and Ch Chadhurst June Melody, both owned by Mrs Ellis and Mrs Britton

An International Champion from France.

C.F.A. Cat of the Year in 1967, female Gr Ch Misty Mornin' Meg, bred and owned in America by Charles P. Milwain and William T. Nix.

The Tortoiseshells, an all-female variety, have been around for a very long time, but unfortunately it is one of the varieties with very little authenticated history. Harrison Weir considered that it was not one of the original Angora or Persian colours, but probably originated through accidental matings between Black Long-hairs with mongrels. A few did appear at the early shows, and some were registered in the first stud books, but practically all were of unknown parentage, possibly produced by accident. By 1900, however, fanciers had begun to realise how attractive Tortoiseshells with their tri-coloured coats could be. They also liked the very mixed variety of kittens which appeared by using different coloured studs. In the late 1800's and the early 1900's the Misses M. and W. Beal became well-known for their Blues, Oranges, Reds and Creams, which they showed under the prefix of Romaldkirk. They used Tortoiseshells in the first place to produce Creams, but liking them very much, afterwards tried to breed them. In so doing, they discovered the fact still well-known today that a Tortoiseshell may have a number of litters without ever having a kitten like herself. However, they did successfully produce Tortoiseshells by mating one of their females, Wallflower, who did well at the shows, to a Cream male, Romaldkirk Midshipmite. One of the resulting Tortie kittens, Snapdragon, was exported to the United States, where the breed is also one of the oldest, and still quite popular today. About the same time, Dr Roper, another successful breeder, managed to produce Tortoiseshells by mating his outstanding black stud, Johnnie Fawe, to his Tortoiseshell queen, Dainty Diana, and bred several this way.

A few years later, Mrs Slingsby's Thorpe Tortoiseshells were frequently among the winners, several being from her Red Self male, Ch Red Eagle of Thorpe. Mrs C. Kennaway also exhibited a number of Tortoiseshells bearing her Garholdisham prefix. Other fanciers at that time included the Hon. Mrs C. Behrens and the Hon. Mrs McLaren Morrison; both owned a number of cats, and produced the Tortoiseshells by various crosses.

In the 1930's, Mrs C. Yeates, whose husband later became Chairman of the Governing Council of the Cat Fancy in Britain, showed Devonshire Duchess and Ch Chintz, and Mrs E. Soame's Ch Ginger-Bell of Barnsley and Miss French's Ch Polly Ebony were also winners at the shows. In recent times, Mrs L. Shepard's Ch Willowglen Lotus Blossom is a good example of the modern Tortoiseshell with good colour and type, and a most promising kitten, Wild Cherry of Carne, owned by the Misses Marshall has taken several firsts as have many of Miss N. Woodifield's Pathfinders cats and kittens.

As stated earlier, it is exceedingly difficult to produce Tortoiseshells to order, and the demand for the attractive kittens is frequently more than the supply. As the Tortoiseshells are female, a black or cream male would make a good stud. A Red Tabby should be avoided, as this may introduce tabby markings which could prove exceedingly difficult to breed out, and would be faulted if a cat was shown. A Red Self male, completely free of markings, from similar parents would be an excellent mate if one could be found. Depending on the stud used, the kittens in the litters may include Creams, Blacks, Blue-creams, Reds, among others, and, if very fortunate, a Tortoiseshell like the mother.

The British Standard calls for clearly defined patchings of red, cream and black, entirely separate, without brindling. White hairs and tabby markings are frowned upon. It is very difficult to breed a specimen with the correct markings, especially in the long coat, as the patches should be evenly distributed, and the head, tail and legs must also be patched, even the ears. Black must never be the dominant colour, as can happen. A blaze, either red or cream, a solid mark running from the nose to the forehead, is liked and certainly adds to the attractiveness of the face. The big round eyes should be deep orange or copper.

The type should be as for other long-hairs, and the coat should be long and flowing, being extra long on the frill and brush. Grooming is important, and powder should not be used, as this may make the colours dull. A good soft bristle brush should be used and a wide-toothed steel comb. The ears and eyes should receive particular attention to make sure that there is no sign of ear mites, or dirt in the corners of the eyes. Intelligent, alert cats, the Tortoiseshells make good mothers, and appear to be very proud of their kittens.

Standards for the Tortoiseshell in North America call for much the same cat as in Britain – there is not the difference in desired coat pattern that we find with the Blue-cream Long-hair, for example.

The Society interested in Britain in the welfare of this variety is the Red, Cream, Tortoiseshell, Tortoiseshell and White, Blue-cream and Brown Tabby Society. There are several Specialist clubs in North America interested in the breed; they too are concerned with both Tortoiseshells and Tabbies.

Above: Head study of Ch Willowglen Lotus Blossom (female), showing well-broken markings on her face. Bred by Mrs. L. Shepard. Below: Lotus Blossom carries a fine coat—an example of a difficult breed to produce to order.

Above, left to right: Ch Bamboo Betula (Tortie Long-hair), Peachy Puzzle (Shaded Tortie), Peachy Porcelain (Cameo kitten). Below: Mrs L. Shepard's Tortie, Willowglen Jacaranda, a kitten with excellent type.

Below: Two young Tortie females, Bruton Bronze Maid and Bruton Beach Girl, owned by Mrs V. Ford and bred by Mrs N. Rosell.

Tortoiseshell and White (Calico)

Long-hair

The three colours of the Tortie and White are clearly distinguishable in this head study of Miss N. Woodifield's Pathfinders Tangled Skein. All Tortie and Whites are female.

It is a pleasure to write about the Tortoiseshell and White Long-hair (known in part of the American cat fancy as the Calico Persian); this is surely one of the most difficult pedigree cats to breed. In the past Tortie and Whites were found in colonies of farm cats, kept in order to keep vermin down; these cats lived and interbred freely. There are no male Tortie and Whites, but the male cats in the farm colonies had Tortoiseshell and White queens in their ancestries–this accounted for the survival of the Tortie and White, still often found on the farms of today.

Although the odd cat of this variety had been exhibited over the years, up until about 1956 a pedigree Tortie and White was unobtainable in Britain–those that were being shown were the result of mismatings. So I took up the challenge on behalf of my favourite cat. I already had several ordinary Tortie and Whites, enjoying a natural life, so I selected the best long-hair, and proceeded to breed correctly, with the aim of producing a top show strain. The first step was to breed into top Champion sires of the right colours–Red, Black, White and Blue (all Persians), to produce males suitable for further breeding; I decided to use the (now recognized) Bi-Colours as the males in Tortie and White breeding; preferably red-and-white and black-and-white, they must be bred from Tortie and White queens.

Meeting this challenge has produced high-class Tortie and Whites, now an established breed, and today the best of the breed can hold their own in the British show world. It is possible to obtain a Tortoiseshell and White with an 8–10 generation pedigree, as in other breeds. But any would-be breeder must know how to reproduce more; the warning is to keep away from cats of solid-coloured breeding, for it is easy to drop back into solid colours, losing the white, although the Bi-Colour male, bred through Tortie and White, will sire, from solid-bred queens, Bi-Colours and Tri-Colours.

At this point we should consider briefly the Blue Tortie and White, sister breed to the Tortie and White, and often coming from the same breeding. Often, if there are two tri-colours in one litter, there might be one of each. Since in all material respects the two varieties are identical, there seems to be no good reason why the Blue Tortie and White should not have been granted Championship status, and there is growing interest in them. It is possible to develop the two lines separately, using the correct bi-colour sires to ensure the development

At four months a promising female kitten, Miss Woodifield's Pathfinders Forget-me-not.

Despite a few white hairs, Pathfinders Tangled Skein is a fine specimen of this all-female variety.

of the characteristics proper to each. The only club in Britain catering for the Tortoiseshell and White is the Red, Cream, Tortoiseshell, Tortoiseshell and White, Blue Cream, and Brown Tabby Society.

The Tortie and Whites have a conformable nature, making very good companions. They are intelligent, they keep themselves well, being very clean, and their coats are not inclined to become matted, as do so many Persians. This is because they have a slightly different texture in coat, with a natural shine, so good for showing, and the white parts are spotless.

Depending on the condition of their housing, diet and general health, the Tortie and White needs little or no bathing. My own experience is that they prefer to live as naturally as possible. They tend to litter in the spring, and from September until after January they can be free – rarely do they call until after January. My preference for my queens is only one litter, usually in the spring, for I find that late kittens are usually the difficult ones, and the mother is often less attentive to a second litter than she was to the first. Queens in the breed usually want their kittens with them, to play with and to look after, until they are quite large. The queens are natural mothers, giving little trouble at kittening time.

The profile of Pathfinders Tangled Skein shows the blaze on the face, which is much sought after by breeders.

When planning breeding I find it best to allow my queens to live with the males, and to maintain familiarity with them by living in adjacent pens which can be thrown into one at the appropriate time. Owing to the shortage of good Tortie and Whites in the litters, it is necessary to look well ahead in planning; indeed for this reason I plan beyond the next breeding season.

My opinion is that in-breeding is wrong; I regard this as most important, it causes many difficulties and produces weak stock and frequently produces bad sires and sterile queens. Occasionally there may come a good kitten, but this does not disprove a rule which I have found to operate in many more cases than not. Even the chance good result seems to pass on faults to its progeniture. I have found that the best results in breeding come from line breeding to the very best

animals, correct in type and with the right pedigree.

The English Standard for the Tortie and White specifies a coat well patched with colour, the three colours, black, red, and cream, to be well distributed and broken, and patched with white. I look for a little patching on the front legs as well. I think that too little white is as bad as too much, and mingling of the colours, instead of the required definite patching, is not desired – it is often the result of solid breeding.

In America there are two counterparts of the British Tortoiseshell and White Long-hair. In C.F.A. the Calico Persian has been appearing in shows at least since 1957, the Standard calling for a white cat with unbrindled patches of black and red, and white predominant on the underparts. In most of the other American associations the cat is known as Tortoiseshell and White, as in Britain; although Standards differ somewhat, that of A.C.F.A. is typical; "The head, back, sides and tail should be black, red, and cream in clearly defined and well-broken patches. The Tortoiseshell-and-White pattern should resemble a Tortoiseshell cat that has been dropped into a pail of milk. The feet, legs, the whole underside and half way up the sides of the body should be white. The 'milk' should have splashed up on the nose and half way around the neck. Any other pattern of Tortoiseshell-and-White should be considered a Particolor and transferred to the Household Pets." The principle difference here is that A.C.F.A. calls for the addition of cream; N.C.F.A. hedge on this point, calling for "Black and red and/or cream in clearly defined and well-broken patches". Thus, cats which fit either C.F.A. or A.C.F.A. Standards may be shown in the same class in N.C.F.A.

The type and formation is the same as for other Persian breeds. According to the British Standard the coat should be long and flowing, extra long on brush and frill. Our cat should have a cobby body, and massive, short legs. The head is round and broad, with small, well-placed, tufted ears. The nose is short and broad, and the cheeks full and round. The eyes, which in this breed are orange or copper in colour, should be large and round.

Pathfinders Forget-me-not at six months. She has won six Firsts and was Best Long-hair Kitten in Show at the Southern Counties Championship Show, London in January 1972.

Turkish *Long-hair*

The Turkish coat is not as full as the Persian long-hair's—Kastamonou Yalali has a fine auburn tail. Owned by Mrs A. Tidmarsh, and bred by Mrs L. Russell.

A second generation male—Van Attila Stambul, bred and owned by Miss Laura Lushington, who introduced the breed to Britain.

One of the two accepted breeds in Turkey, the Van Cat is now known in Britain as the Turkish Cat. Originating in the Lake Van area of south-eastern Turkey, these cats have been domesticated for centuries (in fact for as long as the famous Saluki Hound); they are much loved and prized by the Turks for their exceptional character and unique colouring. Apart from their great capacity for affection and alert intelligence, their outstanding characteristic is their liking for water, not normally regarded as a feline attribute. They not only dabble in water and play with it, but have been known to enter ponds and even horse-troughs for a swim – they soon became famous as the "swimming cats".

I was first given a pair of Van kittens in 1955 while travelling in Turkey, and decided to bring them back to England, although touring by car and mainly camping at the time – the fact that they survived in good condition showed up the great adaptability and intelligence of their breed in trying circumstances. Experience showed that they bred absolutely true. They were not known in Britain at that time and, because they make such intelligent and charming pets, I decided to try to establish the breed, and to have it recognised officially in Britain by the G.C.C.F. – even perhaps to save the breed from eventual extinction in its present form since, although domesticated and privately owned, the cats were then not being bred on a scientific basis in Turkey.

Achieving this goal has been a long and fascinating task, because in addition to the normal trials and tribulations which beset any breeder, in order to find new, unrelated Van cats to enlarge my stock and breeding lines, I have had to return each time to Turkey. The new cats I brought back in their turn all had to go through the mandatory quarantine periods on entry into Britain before they could even begin to establish the four generations required for recognition by the G.C.C.F. In 1969, Turkish Cats were recognised however, and granted full pedigree status in Britain (they are not bred in America), and since then have been eligible for championships. The first Turkish open class Champion was my own cat, Van Alanya.

The breed is strong and adaptable, and when kept as house-pets need not be especially pampered; that is, they can lead the normal life of a domestic cat indoors and outdoors, winter and summer. However, if the cat is a stud to be kept in kennels for breeding, it must be remembered that the indoor temperature should never fall below 42°F, and should, ideally, be kept at 60-68°F; therefore infra-red or other electrical heating should be installed (never paraffin).

Van Celik Burdur—a second generation male. The district of Van is snowed up for six months of the year and these cats are very hardy.

The cats have large appetites and thrive on raw meat and supplementary starch foods, e.g. brown bread or boiled rice; tinned pet food can be given as part of the diet, but fresh meat is an essential part of my own cats' diet. Long-term vitamin deficiency can be harmful, especially in breeding-stock, where lack of thiamine and natural vitamins can cause sterility and impotence.

To vary the diet and to prevent tartar forming on the teeth, cat biscuits can be given, but never as the sole form of nourishment; fresh meat must always be the main meal. Fresh drinking water should always be available, because on the whole Turkish cats do not care for milk. When you are providing four meals a day for a kitten or young cat, you can ring the changes with chopped hard-boiled egg, scrambled egg, a little boiled fish or a little liver, the last two in small quantities

Van Fethiye, an elegant female owned by Mrs Russell.

Kastamonou Yalali in profile.

The Turkish cat's love of water is unique—this kitten is swimming in a river in Turkey.

because they tend to affect the bowels. Many owners have told me of their cat's liking for unexpected tit-bits; by all means give treats, but cats cannot be expected to thrive on table-scraps alone.

Contrary to popular belief, breeding for kittens is not a business which will provide quick and easy pocket-money. Breeding is for people who love animals, and enjoy rearing tiny kittens for the pleasure it gives. Personally, I like a queen to have only one litter a year, even though the litter may only have been two, three or four in number, thereby ensuring sturdy kittens. A queen then very soon regains weight and fitness after feeding her family.

Unlike other long-haired breeds, Turkish cats do not need a lot of grooming, because they have no woolly undercoat, and I have always maintained that using a metal comb too often "electrifies" the fur and encourages it to tangle. If an occasional fur-ball does begin to appear, and if the cat is not for showing, it is quicker and kinder to cut it out, because most cats hate the process of teasing out tangles. Although, on the whole, Turkish cats keep themselves very clean, they really enjoy a bath, provided that a few essential points are remem-

Van Seftali, a nine-month-old female—bred by Miss Lushington.

Right: Van Guzelli Iskenderun with her kitten, Van Kehribar. She was the first registered Turkish cat in Britain, and imported by Miss Lushington in 1955.

114

bered (*see* The Cat in the Home). I know from experience that the Turkish cat will stand purring happily while warm water is poured over its back; the temperature of the water should be the cat's blood heat, 101°F. After the bath, the cat should be thoroughly dried in warm towels in front of a fire, or in really warm sunshine if the climate permits! It must never be allowed to sit about in a wet or even damp condition.

The cat will help to groom itself by dry licking, but gentle brushing in front of a fire, with a bristle brush when the cat is almost bone dry will bring up the fur beautifully. Some cats are sophisticated enough to be dried with a hand-held hair-dryer, but if the cat is timid or exceptionally sensitive to noise, do not attempt it because high-pitched sounds are emitted which the human ear can barely detect and which can terrify a cat or kitten.

The coat of the Turkish Long-hair is striking. The colour should be chalk-white with no trace of yellow. The face should carry auburn markings with a white blaze. Ears should be white, while the tip of the nose, pads and insides of the ears should be a delicate shell-pink in colour. The fur should be long, soft and silky to the roots, without any woolly undercoat. The Turkish cat carries a full brush, medium in length, and auburn in colour with faint darker auburn rings. Ring markings are more distinct in kittens. The colour description given here is the ideal. The Standard points out that, occasionally, some cats may have small auburn markings irregularly placed, but that this should not disqualify an otherwise good specimen in a show. The head of the Turkish is shaped like a short wedge. The well-feathered ears are large and upright, and set fairly close together. The cat has a long nose and round eyes, light amber in colour, with pink-skinned rims. Its body should be long but sturdy, with legs medium in length.

The feet should be neat and round with well-tufted toes. Males should be particularly muscular on the neck and shoulders.

White
(Blue Eyes)

Long-hair

Mrs N. Rosell's Ch Bruton Snokat (male), a fine example of this breed.

Profile of Ch Bruton Snokat showing good type for this variety.

At the first cat shows in Britain, the Blue-eyed Long-haired White cats were among the most numerous, descended as they were from the original Angoras. From the early days of breed registration, they had a breed number, a Standard of Points and were shown in separate classes, achieving a recognised status even before the Blue Long-haired variety, which has since become so much more popular. According to photographs and records, it would seem that the specimens being shown left much to be desired, but even so there were some that measured up to the Standard of the time, which is practically that in use today. We learn from Frances Simpson's *The Book of the Cat* (1903) that, in 1896, a Mrs Pettitt was breeding some specimens which, according to the records, could take their place among the Blue-eyed Whites of today.

Names significant in the history of the breed, from the late nineteenth century and early twentieth, include Lady Marcus Beresford who imported into Britain several cats from America, using them to reinforce her breeding programme. At the same time, Mrs Pettitt was breeding from her glorious collection of Whites at St Leonards, England. Champions arising from these breedings were owned by the Hon. Mrs Clive Behrens, Mr Gay, Mrs Reynold Sams, Mrs Brunton and Mrs Cattermole, and we see the prefixes Swinton, Mayfield, Runnymede, Dunesk and Lotus appearing again and again. In 1931, a very famous male appeared on the show bench, Ch Casino Luck, owned by Mrs Cox-Ife, bred by Mrs Spencer Smith. Although Mrs Smith does not appear to have had a registered prefix, many champions are recorded as having been bred by her; "Lucky" was not only a superb show cat, but a very good sire.

But it was the Orange-eyed White which, by 1938, had become the more popular of the two breeds in Britain. By that time, it had also achieved registration and Championship status, and had taken the place of the Blue-eyed in popularity. After the 1939–1945 War, the

116

A fine show winner: Gr Ch Gallahad's Heritage (male), was Best All-American cat in the 1968 C.F.A. show. Bred and owned by Mrs Blanche Smith.

number of breeders was much depleted; Mrs Cattermole was one of the foremost exhibitors in Britain, with Miss Sherlock (prefix Bircotte) and Mrs Cook-Radmore (prefix Albany). So great was the decline that in 1968 only four Blue-eyed White kittens were registered, and these had all turned up in litters from Orange-eyed sires and dams. Consequently, there are today in Britain very few with the authentic deep sapphire eyes, which were such an attractive feature of their forebears, and good type; some cats with correct eye colour are poor in type, with ears that are too big and high, and noses which are too long. However, a great deal of work is being devoted to restoring to the breed the type which is so admired in the long-haired varieties, the round, broad heads, small, well-placed ears, short, broad noses and strong chins combined with large, round deep-blue eyes. The Black and White Cat Club in Britain, founded in 1902, offers great encouragement to the breeders who work with this most attractive breed.

Although the Blue-eyed Whites have been recognised in America since the first days of the fancy, they have been strongly competitive with the other Persian colours since only about the mid-fifties. It was about that time that Blue-eyed White breeders began to use Blues and Odd-eyed Whites in their breeding programmes.

Gallahad's Faith, bred and owned by Blanche Smith of Pennsylvania, has been called the first modern Blue-eyed White in America. She was the highest-scoring Eastern Persian female in 1958, and All-American Blue-eyed White. She was the result of an Odd-eyed to Odd-eyed mating.

An engaging pair of "Bourneside" kittens, born in 1963, bred and owned by Mrs E. G. Aitken.

Some more recent Blue-eyed Whites who have been very successful in the shows have been Californian Will Thompson's Gr Ch Hirondelle's Nova of Quiksilver (from an Odd-eyed to Blue-eyed mating); Gr Ch Castilia's Surprise, from two Copper-eyed White parents (!), owned by Marcena Myers of Pennsylvania, and Blanche Smith's Gr Ch Gallahad's Heritage, from Odd-eyed to Odd-eyed.

Care of the Blue-eyed Long-haired White is no different from the attention needed by any long-haired, white cat, either for general condition or for showing. Tails often need washing, especially the

Lucy's Kitten, born in 1963, bred and owned by Mrs Aitken.

Mrs Aitken's Ch Bircotte Ursa at two-and-a-half years.

male's tails, for they are usually greasy and, if untended, show a yellow tinge which will disappear when washed in warm, soapy water in which borax has been dissolved. Rinse well, and dust with powder. The queens are usually easy breeders and very good mothers, but have their own ideas as to where the nursery should be. The average litters number three to four kittens, and even when the sire is also a Blue-eyed White, may contain some surprises – the white kittens can have eyes which are blue, or orange, or odd-coloured (one blue and one orange); and the kitten will probably be four to six weeks old before one can be sure of the eye colour. The white kittens seem almost bare of fur when they are born, but within a few days, a definite change is apparent.

The Blue-eyed Long-haired White, although having an ethereal look, is by no means a delicate cat; he is strong and virile with good bone structure. He is also very affectionate, although somewhat shy and nervous with strangers.

Much has been written of the prevalence of deafness in Blue-eyed Whites. Despite more than fifty generations of sincere attempts to breed out this defect, it is as common today as it ever was and appears to be so linked with the genes of blue eyes that deafness must be considered as more or less a normal accompaniment to blue eyes in white cats. As a matter of principle, deaf-to-deaf matings should be avoided. Such matings, however, do occur – either accidentally or otherwise – and when they do, sound-hearing kittens frequently appear. Similarly, sound-hearing to sound-hearing results at best in about 50 per cent sound-hearing kittens, even in Odd-eyed to Odd-eyed matings. In practice, then, avoiding the mating of deaf cats to deaf cats does not seem to be the complete answer to this problem.

The sound-hearing Blue-eyed Whites seem to have the same personality characteristics as all other Persians. Deaf Blue-eyed Whites generally are quieter and, perhaps, more loving. Occasionally, a Blue-eyed White born deaf will acquire hearing during its kittenhood. This sometimes results in a personality change. Often the cat will appear shy and frightened for a period of time until it learns to live with its newly-acquired sense of hearing.

In North America and Britain, the Standards for Blue-eyed Whites are identical with those of all the other Persians except for eye and coat colour. Eyes should be deep blue and coat pure white.

The imposing head of Ch Bruton Snokat.

White (Odd Eyes)

Long-hair

This entrancing variety has one blue and one orange eye, and it seems that only in white cats does this phenomenon occur. They can appear in litters bred from a blue-eyed sire and dam or from one blue-eyed and one orange-eyed parent, and from matings between Blue-eyed and Copper-eyed Whites and between Blues and Blue-eyed Whites; they can be either male or female.

For the breeder, such cats are invaluable as they produce cats of good type; each eye is usually large and of good colour.

The colour was recognized by all American associations early in the 1950's at the behest of Blue-eyed White breeders who found the Odd-eyes invaluable for producing Blue-eyed Whites of outstanding type and eye colour. Most American Standards call for deep copper and deep blue as the eye colours.

An Odd-eyed White, Grand Champion Simbelair Aristocrat, bred by Lois Weston of Ontario, Canada, and owned by Marcena Myers of Pennsylvania, gained thirty-seven Best-Cat-in-Show wins in the period 16th September to 3rd December 1967, a record which still stands for successive wins without defeat.

The breed is not eligible for Championship status in Britain, although in 1968, after representations by the Black and White Cat Club, they were given a breed number and a Standard of Points. Up to that time, little had been recorded about them; they were recognized as White Long-hairs with incorrect eye colour and, if entered in a show, could not achieve a Championship Certificate. In 1967 an attempt was in

Redmire Josephine, female, owned by Miss Sherlock.

Gr Ch Simbelair Aristocrat—an American male who made history by winning Best-in-Show forty-six times in one year, at the age of thirteen months! Bred by Mrs Lois Weston and owned by Mrs Marcena Myers.

119

Redmire Josephine—even in black and white, the odd eyes are clearly distinguishable.

Gr Ch Simbelair Aristocrat.

fact made to have the breed registered as Any Other Colour but with no Championship status, and debarring them from being entered in any other class. This move drew little support from the breeders.

The one great advantage the Odd-eyed seem to have over the other white breeds is that they do not appear generally to suffer from the deafness which seems often to be inherent in white cats, although they can be deaf on the side of the blue eye.

The points of care, grooming and breeding of the Odd-eyed White differ in no way from the Blue-eyed White, and the Standard of Points varies only in the eye colour.

Above: The different-coloured eyes of this female are clearly distinguishable; she has good type, although her ear-carriage is poor.

Dalmond Roames in 1962—a male with an excellent coat, bred and owned by Mrs E. G. Aitken.

White
(Orange Eyes)
(Copper Eyes)

This is one of the most beautiful of long-haired breeds, known in America as the Copper-eyed White Persian, and some of the best examples, exhibited in perfect condition, have been given the highest possible awards on the British show bench in recent years. The breed came into existence in Britain when owners of Blue-eyed White Long-hairs, wishing to improve the type of their cats and given the co-operation of breeders of Blue Long-hairs, mated them to some of the lovely Blues then available. These matings produced Blues and Whites, the latter having blue eyes, orange eyes or odd eyes (i.e. one blue eye and one orange eye). In the late 1930's, the Governing Council of the Cat Fancy decided to recognize the Blue-eyed and the Orange-eyed Whites as separate varieties; once this was done they were both able to compete for Championship status. The Orange-eyed White Persian owes much of its beauty to the Blue Persians whose lovely type and eye colour the breed inherited, and indeed breeders today also outcross to the fine Cream and Black Long-hairs with considerable success.

After the breed was recognised, their popularity rapidly increased and the best of the Orange-eyed Whites achieved success at the shows; by 1960 some breeders had already won the Best Long-hair Kitten and Adult awards at Championship shows in Britain including the National Cat Club show. In this, the largest and most competitive Championship cat show in the world, a First Prize gained in a large class indicates that the cat is very good indeed, while a Best in Show award suggests really outstanding quality. One outstanding cat, Ch Snowhite Herald, has won four Best in Show Long-hair awards, one as a kitten and three

A meticulously groomed six-months-old female, Honeymist White Snowdream, showing a fine wealth of coat and a splendid tail. Bred and owned by Mrs M. Howes.

Neat ears, broad head, firm chin and very short nose: Ch Bullensmede Adrian (male).

as an adult. These and other successes have firmly established the Orange-eyed White Persian until today it is one of the most popular long-hairs in Britain. The Black and White Cat Club caters for the Orange-eyed White in Britain, and offers many cups, trophies and rosettes at the shows.

The Copper-eyed White Persian has been popular in North America since the nineteenth century, indeed the very first listing in the first Beresford Cat Club Stud Book, published in 1889, is a Copper-eyed White. As in Britain, this breed has been very successful in the shows in America, and one White, Mrs Nikki Horner's Gr Ch Shawnee Moonflight, is the only cat to have been three times All-American Cat of the Year – 1960, 1961, 1964. The interests of the breed are looked after by the White Persian Society, which caters for all eye-colours.

Success on the show bench depends not only on having bred or acquired a cat which measures well up to the Standard of Points for the breed, but also on very good presentation, and this applies more to the case of a white, long-haired cat than to many others. A show cat requires bathing to get the coat really white (*see* The Cat in the Home). If care is taken there is no risk of the cat developing a chill, and the addition of a little borax to the water when washing the tail helps to remove undesirable yellow stains. This, of course, must be thoroughly rinsed off and the cat prevented from licking itself until this has been done.

Grooming is particularly important for all long-haired cats, whether destined for the show bench or not. Obviously the aim is to keep the coat free of knots and this can only be achieved by regular grooming. I find all-steel combs which can be sterilized best for this purpose, and the coat is kept clean by powdering either with talcum or chalk-based grooming powder. For very fine white fur the latter is better. The powder is sprinkled through the coat, then combed and finally brushed or patted out. For exhibiting, the fur looks its best after combing through several times with a very fine comb.

Mrs Lois Weston's female, Gr Ch Simbelair Tiffany—a successful cat from America, showing fine type.

Ch Bullensmede Adrian—a typical male profile.

Miss Sellar's Ch Coylum Marcus—said to be one of the world's most valuable cats, he visits the shows with his own security guards.

A female profile: Ferniehurst White Amber, showing a good, firm chin.

122

Showing her fine coat, Ferniehurst White Amber.

Below: Ch Bullensmede Adrian—an impressive all-rounder with a successful show record.

Below: A beautiful example of Australian long-hair breeding stock, Ch Scots Glen Mi Hiland Lad at eight months. Bred in New Zealand and owned by Mr R. Uren of Victoria.

With the White Long-hair, the colour is clean and pure; there is no marking or shading in the fur, and the slightest stain shows; so a very high standard of presentation is required to produce the sparkling white coat which sets off so perfectly the beautiful orange or copper eyes. But the effort is well worth while, and makes this beautiful creature indeed a cat to admire.

The Standard for the breed calls, not surprisingly, for a pure white coat, without mark or shade of any kind. The coat should be long and flowing on the body, with a full frill and brush which should be short and broad. Note the quality of the coat–it should be close, soft and silky, not woolly in texture.

Our Orange-eyed White has typically "British" long-hair type–cobby and massive in the body without being coarse, with plenty of bone and substance, and low on the leg. The head is round and broad, with plenty of space between the ears, which should be small, neat and well covered; a short nose is called for, with full cheeks and a broad muzzle. Orange or copper is the colour of the eyes, which should be large, round and wide open.

The American Standards call for the same type in this breed as for all other Persians, very similar to the British Standard, with eyes of "brilliant copper" (C.F.A.).

Above: Playful male kitten of nine weeks—Honeymist White Snowdazzle, bred and owned by Mrs M. Howes.

Ferniehurst White Amber in playful mood.

Any Other Colour

Long-hair

A pedigree cat or kitten conforming to no set standard may be registered in Britain as "Any Other Colour". Such cats may be the result of experimental or selected breeding, or accidental matings. Classes are put on at the shows for "Any Other Colour", and it is in these classes that new varieties usually make their bow to the public. For example, Cameos (recognized in the U.S.A. but not in Britain), Blue Chinchillas, Brown and Lilac Long-hairs have been seen in this class.

If eventually, the variety does receive recognition, it is entered in its own colour classes, and can, of course, if good, become a Champion then.

The brown and lilac long-hair varieties are even more recent in origin than, say, Colourpoints. The provisional names in Britain, Self Chocolate and Self Lilac Long-hair, were designed to distinguish these varieties from the pointed cats with these colours. Both of the new varieties are in process of full development to the typical long-hair type

Mrs S. M. Harding's Self-Lilac male, Mingchiu Marki.

Blue Chinchilla—an as yet unrecognized variety.

and are not yet recognised by the G.C.C.F. as individual breeds. The first purposeful breeding of these cats occurred in Richmond, Great Britain, and in Holland, but, as with Colourpoints and Birmans, these colour varieties have also turned up in domestic cats free to select their own mates without the intervention of man. In England, Mr B. A. Stirling-Webb bred the first Brown Long-hair.

Since the genes for a brown coat colour were, up to that time, absent in all the long-haired breeds, it was necessary to bring these genes in from the short-hairs – the self-chocolate short-hairs (Havana, formerly known in Britain as the Chestnut-brown). Matings between a long-haired Blue and a Chestnut-brown Short-hair carrying the genes for blue were the first of a series of matings which resulted in the appearance of the first long-haired brown cats. The first Brown Long-hair was exhibited by Mr Stirling-Webb at the National Cat Club show in London in 1961, a few years before his untimely death.

The Brown Long-hair has a rich chestnut-coloured coat, even all over with no ticking, stripes or white hairs. The eye colour ranges from deep copper to orange. Before moulting, the colour changes to tawny brown, and as moulting usually is more advanced on the head than elsewhere, the cats go through a stage with short dark-brown coats on head and shoulders, and longer, moulting, tawny hair still on the body. The Lilac Long-hair is the dilute form of the Brown, achieved by the addition of genes from both parents causing Maltese dilution (blue). Thus a Lilac Long-hair is pure for three recessive characters – long-hair, brown and blue and, if heterozygous for any of these characters or genes, will not be Lilac Long-hair in appearance. The coat colour is even all over and of a pale colour in which both the brown and the blue are visible. Compared with a Blue Long-hair, the difference in colour is very marked; the Lilac is not a pale blue, but a pale, browner version. The eyes are paler orange than in the Brown Long-hair. The first Lilac Long-hairs were produced in Britain in the Mingchiu Cattery where the Brown Long-hairs were also bred. As it was necessary to obtain the brown gene from short-hairs, inevitably undesirable characteristics of type were introduced into the long-hairs at the same time. The best way in which to improve the type of the two new varieties would be to out-cross to the best-typed self-coloured long-hairs and then back-cross or mate two fine carriers together. The procedure is simple but needs space and money, and thus time must pass before appreciable numbers of Brown and Lilac kittens can be produced. Recognition cannot be granted for any variety by the G.C.C.F. until there are three proven generations of like-to-like breeding, which takes some while. Both the Brown and Lilac Long-hairs have crossed the oceans and are being bred by persons who understand how to improve type.

The temperament of the Brown and Lilac Long-hairs makes them as delightful pets as the Colourpoints, as judged by the seven years during which they have so far been bred. Some are quite inseparable from their owners, accompanying them everywhere like a shadow, and sleeping on the bed at night, although the finest coats grow when the cats are fairly cool at night.

As with Colourpoints there is much individual difference in character and behaviour patterns.

Mingchiu Bromsey—a Self-Chocolate female bred and owned by Mrs S. M. Harding.

Short-hairs

Above: Premier Physalis Tangroa, a Seal-point Siamese neuter bred by Mrs V. Paramor.

Mrs I. Johnson's British Blue male, Ch Jezreel Jomo.

Bi-Coloured

*Short-hair
(British type)*

A most attractive Bi-colour with a blue and white coat, Pathfinders Stella, bred by Miss N. Woodifield.

Bi-colours, or cats with two colours in the coats, have been known for a very long time and a number were seen at the early cat shows. Mr Harrison Weir gave details of the many colours possible, i.e. black and white, white and black, brown tabby with white, dark tabby and white, red tabby and white, yellow tabby and white, silver tabby and white, and blue and white. The black-and-white seemed to have been most admired, and he said that the coat should be a dense bright brown-black, evenly marked with white, the feet being white (as in the present day Birmans) with white on the chest and face, that on the latter coming to a point between the eyes. The white had to be pure, with no black. The white-and-black cat should have a black tail, black markings on the head and back, and the rest of the coat pure white. The short-lived Cat Club founded in 1898 drew up a list of the colours of the "English" or "British" cats for the guidance of fanciers and judges and included "Any other colour tabby and white; eyes orange or green." The type was as for the other British cats.

Dr Gordon Stables writing in 1876 said of the black-and-white short-hairs that "a good black and white cat is a very noble looking animal. If well trained and looked after you can hardly have a nicer parlour pet", but he went on to say that "if well treated black and white cats are apt to turn a little indolent and lazy".

In spite of the many admirers of these cats, numbers on the show bench were never very high, and as new varieties and colours appeared, they became very few indeed.

A few years ago, thanks chiefly to the efforts of Miss N. Woodifield, it

An attractive red and white "Pathfinders" female with a good, strong profile and small well-placed ears, wide muzzle and good firm chin.

In mischievous mood—Pathfinders Rinty, a young male bred by Miss Woodifield, carries distinctive patches of black and white and is an example of good "British" type.

was realised that these cats were useful in the breeding of Tortoise-shell and Whites, and eventually they were recognized. Primlington and Tobious, owned by the Messrs H. and J. Biswell, did well at the shows after Bi-colours were first recognized, and Miss Woodifield's Pathfinders cats are always among the prize-winners.

The Standard recognized four colour varieties: black and white, blue and white, orange and white and cream and white, with the markings required to be as those seen in the Dutch rabbit. The description in the Standard was most precise, requiring an exacting pattern with, for example, the mask to be divided exactly in half in colour. It proved impossible to breed cats to this Standard and it meant that hundreds would have to be bred that would be of little use in the hope of producing one to the set pattern. The judges always withheld the Championships and the breeders lost heart.

In 1971 the Standard was revised and any solid colour and white is now recognized, with the patches of colour to be clear and evenly distributed. Not more than two-thirds of the coat should be coloured and not more than one half white. The face, too, should be patched, with a white blaze being liked. Faults are tabby markings, a long tail, green eyes and brindling within the patching. Although the Standard is slightly differently worded, the required type is as for all British Short-hairs (see Black).

Mrs K. Butcher's red and white kittens. Although they are still tiny, they already show clear patches of colouring. The faint tabby markings, considered a fault, will fade with age.

Pathfinder Rinty, with his good coat and colouring, will make a most useful stud for the breeding of Tortoiseshell and Whites.

Black   *Short-hair (British type)*

Mrs I. Johnson's Jezreel Murrey—a fine Black male in excellent condition.

Note Jezreel Murrey's good, firm chin and shortish nose.

The short-haired Black has a long tradition of mystique which persists even today. Seafaring families were, and many still are, very superstitious; a black cat was kept at the seaman's fireside to protect him while away at sea; but a black cat boarding a ship in port was considered an omen of ill-luck or even disaster. The black cat has a long association with witchcraft, too. However, the black cat of ill-omen is traditionally a sinuous, slinky animal – rather like the product of a Siamese mis-mating today; the bringer of good fortune was always a more rotund cat, similar in shape to today's pedigree British Shorthairs, although with greenish eyes, often slanting in shape.

Blacks have been bred to a recognized Standard and shown in Britain from the earliest days of the cat fancy, amber eyes, absence of white hairs, and well-knit type being called for them, just as today. In the late 1800's the eye colour of Mr R. J. Hughes's lovely Amber Queen was acclaimed the best of any black cat seen – she was the winner of many top awards. Mr Hughes bred many fine examples; Ballochmyle Black Bump was a particularly fine cat, later owned by Lady Alexander. There were many more, from this breeder and others.

In the early 1900's the question of out-crossing arose; Mr T. B. Mason, a judge and British Short-hair enthusiast, expressed the belief

Above: Jezreel Myrena (female), bred and owned by Mrs I. Johnson. At ten years old she is still in fine condition, with a good, black coat.

Below: Manana Toodle-Dee, with short, fine fur and a good female head. Bred by Mrs Maddocks.

Below: Head study of Jezreel Murrey, showing well his beautiful large eyes.

that one cross Black to Blue could improve the latter, while firmly advocating that this should be done once only. Suitable females only were to be used for such a cross, and the males neutered. A Black must have sound orange eye-colour; "latent green" eyes can easily be introduced into the breed through mating with a Blue of mediocre eye-colour. Likewise, even then, that the Blue coat may become too dark was a recognized hazard of such breeding, and a warning that only breeders with a sound knowledge of their stock ancestry should practise it. This still applies today.

The First World War put a stop to showing in Britain, seriously curtailing breeding, and Black entries in post-war shows were rather sporadic, greater interest being shown in some of the showier short-haired breeds. The role short-haired Blacks can play in breeding-programmes for Torties, Tortie-and-Whites and, more recently, Bi-Colours, was fully recognized, and this became the more usual reason for breeding a few good Blacks. This was the position until the Second World War further interfered with the Black's progress, as it did with other British Short-hairs.

It was not until the 1950's that we began to see a steadier, if thin, flow of glossy-coated, black short-hairs produced. Type was generally quite good, although eye-colour needed improvement, and this was worked for. We still find in pedigrees today names of lovely cats of that time, for example Ch Roofspringer Melisande, bred by Miss von Ullman, and Ch Bourneside Inky Bit, bred by Mrs Aitken. In Yorkshire Mrs Budd bred several top-class Blacks, such as Ch Nidderdale Black Magic and thus began a period of breeding a few first-rate Blacks by short-haired Red Tabby sires to suitable short-haired dams. Ch Killinghall Black Panther, bred by Miss Hardman, and Ch Aldra's Dark Talisman, bred by Mrs Attwood, come into this group. Mating short-haired Blacks together has produced impressive results in the form of Mrs I. Johnson's Ch Jezreel Maxwell, Ch Jezreel Muffin and others, all progeny of Jezreel Black Mumbo, ex Ch Andersley Allacreiche, a fine sire bred by Mrs Anderson.

Long-hair has been introduced into several recent breeding pro-grammes, a mixed blessing, but in general the future for the breed looks a little brighter, a leading contribution being made by Mrs Johnson's Jezreel prefix, among others. There was quite a good entry of short-haired Black kittens at the National Cat Club's "Centenary of Cat Shows" event at Olympia, London in December 1971, a promise of perhaps many more good pedigree specimens of the breed in the future. The specialist clubs in Britain for the Black Short-hair are the Black and White Cat Club, and the Short-Haired Cat Society of Great Britain and Manx Club Incorporated.

Keeping a Black in show condition can be quite difficult. Daily brushing is essential. Scurf, through lack of grooming, may occur, and greasiness at the tail root can cause discoloration as well. I find that bay rum or a good quality Eau-de-Cologne (just a few drops) brushed into the roots of the coat, allowed to dry, and then hand-groomed with chamois, gives perfect results. Attention to diet, with plenty of good, raw beef and an occasional raw egg yolk, helps maintain the glossy, dense coat. The owner is assisted by the cat himself who is fastidiously clean almost to the point of obsession.

Below: Manana Toodle-Dee.

According to the G.C.C.F. Standard, the coat should be jet-black to the roots, with no white anywhere, and no rusty tinge. Achieving the pure black, glossy coat, with *no* white hairs, is a constant challenge to the breeder. Even with three generations of pure breeding, if this fault exists in the line, it may recur in new generations. It may take almost until early adulthood before this final "unblemished" overcoat is acquired. When choosing which kitten in a litter to breed from, it sometimes happens that what appears to be a good kitten eventually fails on density of colour. The only simple rule when selecting kittens for breeding is to reject those with a lighter or bluish tinge at the hair roots, while keeping for consideration the kitten whose coat may appear slightly rusty on the surface only. Usually this clears and pure black follows. In the summer months one expects a black coat to become rather rusty if the cat is much in the sun. The wise owner will allow sun and fresh air and forego showing, if necessary, during this period. The eyes of the Black should be large, well-opened and really round, deep copper or orange in colour. There should be absolutely no trace of green. Although not actually specified in the Standard, nose leather and paw pads should be black.

Manana Toodle-Dee, her black coat glistening in the sun.

The body type of this cat should be the same as for other British Short-hairs. A well-knit, powerful build is called for, showing good depth of body. The chest should be full and broad, the tail thick at the base, well set, and of a length in proportion to the body. Legs should be of good substance and in proportion to the body, with neat and well-rounded feet.

The head should be broad between the ears, cheeks well-developed, and face and nose short. Ears are small, slightly round at the tops, and not large at the base. The coat should be short, fine and close. The condition of the British Short-hair should be hard and muscular, giving a general appearance of activity.

Mrs M. Maddocks's young male, "Harrison". He has a beautiful, even, dense black coat.

The American (or "Domestic") Short-hair is a somewhat larger and rangier cat than the British Short-hair; the Exotic Short-hair, recognized in America by C.F.A., is a closer equivalent to the British cat, with near-Persian type. Both these American short-haired breeds are covered separately in this book.

Blue-Cream Short-hair
(British type)

Mrs J. Richard's Pensylva Twilight Fantasy, a young, up-and-coming female, with short, close coat, good type and head shape. A striking feature is the distinctive cream blaze on the forehead, much liked by fanciers.

Jezreel Juja is a charming example of this all-female variety, with a well-intermingled coat of blue and cream. Bred and owned by Mrs I. Johnson.

The rarest of the British Short-hair varieties, the Blue-cream was not established until well after the Second World War, which played havoc with the progress not only of this but of other British Short-hair varieties as well.

An early example was Mrs Cattermole's Mingswyk Mysterious Maid, born in 1951 (the breed was shown as A.O.V. at that time) – but this line was not perpetuated. Official recognition was not granted to the Blue-cream by the G.C.C.F. until 1956, and this was achieved largely through the breeding efforts of Mrs P. Hughes, whose Ch Broughton Jane, born in 1955, was one of the most significant early cats, and is to be found in many later pedigrees. Other early cats of note were Ch Jezreel Jamima, bred by Mrs I. Johnson; and three

Head study of Jezreel Juja, showing her good, broad head, and well-placed ears slightly rounded at the tops, and large, expressive eyes.

Champions bred by the late Mrs Attwood, Aldra's Mayblossom, Aldra's Pansyface, and Aldra's Twinkletoes.

Ch Broughton Jane was acquired in 1960 by Mrs Joan Richards as a basis for the Pensylva Blue-cream breeding-programme; this cat produced a long line of first rate short-hairs, beginning with Ch Pensylva Fantasia, sired by the well-known Cream, Ch Aldra's Cream Bunne, followed by Ch Pensylva Pansy, born in the same year, and who has brought to the breed a succession of show awards. By means of accurate breeding records the Pensylva line has been kept quite pure. Jane lived for nearly 16 years, dying in January 1971. Another of her progeny, Int Ch Pensylva Noelle Joyeuse, introduced the British Blue-cream to France – in 1966, her first season in France, Noelle was Best Short-hair in Show, in Paris. Pensylva cats have also introduced the breed to Belgium and the United States of America.

Pensylva Aphrodite (female), bred by Mrs J. Richards—a delightful study of typically "British" type, with short nose and face and well-intermingled colours on face.

The Blue-cream has an important role to play for the short-hair breeder, for a good example, suitably mated, will produce British Blues of particular quality, short-haired Creams, and Blue-creams, all capable of reaching championship status in their own fields. It is fortunate that the Blue-cream was established at a time when care was taken to breed it properly, and accurate breeding records kept from the beginning. The line has thus been kept pure, without recourse to cross-breeding. That is not to say that we have not seen on the show bench cats entered as Blue-creams, but resulting from more injudicious matings, a Russian Blue dam and unknown sire, for example; in 1965 one cat had a Rex sire, mated to a Havana!

135

This Pensylva kitten, bred by Mrs Richards, still has a fluffy kittenish coat, but already showing a good broad head and firm chin.

The interests of the British Blue-cream short-hair are catered for by the Red, Cream, Tortoiseshell, Tortoiseshell and White, Blue-cream, and Brown Tabby Society, and by the Short-haired Cat Society of Great Britain and Manx Club Incorporated. The Blue-cream does not need any special care beyond that given to all short-hairs; given the usual daily grooming, it will be a picture of good health. The only thing to be alert for is the possibility of a hairball during the moult – the cream hairs, finer than the blue, are occasionally responsible for this. During the moult use a fine-tooth-comb to remove loose hair. Generally, however, this problem will not arise in cats which have access to coarse grass, a natural emetic.

The Blue-cream short-hair has considerable aesthetic appeal. According to the G.C.C.F. Standard of Points the coat should be short and fine-textured, with the blue and cream colours softly intermingled, rather than patched. This coat is most attractive, with a resemblance to shot silk, best viewed in daylight. Coupled with large copper, orange or yellow eyes (*never* green) and a sweet personality, this makes for a "prize" cat, whether as a breeding queen or a lovely spayed pet – the spayed Blue-cream is generally a rather larger cat.

Lack of patching in the coat is a most elusive quality, and must be constantly worked for by the breeder. It is worth writing here that in North America the Standard for blue-cream American and Exotic Short-hairs calls for the two colours, blue and cream, not to be intermingled, but to occur in clearly-defined patches. Good patching is probably less difficult to achieve than an intermingled coat, but not easy nevertheless.

The Standard for all matters other than coat and eye colour is the same as that for all British Short-hairs (*see* Black). It is worth bearing in mind that, as the Blue-cream is invariably female, the overall build of the cat will be somewhat daintier than that, say, of a British Blue male.

A Blue-cream queen with good type and distinctive blaze on head—with her young Blue kitten. Owner: Mrs Richards.

British Blue (inc. Chartreuse)

Short-hair (British type)

A female with a good, round head, even-coloured coat and all the required British short-hair characteristics—Fendale Victoria, owned by Mrs S. Beever.

In the early days Blues with short coats were known under a variety of names and the history and development of the British Blue, as it is now known in Britain (in America it is registered with C.F.A. as Exotic Short-hair (Blue) and by most other Associations as British Blue, achieving its first All-American listing in 1961) since the Second World War has been a story of "stop and go". The 1939–1945 period saw the decline and near-extinction of these lovely cats and after the War there was a great shortage in Britain of male British Blues. The consequence was that foreign-type cats were used in breeding programmes. This was almost the death-blow to the desired bone structure; for what we are really looking for in this breed is a blue cat with short, almost plush-like hair, but with near long-hair type.

It was not until the middle and late 1950's that this problem was squarely tackled, when some far-sighted breeders began sending their British Blue queens to selected Blue Long-hair males. This was not a new procedure but was necessary at this time, to recover "bone". Results were good – of course care had to be taken, when placing any long-haired offspring, to ensure that they were not used for future breeding of either long- or short-hairs. However, new breeders today seem reluctant to use a Long-hair out-cross. My own best results came from a mating with a short-haired Black that was long-hair bred. I also tried using a Chartreuse, imported from Belgium; this did not

Full-face of Mrs I. Johnson's female Jezreel Jenny Penn, showing well-developed cheeks and a well-balanced "British" head.

137

Above: An International Champion Chartreuse from France—Bonaventura, with a beautiful, thick coat and yellow eyes.

Opposite page: Jezreel Jandow at six weeks old. A sturdy little male kitten, with the makings of a future champion. Bred and owned by Mrs Johnson.

improve type, although it did produce better coat quality. We are left with the conclusion that the future development of the British Blue, and indeed of all British short-haired breeds, still lies in the occasional out-cross to the long-hairs to retain bone and type.

In France for many years there has been a breed of blue short-coated cats known as the Chartreuse. It is said that they were bred in the first place by the Chartreux monks in the monasteries there. Massive solid cats with broad chests and round heads, they were considered by many to differ from the very similar British Blues, having greyish-blue rather than light to medium blue coats. Although over the years, these differences appear to have vanished, and it is now accepted that standards for the Chartreuse and the British Blue are the same, some judges can still pick out the Chartreuse breed.

There are exceptions to every rule, but the British Blue is normally a very quiet cat, and gives the impression that he would do anything for a quiet life. The Blue is never happier than when sitting by the fire after a romp out of doors, where nature provides the entertainment in the form of birds and mice. Blues rarely leave home in a fit of pique as a Siamese male I once had often did – this cat always seemed to know when I was going out and usually went AWOL at these times. My British Blue would always return home to the rattle of yeast tablets in a tin. If you keep many cats it is impossible to keep them all in the house but you should let them have some freedom to develop their natural instincts. Do not inhibit their spirit of adventure by keeping them indoors or penned all their lives – fortunately I live out of town, so that I can allow my cats more freedom. A cat's character and behaviour is influenced to some extent by its owner, but less so than with other animals. Cats always have a measure of independence and stubbornness that never quite makes you the owner of a cat – always the other way round, and the British Blue is no exception.

Above: Jezreel Jenny Penn with her six-week-old triplets.

Right: A typically "British" male—Mrs Johnson's Ch Jezreel Jomo—a powerful looking cat with short, sturdy legs and full broad chest.

Above: Ch Jezreel Jomo, showing his good broad head and slightly rounded ears.

Care of the British Blue is quite a simple matter – just common-sense awareness of its needs. Feeding is dealt with in full elsewhere in this book; the inner cat requires a little of what it fancies, and it is a mistake to succumb to the demands of a dominant feline. There are three "musts" for my cats that come before the cream and the potato crisps – cod-liver oil, eggs and yeast tablets. Do not be brain-washed by the advertisements – by all means use canned or dried food, but "as well", not "only". At shows in Britain only five points are allotted when judging for condition, but a cat that is not in condition is never a prize-winner. Out of condition, a cat has no bloom to its coat, and coat quality is never right.

Like all cats, British Blues by nature are cleanliness itself, but before you take them to a show a little human help is needed. Being short-coated they are fairly easy to groom. A few minutes hand-grooming keeps them tidy, and habits form in your daily routine whereby you clean their eyes and look into their ears almost unconsciously. Powder helps to clean the coat, but choose one that is not highly perfumed, and make sure you brush it all out before you take your Blue to a show.

The British Standard for the British Blue allows a coat colour of light to medium blue, very level in colour, with no tabby markings, shadings, or white. In fact the colour most favoured in this breed is a mid- or plum-blue. A paler coat colour emphasizes the basic ticking

Manana Tin Tin—Mrs Maddocks's imperturbable British Blue female.

of the hair and gives a speckled effect, less attractive to the eye than that of the slightly deeper shade. In my experience, crossing a British Blue with a British Black has brought out the best coat colour in the kittens. As to coat quality, the Blue is covered by the Standard for all British Short-hairs which requires simply a short, fine, close coat. However, I look for a coat quality different from other "British" varieties – perhaps best described as "plush-like", bringing to mind the old plush table-cloths of our grandmother's day. The eyes of the British Blue should be large and full, copper, orange or yellow in colour.

In all other respects the Standard for the British Blue is the same as for other British Short-hairs (*see* Black).

Above: A litter of Pensylva Blues and Blue-creams, bred by Mrs Richards. Below: Dignified male features of Jezreel Jomo.

Above: From the early days, Lady Alexander's Blue Champion, Ballochmyle Brother Bump.

Left: British Blues make delightful pets as neuters—Mrs S. Beever's Premier Fendale Fidelo.

141

Cream
Short-hair (British type)

Pensylva Gaiety Girl at six months—bred by Mrs J. Richards.

True head shape—Pensylva Gaiety Girl.

The story of the short-haired Cream over the years has been one of mixed fortunes. As early as 1903 Miss Frances Simpson, in *The Book Of the Cat,* noted that interest was generally concentrated on the long-haired rather than the short-haired Cream, and in fact it was not until the late 1920's that this short-hair was even given G.C.C.F. recognition and a breed number. This lack of interest extended to certain other British Short-hair colours, and indeed the situation is to some extent the same today. In the very early days short-haired Creams generally occurred as "sports", undoubtedly from Tortoiseshell queens; when the latter became almost extinct in favour of the Tortie and White, the Cream would have been similarly threatened. The colour of this variety was generally described as fawn, and the pale cream colour that breeders aim at today did not evolve until after the Second World War.

Since the Second World War a number of breeders in Britain have made highly significant contributions to the progress of the Cream. From the early years after the war, it is Mrs J. Cattermole and her

Mingswyk cats, and Mrs I. Johnson, with her Jezreel prefix, who come to mind. In the later 1950's Mrs Attwood's Aldra's prefix came into prominence; this breeder paid particular attention to the improvement of coat-colour. Her best cats came from a short-haired Blue-cream dam – Mrs Attwood understood and made use of the breeding compatibility of the British Blues, Creams and Blue-creams. Her most noteworthy cat, one which still figures in a few pedigrees today, was Ch Aldra's Cream Bunne, a beautiful specimen and worthy sire which, through his daughter Ch Pensylva Fantasia, contributed to Mrs J. Richards's Pensylva breeding-programme.

The most successful British Short-hair neuter of all time is a Cream – Premier Bambi's Mischief, bred by Mrs Hughes and owned by Mrs Richards. This cat is over twelve years old and in 1972 was still winning top show awards. He now reigns over Mrs Richards's highly successful Pensylva cats, which are bred through a three-colour (Cream, British Blue, Blue-cream) breeding-programme; notable names from the Pensylva cattery are Ch Pensylva Pinkerton, Ch Pensylva Prince d'Or, Ch Pensylva Blond Bandit (all males), and Ch Pensylva Flaxen Nymph and Ch Pensylva Pink Champagne (both female). The female of the variety is very rare indeed, due to colour and sex linkage, which needs to be fully understood. Breeding good Creams is not easy, and perhaps this is one reason why, even as recently as December 1971, there was no adult of the breed actually competing in Britain at the National Cat Club's "Centenary of Cat Shows" event at Olympia, London, although some Pensylva cats were on exhibition.

The short-haired Cream is a naturally clean cat, but a special grooming session once a week and the day before a show is recommended, in addition to normal daily brushing; for this a reliable baby-powder should be used to dispel greasiness from the coat – pay special attention to the tail and tail-root. A good mixed diet is recommended, although too much concentration on white fish can cause skin problems. Fresh water and access to coarse grass are important.

The British Standard calls for a rich cream coat, free from barring, and with no sign of white anywhere. Some Creams are far too "hot" in colour, stemming probably from Tortoiseshell or other red ancestry; even mating Cream to Cream for several generations will produce this effect – genetically, after all, cream is a dilute of red. The correct

Above: Bred by Mrs Hughes and owned by Mrs Richards, Bambi's Mischief is the most successful British Short-hair neuter of all time.

Below: Ch Pensylva Blond Bandit; a young stud, nicely balanced with a good even cream coat, difficult to achieve without markings.

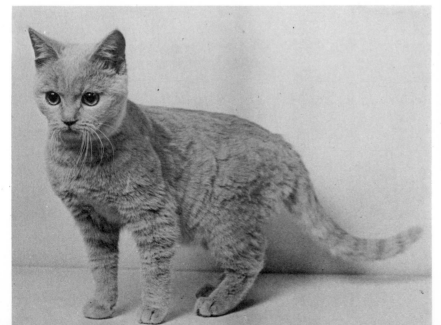

Left: Pensylva Gaiety Girl—the slight rings on the tail are very difficult to breed out.

143

Mrs J. Foster's Jezreel Chaney—a young male with good broad chest and rounded well-set ears.

colour and absence of barring and white markings are best achieved, in my experience, by judicious use not only of the Cream, but of the genetically compatible British Blue and Blue-cream as well. I have found correct colour and clarity in the coat easier to achieve in the females than in the males.

Barring on chest, forelegs, and tail is a hazard which should be constantly recognized by the breeder, and its elimination must be a constant aim. Sometimes as a kitten matures, these markings can be seen to disappear almost day by day. Ghost markings can appear in a normally clear coat, and can be attributed to short-term changes of environmental temperature. A Cream coat is at its best at a constant, moderate temperature.

The G.C.C.F. Standard for the Cream in respect to matters other than coat-colour is as for other British Short-hairs (*see* Black). In fact the Cream's bone structure tends to be a little less massive than, say, the British Blue.

The specialist clubs in Britain for the Cream are firstly the Red, Cream, Tortoiseshell, Tortoiseshell and White, Blue-Cream and Brown Tabby Society; and secondly, the Short-Haired Cat Society of Great Britain and Manx Club Incorporated. The latter, in 1967, was responsible for removing from the Standard the anomaly whereby in the short-haired Cream, hazel eyes were allowable; now the position is as for long-haired Creams – copper or orange eyes only.

A Blue and a Cream kitten produced from a Cream/Blue mating.

Ch Pensylva Blond Bandit, showing a good, shortish nose.

144

Spotted   *Short-hair (British type)*

Ch Culverden Charlotte, female, owned by Mrs J. Higgins. A brown Spottie, with nice head, good width between the ears, big round eyes and well-ringed tail.

The Spotted Cats are thought to be one of the oldest varieties known and many of the wild cats have some form of spotting. In the Egyptian Book of the Dead, the Great God, Ra, is pictured as a spotted cat slaying Apep, the serpent of darkness; and cats with similar markings appear on some of the Egyptian papyrus scrolls, proving that they have been known for several thousand years at least. A mosaic discovered at Pompeii depicts a magnificent spotted cat with a bird in its mouth. In the early 1880's, several domestic cats with spotted coats were exhibited, and John Jennings writing in 1893, said he considered that the Spotted Tabby required but little description, so evidently there were quite a few about at that time. He said the spots should be of medium size, the sharper in outline the better, and "the spots in a grand specimen, should extend in a perfectly uniform manner entirely over the body, feet and tail, and if on the face its value is so much increased". At the beginning of the twentieth century, Frances Simpson wrote that the Spotted Tabby was becoming very rare and was seldom seen at the shows. This was probably because the cats with long coats were coming much into favour, and for a while there was little interest in pedigree short-hairs, many people considering them ordinary pet cats.

Round head and rounded ears of Mrs J. Higgins's brown Spotted male, Zephyr Dionysus.

Although they were referred to as Spotted Tabbies, technically this was incorrect, as "tabby" has always been taken as meaning "striped". Nowadays, the old Standard has been slightly amended, and they are referred to as Spotted cats.

For the next fifty years or so, Spotties seemed practically to have disappeared. They were seen occasionally, usually being neutered pets, the owners considering them nothing out of the ordinary. It was

Above: Pensylva Filigree, a Spotted Lilac, which is an unusual colour.

Right: Ch Culverden Charlotte, showing a short nose and alert expression.

Above: A Spotted cat from France.

Above: The lithe body of Mrs Higgins's brown Spottie female, Ch Zephyr Dionysia, displaying a beautifully defined coat pattern and well-ringed tail, thick at the base, as required by the Standard.

Below: Culverden Magnus, in 1969, showing very clearly his spotted coat. Owner: Mrs E. Towe.

not until 1965 that they reappeared on the British show bench, and the old Standard was revived, with the variety again being recognized.

The first Spotted Cat to be shown for many years in Britain was Culverden Clairedelune, a silver Spotted, and the result of a mating between a pedigree short-haired Black, Marcasite Cachucha, and a short-haired, marbled Silver Tabby, Ch Culverden Maurice; Clairedelune was shown at Cheltenham in 1965, obtained her Championship there and was Best Short-haired Cat in Show. When she was mated later to a pedigree short-haired British Blue, one of the resulting litter was a brown Spotted, now Ch Culverden Charlotte, who has produced several brown Spotteds of excellent coat pattern. In general, the quality of the breed is steadily improving, some of the cats are now showing butterfly markings on the shoulders, and three spine lines in spots – the overall effect is particularly interesting.

Miss Irene Robson who, with her Culverden cats, was largely responsible for the recognition of the breed in Great Britain in 1966, emphasized the importance of correct type. As she pointed out, the Spotted is by definition a "British" short-hair, and so it follows that cats with a long, narrow head, a sinuous body and a whip tail are not good Spotteds, however good their spotting may be. Many hybrid "foreign" cats have wonderful spotted coats, really like ocelots; but although they are very striking, the type is wrong, with their long heads and deeper-set eyes. There is no British Standard of Points for these cats at the present time, and they have to be shown in "Any Other Variety" classes.

The breeder of the Spotted Cat now has a twofold task – to maintain the present quality of type, and, by judicious breeding, to improve the coat pattern still further. There should be more spots and fewer

Zephyr Dionysus—showing clearly his good, clear spotting, powerful body and full, broad chest.

Below: A small kitten owned by Mrs E. Towe, showing guard hairs before spots appear.

A young blue Spotted kitten with spots just appearing in the baby coat. Owned by Mrs Richards.

Zephyr Dionysus—a proud father with his two outstanding sons.

stripes. The spots need not necessarily be round, or all of one shape; some can be triangular, some star-shaped, and some like rosettes, all on the same cat. None of the spots should be narrow, elongated and rod-shaped, like the stripes of a mackerel Tabby. It has been claimed that the Spotted Cat was the original variety of Tabby, but this is unlikely as the coats of the two breeds are so very different. There are now enough good Spotteds in existence to enable breeders to mate Spotted to Spotted, and many are doing this, with rewarding results in the form of more and better spots. Although most of today's Spotted Cats are silver and brown in colour, a few reds, creams, and one or two blue Spotteds can now be seen; the colours, especially of the blues, are very pleasing, but as yet the coat patterns are not very definite.

The British Standard for the breed's coat puts good and clear spotting as the first essential. The spots can be round, oblong or rosette-shaped. Any of these markings may be of equal merit, but the spots, however shaped or placed, should be distinct, and not running into one another. They may be of any colour which suits the ground coloration. Stripes and bars, except on the face or head, are faults in the show specimen.

Eye colour should conform to coat colour, as given in the Standard for the British short-hair.

In all respects other than coloration, the Spotted cat should conform to the Standards for all British short-hairs. That is to say, the body and tail should be well-knit and powerful, with good depth of body and a full broad chest. The tail should be thick at the base, well set, and of a length in proportion to the body. The Spotted's legs should be of good substance, and in proportion to the body, with neat, well-rounded feet. The head should be broad between the ears, with well-developed cheeks, and short face and nose. Ears should be small, slightly rounded at the tops, but not large at the base. The overall effect should be hard and muscular, giving a general appearance of activity. The coat should be short, fine and close.

Tabby, Brown
Short-hair (British type)

Ch Periopal Bubbles—an older female cat showing good head shape and body in a comparatively rare breed. Owned by Mr H. K. Milburn.

Although common among mongrel cats, being found with varying patterns of markings, tabbies are comparatively rare in the pedigree varieties, the Brown Tabby being among the rarest. Even at the first cat shows, Brown Tabbies with the rich sable coat colouring and the correct pattern of markings, as set in the Standard, were few and far between. Any that were exhibited were usually of unknown parentage, without traceable pedigrees.

One name that appears in the early cat books, Ch Xenophon, born in 1892, was a constant winner for many years, being eventually bought by Lady Decies, and was said to have "wonderful colouring and ideal markings". A few years later, Lady Alexander's Ch Ballochmyle Brown Bump, born in 1908, took prizes each time shown.

The numbers continued to be few; several decades later, there were only two entered in the 1939–1948 Stud Book, Stanton Pompadour and Stanton Esther, both with all details unknown, belonging to Miss Wrighton. Later, Miss A. Stubb's Ch Whiston Tabitha Twitchet, by Timothy Titus, a Brown Tabby, and a white mother; Whiston Gorgeous Gussie; and Ch Whiston Tiberius, her half brother, took many firsts at the 1957–1959 shows. Miss B. Milburn showed Brown Tabbies for many years in the late 1950's and, on her death, her cats were transferred to her brother, Mr H. Milburn, who bred and showed several with pure Brown Tabby breeding, a great achievement. These included Ch Periopal Bubbles, Ch Periopal Easter Munday, Ch Periopal Silken Firefly and Ch Periopal Squeak. At the present day shows, Mrs Absalom's Ch Brynbuboo Brown Peter is a fine example of what is required in a pedigree Brown Tabby, and he has also sired a number of outstanding kittens, while Mrs J. Higgins's Zephyr cats and Mr M. Warde's Sherada cats are also doing well. In fact, the present time appears to be the heyday of the Brown Tabby· Short-hairs in Britain, and it is hoped that this trend will continue.

The short-haired Brown Tabby is an excellent show cat; it is not only easily prepared but, in addition, it is a complete extrovert and loves attention. Of course, a comparatively rare variety such as this has more opportunities for high awards on the British show bench than some of its more numerous cousins.

Grooming of a short-haired Brown Tabby is very simple and also very rewarding. My normal daily routine consists of a good stiff brushing and combing and, in the moulting season, a wipe over with a damp chamois leather to finish off. If the cat is to put in an appearance at a show, about three days beforehand I give the coat a good overall rub with a special grooming preparation, and brush until dry. After this, really thorough and repeated brushing will impart a lovely sheen to the coat, and bring out the pattern of markings. Give plenty of hand-grooming as well, making sure that your hands are clean first,

A European Brown Tabby.

Left: Ch Westways Alice owned by Mrs A. Sayer—a female with a good profile and typical British head.

149

otherwise the coat will become greasy. A quick clean with a cotton bud in the ears and that is all the show preparation needed – you will find that the finished product is well worth the effort, and the judges will admire the results as much as you do.

There are no special breeding problems with this variety – the queens appear to be "born mothers"; their strong maternal instinct carries right through until the kittens are adult. The Brown Tabby queen is usually the undisputed "Boss Cat", taking precedence over the stud. The male tends to be less aggressive; this does not mean that he lacks courage – far from it, but he would not start an argument. He is a virile stud-cat, gentle and affectionate, but not really a "lover", for once he has done his duty by his queen, he wants to be off and about other matters of interest!

The kittens are a delight from the moment they are born. Their little "pansy" faces with the tiny pattern of markings immediately give them character. Usually one has to wait a while for all the colour to come through, and sometimes for some of the tail and leg markings, but normally with a short-haired tabby, one can see from birth which kittens are the best. They usually have good appetites and are very playful little creatures, very fond of their own "family". Usually exceptionally clean in their toilet, they are very easy to house-train – if shown the litter tray, they will always go to it until old enough to go outside and use the garden.

There is very little difficulty in selling a Brown Tabby short-hair, although the general public still needs a certain amount of education in what to look for in a pedigree specimen. The Tabby Cat Club was formed in 1968 and is now flourishing, and one of its aims is to further the interests of the pedigree tabby, as well as to give help, advice and information to owners of tabby cats in general.

Looking at the short-haired Brown Tabbies at today's shows in Britain, I have the impression that while head type and markings usually conform to the officially recognized Standard, the colour very often does not. One rarely sees the lovely, rich, russet brown which calls the jungle to mind, and which sets this cat apart from his less exalted cousins.

The Standard in Britain calls for very dense and black markings, quite distinct from the ground colour, which is described as a "rich sable or brown", uniform throughout and completely without white markings.

A definite butterfly mark on the shoulders is required. The tail must be ringed from base to tip, as should the legs. On the chest there should be two necklaces or "mayoral" chains, and the flanks should carry swirls of oyster pattern; the chin should be cream or brown, and not white – a white chin is a bad fault which breeders are doing their best to eliminate. The eyes may be orange, hazel, deep yellow or green. Although it does not appear in the Standard, a good tabby should always carry the "capital M" on its forehead, and appear to be wearing spectacles; this gives the tabby face a touch of distinction which – in the eyes of every tabby enthusiast – is lacking from the self-coloured cat.

In respects other than colour and markings, the short-haired Brown Tabby should meet the same description as all other "British" short-hairs (see Black).

Good body shape and legs of Ch Westways Alice, showing whorls on the flanks and "chains" around the neck.

Opposite page: Ch Westways Alice has a beautiful head shape, well-placed round-tipped ears and well-defined markings on head.

Two of Mrs S. Higgins's kittens, age ten days and a few weeks. The markings are not yet distinct, but beginning to appear in the older kitten.

Tabby, Red

Above: Peerless Firecrest, a male bred by Mr M. Winder and owned by Gary Menezes—showing well-knit body and well-rounded feet.

Below: Vectensian Crunchie, female, bred by Mrs P. Hoare and owned by Mrs Menezes. A red female tabby is thought by many not to exist, but can be produced from pure breeding.

The short-haired Red Tabby, given its correct colour and markings, is one of the most striking of cats in its appearance, and has an intelligent and affectionate nature to match. Unfortunately, it does not appear to be much in favour with breeders and exhibitors in the United Kingdom these days, as evidenced by the invariably small numbers appearing at shows. It has been in the past, and still is, bedevilled by its public image of "ginger tom next door", or "marmalade cat" whereas a Red Tabby of the correct pedigree is certainly neither ginger nor orange-coloured.

There are several widely-held, but erroneous, beliefs regarding tabby cats, particularly in country districts in Britain. One is that the word "tabby" means "female"; in actual fact the derivation is probably from the resemblance of the tabby markings to those on a watered silk originally made at Attabiy, Baghdad, in ancient Persia, now Iran and of course applies to both sexes. Another, conflicting, tradition, still strongly held in many districts, has it that all *Red* Tabbies are *male*. Not so, but it is true that red-to-red matings produce more males than females – the proportion has been observed generally to be two to one; as any female resulting from blacks mated to reds will be tortoiseshells, the number of Red Tabby females naturally occurring in mixed colonies, say of farm cats, is likely over a period of time to decrease to vanishing point. Hence this particular belief.

Red Tabby short-hairs are sometimes mated to long-haired Red Tabbies, to improve eye or coat colour, but this practice has the disadvantage that the short, fine and close coat essential for short-hairs is lost in some of the progeny, and this quality is difficult to recover. A Red Tabby dam mated to a black sire will produce red males and tortie females, and a Red Tabby sire mated to a black dam will result in black males and tortie females; to produce Red Tabby females it is necessary to mate red to red, or to mate a tortie female to a red or cream sire.

There are few mentions of any specific Red Tabby cats in the early books on cats, although Gordon Stables writing in his book *The Domestic Cat* in 1876 does say of them "They are the prettiest of pets and the honestest of all cat kind. They are such good ratters that neither mice nor rats will frequent the house they inhabit". Harrison Weir included them in his Points of Excellence, the standards he set out for the judging of cats at the first shows. They came under the heading of "Chocolate, Chestnut, Red or Yellow Tabby, Striped, Short-hair", but he says little about them in the actual text of the book *Our Cats and All About Them* printed in 1889.

Mrs E. Soame, writing as late as 1933, said "There is little to write about this breed. They are very scarce, and the few there are, are of a pale sandy colour". She does mention Ch Rufus Superbus, bred by Miss Bretherton and owned by Lady Alexander, and Ch Clayton Masher belonging to Mr Clough, as being among the winners.

Short-haired Red Tabbies may not make up the largest contingent at cat shows, but the last twenty years have nevertheless seen some splendid examples – Ch Stanton Red Elf, bred by Miss Wrightson in 1945, is on many a pedigree, as are the Rivoli cats bred by Miss Bridgford, and Ch Vectensian Copper-Eyes and Ch Vectensian Anaconda, bred by Miss Pat Tucker (now Mrs P. Hoare); there are many others, the Barwell, Nidderdale and Killinghall prefixes figuring prominently. Many of these cats have been mated to black or tortoise-shell, to produce very good and successful progeny of these complementary colours. Latterly, good Red Tabby short-hairs have been bred by Mrs H. Woollin, notably her Ch Tip Top and Ch Golden Glory, and cats under the prefix of Peerless, bred by Mr Norman Winder, are making their mark.

The Red Tabby is red, not ginger or orange – the ground colour of the coat should be as rich a red as possible, and the markings an even deeper tone, a dense, dark red, not mixed with the ground colour, and quite distinct from it.

The correct markings are three dark red stripes down the back, with an oyster-shaped pattern on the sides of the body. On the back of the neck is a "butterfly" mark – attributed by legend to Mahomet! One or more clear markings encircle the neck and throat, and bracelet markings adorn the legs. The tail is ringed evenly all the way down to the tip, which should preferably be of the darker colour. The forehead shows pencilled markings running down to the base of the nose, and the cheeks have heavier markings converging to a point below the ears. White patches or hairs anywhere are completely taboo. At birth the markings are quite clear but they quickly disappear and for

Peerless Firecrest.

Peerless Firecrest—a beautiful head study of this old British variety. Good expressive eyes and slightly rounded ears.

153

Vectensian Crunchie has a good female head and body shape, but markings are not well-defined on the body.

Below: George—a male kitten sitting in the sun. Still with a fluffy kitten's coat but tabby markings beginning to appear. Owned by Mrs S. Crabb.

Killinghall Red Spark, bred by Miss G. Hardman, was not shown as an adult, so did not become a Champion, but his markings and type are exceptional.

several weeks the kittens are a rather pale self colour. This can be a disappointment to a novice, but gradually the colour deepens and the markings reappear, though they may be somewhat confused and blurred; in due course the kitten coat gives way to that of the adult, and the markings become clear.

The Red Tabby comes also in the "Mackerel-striped" form. Here too the markings should be as dense as possible, distinct from the ground colour. The darker rings should be as narrow and as numerous as possible, running vertically from the spine towards the ground.

The G.C.C.F. Standard for the short-haired Red Tabby, in regard to matters other than coloration, is as for other British Short-hairs (*see* Black).

The Short-haired Cat Society founded in 1901 and now known as the Short-haired Cat Society of Great Britain and Manx Club Incorporated is one of the specialist clubs interested in this variety, as is also the Red, Cream, Tortoiseshell, Tortoiseshell and White, Blue-Cream and Brown Tabby Society.

Tabby, Silver
Short-hair (British type)

Mrs M. Greenwood's Ch Gringo Silver Peregrine, a male with dense black markings on a coat of silver and showing a good British-type head.

The derivation of the term "Tabby" is given elsewhere in this book. The distinctive coat pattern is possibly one of the oldest and most familiar. References were made in Roman times to the Tabby, but only in modern times have the variations been recognized; the marbled, the mackerel and the spotted variety (*see* Spotted). Recent, additional information is difficult to discover as many records were destroyed during the Second World War, forcing contemporary writers to refer to old books.

The colour variations usual in marbled tabby cats are brown, red and silver; for mackerels silver and occasionally blue. Silvers should have dense markings on pure clear silver, and in the best specimens the markings have the appearance of black velvet, making a very striking effect. In all cases the markings must be clear and distinct, providing a decided contrast. Of all the tabby breeds, the Silvers are perhaps the most showy and popular. They are gentle, shy and affectionate. The females have pretty "smiling" faces, and they get on well with other breeds, especially the Siamese.

There seem to be more definite links between the Silvers and the famous cats of the past than there are with other tabby breeds. As far back as 1870, according to books and show catalogues of that time, Silver Tabbies were highly regarded, some were priced as much as £50 ($130). Among famous Silvers of pre-war days, the ancestors of the significant queens and sires of today, were Silver King, Sure Again, James II, Ch Shelley, Sweet Phyllis and many more; and there was the

Mrs Menezes' Taishun Sequin. The head of this female shows correct face markings and pencilled "M" on the forehead.

famous neuter, Silver Penny, owned by Mrs Burls, winner of over thirty first prizes in the days before Premier Certificates were awarded to neuters.

Since cat shows began again after the War, in 1946, many Silvers have been shown and they remain great favourites. The War caused a great run down of quality specimens in this breed, as with many others. The situation was perhaps not so bad in the U.S.A. as in Britain, where only one pedigree female could be found. This female, registered as Hillcross Silver Lady, was about eight years old, and descended from two short-hairs well-known in Britain, Silva Jim and Silva Laurel. Tigger, as she was known, was mated to a Silver male of no known pedigree and, through him, founded the Silver Tabby breed as we know it in Britain today. Tigger was a beautiful little cat, who became Champion in three successive shows. A male from her final litter was the well-known Ch Hillcross Silver Flute, a lovely cat for type and colour, who became the sire of many winners.

In 1948, a Silver female of obscure parentage contributed to the post-war re-establishment of the breed. She was Ch Starlight of Silverleigh, owned by Miss Bracey. Starlight was mated to the long-haired Silver, Robert of Silverleigh, and produced a litter of three short-haired female Silver kittens, all subsequently mated to Silver Flute. A little later, Miss Peters bred a good Silver, Silver Lute of Blagdon, who further influenced the improvement of the breed, and the stock in Britain was further strengthened by the import from France of Bellever Calchas d'Acheux. This cat was the last of a famous pre-war French strain which consistently provided winners under English judges, who had high regard for the French Silver Tabbies, for their excellent type and dense markings on a pure silver ground.

It is interesting to note that these excellent features were maintained by the French breeders by using a short-haired Black in every fourth generation, and this practice has been followed also by a few English breeders, with satisfactory results. A short-haired Smoke kitten will

157

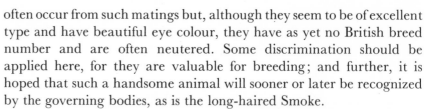

often occur from such matings but, although they seem to be of excellent type and have beautiful eye colour, they have as yet no British breed number and are often neutered. Some discrimination should be applied here, for they are valuable for breeding; and further, it is hoped that such a handsome animal will sooner or later be recognized by the governing bodies, as is the long-haired Smoke.

In Britain for the past sixteen years at least, the famous Culverden and Hillcross strains have produced only pure short-hairs, and the famous names, to be found in most present-day pedigrees, include Chs Culverden Ceinwen and Maurice, Chs Hillcross Silver Petal and Silver Lace, Chs Silverseal Antony Rowley and Oriel, Ch Perrington Silver Rose, Ch Elvaston Silver Careta, Chs Millstar Alexander and Silver Beauty, to name but a few.

In Britain, the interests of the Short-haired Tabby varieties are served by the Short-haired Cat Society of Great Britain, and there is also the Tabby Club, whose members sometimes breed both long and short-haired Tabby cats.

The Standard for type and scale of points in Britain is the same as

Above: Ch Hillcross Silver Petal, female bred by Mrs E. Towe.

Above: Mrs Towe's Ch Hillcross Silver Jacaranda.

Taishun Sequin with correct tabby markings—butterfly on shoulders and stripes on back.

that apportioned for other British Short-hairs (*see* Black). The markings, the great distinctive feature of the Silver Tabby Cat, should be dense black, without any mixture with the ground colour and quite distinct from it. The ground colour should be pure silver, uniform throughout, without a trace of white anywhere on body or tail.

The eyes should be round, well-opened, and green or hazel in colour. Distinctive features regarded as ideal in the Silver Tabby are the black saddle, often referred to as the butterfly, separated by a silver line from the three distinct parallel lines on the back; the large lateral black ring with black centre on the flanks, and the completely joined neck rings.

The mackerel-marked form of the Silver Tabby short-hair is somewhat rare. The markings should be as dense as possible, and quite distinct from the ground colour. The rings should be as narrow as possible, and numerous, running vertically from the spine downwards; the pattern is very reminiscent of the fish, hence the name. In all Tabby cats, the tails should be neatly ringed, and an unbroken ring on the chest, or more than one, is most desirable.

Miss I. Robson's Culverden kittens at about four weeks old—still with baby coat; markings not yet distinct.

Mrs Towe's kittens—one a future "Spottie" and the other a Silver Tabby, already with good pattern of markings.

A lively litter of promising kittens bred by Mr A. Pearson.

159

Tortoiseshell

Short-hair (British type)

A playful specimen of a very rare variety—Miss N. Woodifield's young female Pathfinders Brownie has attractively patched fur and good body and head shape.

The Tortoiseshell is one of the oldest varieties known – but nevertheless has very little recorded history. Looking down the ages, it seems always to have been with us, the loved companions of statesmen and kings, providing inspiration for artists and poets.

Appearing over the years often on farms and resulting from indiscriminate matings, the Tortie is difficult to breed to order; even when Torties do appear they are often too dark or too light. It is a female-only variety, and males born usually prove infertile, and this complicates breeding further, although it is interesting to note that in the National Cat Club Stud Book for 1900–1905 are two Tortoise-shells, Ballochmyle Samson and King Saul, which both apparently sired; whether or not they were in fact true Torties as we know them today, one cannot say with certainty.

The early years of the century produced over twenty prize-winning females; but since then, numbers of this variety on the British show bench have always been small; recently however, Mrs Budd's Ch Nidderdale Sprite, and Miss G. Hardman's Ch Killinghall Tortella have done well and helped to revive interest in the variety. The sire for a Tortoiseshell can be black, red or cream but never a male with tabby markings as he would certainly give his tabby bars to his progeny. This is a bad fault. Kittening is an easy business for this breed and the Tortoiseshell is a very good mother. After a wait of sixty-three to sixty-five days, she will produce her kittens quite easily in her box which has been carefully placed in a quiet secluded place away from light and draughts. When born, the best Torties are quite dark, but as they grow older the colours become much brighter. The kittens start to move around the box after three days and eyes will start to open about the tenth day.

Mrs I. Johnson's Jezreel Debby, a lovely female Tortoiseshell, with outstanding British type, body shape and good tail. This all-female variety has a striking coat of black and red (light and dark) and is exceedingly difficult to produce "to order".

Above: A successful show Tortie; Ch Cathis Torti-Queen bred by Mrs K. Vickers and owned by Mrs G. A. Genty.

Below: Profile of Jezreel Debby.

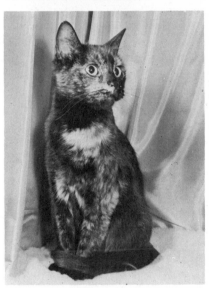

Tortoiseshells, when spayed, make wonderful house pets and can still be shown in Neuter Classes. A more loving and rewarding companion has yet to be found.

The Tortoiseshell Short-hair is an easy cat to prepare for show or exhibition providing of course that it has had a daily brush and hand grooming. Its coat should be fine and glossy. Ears must be cleaned gently, feet and tail sponged and dried. If by chance the coat is soiled, brush in fuller's earth powder and rub in well, then brush out thoroughly until all powder is removed.

The coloured patching on a Tortoiseshell cat must be of three colours only: black, light red and dark red. These patches must be clear and separate over the entire body. There must be no white hairs – no tabby or brindled markings. The large round eyes may be orange, copper or hazel and each paw and the tail must have its share of all three colours. A red blaze on the face is desirable

For matters other than coloration of coat and eyes the Tortie should conform to the same Standard as other British Short-hairs (*see* Black).

The two specialist clubs for the variety are the Red, Cream, Tortoiseshell, Tortoiseshell and White, Blue-Cream and Brown Tabby Society and the Short-haired Cat Society of Great Britain and Manx Club Incorporated.

Tortoiseshell and White

Short-hair (British type)

All Tortie and Whites are female—Miss N. Woodifield's Pathfinders Mary is a fine example.

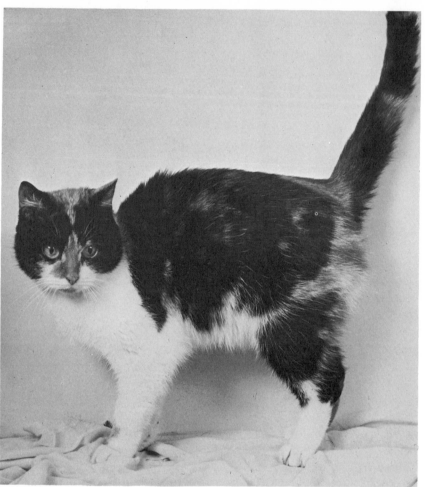

Below: Pathfinders Mary—a well-marked face with full cheeks and rounded ears.

The Tortoiseshell and White, with tri-coloured coat of black, light and dark red patches, evenly balanced with white, is one of the most striking of the British-type short-hairs, and one of the oldest varieties known. It may seem strange, therefore that it has little or no recorded history, but as it is generally a female-only variety, many of the early Tortie and Whites were "of unknown parentage".

Featured frequently in paintings over the years; particularly liked by the Japanese; once known as Spanish cats, as so many were seen in that country; long ago known as the Chintz and White in Britain; and still called Calico in the United States, it is still a variety that has more or less been taken for granted. It probably occurred in the first place, and still does, on farms from mixed matings from the various coloured cats around. It is particularly liked by farmers for its rat and mouse catching activities.

Tortoiseshell and Whites appeared at the early cat shows in Britain, where Lady Alexander exhibited a number bearing her Ballochmyle prefix, but with few details being given of the breeding. Of particular interest was a cat she entered in the 1912 Crystal Palace Show, a male,

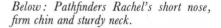

Ballochmyle Bachelor. The judge's report makes no mention of the fact that Tortie and Whites are usually female, and that a male was unusual, but just says that Bachelor "was a really good exhibit regarding patches, particularly the black". He was still winning in 1914, but does not appear to have sired any kittens. Mrs Budd registered Bits and Pieces in 1938. She was by The Aristocrat, a Blue Long-hair, and Liselotte of Coryton, a Tortie and White, and illustrates well the unusual cross-breedings that produce this variety. At the first shows after the Second World War, Mrs Axon's Ch Noxa Teena did well at the shows; all particulars about her were unknown. It is interesting to note that a Tortie and White male was registered in 1944, Clown of Carne bred by Mrs Newton, but it is not known whether he sired

Below: Pathfinders Rachel's short nose, firm chin and sturdy neck.

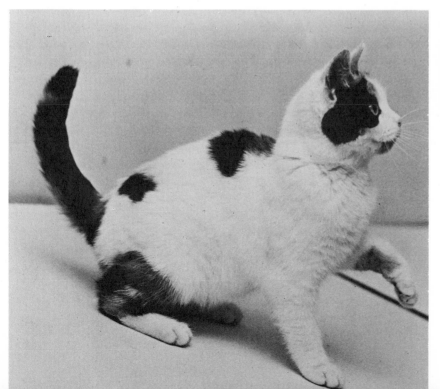

Left: Although this cat has definite coloured patches, there is far too much white in the coat, which would be considered a fault if shown. However, it shows good "British" type and a nice head.

163

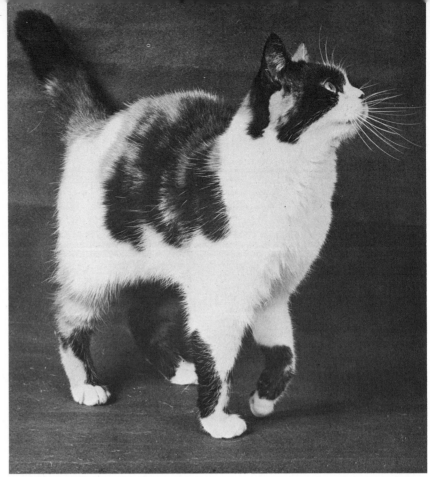

A most attractive Tortie and White, but with rather too much white and some brindling, i.e. white hairs in the coloured patches.

Below: Female kitten bred by Mrs K. Butcher. Although she still has a fluffy kitten's coat, she is already showing distinct patching and definite blaze on forehead.

In the 1963–1968 Stud Book, there are over twenty Tortie and Whites entered, many bearing the Pathfinders prefix belonging to Miss N. Woodifield, who has been most successful with her breeding programme. This has involved the use of the fairly recently recognized Bi-Colours, and has resulted from carefully planned breeding, in the production of more Tortoiseshell and Whites to order than has ever before been possible.

The specialist club particularly interested in this variety is the Red, Cream, Tortoiseshell, Tortoiseshell and White, Blue-Cream and Brown Tabby Society.

Tortie and Whites are usually very good mothers, and the litters they produce contain a colourful variety of kittens.

The type of the Tortie and White should be the same as that of the other British Short-hairs (*see* Black). The coat should be red and black on white (which should never predominate); the colour should be in distinct patches – there should be no brindling or tabby markings. A white blaze is desirable. Eye colour should be copper, orange or hazel.

Pathfinders Sybil, a bi-coloured queen owned by Mrs Butcher, with her litter of two Tortoiseshells and two Bi-Colours.

164

White   *Short-hair (British type)*

Short-haired British Whites are recognised, like their long-haired cousins, in Blue-eyed, Orange-eyed and Odd-eyed varieties. Over the years, cats with short white fur have always been portrayed in some form or another, appearing in fairy tales such as *The White Cat* written as long ago as 1682 by the Comtesse D'Aulnoy, with the little cat being turned into a princess; they have been featured in ballet, as in Tchaikovsky's *The Sleeping Beauty*; in paintings by many artists, notably the *Chat Blanc* by Géricault; and have not been forgotten by poets even as far back as the eighth century, when an Irish monk dedicated a poem to "Pangur Ban, my white cat":

> I and Pangur Ban, my cat,
> Tis a like task we are at,
> Hunting mice is his delight,
> Hunting words I sit all night.

There is the old rhyme, too, which really refers to the fact that black cats are said to be lucky, but which may nowadays be more of interest to would-be slimmers:

Ch Dellswood Saint, an orange-eyed White male, with a fine pure white coat, strong legs and well-rounded feet.

Profile (above) and full face study (below) of Dellswood Saint, showing clearly the well-developed cheeks and broad head of a stud cat.

Kiss the black cat,
An 'twill make ye fat,
Kiss the white ane,
'Twill make ye lean.

Represented in pottery and porcelain in many countries and now frequently seen in television advertisements, it is surprising to discover that, in fact, short-haired white cats are really quite rare, and have always been so. A few did appear at the early shows and it is said that in 1898 two were imported into Britain from Japan; there, they were much favoured, being symbols of purity.

Harrison Weir writing in 1889 said of the White—"This of all, as it depends entirely on its comeliness, should be graceful and elegant in the outline of its form and also action, the head small, not too round nor thick, for this gives a clumsy, heavy appearance, but broad on the forehead, and gently tapering towards the muzzle, the nose small, tip even and pink, the ears rather small than large, and not too pointed, the neck slender, shoulders narrow and sloping backwards, loin full and long, legs of moderate length, tail well set on, long, broad at the base, and gradually tapering towards the end. The eyes should be large, round, full and blue". This description, with the exception of one or two points, such as the tail, is very much as required in the modern Standard.

In the first Stud Books, almost without exception, all the white cats were of unknown parentage. Lady Alexander owned, and showed, several in the early 1900's—Ballochmyle Snow King, Ballochmyle Billie Blue Eyes, Biddy Blue Eyes and Ballochmyle Snow Bump, while Dr Prior showed Snow Lassie. One judge's report on her after a show in Glasgow in 1912 was "a typical short-hair, excellent in shape and texture of coat, pure colour, large deep blue eyes". At the National Cat Club Show held at the Crystal Palace, London, in December 1910, the Best Short-hair in Show was Mrs L. Westworth's Blue-eyed Don, of unknown pedigree. He was offered for sale at £25 (over $60), which was a very high price in those days, when the price for short-hairs was usually about £1–£2 ($3–$6).

Further study of the Stud Books over the years show that there was very little increase in numbers, and only three were entered for 1939–1948. There is one male, Stanton Orlando, from an unregistered male and a White mother, Susannah Meadowsweet, who is also entered, Orlando being owned by Miss Wrighton and Meadowsweet by Mrs Harrison, who bred Orlando. Ch Amorel of Coryton, a female, the third entry, was bred by Mrs Sharman and took prizes at many of the shows prior to the Second World War.

The Governing Council of the Cat Fancy's Stud Book for 1963–1968 shows the greatest increase of all time in the White short-hairs, with as many as thirty being entered, the numbers being almost equally divided between the Blue-eyed and the Orange-eyed. Since the publication of the above, the Odd-eyed Whites have been recognized in Britain, but have not yet been granted Championship status. In the early 1960's, Lady R. Glubb registered several bearing the Heartsease prefix, and Mrs L. Parker bred a number with her Pinewood prefix, while Miss A. Codrington's Watermill Lilywhite Boy sired a number of white kittens. Ch Dellswood Saint bred by Mrs C. Betts is one of the most notable present-day winners.

As in the long-hairs, there is an element of deafness connected with those with blue eyes, but if a white kitten has a dark smudge on its head

Below: Dellswood Mischief, a five-months-old female, bred by Mrs C. Betts. Her eyes are already changing to orange —all kittens have blue eyes when they first open.

Ch Dellswood Saint, showing his powerful body and full, broad chest, as required in the Standard for all British Short-hairs.

between the ears, it is said to be an indication that it has good hearing. The dark smudge usually disappears as the kitten grows. It is not easy to tell for several weeks which kittens will have the orange eyes and which the blue, as all have blue eyes when first they open. After about nine to ten weeks, those with blue eyes will usually stay that way, and of course the odd-eyes, one orange and one blue, are readily apparent. These frequently have good hearing, as do those with orange eyes.

A White stud is useful for mating to Tortoiseshells, and Tortoise-shell-and-Whites. When mated to Blacks, Creams, Blues and Reds, Bi-colours may result, and mated to a White, further Whites can be produced.

Careful grooming is an essential for the Whites, particularly in show cats, as yellow staining and dirty fur would be faulted by the judges. Some breeders bath their exhibits with a baby shampoo several days before a show, making sure the fur is completely dry before the cat is allowed out, as cats catch cold easily. Others prefer to use talcum powder sprinkled well into the fur, and brushed completely out, the coat being polished with chamois leather or a piece of silk afterwards, to give the fur a sheen.

According to the G.C.C.F. Standard, the Whites should have a short, fine close coat, which should be pure white, untinged with yellow; the big, round eyes should be deep, sapphire blue in the Blue-eyed; and golden orange or copper in the Oranged-eyed; the Odd-eyed White has one eye of each colour.

In all respects other than colour, the White should conform to the same Standard as all British Short-hairs (see Black); the type of the Whites is often very good, with the correct broad head, well-developed cheeks, small ears, and short nose and face.

Two "Dellswood" kittens—one with odd-eyes, the other will have orange; the difference can be seen distinctly.

Dellswood Opal, female, an odd-eyed White, with one eye orange and one eye blue. The smudge mark on the head means she should have good hearing. Breeder: Mrs Betts.

169

Siamese, Blue-point

Short-hair

Mrs H. Buttery's Taurus Kock-a-Leekie, a male with a good length of body and desired whip tail.

The Blue-pointed Siamese was the second Siamese variety to gain recognition in Great Britain by the Governing Council of the Cat Fancy. It is now almost as well known as the first and best known of the Siamese breed, the Seal-point. Although recognized only comparatively recently, there is evidence to indicate that some Blue-points reached Britain from Siam (now Thailand) very much earlier. An example is thought possibly to have reached Europe in 1896, when it was exhibited at the Holland House show in London, by an Englishman who had brought it home from Siam. Because of its blue colour, Mr Louis Wain, who was judging, refused to recognize it as Siamese – the generality of Siamese were seal-coloured at that time. However the owner declared that there were others of the same colouring and type in Siam. Whether this cat was what we now know as the Blue-point is still a matter for conjecture – in fact it has been suggested that this cat was the first Korat seen outside of Siam. However it is recorded that a Blue-pointed cat did appear in the Siamese Cat Club register in 1894, and sixteen were registered before 1927, one being an import to Britain.

It is known that Blue-point Siamese were appearing in North

170

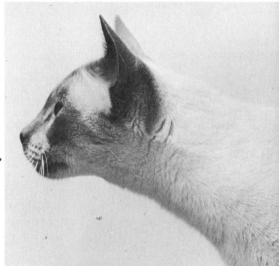

Bitchet Ratimia—a female with well-set ears and the alert expression typical of the breed. Bred by Mrs H. Philpot.

Below: Profile of Bitchet Ratimia—her long neck, firm chin and typical feminine look are shown to good advantage here.

America shows in the 1920's in direct competition with Seal-points – both being placed in the undifferentiated "Siamese" classes. In January 1932, however, at the Boston Cat Club (C.F.A.) show, there was a separate Blue-point class indicating that by that time the colour had earned championship recognition in the C.F.A. Many of the early American Blue-points were descendants of the English import, Siamese Star Adamina, a Seal-point who was sent to Mrs H. E. Naatz by Mrs C. Fisher in 1925.

The history of the Blue-points now enters a long period of gradually increasing popularity in Great Britain. The first Blue-point Champion, Sayo of Bedale, was bred by Phil Wade and owned by Mrs G. Hindley as early as 1937. They gradually increased in number and attracted much interest from breeders and public alike. An important event occurred in 1944, when Mrs Hindley founded the Blue-pointed Siamese Cat Club, the breed's first specialist club in the British fancy. She was joined by Major and Mrs J. C. Rendall, and the fact that the club still thrives some thirty years after its intial foundation bears witness to their great contribution to the breed's progress. In 1948, Ch Pincap Azure Kim was Best in Show at the Siamese Cat Club Show.

It is often said by its many owners and breeders that the Blue-point is, of all the Siamese, the most gentle and affectionate in temperament.

171

Taurus Kock-a-Leekie, with well-set oriental shaped ears and good length of head.

Profile of Taurus Kock-a-Leekie. His mask is completely blue, and he shows a slight sign of the jowls usually developed by males used for stud work.

This is quite an asset in both pet cats and pedigree breeding-stock – and on the show bench an equable disposition is desirable and makes the task of both judge and steward a pleasure to perform.

If you decide to take up breeding, follow the usual principles in selecting your stock; that is, bear in mind what you want to see in the progeny, and in the first place make absolutely sure that the queen to be used is healthy and the best you can obtain. She should have as good a pedigree as possible, as should the stud, and both parents should have the right pleasant disposition, as this also will be inherited by the offspring. Neither male nor female should show faults, such as incorrect eye colour, a squint, or definite kink in the tail. Breed to like-colour; it is of prime importance if one is to achieve the high standard desirable.

The Blue-pointed Siamese is normally quite healthy in its constitution, and provided that it is well cared for, handled correctly and given the right food, it will live to a good age.

All the usual feeding rules apply; it is often found that individual cats have their own fads about food – if this is the case, it is reasonable to allow them their particular whim or fancy, provided of course that no harm will result. One famous Blue-pointed stud cat was known to be very partial to yeast extract on brown bread, and expected this every day without fail!

The cat will require little special care beyond a light brushing each day followed by a smoothing down of the coat – I use soft suede-leather gloves. Inspect the ears, and if there is a deposit of wax in them dip some cotton wool in olive oil, squeeze it out, put a little on the end of an orange stick, and then *very gently* just remove any obvious traces. Do not probe right into the inside of the ear as this might very easily cause distress and permanent damage. These small attentions are particularly important if a cat is to be exhibited; no one likes to see an unwell, uncared for and ill-prepared cat on the show bench. Indeed, as is frequently the case, a cat out of condition may not even pass the veterinary examination.

The Blue-point classes make a wonderful sight at the shows, whether male, female or neuter. Incidentally, it often happens these days that the very best and most striking cats are to·be found among the neuters, who often seem to possess an extra quality all of their own.

The Blue-point, conforming fully to the Standards, is one of the most striking of all of the Siamese colour-dilutions; in type and shape it should correspond to the other varieties in all respects, and it is in the colour that the difference is to be found. The points (i.e. mask, legs, ears, feet and tail) of the perfect Blue-point should all be of the same even blue colour. The body colour should be a glacial white, shading gradually into the blue on the back, the same cold tone as the points but of a lighter shade. The eyes should be a clear, bright, vivid blue, but not too deep in tone.

It is a rare event indeed these days to see a Blue-point with exactly the right coat colour. Breeders have become all too aware in recent years that we have to some extent succeeded in perfecting Blue-point type, but in doing so have had to breed to other Siamese colours, which has meant the sacrifice of the pale coat colour. Furthermore the points colour is not always of the desirable blue shade, but often appears as a dark "gunmetal", or "slate" grey.

In other respects the Blue-point should conform to the Seal-point standard which requires a medium-sized build, a long, svelte body with proportionately slim legs. The hind legs should be slightly longer than the front, with small, oval feet. The tail should be long and tapering, either straight or *slightly kinked* at the extremity. This kink is permissible at the present time.

The head should be long and well-proportioned, with width between the ears; in shape the head is a wedge, tapering in perfectly straight lines to a fine muzzle. The ears should be wide at the base, rather large and pricked. The eyes should be oriental in shape, slanting towards the nose, without any tendency to squint. The coat of the Siamese is very short and fine in texture, glossy and close-lying.

In America the type, pattern and fur length specifications are identical for all Siamese–only the coat, nose leather and paw pad colours are different. The C.F.A. standard calls for, in the Blue-point, "Body bluish white, cold in tone, shading gradually to white on stomach and chest. Points deep blue. Nose leather and paw pads: slate colour."

Siamese, Chocolate-point

Mrs H. Buttery's Samsara Whisper—a beautiful Siamese queen, combining pale coat and well-matching points with a good body and tail.

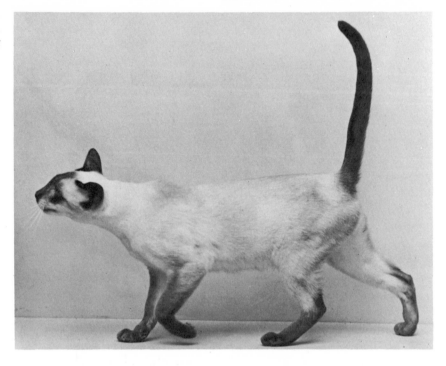

Profile of Craigiehilloch Chomarcus.

Although Chocolate-points have a long history they did not, in fact, gain official recognition in Britain, and a Governing Council breed number, until 1950.

Many of the early Seal-points, or Royal Cats of Siam, carried the genes for chocolate points and indeed frequently produced charming kittens of this type in their litters. Unhappily such kittens were not favoured in those early days, although it is difficult to understand why. They were referred to as "the pale ones" or "bad seals". Today it is a very different story, thanks to the foresight, tenacity and love of the breed shown by some of the early breeders, such as Miss Wentworth Fitzwilliam and Mr Stirling-Webb.

In Britain there is a specialist Siamese Club, the Chocolate-pointed Siamese Cat Club, catering exclusively for the Chocolate-pointed variety. Among other facilities the club offers classes and trophies at all Championship shows. It was founded in 1954 by a group of enthusiasts who wished to see their favourite variety of Siamese brought to public notice and to ensure the breeding of the variety in much greater numbers. In the early fifties it was cause for comment if three Chocolate-points appeared in a class at a show, and six would cause great surprise. Today it is different; a large proportion of the club members are enthusiastic breeders, all anxious to combine type and colour to produce the perfect cat.

Chocolate-points are one of the very popular Siamese colours in America. They were recognised in the 1950's by most associations, and appeared first in the All-American listings in 1953.

A Chocolate-point of good type, with the correct milk-chocolate

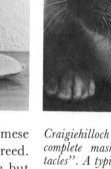

points, ivory body and vivid blue eyes, is one of the loveliest of Siamese varieties but, unfortunately, it is also one of the most difficult to breed. Very often the breeder ends up with a kitten of excellent type but having the wrong colour points, cold and dark, with the body colour starting to shade, faults that have gained the description "bad seals".

It is very often the case that the cat having the correct milk-chocolate shade of points was, when a kitten, showing the least definition in mask and stockings – a late developer in fact, as far as coloration is concerned. Chocolate-points do not in fact develop their points nearly as quickly as Seal-points, and those having a complete mask and stockings when young will almost certainly become much too dark when they reach adulthood. Furthermore, it is by no means certain that the promising pale-pointed kitten will develop the required complete mask and matching ears and stockings. It is not uncommon for an adult of fifteen months or more still to retain the white whisker pads and chin, and the pale legs, features that are often slow to disappear, showing real colour only on the ears and nose. It should also be noted that, like the Seal-point, the adult Chocolate-point is usually at its best around Christmas; during the summer these cats are much affected by the sun and tend to lose colour. I have possessed several cats which have shown distinct signs of sun-burn on the sides of the face below the ears, and have even slightly peeled in very hot weather, although they did not seem unduly upset by it.

Chocolate-points are very easy indeed to prepare for showing; their coat texture is extremely responsive to grooming; it is seldom coarse or harsh, and has a lively sheen. Nothing special need be done to the

A playful Praha kitten, bred by Mrs E. Fisher, showing good pale body and beautifully defined points.

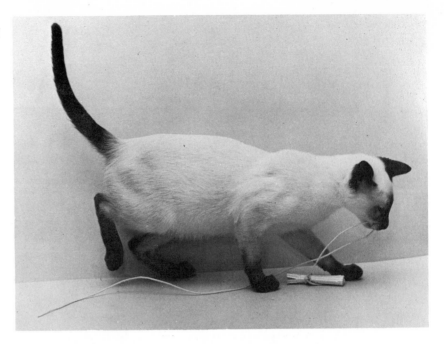

animal, just the normal grooming – a few minutes regularly each day should be sufficient to keep its coat looking as it should.

Chocolate-pointed kittens are most attractive, having a fairy-like ethereal look about them, with their pale points and very light-coloured bodies. They are very much in demand, probably because they have not yet bred in the same numbers as the other colours of Siamese.

In the breeding of Chocolate-points, it has been found that the best kittens come from two good Chocolate-points, or from a Chocolate-point and a Seal-point carrying the chocolate factor, but without the blue factor. It is considered that the introduction of blue into the Chocolate-point variety, which was inevitable when it was used with

Samsara Whisper—her ears forming a triangle with the wedge-shaped head, giving the required marten look.

Seremban Samson—a delightful male kitten at four weeks, bred by Mrs A. Aslin.

Mrs Philpot's Tyko Little Flirt—a beautifully co-ordinated female, giving perfect balance.

Blue-point for Lilac-point breeding, has been much to blame for fostering the undesirable cold tone in Chocolate-points. Chocolate-points of better colour were being bred in the 1950's, when few of the animals carried blue, than since the early 1960's, although type has definitely improved in the modern Chocolate-point. The loss of Ch Bolney Kien in 1966, possibly the last Chocolate-point stud cat without the blue factor, was a great loss to the future of the variety. Bolney Kien had excellent type and beautiful colouring, reminiscent of his grandfather, Ch Craigiehilloch Chozaro; who figures in most Chocolate-point pedigrees way back, and of course, carried no blue. It used to be true to say that two Chocolate-points (recessives) bred together would breed true, but this cannot be said today – in a recent litter I had four Lilac-points and three Chocolate-points, from a mating of two Chocolate-points!

The standard requires that the body of the Chocolate-point should be of an ivory colour overall, and shading should be to the colour of the points. Points should be the colour of milk chocolate; ears mask, legs, paws and tail should all be of the same colour, and the ears no darker than the other points. The eyes should be a clear, bright, vivid blue.

Standards in the various American associations differ in wording somewhat, but it would appear that all visualize the same cat as is called for in Britain.

An important male figuring in many pedigrees, Ch Craigiehilloch Chozaro, bred by Mrs D. Clarke.

Below: As a kitten, Gr Ch Bibury Café au Lait, an outstanding Australian queen bred and owned by Mrs M. Batten.

Samsara kittens—an extremely promising litter.

177

Siamese, Lilac-point

Ch Physalis Chulalongkorn, a well-muscled male bred by Mrs V. Paramor. He is in the peak of condition, with good pale body colouring and well-defined points.

Mrs H. Buttery's Ch Edwardian Magnolia—a female showing a lovely straight profile, as required by the Standard, firm chin and good slender neck.

History does not give us precise dates for the beginnings of the Lilac-point. In 1896 a Blue-point, owned by Mr W. Spearman was disqualified from the Holland House Show in Britain because it "was not quite blue". This animal may have been a Lilac-point. It is also said that the breed was first seen in America, but it is to Mrs A. Hargraves in her cattery in England in 1955 that the credit must go for the first recorded birth. In a litter of kittens, of which both parents were Blue, there appeared a wonderful Lilac-point.

A Lilac-point Siamese has delicate lilac-grey points, with pink pads to the feet, and a faded rose-coloured nose of leathery appearance. The breed has vivid blue eyes and almost glacier-white bodies. An interesting point about the lilac is that the breeder can put lilac to lilac, and they will breed one hundred per cent correctly. Recognition by breeders that a dilute Blue-point Siamese was appearing in some of their litters probably traces back to about 1950 in North America. By 1954 the C.F.F. and A.C.A. had accepted these "Frost-point" Siamese (as they were then known) for championship competition and the first Frost-points gained All-American recognition in 1955. Acceptance in all associations followed within a few years but the name has gradually become Lilac-point in all associations but A.C.F.A.

Lilacs have travelled a long way since 1955; they have lost their big, awkward heads and pale eyes and, from having hardly any points on feet or legs, they now have frosty points showing greyly, with pink undertones and foot pads of lavender pink.

Ch Edwardian Magnolia is an excellent example of breed type in the Lilac-point, with well-set flaring ears and good position of eyes.

Ch Physalis Chulalongkorn shows fine type and the confident look of a Champion.

While it is true that great attention must be given to every type of Siamese, it is even more necessary with the Lilac, because of its delicate colouring. The breeding is a tricky business unless you follow certain, carefully considered lines. The first requirement is to have strength of line in both stud and queen; type can be disregarded in this first commencement of your line. When you have completed your first breeding then is the time to observe for faults and to select from the litter the progeny which are perfect for your breeding purpose.

The queen selected for your next breeding need not be special, as long as she fulfils the obvious health qualifications – and it must not be forgotten that the condition of the mother conditions in turn the kitten which is to become a good queen. During pregnancy the queen should be fed on proteins, no bulk to "fill-up", and she should be groomed well and treated comfortingly. It is essential that the queen is taken to her maternity ward several times a day so as to become familiar with it. When the time for confinement arrives there is one very important point to be observed by owners; especially where maiden queens are concerned the owner must never panic and must maintain an atmosphere of calm. Every evidence of nervousness on the part of the owner is apprehended by the queen and all sorts of complications may occur. Another important point is that should your queen have been in labour without result for more than, say, two hours, expert veterinary attention must be obtained as soon as possible.

Maiden queens often have large litters, from five to eight kittens,

Siamese, Lynx-point
see page 191

Premier Physalis Shagrayn, bred by Mrs Paramor—at three-and-a-half months this neuter has a typical Siamese expression.

Promising five-days-old kittens, with eyes just beginning to open. Bred by Miss I. Wiseman.

and if this does occur she will need help in both feeding and grooming. Kittens are often mistakenly allowed to remain too long with the queen before weaning. This can be left for as long as eight weeks but it is best to start the operation after four weeks.

My approach to showing the Lilac-point is to bathe the cat in warm bran, rubbing it in gently to clean out any impurities in the coat and to make it glossy. The morning of the show the coat is rubbed down with talcum powder or white fuller's earth and brushed out thoroughly. At the show the coat is rubbed down with the bare hands, and any discharge removed from the eyes and ears.

The Lilac-point must be of medium size with well-proportioned legs, the back legs being slim and slightly longer than the front; the feet small and oval-shaped. The tail is long and tapering. The head is well proportioned, with definite width between the eyes, which are oriental-shaped, sloping towards the nose, brilliant deep blue in colour. The ears are rather large and wide at the base. The coat is off-white (magnolia), shading to the tone of the points, which are of a faded pinkish lilac colour; it is short and fine in texture, glossy, lying close to the body.

The American Standards for the Lilac-point are the same, on matters other than colour, as for all other Siamese. Standards, depending on the association, call for a milk white or glacial white body with points of frosty grey with pinkish tone. The nose leather in the A.C.F.A. Standard should be a translucent old lilac hue at the tips with frost pads of a coal pink colour. In C.F.A. the nose leather and paw pads should be lilac pink. According to both standards, eyes should be deep vivid or brilliant blue.

Siamese, Red-point and Tortie-point

Mrs D. White's Ch Ilona Firefly—male with strongly marked mask and points. The slight barring or stripes on the mask are not now deemed a fault, as it does tend to appear in this variety.

Fine profile of Pitapat Shane, a male with a good straight nose and firm chin. Owned by Mrs A. Sayer; bred by Mrs W. Holt.

Although Red-point and Tortie-point Siamese have separate breed numbers in Britain, and are treated as two entirely different breeds as far as showing is concerned, they are in fact very closely allied, and form part of the same variety. There are no Tortie-point males, and Tortie-point females are produced when a Seal-point female is mated to a Red-point male, from Tortie-point mated to virtually any other colour Siamese, and from Red-point female to Seal-point male.

Red coloration in the cat, known by the geneticists as "yellow", is a sex-linked factor. This is simply explained in that the gene responsible for red is carried on the X chromosome of which each female has two, and each male only one, his chromosome pair being completed by a Y. Therefore if an ovum is fertilized by a sperm carrying X, the

two matching chromosomes give a female and, if by a sperm carrying Y, the X and Y combine to give a male. As the red colour gene is only carried on the X chromosome, the colour of a kitten from a mating in which one or both parents is red is, therefore, related to its sex.

The practical effect can be shown by mating a Seal-point female and a Red-point male. All the male offspring will be Seal-point as they have received their father's Y chromosome in order to be male, and this cannot carry the red factor; but the females will be Tortie-point because they have their father's X chromosome carrying red, and the X chromosome from the mother, carrying black (seal). If these Tortie-point females are mated to a Seal-point male, the progeny can include Seal-point males and females, Red-point males and Tortie-point females. If a Tortie-point female is mated to a Red-point male, however, both father and mother can provide the necessary X chromosome carrying the red gene, for a Red-point female to be possible.

Should the Red-point and Seal-point parents also carry other colour factors such as Blue-point or Chocolate-point or both, the permutations of colour expectancy in the offspring are many. When Red-point is mated to Red-point, only Red-point kittens can appear.

Throughout the 1940's and 1950's, some dedicated breeders struggled for the development and acceptance of the Red-point, notably Mrs Alyce de Filippe in the U.S.A. and Dr Nora Archer and Miss Ann Ray in Great Britain. They all experienced setbacks in breeding the required number of generations of like-to-like matings to achieve breed recognition, with lack of "foreign" type, heavy bone structure and pronounced tabby markings on masks and tails.

The preliminary cross in the U.S.A. was made between a good Seal-point female and a Red Tabby long-hair male, and in England between a half-Siamese tortoiseshell and a Seal-point male. The biggest mistake made by these early pioneers was in carrying out the like-to-like matings between the early Red-points, rather than in back-crossing to Siamese Seal-points of excellent type. They tried to avoid the production of the Tortie-point females which are inevitable by the back-cross method, and went all out for colour at the expense of type. This was probably

Ch Amanda Rose—an excellent example of a Siamese head, with Oriental-shaped eyes, long nose, and strong chin.

Below: Two of Mrs White's Catherstone kittens—a promising pair with good wedge heads and well-set ears.

why it was not until 1966, after the formation of a specialist breed club by several progressive breeders the previous year, that this fascinating breed was accepted by the G.C.C.F. and granted Championship status. In the U.S.A., however, these cats were recognised in 1956, but as the Red Colourpoint Short-hair, and not as a variety of Siamese; this controversy still reigns today, with some associations recognising the Red-points and Tortie-points as Siamese, and others, including C.F.A., recognizing them along with Lynx-points (Tabby-points) under the separate breed classification of Colourpoint Short-hairs.

The increased genetic knowledge of the breeders of the late 1960's resulted in great strides in the type and eye-colour of both Red-points and Tortie-points at shows on both sides of the Atlantic, but very little

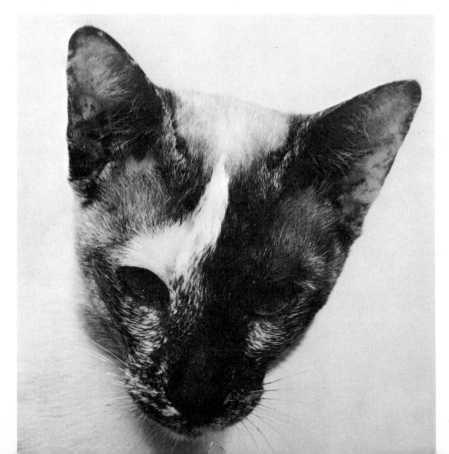

Ch Pitapat Sequins, a female with an excellent wedge-shaped head, showing the desired blaze and good tortoiseshell markings on face. Owned by Mrs White; bred by Mrs Holt.

Profile of Ch Nikaed Minerva, female owned by Mrs M. Gamble, with well-shaped head and distinct tortie markings.

selection seems to have been made for the improvement of colour, or the reduction of the ghost tabby effect seen in most cats exhibiting the red factor. Some typy winning Red-point Siamese have very little colour at all except on ears and tail, and many have completely white legs and pale masks. The factor which restricts the colour to the points in Siamese has a diluting effect on that colour so that we never get true Black-points, for example; they appear dark brown and are known as Seal-points, although "seal" is genetically black. Red-points have an added disadvantage in that the factor which masks the tabby effect in all other cats does not operate in the red series, and so all Red-points appear tabby to a greater or lesser degree. Breeders must be encouraged to work harder for the improvement of the colour in this breed, which may best be achieved by the introduction of Chocolate-point studs every second or third generation. The females thus produced will be Tortie-point, either Seal- or Chocolate-Tortie depending on the colours carried by the dam, but cats carrying blue are best avoided, as it has seen that the blue factor when carried by Red-points can result in a high degree of diffusion of the points colour into the coat. Lilac-point should only be used in Red-point breeding programmes when it is desired that Cream-points may eventually be produced. Tabby-points should not be mated with Red-points as it is impossible to distinguish by appearance alone between a Red-point Siamese and a Red Tabby-point Siamese, and test matings must be carried out before the kittens thus produced can be genuinely registered as one or the other.

A good specimen of the Red-point Siamese is a most beautiful animal with a gleaming white body, any shading visible a delicate apricot shade. The ears, mask and tail should be bright reddish-gold, and legs and feet may be bright reddish-gold or apricot. Eyes should be bright, vivid blue in colour, and barring on mask, legs and tail is not considered a fault in this variety. The coat should be short, fine and silky

Ch Nikaed Minerva, with good body colour and excellent distribution of patching in the points.

and the fur glossy and close-lying. Kittens are generally paler all over.

In all other features, the Red-point Siamese should conform to the Seal-point Standard.

The Tortie-point Siamese is always female; she conforms in every way to the Seal-point Standard apart from colour, and in turn may be found in four shades, although until recently only Seal-Tortie points were eligible for competition for Championship status in Britain. No two Tortie-points are ever found alike in appearance due to the haphazard distribution of the red among the darker areas of the points. The nose leather and pads should match the equivalent solid colour Siamese, and the points must have clearly visible red or cream patches among the darker areas. Many Tortie-points exhibit heavily shaded bodies, and this is a fault to be bred out by selection for it is found that Red-points bred from such queens invariably develop heavily-shaded coats in maturity.

Very recently the Chocolate, Blue and Lilac Tortie-points have been given full recognition in Britain. These, and in particular the Chocolate Tortie-points, are especially valuable in Red-point breeding programmes. The chocolate factor underlying the points colouring in the Red-point kittens produced by a suitable Chocolate Tortie-point gives an added intensity to the red and also seems to eliminate to some extent the tabby barring so often seen in this variety.

Genetically merely diluted tortoiseshell, the Chocolate, Blue and Lilac Tortie-points are always female and the basic points colour is mixed with correspondingly diluted red, which appears as cream in varying depths of colour. These varieties are also known as Chocolate/Cream-point, Blue/Cream-point and Lilac/Cream-point, respectively.

The Chocolate Tortie-point has an ivory body with points of a definite warm brown intermingled with rich cream. The nose leather and pads are either deep rose or flesh pink, or a mixture of the two colours depending on the distribution of pigmentation beneath the skin. In the Blue Tortie-point, the body is white, shading to a pale cold grey and the points are mottled deep slate-grey and pale cream of a cold tone. The nose leather and pads are deep blue-grey or pink, or variously mottled as in the Chocolate Tortie-point, and as the blue factor in the Siamese cat has the effect of diffusing the points colour into the coat, a faint, mottled, blue tortoiseshell effect is often seen in the coat of this variety on maturity. The Lilac Tortie-point is a misty white cat with points pastel tinted in the palest blue-grey and pink tone on ears and tail, the mask and legs being barely shaded. The pads and nose leather are pale pink and grey, mottled according to the pigment distribution.

For those who like to own a completely unique-looking cat, the various Tortie-points are ideal as no two are ever alike; some have quite bizarre expressions when the predominant colour runs down the face, bisecting it with a distinctive blaze, and some have one profile predominantly dark, and the other of a lighter tone, giving an attractive harlequin effect.

Red-point and Tortie-point Siamese are an asset on the show bench, creating great interest by their startling appearance, and a delight in the home, but their breeding should not be undertaken by the novice until many of the present problems have been resolved.

Above: Solitaire Emeraude, bred by Mrs A. Sayer, with good type, fine slender tail and well-broken points.

Below: A promising young kitten of this all-female variety, with large well-marked ears and points on legs just appearing. Breeder: Mrs Sayer.

Pitapat Sequins, with marbled tortie markings on head and legs and beautiful body shape.

Siamese, Seal-point

Mrs A. Sayer's Solitaire Sheba (female) showing a long and well-proportioned head, well set on slender neck. A good contrast between body colouring and points.

Below: Probably a Siamese, the cat observed by Peter Simon Pallas during exploration of the Caspian Sea area in 1794.

The origin of the Siamese cat is obscure. It is probable that the cat seen by the German naturalist and explorer Peter Simon Pallas, during his exploration of the Caspian Sea in the late 1700's, was a "Siamese".

It was said to be the offspring of a black cat and described as having a light chestnut-brown body colour, black at the back especially towards the tail and paler along the sides and belly, with a black streak running along and surrounding the eyes and ending in front of the forehead. "The ears, paws and tail are quite black. It is of a middle size, has somewhat smaller legs than the common cat and the head is longer towards the nose." Perhaps this cat was one of the first to show the genetic mutation restricting the colour to the points – the Siamese coat pattern.

It is generally held that these cats are of Eastern origin and there are many legends about them. Some say they were Temple cats, others think they were bred from an albino cat given to the King of Siam,

crossed with the Temple cats and bred in the Royal Palace.

This "cat with a difference" is said to have been introduced to Europe in the 1880's. Mr Owen Gould brought a pair, Pho and Mia, to England in 1884; their progeny were exhibited by his sister, Mrs L. Veley, at the 1885 Crystal Palace Show in London. Others are known to have gone to Belgium, New York, and Sydney, Australia.

However, they had been known in England some years before this; two were entered at the Crystal Palace Show in 1871. Descriptions of these cats at the time ranged from "an unnatural, nightmare kind of cat", to "singular and elegant in their smooth skins, and ears tipped with black, and blue eyes with red pupils". Accompanying sketches showed round heads and heavy bodies, almost "British" type. In 1872 Lady Dorothy Nevill exhibited a "pure Siamese" under "Short-haired Unusual Colour She-Cats", and over the next three years Mr J. Walter's Mymie also made appearances under the same description.

Above: Mrs Saunders's Ch Supra Cassandra, a good male with noble head, alert and intelligent expression.

Below: This Siamese shows beautiful contrast between coat and points, but has what is known as "old-fashioned" type.

Among early winners were Mrs Robinson's Wankee, Lady Vyvyan's Tiam-o-Shian IV, and Mrs Parker Brough's Koschka.

In the 1890's and early 1900's Seal-points were sent to North America from Britain, France, Japan and also Siam. Most of the present American strains, however, trace back to English forebears. Mrs A. Hoag owned a Seal-point, Chone, born in 1899 and believed to be the first American-born Siamese, and her Madison California was one of the first Siamese to win a Championship in North America. However, the breed remained relatively rare until after the Second World War. Now on both sides of the Atlantic, numbers of registrations outstrip those of all other breeds.

The characteristic feature of this breed is the coat-pattern, i.e., the restriction of colour to the "points", the mask, ears, legs and tail. The Seal-point Siamese cat has dark brown points contrasting with the creamy-fawn body and it is the Seal-point that first comes to mind when Siamese cats are mentioned. Siamese kittens are born white and only gradually does the colour come to their points, showing first as a dusky smudge on the nose.

The Siamese cat is robust and should not be molly-coddled. It should be fed well, but not over-fed and allowed to become fat. Daily grooming with a soft brush and comb is appreciated by these cats, followed by hand grooming or stroking. This removes loose hair and keeps the coat lustrous. Siamese cats are normally prolific and breeding them can be a pleasurable but expensive hobby. One should only breed from healthy stock of the highest quality. Siamese queens can be very noisy in season but should not be mated until at least nine months old or after the third "call".

Siamese are devoted to their owner and thrive on human companionship, indeed many will fret if left alone. They will follow you at heel

Early American Champion—Siam de Paris (above) and an early British Champion—Wankee (below). Note the rounder heads characteristic of Siamese in the early days of the fancy.

Above: Sheba—a beautifully balanced and well-proportioned female.

Right: Shushilla Kristina, female, owned by Mrs Sayer, with good, wedge-shaped head and almond-shaped eyes.

or run ahead and hide, waiting to spring out as you get close, loving to play hide-and-seek. If accustomed when young, they will walk on a lead, holding their head proudly, tail erect. They will entertain you with their antics, leaping in the air, turning somersaults like any circus clown, walking on tip-toe, stiff legged, fur on end and tail like a bottle brush, warning off any would-be enemy. They are keen conversationalists and have different tones to express their needs and views, and are adept at getting their own way.

The Siamese voice has great range, from a deep, bass growl to a high pitched screech, and a female in season, calling for a mate, has to be heard to be believed. Not all Siamese, however, are noisy, but all are clever and can make themselves understood. They are intelligent and readily trained; they will obey your command – if it so suits them – or openly defy you, knowingly and with arrogance. They are great hunters, and thieves, but honest thieves, ready to snatch a mouthful under your very eyes. Often they will bring their catch to you for admiration and praise. They are inquisitive and cannot resist exploring sheds and open windows, sometimes with dire results. Siamese cats can be destructive, they delight in "stropping" on your best chair, or climbing up the curtains to sit high on the pelmet, but they are intelligent and soon learn the meaning of NO and can with firmness and persistence be trained to strop on a tree trunk or scratching board. Siamese will only be vicious if they have been teased or treated cruelly and badly; treated as an equal, they will respond with loyalty and affection, give you a maximum of love and devotion and will demand of you whole-hearted attention in return.

The cats are judged by a Standard of Points which was first drawn up in 1902 by the newly formed Siamese Cat Club as an ideal for breeders to aim at. It was based on the "Royal" Siamese and our present-day

Above: Siamese showing "spectacles", which would be faulted if judged.

Below: An example of "strabismus" or "squint"—a disqualification fault on the show bench.

International Champion from France— Saphir.

Ora Song—another French International Champion.

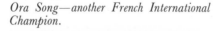

Above: Once of Australia's famous studs and the sire of many champions, Gr Ch Koa Prince Valiant, bred and owned by Mr K. Anderson of Queensland.

Above: Two appealing Manana kittens at six weeks. Breeder: Mrs C. Maddocks.

Below: Noelle, a promising young kitten bred by Mrs E. Christmas.

Standard has evolved from this. Sixty years of selective breeding has resulted in great refinement of type and shape, and certain features such as a kink in the tail, once desirable, are now considered less so, while a squint or a white toe or toes are definite disqualifying faults on the show bench. The British Standard requires a beautifully balanced animal, medium in size, with a long svelte body and proportionately slim legs, and a long tapering tail. The hind legs should be slightly higher than the front, and the feet small and oval. The head of our show cat should be long and well-proportioned with good width between the ears, and narrowing in perfectly straight lines to a fine muzzle. The ears themselves are rather large and pricked, wide at the base. The mask should be complete, connected by tracings with the ears, the eyes a deep blue, a green tinge to be considered a fault. The cat's expression should be alert and intelligent. American Siamese Standards differ only in minor wording from that of the English Standards and all of them describe essentially the same cat.

There are thirteen clubs in the United Kingdom catering for Siamese alone; the oldest and largest is the Siamese Cat Club, founded in 1901. It has over eight hundred members throughout the world. Sir Compton Mackenzie has been its President since 1948 and takes much interest in the Club. Originally only Seal-points were catered for but today all colours are represented and each one has its own club. In America there are several societies devoted to the welfare of the Siamese, the most influential being the Siamese Cat Society of America which was founded in 1909.

Seal-point Siamese are now bred and exhibited in many overseas countries. Probably the United States of America today has the greatest number, but Australia, New Zealand and South Africa have well-established Siamese cat fancies developed largely from stock exported from England. Canada looks more to the United States of America and there are, today, an increasing number of American-bred Siamese cats in Europe. Seal-point Siamese are still the most popular of all the different-coloured points. They hold their own by numbers at all British shows; more Seal-points are registered and by and large, most of the top Siamese honours are still taken by Seal-point cats.

An alert, well-developed litter, with good heads and masks already well-coloured. Breeder: Mrs Y. Kite.

Mrs A. Wilson's Ch Redleaf Benni, a male with good head and strong jaw line, showing well-developed jowls.

A prize-winning queen in the early stages of pregnancy—Mrs Sayer's Shushilla Kristina.

Siamese, Tabby-point (Lynx-point)

Ch Reoky Jnala, owned by Mrs A. Sayer—a Tabby-point male with chocolate markings, showing a good distribution of stripes on points and good body colouring.

The Tabby-point Siamese have an interesting story which starts as early as 1902, when they are mentioned as "Any Other Colour Siamese Tabby" in Frances Simpson's book *The Book of the Cat*. Much more recently, they appeared in Scotland and there are photographs of them dated 1944-49, when they were called Silverpoint Siamese. However, they did not become widely known or popular until 1960 when a Seal-point Siamese queen, Lady Me, owned by Miss Eileen Alexander, slipped out and found her own mate. Immediately on her return, she was mated to Mrs M. Buttery's Seal-point, Druid and among the five kittens of this dual mating was one Tabby-point female—Patti. This unusual Tabby-point Siamese queen was mated to Mrs Buttery's Seal-point, Samsara Saracen, and four of the six kittens born were Tabby-points. These kittens were so well marked and of such fine Siamese type, it seemed a good idea to introduce them to the cat fancy, and they were shown at the 1961 Croydon Cat Club Show in London. Here they had the good fortune to be seen by Mrs G. Hindley, who was so attracted by them that she bought a female—Tansy—and has had many kittens from this queen, doing so much to popularize them and in getting them recognized as Siamese in Britain. Mrs M. Hudson also bought Faux Pas to be the first Tabby-point Siamese stud.

Another Tabby-point was discovered in the early 1960's—Mrs Pears's famous Miss Tee Kat who, mated to Mr R. Warner's Spotlight Troubadour, produced Mister Buttons, used as an unrelated mate for Patti, and Praline, taken by Mr and Mrs Warner and the

Prestwick Pervenche, bred by Mrs G. Hindley and owned by Mrs N. Hardy.

Mrs Saunders's Lymekilns Hifua—a beautiful female profile with good tracings.

foundation of their beautiful Tabby-points to-day.

Their name has given rise to much difficulty as "Tabby-point" was considered by breeders to be too ordinary for such attractive cats. Lynx-point was suggested, and is still used in U.S.A. and some parts of Australia, New Zealand (and Canada). Attabiy was also tried, being the original name for the tabby cat in Persia, but again this led to more difficulties and impolite versions such as "Atta-boy". Shadow-point was another name liked by many breeders and used for some time. Finally the Siamese Cat Club Committee decided that these cats should be called Tabby-pointed Siamese, but that they should *not* be classified with the solid-colour-pointed Siamese, and that they should be given a different breed number to distinguish them as variegated-pointed Siamese. In 1966 they were granted recognition by the Governing Council of the Cat Fancy as Tabby-pointed Siamese. In the U.S.A., the Lynx-points are recognized by some associations as Siamese, while in others they are classified with the Red-points and Tortie-points as a separate short-haired breed known as Colourpoint Short-hairs. Britain now has two specialist clubs for the Tabby-points, both founded in 1964. In January 1967 the Shadowpoint and Progressive Breeders Cat Club became the Tabby-point Siamese and Progressive Breeders Cat Club and in July 1969 the Lynx-pointed Cat Club became the Tabby-Pointed Cat Society.

Great care should be taken with breeding programmes to preserve the outstanding Siamese type, and only the best show quality cats should be used. All Siamese, in my view, carry the genes for tabby patterns but show little or no evidence of this unless they are either Tabby-points or Red-points. It is possible to breed Tabby-points from any

Above: A Tabby-point bred by Mrs Pears.

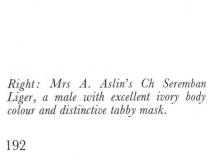

Right: Mrs A. Aslin's Ch Seremban Liger, a male with excellent ivory body colour and distinctive tabby mask.

Siamese queen if a Tabby-point stud is used and vice versa. Tabby-points with badly non-matching points should be avoided, and also mating like to like for several generations, so that their excellent Siamese type may be preserved; for these Tabby-points have not only produced wonderful type, but have improved the health generally of the Siamese. A Tabby-point queen, mated first to a Lilac-point stud, usually shows by her kittens what solid colours, if any, she carries genetically and can, therefore, be mated to that particular solid-colour-pointed Siamese and produce healthy kittens of good type. Some Tabby-point queens produce only Tabby-point kittens, whether mated to seal, blue, chocolate or lilac, but mated to a Red-point, they produce the Tortie Tabby-points and the Red Tabby-points, usually of excellent Siamese type; but this mating should not be encouraged as it has misleading results, for it is very difficult to distinguish between the Red-point and the Red Tabby-point.

The Tabby-point Siamese has a delightful character, friendly and intelligent as all Siamese are; they are very affectionate and make excellents pets for old and young alike. It is a medium-sized cat, virile and muscular, but dainty in appearance and with a firm, close-lying coat. Siamese in type, it has a long and svelte body, with proportionately slim legs and small oval feet. Its tail is long and tapering, and it has a long, graceful but strong neck. The Tabby-point's head is wide at the top, tapering to a pointed nose, long and clearly-defined, with a strong chin. The eyes are oriental in shape, slanting towards the nose. There is a good width between the ears, which are large and pricked, and wide at the base.

As with all Siamese, colour is restricted to the points, the basic

A "Rathglass" queen and litter of Tabby-point and Seal-point kittens. Owned and bred in Australia by Mrs M. Batten.

Above: A queen with two most attractive kittens. Breeder: Mrs Pears.

Left: Profile of Ch Seremban Liger, showing well-set eyes and ears and typical spotting on whisker pads.

193

A group of Australian-bred Tabby-points.

colour of which may be seal, blue, chocolate, lilac, tortoiseshell or red. The general body colour should be pale and free from mottling or tabby markings; the colour conforming to the recognized Siamese Standard for the particular points colour in its solid (i.e. non-tabby) form. The colour of the ears should be solid, with a distinctive "thumb mark". The Tortie Tabby-point is sometimes an exception to this rule—here the ears can be mottled with red and/or cream, as in the Tortie-point Siamese.

On the face, the mask should bear clearly defined stripes, especially round the eyes and nose, with distinct markings on the cheeks, and darkly spotted whisker pads. The legs should carry varied-sized broken stripes with solid markings on the back of the hind legs. Tortie Tabby-points carry some mingled red and/or cream patching on the legs, mask and tail. The tail should have well-balanced varied-sized clearly-defined rings, ending in a solid tip. Eyes should be brilliant clear blue, the lids dark-rimmed or toning with the points, nose leather conforming to the recognized Siamese Standard for the particular colour of points, or pink.

The kitten on the right of this pair is still showing the baby coat. Breeder: Miss Gamble.

194

Siamese, Any Other Colour

Triple Champion White Sheik of Avio, an All-American Albino Siamese male, owned by Mrs Thelma Harrington.

The most ethereal in appearance of all Siamese cats are the dilutions in the red series, which, with the exception of the Tortie-points, are all grouped together in Britain by the Governing Council of the Cat Fancy at present. This group consists, besides the Tortie-points, which are recognized separately, of the Cream-point Siamese; the Red and Cream Tabby-points; and the Tortoiseshell Tabby-points which can be either Seal, Chocolate, Blue or Lilac.

All the dilute forms of Siamese conform in type to the normal Siamese standard as regards size, shape and bone structure, and all have definite blue eye-colour, the shade varying in intensity according to the predominant colour visible in the points; for example like a Chocolate Tortie-point, a Chocolate/Tabby Tortie-point should have

Siamese, Tortie-point
see page 181

195

eye-colour of the same shade as that seen in the Chocolate-point Siamese.

Cream-point Siamese can be either male or female and the body colour is a warm shade of white; the legs and face are the colour of clotted cream and the ears, nose and tail are a pale warm apricot shade, with nose leather and pads of flesh pink.

Red Tabby-points can be either male or female and are indistinguishable by eye alone from Red-point Siamese, and this can, and has, led to difficulties within the breed. Red, when present in any cat, appears "tabby" whether it is so genetically or not; and if from a Tabby-point sire or dam, only test-mating can determine whether the cat is "tabby" or "self". The same remarks apply also to Cream Tabby-points. Tortie/Tabby-points carry all their genetic make-up on the surface. Always female, they can be bred in any of the four basic Siamese colours.

The Seal Tortie/Tabby-point has red tabby on cream, and black on silver patching and intermingling on the points, in random areas of distribution, with banding showing on the tail and legs and distinctive tabby lines on the forehead and cheeks. The whisker pads also often appear to be spotted in the typical "tabby" manner.

Chocolate Tortie/Tabby-points are similar to Chocolate Tortie-points with the addition of tabby markings especially apparent on the cream areas. The Blue Tortie/Tabby-point resembles the Blue Tortie-point, again with the tabby markings more apparent on the cream areas, but the Lilac Tortie/Tabby-point is very hard to distinguish until about six months of age, as the barely visible points carry only ghost tabby bars, and it cannot be ascertained whether these are temporary and will clear with maturity, or develop more strongly.

As household pets, these Siamese varieties are particularly appealing, their pastel shades complimenting the decor of any home. Vocally and temperamentally toned down from the extroverted Seal-point, they make wonderful companions for dogs, and are particularly good with young children.

Cream-point mated with Cream-point give only Cream-point progeny, and the Red Tabby-point also breed true, but the dilute Tortie/Tabby-point females are much more complex in their production, and there are many permutations of matings which can produce them. The breeding of this series of Siamese should only be undertaken by the experienced cat breeder with a good working knowledge of genetics, or with guidance from a specialist club. Even the most knowledgeable breeder can find it difficult to determine the points colour of some of the young stock for registration purposes, when the colour factors of the parents make it possible for such a wide variety to be shown in one litter.

A variety known in America but not in Britain is the Albino Siamese; this cat shows a complete lack of pigmentation caused by a genetic change, with a white coat, pink skin, and a pink under-tone to the eyes.

Abyssinian
(Abyssinian, Ruddy)

Short-hair

Like many of the best-established breeds, the Abyssinian is of uncertain origin, although this slender, sleek-looking animal is looked upon by zoologists and geneticists as one of the oldest, with its agouti coat markings, like those displayed by the *Felis caffra*. It is certainly the breed most resembling the cats worshipped by the ancient Egyptians, whose bronzes and frescoes portray the litheness, long body, whip-like tail, large eyes, and alert ears which are distinguishing features of the best type of Abyssinian today. The first reliable reference to the cat we know as the Abyssinian dates from 1868, when a military expedition led by Lord Robert Napier returned home from Abyssinia with the first cat of this breed to be seen in Great Britain. It was given the name Zula, after the port at which the advance party had landed.

The appearance of this cat, with its ticked, ruddy coat, was unusual and attempts were made to create from it a breed which would reproduce its essentially "foreign" characteristics. It is a certainty that the Abyssinian we know today is the result of careful cross-breeding with selected native British cats.

Other, undesirable, colours were added to the coat – in the early days indiscriminate crossing produced coats that were silver instead of

Ch Taishun Leo, an outstanding stud with the noble look of an older male. He still has an excellently ticked ruddy brown coat and keen, alert expression.

197

Mrs E. Menezes' Taishun Chula (female) with well-shaped body, long tapering tail, small feet and black colouring extending up the back of the legs.

ruddy. There was inevitably confusion as to correct type and colour; a different type of bone structure was introduced, and part of the "Abyssinian" type was lost. When, in 1882, the Abyssinian was recognised in Great Britain as a separate breed, both Harrison Weir and Louis Wain, the foremost judges of their day, expressed their doubts and suggested the description "Abyssinian-type". They considered that it was possible for Abyssinian-type kittens to appear as the result of chance matings between ordinary tabby cats, and therefore the Abyssinian should not be looked on as a separate breed.

The arguments continued for some years, and at the beginning of this century the name Abyssinian was dropped, at least for a while, the cats being known variously as "Ticked", "British Ticks" and "Bunny Cats". The numbers increased very slowly, the 1914–18 War causing the cessation of breeding by several fanciers, and it was not until 1929 that the Abyssinian Cat Club was formed in Britain and a Standard of Points adopted, essentially the Standard in use today. The first president of the Abyssinian Club was Mrs Gordon Stables; her husband, Dr Gordon Stables, was author of the book *Cats, Their Points and Characteristics* in which, so far as is known, the Abyssinian received its first mention in print.

Numbers of this breed appearing on the show bench would indicate popularity comparable to other "foreign" breeds; but, due to the

Above: A ten-month-old female from Canada, Gr Ch Chota-Li Kahina of Phaulkon. Bred by Mrs E. Field and owned by Mrs S. Mayer of California.

Ch Chota-Li Jester—a male, bred in Canada by Mrs Edna Field, and owned by Miss Cheryl White of Illinois.

relatively small litter size, compared with the more prolific Burmese and Siamese (the Abyssinian normally produces about four kittens), supply does not always equal demand.

There is no lack of outstanding cats to maintain the standard of the breed – leading examples are the female Ch Heatherpine Juanita, and the male Ch Contented Amigo, both owned by Miss F. Bone and bred by Mrs I. Earnshaw and Miss I. Wiseman respectively; 1964 saw the birth of a kitten later to prove unbeaten in any open class, Ch Taishun Leo, owned and bred by Mrs E. Menezes; he was the sire of numerous champions all over the world, including Ch Taishun Solo, owned by Miss Wiseman, and one of the leading Abyssinians of the 1969–71 show seasons in Britain.

The American story began in 1909, when Miss Jane Cathcart of Oradell, New Jersey, imported from England Chs Aluminium and Salt, thought to be "Silver" Abyssinians, but it was many years before the breed became at all popular. In 1934, Mrs Gardner Fiske of Boston imported Woodruffe Ena and Woodruffe Anthony, bred in England by Major Sidney Woodiwiss; Ena subsequently came into the possession of Mary E. Hantzmon of Washington, D.C., who, in 1937, mated her to her newly-imported male, Ras Seyem, also bred by Major Woodiwiss.

With the progeny from this pair, the Abyssinian at last became

Gr Ch Chota-Li Cricket of Phaulkon, a Canadian Ruddy Aby female, sired by one of the top Aby studs in Canada, Gr Ch Chota-Li R.S.T. Bred by Mrs Field and owned by Mrs Mayer.

Above: Ch Taishun Leo, with brilliant almond-shaped eyes and a good profile.

Left: Ch Taishun Leo—note his well-developed male head, with large, well-tufted, pointed ears; broad at the base.

199

firmly established. It is now third in North American registrations, following the Siamese and the Burmese, and numbers are far greater than in Great Britain. The Abyssinian Cat Club of America and the United Abyssinian Club are the two strongest specialist groups; the latter has published *Journey from the Blue Nile*, an authoritative history of the Abyssinian which documents that, in about 1960, a native Ethiopian cat matching the Abyssinian Standard to a remarkable degree was brought from Addis Ababa by an American family – their own local house-cat had given birth to it, suggestive of the authenticity of the Abyssinian's historic background.

The lithe, svelte outline and large ears of the Abyssinian give it a typical "jungle" appearance; it is an active, friendly cat, highly intelligent, with a personality all of its own – an asset to any home. Moreover, the grooming of these lovely cats is very simple. With their short, close coats, a fine tooth-comb will soon remove any loose hairs. I brush the coat with a soft or rubber brush, and then gently wipe it with a damp chamois leather, finishing off the grooming session with a dry chamois or a piece of silk. Every day, you should stroke the cat's fur with your hands – this helps to give the coat a lovely sheen.

If you intend to show an Abyssinian, it is no use leaving the grooming

Above: Mrs Menezes' Ch Contented Penny (female) in profile, with large, alert pointed ears and almond-shaped eyes. Her coat is excellently ticked, with no white or bars.

Ch Contented Bambino, female, bred by Miss I. Wiseman—a dainty queen with foreign-shaped head on slender neck.

until the last few days before a show. Grooming should be a regular feature in your cat's routine. Some cats can be upset by travelling and be of a poor colour on the morning of the show; but by afternoon when they have settled down, they can look quite different, much richer in colour.

Not all queens are necessarily suitable for breeding – as with any other breed, an Abyssinian queen should be spayed if she shows any serious faults according to the Standard. White fur on parts of the body other than the chin, between the hind legs, for example, or heavy rings on the tail or hind legs, should rule out an Abyssinian queen for breeding purposes. If kittens of quality are expected, the good and bad points of both parents have to be assessed, the good points of one compensating for the bad points of the other.

As we have mentioned, the Abyssinian does not usually have a large litter, four or five being the average, although some queens have had six or seven kittens at one time. When they are born, some kittens have very dark coats, with dark marks on their stomachs, and bars on the front legs. Some have a necklet slightly darker in colour than the rest of the coat. Often, when adult, they are hardly recognisable as the same animals, as all markings disappear and coat colour and ticking changes to the rich ruddy colour required in an Abyssinian. The ideal kitten is one free of any barring or white, with a rich, ruddy coat colour, well ticked, and a lithe, svelte outline. The ticking starts to show when the kitten is about a month old. A rich pigmentation all through the fur is desirable.

The fine ticked coat of the Abyssinian is unique among cats. Each hair has two or three distinct bands of colour, the whole blending into an effect often compared to a Belgian hare. The coat, according to the British Standard for the "standard" variety, known as Ruddy in the States, should be ruddy brown, ticked with black or dark brown. Double or treble ticking is preferable to single ticking. There should be no bars or other markings except that a dark spine line will not militate against an otherwise good specimen on the show bench. The inside of the forelegs and the belly should harmonise well with the main colour, preference being given to orange brown. Distinct bars and rings on legs and tail, and a white chin, are undesirable; no other white markings are permissible.

The Abyssinian's head is long and pointed, with ears comparatively large and broad at the base, set as though "listening". Its eyes are large, bright and expressive, and green, yellow or hazel in colour. The tail is fairly long and tapering, and the feet small, with black pads. This colour also extends up the back of the hind legs. A judge, the British Standard points out, must not attach such undue importance to the absence of unwanted markings that he fails to give due weight to other qualities.

The Standards of the North American associations differ from the British in some aspects of type. The American head is (to quote from the C.F.A. Standard) "a modified wedge without flat planes; the brow, cheek and profile lines all showing a gentle contour". The muzzle is not sharply-pointed. Eyes are almond-shaped, gold or green in colour – the Standards of some of the other associations, including A.C.F.A., call for gold, green or hazel eyes.

Leading Australian Aby stud—Gr Ch Araya Pasha, bred by Mr P. Wellwood and owned by Mrs G. Jenkins.

Taishun Cherokee, a five-months-old male, with good type and well-proportioned body on slim legs, and with small, well-shaped paws. Bred by Mrs Menezes.

Abyssinian, Red *Short-hair*

For as long as the Abyssinian breed has been officially recognised, there has, from time to time, appeared in a litter an odd kitten of other-than-normal colour. It will be held by some breeders that the new shades have been introduced intentionally, but my own conviction is that the Red Abyssinian did not originate in this way – indeed I have been given to understand that a red kitten appeared in a litter of Abyssinians as long ago as 1880, although nothing is known of the breeding.

The colour of today's Red Abyssinian is due to a special red gene which is recessive, which means that for a red to appear in a litter, this gene must be present on both sides. A queen with normal colour may carry red, and may never produce a red kitten because she has not been mated to a male carrying red. If the male is normal in colour but carries the red gene, the female will produce both red and normal progeny in the litter. In my experience, I have never seen a normal kitten born to two red parents – only by mating red to red can one be sure of producing an entirely red litter.

The strength in Britain today of the beautiful Red Abyssinian must be largely attributed to the pioneer work of the late Mrs Dorothy Winsor, for it was mainly due to her untiring efforts over many years, patiently breeding red to red, that the new breed gradually became known. In 1959, she acquired a red female, Merkland Yilma, from Lady Liverpool, and later another female, Merkland Sheba; she was also able to take a red male, Taishun Khepha, from Mrs E. Menezes

and, together, these formed the basis of the breeding programme, which progressed despite many setbacks, at a time when most breeders would give away any kitten with other-than-normal coat colour.

In 1963, the Red Abyssinian was officially recognised in Britain. In that same year, I obtained a red female in a litter of five, of which four were the normal colour, this from a normal queen mated to a red male. This kitten later became Ch Bernina Heidi, the first Red Abyssinian to achieve championship status in the U.K. The Red Abyssinian was recognised by the larger American associations, too, in 1963, and the first All-American Red Aby (1964) and first Champion was Du-Ru-Al's Sorrel Sultan, owned by Alma Cowell of Detroit. In America, as in Britain, the Red Abyssinian is catered for by the same specialist associations as its "normal" cousin.

The Red Abyssinian is no harder to rear than any other pedigree cat and my experience is that they kitten and look after their young like good mothers. As soon as the kittens are born, their colour is easy to determine, for a red kitten always has pink pads while the normal has black; the black pigment is missing in the Red.

My own method of routine grooming is to administer a good rubbing-down with damp rubber gloves. This removes all loose hairs, and coats assume a glossy sheen. For special show grooming, I rub bay rum over the coat maybe a day or two before a show, as this removes all unwanted grease; bay rum should not be used regularly, however. Special care must also be given to ears. Then just before putting them

203

Miss Wiseman's Contented Ras, with a beautiful red ticked coat free from markings, and good length of body and well-shaped head.

Above: Ch Madrigal Dougal in profile, showing well-placed large ears, broad at base, and firm chin.

in the show pen, I give my cats a final rub with the silk scarf that has been around my neck, which gives a final polish to the coat.

The British Standard for the Red Abyssinian is the same in every respect as that for the normal variety, except in regard to colour, which should be rich copper red on the body, doubly or preferably trebly ticked with darker colours. Lack of distinct contrast in the ticking is a fault. The richer the body colour the better – a pale colour is a bad fault. The belly and inside of the legs should be deep apricot to harmonize. The tip of the tail is dark brown, and this colour may extend along the tail as a line. A spine line of deeper colour is also permissible. As with the standard variety, a white chin is considered undesirable on the show bench, while other white markings are definitely not permitted. The nose leather is pink; pads are pink, set in brown fur which extends up the backs of the legs. Eye colour, like that of the normal variety, is green, yellow or hazel.

Ch Taishun Sabrina, now in the U.S.A., protecting her Aby kittens; one Red and one with "standard" or "ruddy" colouring.

204

American Short-hair

The American Short-hair (or Domestic Short-hair, as it is sometimes known) is the oldest domesticated short-haired breed in North America, with some of its ancestors arriving with the early Puritan families from Britain. These cats were brought along for a purpose and they certainly earned their keep. They were great rodent hunters and protected precious grain as well as being the family pets.

It is known that no similar cat was established in North America before the era of Columbus, and it has been reported that at least one cat arrived on the Mayflower. So, these cats are entitled to the name "American Short-hair", for even though the breed did not originate in North America, they are every bit as American as any immigrant!

Contrary to the carefully controlled conditions under which many of the contemporary breeds have seen their beginning, the formative years of the American Short-hair were subjected to the pitiless laws of

Quad Gr Ch Go-Seek-Us Ike—a Silver Tabby male. He has won numerous association awards, including Highest-Scoring All-Eastern Cat and Best All-American Short-hair, 1970. Breeder and owner: Jessie James Mayer.

natural selection, hence the particularly tough and hardy qualities the breed now exhibits. Noted for their health, strength, stability, even temperament, affection and intelligence, it is small wonder that they are great favourites.

Breeders who foresaw a future in the cat fancy for the American Short-hair undertook the job of selective breeding and have established a standard of high quality. In the last decade, it has not been an uncommon sight to see the breed taking top awards at cat shows throughout North America and interest has grown in leaps and bounds.

The Silver Tabby is one of the American Short-hair colours that has contributed greatly to the upsurge of interest in this breed and many lovely examples are seen today. A Silver Tabby, Gr Ch Shawnee Trademark, owned by Nikki Shuttleworth of Kentucky, was 1965 All-American Cat of the Year. Another popular colour in America is the Red Tabby, which is somewhat larger and rangier than its British counterpart. The Brown Tabby is a less popular colour, but it consistently appears in the All-American award listings and from time to time wins association-award recognition. In 1971 C.F.A.'s leading short-hair was the Mackerel Brown Tabby Gr Ch Male Man of DeTracy, owned by Mr and Mrs Tracy W. Tucker of California.

There are classes for both the "Classic" tabby, and for the "Mackerel", which carries the striped tabby pattern. Associations other than the C.F.A. also recognize Tortoiseshell and White and Parti-colour Short-hairs.

Some twenty odd years ago, I was amused and surprised by a neighbour who owned what almost everyone called "just a black cat". Each year, just before the big Canadian National Exhibition cat show, which was held annually in Toronto, his owner would haul "Tom" into the house and unceremoniously give him a good bath. He was transformed overnight – and without the help of a Fairy Godmother – into a show cat! He was a handsome sturdy black cat, who had somehow managed to keep his ears intact during his many back-yard fights. Every year, he came home with rosettes and trophies, his owners justifiably proud of their "show cat". Next day, Tom was back outside, tending to his chores of keeping the garden and tool-shed free from mice.

Tortie American Short-hair female, Gr Ch Rococo Ruby Begonia; was C.F.A.'s Best American Short-hair in 1969. Breeder and owner: Jim Shinkle.

The breed has come a long way since then, but basically, the cats have not changed. They are still born hunters, their hard, thick coats protecting them from cold, rain or thorny bushes. Some fine examples are occasionally produced by chance matings and one sometimes sees some of them as lovely exhibits in the Household Pet classes. However, offspring of matings between Long-hairs and Short-hairs are ineligible for showing either as Persians or American (Domestic) Short-hairs.

Nevertheless, the credit for the popularity and quality of the American Short-hair must go to the devoted breeders who have carefully guided the breed to one of the top places in the Cat Fancy today, and buyers expect to pay as much for a show-type kitten of this breed as they would for any other.

The American Short-hair is described by the Standard as giving the general effect "of the trained athlete, with all muscles rippling easily beneath the skin, the flesh lean and hard, and with great latent power held in reserve".

It has a large head, full-cheeked, giving an impression of an oblong just slightly longer than wide, and a medium-length neck, gently curved, and the same width for the entire length. The muzzle is squared, and stud cats have definite jowls. A firm, well-developed chin is called for, forming a perpendicular line with the upper lip. The wide set ears are slightly rounded at the tips, and not unduly open at the base, while the eyes too should be set well apart, round and wide with a slight slant to the outer aperture; they should be bright, clear and alert.

A fine example of a rare variety—Gr Ch Adam's Rib Moonshot (male), a Cream Mackerel Tabby, bred and owned by Adam Frecowski of Illinois.

This is a powerfully-built cat; the body should be medium to large, well-knit and hard with a well-developed chest and shoulders. At the same time, as the Standard points out, there should be no sacrifice of quality for the sake of mere size. Legs should be medium in length, firm-boned and heavily muscled, showing the breed's capabilities for easy jumping. The paws should be firm, full and rounded, with heavy pads; five toes on the front paws and four behind. The tail is of medium length, and heavy at the base; although it appears to come to an abrupt, blunt end, in structure it has the normal, tapering final vertebrae. A very short or kinked tail is a fault.

The coat should be short, thick and even, and hard in texture. In

A Brown Tabby male with good distinct markings, Gr Ch Bi-Zi Beauregarde of Ru-Bee. Owner: Bert E. Rees.

the winter it will be somewhat heavier and thicker. The coat should not be long or fluffy.

A cat will be penalized on the show bench for excessive cobbiness or ranginess, obesity or boniness; it should be springy in movement, with lithe, rippling muscles.

There are variations between the American (Domestic) Short-hair and the British Short-hair. The nearer counterpart of the British Short-hair in America is C.F.A.'s Exotic Short-hair and this was developed by cross-breeding Persians and American Short-hairs, together with other Short-hairs.

The American (Domestic) Short-hair is different in several ways from the Exotic. For example, they have an "oblong head" rather than the Exotic's "round and massive head with great breadth of skull". The Domestic's body is of "medium" build rather than "cobby" like the Exotic, and its legs are to be of "medium length" rather than "short, thick, and strong" which is required in the Exotic. Other associations' Standards for the American (Domestic) are similar to C.F.A.'s, and in the associations which recognize the British Blue (A.C.F.A. and A.C.A., for example) the same characteristics are required.

The American Short-hair is recognized in the following colour varieties: white (blue-eyed, copper-eyed, and odd-eyed), black, blue, red, cream, chinchilla, shaded silver, black smoke, blue smoke; five tabby colours – silver, red, brown, blue and cream, all recognized in classic or mackerel form; tortoiseshell, calico and blue-cream. Bi-colours are also bred.

American Wire-hair

Short-hair

The first record of an American Wirehair was in 1966, when a strange-looking little kitten appeared in a litter of kittens from ordinary farm cats. The owner of the farm contacted Mrs William O'Shea – a Rex breeder – and told her about this remarkable kitten. Mrs O'Shea purchased the kitten, along with a normal-coated litter sister. The little female looked like any normal, healthy little brown tabby-with-white kitten, but her red and white brother was different. His coat was very wiry, resilient and even coarser than that of a Wirehair Terrier. In the hope that this attractive type of cat could be reproduced, brother and sister were bred and produced four kittens, two normal-coated and two wire-haired, both of the latter being red and white. The female red and white kitten carried many of the father's characteristics, with tightly curled coat on the head and having the same long-legged appearance.

The original male – named Council Rock Farm Adam of Hi-Fi – was later bred to an unrelated Blue-eyed White Domestic Short-hair; and this litter again produced two Wirehairs in a litter of four. This clearly indicated that the Wirehair gene is not a simple recessive like the Rex.

For the first Wirehair-to-Wirehair breeding, the red and white female from the first litter was bred back to her father and produced two red and white Wirehair kittens – strong and healthy and just covered with tight, coarse, curly, wiry hair! Several breeders are working with this new breed and some are appearing in shows where they cause quite a sensation.

The Standard proposed by the American Wirehair Cat Society for the breed describes it as "a spontaneous mutation of the domestic cat. The only difference between the domestic and the wirehair is the coat". Indeed, in respect to matters other than the coat, the proposed Standard follows closely that of the American (Domestic) Short-hair.

However, the coat of the Wirehair (which comes in all American Short-hair colours) should be medium in length, coarse, stiff and wiry to the touch – it should be fairly dense. From the top of the head, across the back, sides and hips, and along to the top of the tail, the coat is wiry, but it is less coarse on the underside of the chin and on the chest and abdomen.

Hi-Fi's Amy of Katzen Reich, a red and white female from the first registered litter of Wire-hairs born in the world. Her sire is the Wire-hair mutant, Council Rock Farm Adam of Hi-Fi. Bred by Mrs William F. O'Shea, and owned by Dr Rosamonde Peltz.

Burmese, Blue *Short-hair*

Ch Belcanto Floria Tosca, female, showing a good silvery sheen to her coat, an elegant body and long, slender neck. Owned by Miss Mack.

Head study of Ch Arboreal Blue Leela, female, owned by Miss Mack.

The Blue Burmese has not been with us very long; in 1955, a British-bred Brown Burmese cat, Chinki Golden Gay, produced a litter of four kittens, one of which was much lighter in colour than the other three, which were normally-coloured. Golden Gay was a daughter of the American-bred Brown Burmese, Casa Gatos Darkee, one of the original breeding stock for the Brown Burmese in Britain; the litter containing the odd-coloured kitten was the result of Golden Gay having been mated back to her father.

At first, this unexpected event seemed to cast doubt on the genetic status of Brown Burmese, but more mature consideration led to the theory that the odd-coloured kitten probably was the "blue-diluted" form of the Brown Burmese coat colour.

The work of Dr Thompson and others (*see* Burmese, Brown) had already shown conclusively that the Burmese and Siamese coat pattern genes which, when associated with genetic black, gave respectively Brown Burmese and Seal-pointed Siamese, were members of the same albino series. It was therefore reasonable to assume that the same recessive blue-dilution factor, which modified Seal-pointed Siamese to Blue-pointed, could similarly be associated with Brown Burmese to give a blue-diluted form. However, since Seal-pointed Siamese had been used as out-crosses in the basic work on Burmese, it was possible that one of them, or even the original hybrid, Wong Mau herself, had carried the recessive blue-dilution factor, which had then been transmitted to the "pure" Burmese. Because of its recessive character, the diluted colour would be expressed only in individuals which had received the dilution factor from both parents. Thus, if Casa Gatos Darkee was carrying blue dilution, he could have passed on the recessive factor to his daughter. Then, when father and daughter were mated together, it would be expected that some of the kittens would receive the recessive factor from one parent only, and would be the normal colour, and some would receive the factor from both parents, and would be the blue-diluted colour. Increasing support came for this theory as the kitten grew up and her coat colour developed to a bluish grey. Appropriately, she was registered as Sealcoat Blue Surprise.

By 1960, six litters from blue-to-blue matings had been produced, representing twenty-six kittens and three generations of pure breeding; a documented case for the recognition of Blue Burmese was submitted to the Governing Council of the Cat Fancy in Britain, by the Burmese Cat Club, on the general basis that Blue Burmese were in the same relationship to Brown Burmese as Blue-pointed Siamese were to Seal-pointed. The breed was recognised in June 1960.

At the time of writing, all British-bred Blue Burmese cats are descended from Ch Casa Gatos Darkee, or from a Burmese/Siamese hybrid cat, China Tan Tockseng, brought into Britain around 1960 by Mrs Grove-White. The American United Burmese Cat Fanciers has been unable to agree with the above conclusions, and considers the Brown (or Sable) variety to be the only Burmese cats, but within the last few years, some of the American registration bodies (N.C.F.A., C.C.A. and C.F.F.) have recognised Blue as a colour variation of Burmese. In general. Blue Burmese have not so far made as much

Above: The first Blue Burmese, Mr V. Watson's Sealcoat Blue Surprise (female, centre) and her litter brothers.

Below: This fine Blue Burmese lives in France, but is of English breeding.

Above: A typical stud with a good sheen to his blue coat and a fine chin—Mrs R. M. Pocock's Ch Buskin's Blue Sonya.

Left: Ch Lydeard Princess Bluebell (female) has a pleasing expression, large lustrous eyes and good medium wedge shape to Standard. Owned by Mrs Warren-Hurlock.

211

Above: Linlinkye Blue Bell and Blue Blossom—two very promising, self-possessed five-months-old kittens.

Below: Vanya and her kittens—bred by Mrs Boydell and Mrs P. A. Lloyd.

Three generations of Blue Burmese—left to right, Belcanto Daphne, Ch Arboreal Blue Leela (grandmother) and Ch Belcanto Floria Tosca (mother).

progress in the U.S.A. as they have in the U.K., since there were comparatively few breeders interested until recent years.

There have, however, been Blue Burmese All-American winners every year since 1966, the first awards having gone to International Champion Santhone Ju-Jitsu, owned by Margaret Francis, and to Ch Ballard Sipora of Mingala, owned by Mrs C. Prymus.

The coat colour of the Blue Burmese is, in fact, different from that of other blue cats. Compared with Russian Blue and British Blue, it is a paler shade of grey, with a slightly warmer (i.e. less bluish) tone, appropriately described as "antique silver". The British Standard specifies "predominantly bluish grey, darker on the back, the overall effect being a warm colour with a silver sheen to the coat – the tail the same colour as the back". As with the Brown Burmese, a few white hairs, while undesirable, may be permissible. There should be no white patches or tabby markings, although kittens are usually of lighter colour, and young kittens may show tabby bars. The American Standards for the coat are similar, describing the colour as "rich, sound, even blue-grey of velvety texture characterised by a high sheen on the coat, giving an illusion of irridescence".

The coat itself should be short, fine in texture and lying moderately close to the body. There is a difference in texture between the coats of Brown and Blue Burmese, and this is acknowledged in the British Standard for the Blue. In the case of the Blue Burmese, in common with blue-diluted forms of some other breeds, the coat is not quite so fine in texture, does not lie quite so close to the body and does not have such a high sheen. Both the British and the American Standards call for Blue Burmese to have the same type as Brown.

The eyes of the Blue Burmese should be yellowish-green to yellow in colour according to the British Standard – yellow to gold according to the American; really green eyes are a serious fault. Burmese eye colour is of low intensity, and hence the apparent colour is considerably influenced by the strength and colour of the light in which it is viewed; the British Standard recommends that eye colour be assessed in daylight.

Burmese, Brown
(Burmese, Sable)
Short-hair

Mrs Warren-Hurlock's Ch Mauresque Chola, an outstanding Brown Burmese queen, with her eight-weeks-old son—a future Champion. The difference is clearly visible between the adult and kitten coat colouring.

The story of the Brown Burmese begins in 1930 with a cat called Wong Mau, which was taken from Burma to the U.S.A. by Dr Joseph C. Thompson of San Francisco. American cat fanciers of the day were inclined to regard Wong Mau as a specially dark Siamese; Thompson disagreed. She was, in his view, distinctly different from Siamese, and in conjunction with some other breeders he decided to carry out breeding experiments to settle the doubts on a scientific basis. These

Mizpah's Ferdinand of Brierwood—an International and Septuple Grand Champion, and Octuple Champion; was Best Cat in Show 119 times—an international world record—and was All-American Cat of the Year in 1967. Bred by Vivian E. Chartier and owned by John E. Baker of Pittsburgh, Pa. Note the more rounded, less "foreign" type called for by the North American Standards.

Profile of Ch Linlinkye Miatango (male), with a good break in nose and a superb strong chin. Owned by Mrs Warren-Hurlock.

investigations demonstrated that Wong Mau was, in fact, a hybrid of Siamese with a previously-unknown dark-coated breed to which was given the name "Burmese". Mated to Siamese, Wong Mau produced Burmese/Siamese hybrids and pure Siamese, the darker-coated, pure Burmese cats only appearing when Burmese/Siamese hybrids were mated together.

The darker-coated Burmese bred true, and the Burmese breed emerged with its own distinct identity. On the evidence of Dr Thompson's experiments, the Burmese was recognised in the United States in 1936 as a new show breed, although in the early days interest was mainly confined to the West Coast. With hindsight it seems very probable that Burmese/Siamese hybrids were, in fact, imported into Great Britain in the early days of Siamese imports, around the turn of the century, without being recognised for what they were.

The difference in appearance between Burmese/Siamese hybrids and pure Burmese are most obvious in kittens and young cats; in the hybrid, the points are obvious and the body colour is paler. With increasing age the body colour of the hybrid darkens and the differences become less apparent, but it is still easily possible to distinguish between the two. In the early days of the breed in America, when hybrids were of necessity being produced, the demand for pure Burmese outstripped the available supply and, by 1947, through ignorance or otherwise, hybrids were being shown and sold as pure Burmese. In that year, and for this reason, C.F.A. withdrew its recognition of Burmese and only restored it in 1953, when the situation had been brought under control by the Burmese Cat Society of America. By 1953 Burmese had also been recognised by A.C.A., C.F.F. and U.C.F. Some of the early American breeders of Burmese were Mrs Gerst (Gerstdale), Mrs Alexander, Mrs Merrill Stevens (Tung Wong), Miss Winifred Porter (the Farm), Mrs Nan Pyle (Hassayampa) and Mr and Mrs Donald Came. In 1950, the Cames sold out most of their cats to Mrs Blanche

Warren of the Casa Gatos Cattery. The first American specialist club was the Burmese Cat Society of America, of which Mr and Mrs Warren were President and Secretary respectively.

A good head shape—Arboreal Sitta, showing nicely placed ears, good eye shape and fine whiskers.

The pure-bred Burmese did not appear in Great Britain until well after the Second World War, when Mrs L. France imported from America four West Coast cats, Ch Laos Cheli Wat, Chindwin's Minou Twm (females, 1949), Casa Gatos da Foong (male, 1949), and Casa Gatos Darkee (male, 1953). Another American male important in the establishment of the Burmese in Britain was Darshan Khudiran, imported by Mrs C. F. Watson in 1957. In the United Kingdom the Burmese Cat Club, which caters for all colours of Burmese, was formed in 1954 by Mr V. Watson. At first, the Burmese were rather susceptible to respiratory infections which led often to chronic catarrh. This tendency has, fortunately, now disappeared as the cats have become acclimatized, and generally speaking Burmese cats are tough, hardy and very healthy. Breeding is without special complications – the kittens are usually strong and develop rapidly.

Ch Casa Gatos Darkee, one of the original Brown Burmese imported into Britain.

When mature, the Brown Burmese has a rich, dark, seal-brown body colour, shading to a slightly lighter colour on the chest and belly. There should be no white or tabby markings. White hairs are undesirable – although a few may be permissible, a definite white patch is not. Ears, mask and points should be only slightly darker than the back coat, and indeed mature cats showing decided contrast are not eligible for top British awards.

In young adults and older kittens, all coat colours may be slightly lighter and greater contrast is allowed between body coat and points. Young kittens will generally be lighter still and may show tabby bars.

Miss M. Mack's Belcanto Zigeunerbaron —a young male showing good head and firm chin. Good temperament is important in a stud.

The original U.S.A. Standard was revised in 1951 by the Burmese Cat Society. The British Standard of 1954 was based on this, and remains substantially the same to this day; it clearly calls for a foreign-type cat, which is logical for a breed emanating originally from the East.

The present British Standard requires a well-muscled cat with no fat – the Burmese has a typical firm feel when handled. The medium-sized body is elegant, long (but not as long as Siamese) and svelte, and the neck long and slender. As with Siamese, the legs should be proportionately slim with hind legs slightly longer than the front, and with small, oval feet. The tail should be long and slightly tapering, although a whip tail is undesirable, as is a very slight, scarcely visible kink at the extreme end, although this *may* be permissible in a cat of otherwise superlative quality.

The Burmese face is wedge-shaped, but shorter, blunter and wider at the jaw than Siamese. The top of the head should be slightly rounded, the profile showing a firm chin and a break at the top of the nose. The relatively large ears should be wide at the base and slightly rounded at the tip, and outer line of the ears continuing the wedge shape of the face. A jaw pinch is a fault.

A sign of good health is a glossy sheen on the coat, which should be short, fine-textured and lying close to the body.

A consistently good litter of Burmese kittens at eight weeks.

Green or blue-green eyes are a fault in the Brown Burmese; ideally they should be a clear, fairly intense golden yellow, although the majority of Brown Burmese today have chartreuse-yellow eyes.

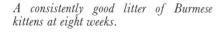

A male kitten bred and owned by Mrs Dell—Kupro Bronze Boy. His coat shows ghost markings which will disappear as he grows older.

It seems possible that in the process of selection, American breeders have placed the greatest emphasis on a deeper yellow eye colour, tending to sacrifice foreign type in doing so. In 1959, the U.S.A. Standard was changed, calling now for a cat of British/Domestic short-hair rather than "foreign" type – "body medium in size, muscular in development and presenting a somewhat compact appearance . . . amply rounded chest with back level from shoulder to tail, legs well-proportioned to body with round feet". The current U.S.A. Standard also calls for a more rounded face and medium-sized ears, tilting slightly forward, and broad at the base. The eyes should be wide apart and, according to the British Standard, almond shaped and, according to the U.S. Standard, round.

Mrs Warren-Hurlock's eight-weeks-old kitten showing great promise, with good, rounded skull and in first-class condition.

Left: "Gossip", a female bred in Canada by a Canadian sire of an English dam, bred by Mrs Clarkim and now owned by Mrs P. A. Lloyd.

217

Burmese, Other Colours

A blue-cream Burmese, Kupro Silken Sophina, owned by Mrs J. Dell.

At the time of writing, the Burmese breed includes the following colours – cream, blue-cream, red, tortie, champagne (a colour known in Britain as chocolate), and platinum (lilac in Britain). The Browns and Blues have, for some time, had their separate recognition in Britain by the Governing Council of the Cat Fancy, and, in 1971, they were joined by the Creams and Blue-creams. Although recognition is being sought for the other colours, they must, for the time being, be included in the Any Other Variety category. The Burmese of North America have not yet officially assumed the coats of many colours sported by those in England. The two largest associations, C.F.A. and A.C.F.A., do not even recognise the Blue Burmese or the Champagne, but these colours do have championship status in most of the smaller registries and have been earning All-American wins since 1965. American fancy-wide recognition of these new colours, however, is still several years away. In Britain, there is a native breeding programme for creams, blue-creams, reds and torties, while the British breeding programme for chocolates (champagne) and lilacs (platinums) is linked to animals imported from America.

The story of the Creams and Blue-creams in Britain began in 1964, from a chance mating between a Blue Burmese and a Red Tabby. Among the original litter was a tortie "half-Burmese" which was kept for breeding, the aim being eventually to produce Red and Cream Burmese. A second string was necessary to the plan and, keeping in mind the desired end-product, a brown queen was mated to a Red-pointed Siamese. This mating produced a tortie hybrid female, and she was mated eventually back to a Blue Burmese male. Thus the blue

Burmese, Sable
see page 213

factor was now present in both pedigrees, and it was genetically possible for no less than eight colour types to appear in subsequent litters, although only half would be pure Burmese, the remainder being hybrid. In the event, fewer than the possible eight colours turned up, but among these were one tortie female and two blue-cream females, all of which were capable of producing Red and Cream Burmese. (Torties and blue-creams are always female; if a male did appear it would almost certainly be sterile.) The breeding programme was enlarged when other breeders joined it to establish the new colours in cats which were one hundred per cent true Burmese. Cream females were mated to a number of blue Burmese males – if instead a brown male is used, red and torties result; if the brown male carries blue, then cream and blue-cream could reappear and, in fact, the numbers of creams and blue-creams has far exceeded the number of reds and torties. This has led to the earlier recognition by the G.C.C.F. of the creams and blue-creams. It was felt that after six years, covering four or more generations, carefully selected, the true Burmese characteristics had been established in creams and blue-creams.

Profile of Mrs Dell's Kupro Cream Kismet (male), showing good nose break and perfect eye and ear setting.

The body shape is the same for creams and blue-creams as for Burmese generally, and so is the head and ears. The body colour of the Cream Burmese is a rich cream, shading to a lighter cream on the chest and under parts. There should be no spots or tabby markings, but if the cat is otherwise excellent, small indeterminate markings are permitted. The ears should be slightly darker in colour than the coat on the back. There should be no white patches. Kittens may be slightly lighter. The eye colour can be any shade of yellow to amber; green eyes are judged as a fault. The blueish eye with which kittens are born may remain longer than it does in Brown and Blue Burmese.

The coat should be short, finely textured, lying close to the body, and with a definite sheen. The coloration of the blue-cream differs from the cream in that it has blue and cream intermingled, without any obvious bar markings; but colour in this breed is deemed to be less important than type.

Cream Burmese female, Kupro Cream Carina, with dainty female head, correct width of ears, large lustrous eyes and sound colour.

The Chocolates (Champagnes) and Lilacs (Platinums) have been evolved in a different way. As recently as 1969, several cats were exported from America to Britain, coming from breeders in both sides of the country, the West and East Coasts. Some of these animals were actually chocolate (champagne), and some were Brown Burmese carrying the chocolate factor in the same way as the blue is carried. These cats were imported into Britain for the purpose of improving British stock by mating the chocolates of both sexes to brown, blue and to brown Burmese carrying blue (it must be understood that careful records are kept of all matings, and the genetical possibilities for colour in each mating are fully understood). In fact, by the second generation of matings from these imported animals, it became apparent that some of the American stock carried not only the chocolate factor, but the blue also. Although the programme is generally aimed at improving British stock, it was hoped by the British breeders that the missing colour, lilac (platinum) would be achieved. It was known that this could be brought about by mating together two of a brown-carrying chocolate-and-blue-litter (from a chocolate/blue mating) or from other matings of chocolates-carrying-blue and blues. The programme

is very recent, but even at the time of writing, several lilac (platinum) kittens have been born.

The present-day generations of both programmes, the chocolate (champagne) and the lilac (platinum) Burmese, contain sturdy kittens, displaying the fearless and active character and characteristics of the Burmese as we know them, and it is to be hoped that all Burmese of the new colours will maintain the existing characteristics of the breed. The object of both programmes in Britain is to bring the colours to perfection in as good a Burmese type as possible.

The Standard, or the description which has been put forward in Britain for adoption by the governing body, for chocolate and lilac Burmese follows in all points except that of coloration the Standard for the generality of Burmese.

Two fluffy kittens, well-coloured and with good unmarked coats—Kupro Cream Jasmine (female) and Kupro Cream Cosmos (male). Bred by Mrs J. Dell.

Egyptian Mau *Short-hair*

The most ancient cats in history were worshipped by the Egyptians in the nineteenth dynasty. The Egyptian *Book of the Dead* includes the Papyrus of Hunefer, a royal scribe of that time, which shows *"Ra"* the Sun-God in the form of a spotted tabby cat, slaying the serpent Apep. This cat and others in bronze and tablet pictures are of what we would call "good foreign type", and when the coat pattern is clearly shown, it is either spotted or mackerel tabby, or midway between the two. Many bronzes show a scarab beetle amulet placed carefully between the cat's ears, but this beetle mark is a natural pattern in some tabby cats, and it is thought that the bearing of this mark – by the common cat of that time – was a causal factor in the choice of the cat as an object of worship.

During the development of the Tabby-pointed Siamese in England, some "foreign" tabbies were produced, which were discarded from the breeding programmes as soon as there was sufficient "pointed" stock available. These showed a remarkable resemblance to the Egyptian Solar Cat, and one of these, Panchusan Zerina, was taken by Mrs Sayer of the Solitaire Cattery as a foundation queen for a programme designed to re-create the cat of the Ancient Pharoahs. Back-crosses to Siamese are necessary at all stages of the development of this breed to maintain type, although top quality Havanas are also being used to produce the bronze or chocolate variety.

The breeding programme at Solitaire, the only English cattery breeding this variety, should be completed in 1973, when application will be made to the G.C.C.F. for acceptance of the Standard and the granting of a breed number and Championship status.

The American strain of the Egyptian Mau is reputed to have

Solitaire Rah-Tu, a bronze Egyptian Mau (male), bred by Mrs A. Sayer.

Profile of Solitaire Rah-Tu shows a long and well-proportioned head, narrowing to a fine muzzle.

Above: Solitaire Rah-Tu—the nose leather tones in well with the body colouring.

Below: Mrs Sayer's Solitaire Egyptian— a second generation cat showing clearly the "scarab" mark between the ears.

Fatima's "Sequin" of Polka Dots—a four-month-old male kitten (right), with two female companions. Owned by Suzanne Schwetley of New York.

originated in the early 1950's from two cats acquired in Cairo, Egypt, who reached the U.S. via the Lebanese Embassy in Rome, Italy. Somewhat similar patterns have been produced in America by cross-breeding various of the "domestic" and "foreign" short-hairs and they are known by such names as the Bristol and the Ocicat, but the Egyptian Mau breeders have attempted to maintain a pure line from the original imports. The Egyptian Mau Breeders and Fanciers Association is working hard in America to spread information on the breed, and already several of the governing associations have accepted the breed for Championship classes.

The Egyptian Mau (Mau is Egyptian for "cat") is just a Siamese in disguise. He has all the traits of any Siamese cat, but a slightly quieter voice. He is a very elegant and loving cat, rather dog-like in his devotion to his humans. The bronze variety, upon which the greatest interest is centred in Britain, is extremely beautiful, with bright chestnut markings on a warm fawn base colour. The spots and stripes are very clearly defined, and the "scarab" mark aimed at in Britain is complete with body, six legs and antennae. Tail and legs are boldly ringed, and eye-colour is opal-green.

A Standard has been proposed in Britain, calling for a short, soft and glossy coat with clear mackerel-tabby or spotted markings on a paler ground colour. Nose leather and paw pads should tone with the coat colour. According to this Standard, the head should be long and well-proportioned, narrowing in perfectly straight lines to a fine muzzle.

There should be good width between the large pricked and pointed ears. The distinctive "scarab" mark should lie between the ears – lack of it is a fault. The Egyptian Mau has a long body, muscular and sinuous and of medium size. Legs should be slim and dainty with small oval paws, the hind legs slightly longer than the front. The tail should be very long and whipped, with no kink. The Mau's eyes should be green, yellow or hazel, oriental in shape and setting – they should not be round.

This Standard is different from that recognized in America, which calls for slightly less "foreign" type – eyes should be oval and slanting, but "oriental" eyes are a fault. This Standard does not allow "mackerel tabby" coat pattern, nor does it mention the scarab mark between the ears. The Mau is recognized in America in two colours – silver (sloe-black markings on a pale silver ground) and bronze (contrasting dark brown markings on a light bronze ground).

Exotic Short-hair

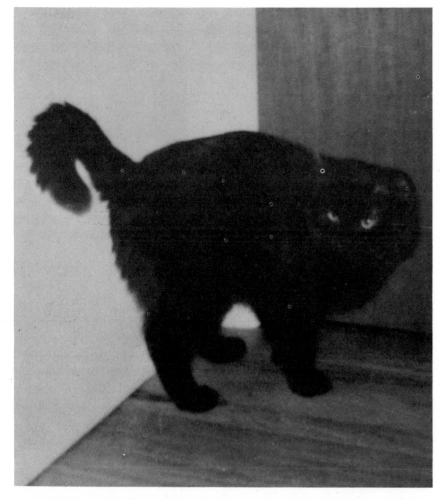

Gr Ch Leprechaun's Tepas Tea, a Black Exotic Short-hair male, bred and owned by Nancy and Robert C. Lane Jnr.

One of the newer short-haired breeds in America, the Exotic Short-hair was accepted into championship competition by the Cat Fanciers' Association in 1967. At present this cat is only recognized by C.F.A., but other associations are, however, considering it for recognition. Gaining popularity with both long-hair and short-hair lovers, this breed, like the British Short-hair, combines the Persian type with a beautiful short coat. Although the fur has the texture of a Persian, it is no longer than that of an Abyssinian. In short, as the originator of the breed – Mrs Jane Martinke – describes it in one of her articles, it is "a mod Persian in a mini-skirt".

The Exotic Short-hair is a hybrid, deliberately produced by breeding a short-hair and a Persian. Any short-hair breed may be used and usually it is an American Short-hair. However, some breeders prefer to use Burmese, as the Standard for Burmese in North America calls for a rounded head, broad chest and compact body which are all steps towards the desired type for the Exotic Short-hair. As long-hair is recessive to short-hair, the required effect of a short coat on a Persian-type body is not too difficult to obtain. The Exotic Short-hair may also be produced from two short-hairs with sufficient Persian in the background for the desired type to emerge, as it is created through the use of dominant characteristics.

In America, offspring of matings between long-hairs and short-hairs are ineligible for showing either as Persians or American Short-hairs. Cats from such matings are permitted to be shown in the C.F.A. as Exotic Short-hairs only. The acceptance of this cat as a separate breed also provided a place for the American Short-hairs which – for various reasons – had Persian in the background. For several years cats in this class that fitted the Exotic Short-hair Standard could be transferred – with the permission of the owner – to their rightful category. It was the only breed that was allowed the privilege of retaining, after it had been transferred, any wins previously made.

Careful breeding can produce excellent examples of the breed and some good ones are catching the judges' eye and taking the coveted wins in the championship classes.

Exotics are strong, sturdy, healthy and affectionate cats and are readily accepted, both as show cats and as ideal pets. Grooming is no problem, as the coat will not mat. The usual light grooming required by most short-hairs is sufficient to keep the Exotic Short-hair looking most attractive. A good specimen is truly breath-taking, although to thoroughly appreciate its full beauty, one must hold the cat and sink one's fingers into the luxurious and unique kind of fur.

Apart from the description of the coat, which should be medium in length and soft in texture, the Standard for the Exotic Short-hair is in most respects the same as that for the Persian in North America, and calls for a round, massive head with great breadth of skull. The face is round, as is the underlying bone structure. The head should be well-set on a short, thick neck. The nose should be short, snub and broad (note the omission of the nose-break called for in the Persian Standard), and the cheeks full and well-developed. The jaws should be broad and powerful. Small, round-tipped ears should tilt forward; they should not be unduly open at the base. Set far apart and low on the head, they fit into, but do not distort, the rounded contour of the head. The brilliant eyes should be large, round and full, set far apart.

A cobby body is called for; it should be low on the legs, deep in the chest, equally massive across shoulders and rump, and with a short well-rounded middle piece. This cat is large or medium in size, but as the Standard makes clear, quality is the determining consideration rather than size. The cat should have a level back, and short, thick, strong legs. Forelegs should be straight. The paws should be large, round and firm with the toes carried close; there are five toes in front and four behind. The tail should be short, but in proportion to the body length; carried without a curve, it should be at an angle lower than the back, and without kinks or abnormalities.

The colour classifications are the same as for the Persians; that is white (blue-eyed, copper-eyed or odd-eyed), black, blue, red, cream, chinchilla, shaded silver, shell cameo, shaded cameo, black smoke, blue smoke, cameo (red) smoke; classic and mackerel tabby patterns in silver, red, brown, blue, cream and cameo; tortoiseshell, calico (tortoiseshell and white) and blue-cream. Bi-colours (black and white, blue and white, red and white, cream and white) have been accepted as of May 1st 1972.

Opposite page: A Silver (Chinchilla) Exotic Short-hair owned by Doris Walkingstick.

224

Foreign Lilac (Foreign Lavender)

Short-hair

Solitaire Amethyst (female) at eleven months. Owned by Mrs Sayer.

The Foreign Lilac, or Foreign Lavender as it is sometimes known, is one of the self-coloured cousins of the Siamese. It is an attractive cat, and appears in ever increasing numbers at British shows. It is also found in the United States of America, where it is already recognized by several of the smaller governing associations. This cat has Siamese type, green eyes, and a coat of a sound, faded-lavender shade all over.

In character, the Foreign Lilac is super-Siamese with all the advantages, and none of the disadvantages. This is a gentle but demanding cat, soft-voiced but firmly insistent on having his own way. The kittens are born the same colour as the adult, but the coat is dull and rather fluffy in appearance, with tabby markings often showing just under the surface of the coat and on the tail. These quickly disappear, although ghost tabby rings may be apparent on the tail throughout kittenhood.

Show preparation is quite easy, for the antique-velvet appearance of the lavender coat can only be produced by excellent feeding and adequate exercise. Old hair should be groomed out daily with the hand, and a firm pad of cotton wool used with a strong sweeping motion along the flanks will stimulate the circulation in the muscles, and put a dull sheen on the coat. Foreign Lilacs usually show well, as they love human company and have exhibitionist tendencies. They are hardy, and love outdoor exercise all year, but must not be allowed to become damp or chilled. Dappled markings may appear along the flanks during hot summer weather, but these will disappear with the growth of the winter coat.

Foreign Lilac short-hairs have cropped up naturally over the years during the development of the Havana brown. To produce lilac, both parents have to carry the blue and the chocolate genes, so it can be seen that this is an elusive colour.

Mrs E. Fisher exhibited a lovely lilac in the 1950's, Praha Allegro Agitato, but he was neutered when no stud work could be found for him. Mrs Hargreaves also bred lilacs when working for Havanas, but did not pursue a breeding plan with them, and it was only in the late 1960's that a few progressive breeders decided to work seriously on this variety. Several breeding programmes were drawn up and, by 1970, first and second generation lilacs of extremely good type and colour were already drawing attention to the A.O.V. classes at shows. Mrs Betty Harrison and Mrs Angela Sayer are currently breeding down four separate lines in order to produce the third and fourth generations of the Foreign Lilac so as to reach G.C.C.F. recognition standard with the minimum of in-breeding. One useful line stems from an off-shoot of a former Rex breeding programme; Mallorca Li-Ming, one of a litter of Foreign Lilacs from a lilac dam, was Best in Show at the Gwynedd Cat Club's first show in 1970, and her daughter, Solitaire Lavendula, was best kitten. The top scoring Foreign Lilac male for show season 1969/70 was Mrs Wilding's Dandycat Ivanhoe bred from her champion Havana queen and a lilac-point male.

Another lilac male exhibited at this time was Mrs Garnett's Malewa Julius, who was unfortunately killed before he had sired many kittens. Mrs Sayer's Solitaire Amethyst, daughter of a champion Havana queen, was mated to Ivanhoe's son, Solitaire Bilberry, to produce the

Mrs Sayer's Solitaire Amethystine (female) in profile—the first winning Lilac of a like-to-like mating; was nominated Best-in-Show the first time she was exhibited.

Head study of Solitaire Amethyst.

227

Full face of Solitaire Sylvano.

first winning lilac of a like-to-like mating, Solitaire Amethystine, an exquisite kitten nominated for Best in Show the first time exhibited. Mrs Harrison has bred lilac kittens with the sought-after faded-lavender coat colour – Harislau Echo, Eloise and Estralita will be invaluable in the development of the breed.

The show season of 1971/72 saw the first classes to be put on specially for this variety. Special classes at big cat shows are the best boost it is possible to give a new variety. They give the general public a chance to see the new cat, and ensure that the breeders are keeping their standards and quality high; they also act as a morale-booster to a progressive breeder who often feels that he may be working alone and unaided, and wonders if it is all really worth-while.

The proposed British Standard of Points for the Foreign Lilac Shorthair calls for a soft and glossy coat, frost grey in colour with a pinkish tone, and sound and even throughout. Tabby markings are a fault, although young kittens may show ghost tabby markings. There should be no tendency to "British" type – the head should be long and well-proportioned, narrowing in straight lines to a fine muzzle. A strong chin is called for, and good width between the large pricked ears. Nose leather should tone with coat colour. Eyes should be oriental in shape and setting, and green in colour; in the adult cat yellow or hazel eye colour is a fault, although in kittens, the eyes may show a blue or yellow tinge.

The body should be long, lithe and graceful, medium in size, with slim, dainty legs and small, oval paws. Pads should be pink. The tail should be long and tapered without any kink.

In Great Britain, the interests of this new variety are catered for by the Foreign Lavender Group; the Colourpoint, Rex-coated and A.O.V. Club; and the Foreign Shorthair Cat Club.

Solitaire Sylvano, a male owned by Mrs Sayer, showing the required long well-proportioned head.

228

Foreign White *Short-hair*

The Foreign White Short-hair is merely a Siamese wearing a white overcoat as disguise. The white colour is due to a dominant gene, which makes it impossible to determine by eye what colour actually lies hidden beneath this "overcoat"; Siamese cats of different colours were used in the preliminary matings to establish the breed, and it is only by test mating of progeny that the underlying factors can be proven.

The excellent type apparent in the majority of Foreign Whites is an object lesson in the advantages of selective breeding technique, and could well be noted by any breeders embarking on the development of a variety. Siamese, mated more carefully, and with more regard for the merits or short-comings of the stud male, could also be much improved by this form of selection, and fewer dark-coated, weak-chinned and frail specimens might then be seen on the show bench. Basically, cats for Foreign White breeding were selected for their excellence of "foreign" type and fine bone structure, and no cats that exhibited faults that might prove difficult to eradicate later, such as weak chins and small ears, were used in the breeding programmes, and great emphasis was placed on perfect hearing as it was well-known that many ordinary blue-eyed white cats were deaf.

It was by coincidence that, in 1962, three independent breeders in Britain had virtually identical thoughts on the development of a

Above: Mrs M. Macaulay's Heatheral White Tornado; a mature male, with the slightly heavier masculine bone structure and a very good pure white unmarked coat.

Below: Head study of Heatheral White Tornado, showing an extremely long, straight nose. A well-developed strong male head, with stud jowls.

Florentine, a six-month-old male kitten with a beautiful wedge-shaped head and almond-shaped eyes. Owned by Mrs M. Hyde.

Showing the extreme "foreign" body length—Hihoe Persuasion in action. A female owned by Mrs Macaulay.

white cat of extreme "foreign" type. They were Miss Elizabeth Flack of Northern Ireland, and Mr Brian Stirling-Webb and Miss Pat Turner, both from the South of England. Miss Flack's Seal-point queen had mis-mated and had produced two golden-eyed white males and a blue-eyed white female, which were considered so typy and attractive, that she decided to breed from the female, El Maharanee Saengdao, who became the foundation queen of the Irish strain of Foreign White Shorthairs. Brian Stirling-Webb had mated a non-pedigree white short-hair to a Siamese Seal-point male to provide an out-cross for his work in the Devon Rex programme in 1957, but he was persuaded by Mrs Mary Dunnill to use the white hybrid female from this mating to establish a strain of white "foreign" cats–also during 1962. It was in this provident year, too, that Miss Turner was so intrigued by the effect of some over-exposed photographs she had taken of her lovely Lilac-pointed Siamese queen, showing her as a pure white Siamese without any visible points, that she drew up a breeding programme using her considerable genetic knowledge to produce such a cat in reality.

These three breeders each bred along carefully formulated and remarkably similar lines. It was not until 1964, when Mrs Dunnill visited Miss Turner and told her of Mr Stirling-Webb's results, and publicity resulted from the discussions regarding Miss Flack's white kittens by the Ulster Siamese Cat Club, that they were brought into contact with each other.

By the spring of 1965, eight breeders were actively engaged in a co-operative breeding programme, involving careful selection and back-crossing to line-bred Siamese for several generations. The name Chinese White was originally chosen, but dropped later in favour of the genetically more accurate designation Foreign White Cat. A provisional Standard of Points was drawn up and submitted to the G.C.C.F. in 1966; as it was evident that a good working knowledge of the genetic factors involved was necessary, the Foreign White Cat Society, formed specially in May 1965, recorded all data and pedigree records of all stock produced, and was available then as now (it was affiliated to the G.C.C.F. in 1971) to advise on breeding policy. Most non-white kittens produced were neutered before going to new homes, and only the very best of the white offspring were kept for breeding further generations.

Many problems beset the breeders in the early days of this variety; in two of the programmes a high incidence of deafness occurred and it was decided to discontinue these strains, and in other lines, a degree of head smudging, long coarse coats and indeterminate eye-colour were defects to be bred out. Excellent type was produced very quickly and was soon fixed in the breed, and the new wave of fanciers who brought in third, fourth and fifth generation stock had none of the problems that plagued the pioneers.

In 1966, the Foreign Whites seen in the A.O.V. show classes were of very high standard and strikingly attractive, resulting in three separate nominations for Best in Show awards, and although the show manager in each instance disqualified these exhibits, as they were of an unrecognized variety, the following year a Foreign White kitten, Miss Flack's Scintilla Tseng-Hsi, made catdom history by being voted Best in Show Short-hair Kitten at the Hertfordshire and Middlesex

Championship Show at Alexandra Palace, London. Other Foreign White cats have achieved Best in Show awards since then, no mean feat for a variety without breed number or championship status.

Foreign White Short-hairs outnumber all other new varieties in the A.O.V. classes at our championship shows in Great Britain, their similarity to one another proving how carefully they have been bred to their provisional Standard. The Foreign White is a medium-sized cat of foreign type, well-balanced, fine of bone, lithe, sinuous and of graceful proportions. The head, both full face and in profile, is wedge-shaped, with large pricked ears and an alert, intelligent expression. The close-lying, finely textured coat must be pure white and the pads and nose leather should be pink. The slanting, oriental eyes must be bright blue, and there must be no tendency to squint. Faults sometimes seen in the Foreign White, and to be avoided in breeding stock, are heavy bone structure giving a cobby appearance, roundness in the head, and kinked tails. Cats with green, grey or odd-coloured eyes should also be discarded from breeding programmes. Another fault, which is some-times seen in this breed, is the formation of pigmented areas in the nose leather, forming tiny black spots which increase in size as the cat ages. This problem is also encountered in the Red-point Siamese, and is frequently seen to a much greater degree in red tabby cats of unknown parentage. It is possible that the red factor, masked by the dominant white coat, is involved and may have to be tested for, and possibly removed from, future generations.

Above: Profile of Hihoe Persuasion at the peak of fitness. Note the good straight nose, level mouth and firm chin.

Above: Although unrecognized as yet, selective breeding has developed this variety with near-perfect foreign type. Hihoe Persuasion has a completely unmarked short, fine coat and good wedge head shape.

Left: Hihoe Persuasion showing well-set blue eyes and large pricked ears, wide at base.

Havana
(Havana Brown)

A dainty queen with a beautiful glossy chestnut brown coat—Mrs A. Sayer's Solitaire Pikake, with a complete lack of shading on the points.

The lithe and graceful Havana is one of the rarest of the recognized breeds. It is genetically a self-coloured chocolate Siamese, and therefore of extreme "foreign" type, with a burnished dark chestnut-brown coat; and the greenest of green eyes.

The earliest records of the existence of a self-brown cat date from 1894, when a pioneer English cat fancier named Mrs French imported, probably from a European country, a chocolate-coloured queen called Granny Grumps and bred from her a male kitten, Master Timkey Brown. These cats were described by a contemporary writer as "Siamese, with coats of burnished chestnut, with greeny blue eyes". Other imports were made; in particular a brown queen, Adastra, was brought to England by a Sister Stockey – this cat is in fact reputed to be the forebear of many of the best Chocolate-pointed Siamese of today. Such imports were rare, however, and brown cats were still considered most unorthodox in Great Britain. In continental Europe, on the other hand, brown "foreign" cats were more popular – in Leipzig in 1923, a chocolate "self" male, owned by a Frau Koch, was reported to be at stud, and brown "Swiss Mountain Cats" figure in many accounts.

We hear nothing more of the self-coloured brown cat until 1939, when reports were published by two writers on the cats of the day, one describing a "very dark Siamese, almost black", and the other "chocolate-coloured Siamese, that is, the same colour all over". Other writers referred to "brown cats, having points like Siamese". These reports are not very clear, but it is surmised that in the 1930's no distinction was made between the self-coloured chocolate cats, and brown Burmese/Siamese hybrids; they were shown in the same classes at shows and bred together haphazardly, due to the general lack of genetic knowledge among breeders of the time. This would certainly account for contradictory descriptions of coat and eye colour; the progeny of such indiscriminate mating of cats with widely different genetic backgrounds would certainly not "breed true", and indeed only black and Siamese kittens would have been produced; one can understand how breeders might have been tempted to revert to the more straightforward pure Siamese and Burmese breeds.

This was the position until 1951, when in England the Baroness von Ullman made a study of chocolate gene inheritance in cats, and then planned a programme for the breeding of a self-chocolate cat of "foreign" type – the Havana as it is known today. Preliminary matings were between her Chocolate-pointed Siamese male and a black "alley cat" of reasonable type. After consultation, Mrs A. Hargreaves decided on a similar scheme using her own Siamese and Russian Blue breeding stock. Mrs E. Fisher became interested, and the three breeders carried out a carefully planned programme. Meanwhile Mrs Munro-Smith, conducting experiments aimed at producing the Colourpoint Persian, had mated a Seal-point queen and a black Persian. One of the resulting black short-haired females, Susannah, was mated to a Seal-point stud, Tombee.

In the litter born on October 24th, 1952, was a self-chocolate male kitten, later to be registered as Elmtower Bronze Idol, and this kitten was the first of the present day Havanas. For this kitten to have appeared the elusive chocolate gene must have been present in both Seal-pointed Siamese used in Mrs Munro-Smith's experiments.

The second Havana male to be bred was Praha Gypka, born June 1953; Laurentide Brown Prior arrived later in the year, and Roofspringer Peridot the following year. These four males formed a healthy basis for the development of the breed in England. Mrs J. Judd joined the breeding group, starting an out-cross line under the Crossways prefix, and by 1956 numbers had increased sufficiently for two promising kittens, Roofspringer Mahogany (female), and Laurentide Brown Pilgrim (male), to be exported to Mrs Peters in California – the introduction of the Havana cat into the U.S.A.

Although not very popular in the U.S.A., the Havana Brown, as it is called there, nevertheless has a nucleus of devoted supporters. The cats exported to Mrs Peters came into the possession of Mrs Elsie Quinn of California and Roofspringer Mahogany Quinn appeared in the All-Americans every year from 1960 to 1965 along with many of her descendants.

There are fine Havana Browns shown in America today, many of which are winning high show honours. The Havana Brown breeders of Eastern America and the Western Havana Brown breeders are working together for the benefit of the breed.

In 1958, after the required three generations of like-to-like breeding, and with yet more breeders participating, the Havana breed was firmly established in Britain and given official recognition. Presumably in order to avoid confusion with the Havana rabbit, and against the wishes of the breeders, the new breed was given the name Chestnut Brown Foreign Short-hair; this name was used until 1970, when the

Above: Ch Solitaire Aloha, a worthy female champion at ten-and-a-half months. She has a long, well-proportioned head, an elegant neck, good, firm chin and well-set ears. Bred by Mrs Sayer.

Below: The characteristic enquiring look of a healthy, lively Havana—Ch Solitaire Aloha.

Gr Ch Z.Z.'s Georgette of Sidlo, a female Havana Brown from California owned by Mrs Dallas Sidlo.

233

Above: The good head shape and straight profile of Ch Solitaire Maneki Neko. The wide base of the ears are typical of the variety, as is his alert expression. Bred by Mrs Sayer.

Below: Solitaire Tiare Tahiti at three months and showing great promise. Bred by Mrs Sayer.

Below: Ch Solitaire Aloha with her five-week-old playful twins, still showing slight ghost tabby marks and a few white guard hairs, which will later disappear.

Governing Council in Britain agreed to the use of the name Havana once again.

In the early 1960's England's first champion was Mrs Davis's Cross-ways Honeysuckle Rose. Then, later in the decade, numbers on the show benches declined, although breeders such as Mrs Sybil Warren assured the continuance of the breed. It was found that continued breeding of like-to-like was producing a gradual, but noticeable, loss of size and stamina in the breed, together with the development of yellow eye-colour, and a melanistic coat. The early 1970's however brought a new wave of young fanciers, and outcrosses to Chocolate-Pointed Siamese have had an effect – Havanas of extreme type and the true green eye colour began to appear on the show bench, even winning Best in Show awards, and so obtained much-needed publicity for what could have become something of a neglected breed.

The interests of the Havana are catered for in Britain by the Short-Haired Cat Society of Great Britain and Manx Club Inc., the Foreign Shorthair Cat Club, and the Chestnut Brown Group.

The Havana will always remain the cat for the connoisseur and one would never expect to see Havanas as popular at the shows as Siamese, but he is a charming cat, full of character and with an exceptionally sweet and considerate nature. He has a voice that is neither raucous nor effeminate, and although mischievous, he is rarely wantonly destructive. He is super-intelligent, and always, whether in repose or in motion, aesthetically pleasing. He repays a careful upbringing with life-long friendship and good health. Although he is hardy and likes to play outside in all weathers, having a special penchant for deep snow, he must not be allowed to become too chilled, and is susceptible to draughts and damp conditions. Being so extrovert by nature, he is a natural showman and loves a day at a cat show, being admired and handled by all and sundry. A hot summer will dapple his coat, and bleach his tail hairs to a deep ginger tone, but the benefit of the vitamins absorbed from the sun-light will far outweigh any show points he may lose, and his coat will grow through to its correct colour with the autumn moult.

The Havana is easy to maintain in the peak of condition by feeding a correctly balanced diet, and giving plenty of exercise. He rarely seems to suffer from looseness of the motions caused by the inability to assimilate milk which affects his Siamese cousins, and can drink milk almost with impunity, which helps to improve the texture and sheen of his coat. He may be "strapped" as one would groom a thoroughbred horse, making a firm pad of cloth or cotton wool, and applying it firmly to the coat along the muscles of the body with a hard sweeping motion. This method must not be used on young kittens or pregnant queens, but older cats and especially the stud males love this procedure, and purr and lean towards the grooming action with pleasure. This method of grooming increases the blood flow, toning the muscles and imparting a glow to the entire coat.

The Havana queen is normally an excellent mother, producing on average, five even, healthy kittens at an easy parturition, which are forward, opening their eyes around the third day, and tumbling out of the maternity box at four weeks in search of solid food. They rarely appear to suffer from gastric upsets at weaning as do other "foreign"

breeds and also appear to have a certain natural immunity to upper respiratory ailments. In all, the Havana is the epitome of the perfect "foreign" cat, a healthy, lively, happy creature of iron muscle under an exterior of soft brown velvet, with the ability of almost human expression from fathomless gooseberry-green eyes.

The coat of the Havana is, according to the British Standard, any shade of rich chestnut brown, short and glossy, even and sound throughout. Whiskers and nose should be the same colour as the coat, and the pads of the feet are a pinkish shade.

"Foreign" type is called for in Britain, with a long, well-proportioned head, narrowing to a fine muzzle. The ears should be large and pricked, wide at the base and with good width between; eyes are green. The body should be long, lithe and well-muscled, and graceful in outline, on slim and dainty legs. Hind legs should be slightly higher than front legs. The paws should be oval and neat, while the tail should be long and without any kink.

The American Standards for the Havana Brown call for a whisker break, and a distinct stop at eyes when viewed in profile. The eyes should be oval in shape – for the overall type called for in America is less extremely "foreign" than in Britain. Havana Browns are penalized for an excessively melanistic (i.e. black) coat.

Above: Ch Solitaire Maneki Neko, pictured here at only eight months, with typical muscular body and good, smooth close-lying coat. His head has still to develop the true masculine look.
Below: Slight jowls are now appearing— Ch Solitaire Maneki Neko.

Japanese Bobtail

An appealing group of Japanese Bobtails owned by Elizabeth Freret. This variety has been recognized provisionally in America by C.F.A.

This breed has existed for centuries in Japan, for which evidence may be seen in the many prints, paintings and sculptures, both ancient and modern, in which they are portrayed. They were obviously held in very high esteem by the Japanese people and there is even a temple in Tokyo whose facade bears pictures of the "Mi-Ke" with paws up-raised – a symbol of good fortune.

One of the noticeable characteristics of the Japanese Bobtail is their "clannish" nature. The family ties are very strong and a mother cat will remain very attentive to grown kittens and, although they get along well with other cats (of their own or other breeds) they will keep in little family groups, sleeping and playing together. They have impeccable habits, particularly the females, who make excellent and devoted mothers.

A very quiet breed normally, they will speak when spoken to and will hold quite a conversation. Adding to their attractive appearance is the delight of the colourful, practically non-shedding coat, which is soft, silky and longer than most of the other short-haired breeds.

The first breeding pair of Japanese Bobtails were sent in 1968 to the United States from Japan by Mrs Judy Crawford, an American who had been raising these cats while living in Japan. At that time, she had been working with the breed for about fifteen years and was delighted to know that American breeders were interested in helping to establish the breed outside Japan. The first two to arrive were Madam

Butterfly, a pretty calico (tortie and white), and Richard, a handsome red and white male, and they were sent to Mrs Elizabeth Freret in Virginia, U.S.A. Mrs Crawford later returned to the United States, where she is continuing to raise the Japanese Bobtails, having about thirty-five – many of them unrelated. By placing kittens in the hands of reliable and interested breeders, the first breeders in North America soon spread word of the endearing charms of the breed, and Bobtails are rapidly gaining popularity. The formation, in 1970, of the International Japanese Bobtail Fanciers Association helped to form a centre of information as to the stud cats and bloodlines that were available to breeders and fanciers. The members were from Japan, Canada and the United States and their services included a newsletter. The Bobtail has obtained provisional status in C.F.A., and is on the way to full championship recognition. It is not bred in Britain.

One of the most characteristic features described in the Provisional Standard is the set of the eyes. These are set at a pronounced slant; combined with the high cheek bones and the long parallel nose, they give a distinctly "Japanese" cast to the face, in profile especially, quite different from the other Oriental breeds. The big eyes are oval, wide and alert. The long, finely chiselled head, according to the description, forms an almost perfect equilateral triangle, with gentle, curving lines; a short, rounded head is a fault. The body type of the Japanese Bobtail is unique – it fits into neither the "foreign" nor "domestic" category; this is a medium-sized cat, with long, clean lines and bone structure; although well muscled, it is slender rather than massive in build.

The back legs are higher than the forelegs – however, when the cat is standing relaxed, the hind legs bend, so that the back remains nearly level rather than rising towards the rear. However, the Japanese Bobtail is in no way related to the Manx, and carries none of the lethal genes that sometimes affect the Manx. When the cat stands, the forelegs and shoulders form two continuous straight lines, close together. The tail of the Japanese Bobtail is distinctly different from any other breed, extending only two to three inches from the body, although the tail bone, if straightened out to its full length, might be four or five inches long. The tail bone is usually strong and rigid rather than jointed (except at the base) and may be either straight or composed of one or several curves and angles. Usually carried upright when the cat is relaxed, the tail bears hair somewhat longer and thicker than that on the body, growing out in all directions, creating a "pom-pom" or "bunny-tail" effect (somewhat resembling a chrysanthemum!) commencing at the base of the spine, and camouflaging the underlying bone structure. The coat pattern is usually exceptionally clear-cut, with distinct edges, and the brilliance of the colours and design calls to mind the artistry of the Japanese people.

The Provisional Standard specifies that, in keeping with Japan's traditional "Mi-ke" cats, which are tri-coloured (black, red and white), colours should be limited to those tending to produce tri-coloured females; the solid colours (black, red or white); the bi-colours (black and white, or red and white); the tri-colours (black, red and white, or tortoiseshell and white); and tortoiseshell (black, red and cream).

Korat

Quad Ch Larlin's Sukisari of Margus, owned by Marjory S. Hoff.

The Korat Cat, or Si-Sawat, as it is also called in Thailand, is one of the very few cats now being bred in its ancient natural form, in the Western world as well as in its native Thailand. Si-Sawat is a compound Thai word meaning a mingled colour of grey and light green, while Sawat means good luck or prosperity. Hence the link between the Korat's silvery-blue colouring and its traditional "lucky" quality. Its origin is believed to be the Malay Self-Blue and for want of evidence to the contrary it has been suggested that the Korat is the forerunner of the Blue-pointed Siamese. Despite its long history, the Korat has not been seen very much outside Thailand.

The earliest known illustration of a Korat is to be found in the ancient *Cat-Book Poems*. This book of paintings of cats, each with its own descriptive verse, is believed to have been composed during or even prior to the Ayudha period of Thai history (1350–1767). When the glories of Ayudha were destroyed and the city fell, many art treasures and documents were vandalized or stolen, and the identity of the artist and the poet who recorded the ancient cats of Siam was lost. During the reign of King Rama V (1868–1910) a high-ranking monk, Somdej Phra Buddhacharn Buddhasarmahathera, copied some of the cats from the *Cat-Book Poems* on to a long strip of papyrus. This *Smud Khoi* ("papyrus book") hangs in Bangkok's National Museum. The drawings in both these manuscripts are stylized, depicting cats considered assets in the house because of their beauty, disposition, and the good (or bad) luck they bring. Among these are the "Copper" or Burmese, and the Vichien Mas, or Seal-pointed Siamese, as well as the Korat. This verse, written probably four-hundred years ago or more, describes the Korat as well today:

The cat Mal-ed has a body colour like Doklao.
The hairs are smooth with roots like clouds
    and tips like silver.
The eyes shine like dewdrops on a lotus leaf.

Mal-ed means seed: there is a wild fruit in Thailand, the Look Sawat, whose seed is silvery grey with a greenish tinge. Dok means flower and Lao is a kind of wild herb with silver-tip flowers like lemon-grass. Mal-ed and Doklao are popular names in Thailand for the Korat.

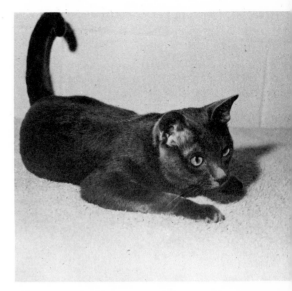

Above: Ready to pounce—Dbl Ch Si Sawat's Sumatra of Si-Kiu.

The first reference to the exhibition of a Korat in the western world is perhaps to be found in *Cats: Show and Pet* (1912) and *Our Cats and All About Them* (1930) by C. A. House. Mr House reports that a young Englishman, a Mr Spearman, just home from Siam, exhibited a Blue Siamese at a National Cat Club show in the grounds of Holland House, London in 1896. The judge refused to recognize it as a Siamese, but Mr Spearman argued that there were others in Siam, from where he had brought it. In 1906 a Mr Robins of New York City attested to the existence of the silver-blue cats in Korat, and according to the *Journal of Cat Genetics* Korats were present in the U.S.A. some years later, in the 1930's.

Today's story of the Korat in the West begins with the arrival of a pair in America in 1959. Other Korats were imported, and the breeders formed themselves into the Korat Cat Fanciers Association, an unaffiliated club, in March 1965. This body formulated certain pledges governing the sale of Korats, and started the private listing of census details of cats – imports, births, placings and deaths, and quality details. K.C.F.A. members are pledged to maintain the purity of the breed, and specific documentary evidence is required in relation to cats claiming to originate in Thailand. The Korat is indeed the "Cat with the Passport". True Korats are available only from the breeder, not in pet shops. Many of the important early Korats in America and Canada figure in pedigrees not only on that continent but also in South Africa, South Australia and the Netherlands. The breed is still comparatively unknown in Britain.

Below: Ch and Int Ch Si Sawat's Soon Soon Sam, a male bred and owned by Mrs R. Negus.

The breed was first recognized by the American Cat Association, followed by the National Cat Fanciers Association and United Cat Federation, all in April 1966. Korats first competed for championship and show honours in June 1966, at King of Prussia, Pennsylvania, at a show sponsored by the A.C.A., with nine Korats present. Korats were then recognized in turn by the Cat Fanciers Association (1966), the Canadian Cat Association (1966), the American Cat Fanciers Association (1967), the Cat Fanciers Federation (1968), and the Crown Cat Fanciers Federation (1969), and by the governing bodies in South Africa and South Australia. As numerous Korat cats have made their way into America, many brought home by Service personnel, interest has flourished among breeders; three more specialist clubs are the C.F.A.-affiliated Si Sawat Society and the Sa-Waat-Dee, and the C.F.F.-affiliated Korat Fanciers of the East.

Males of the breed are renowned as fighters in Thailand. In remote

239

Opposite page: A male Korat with a fine show record, Mrs Negus's Gr Ch Si Sawat's Sunan.

Below: Mahajaya Ling Dum (female), born in 1966. Bred and owned by Mme Ruen A. Rajamattri of Bangkok.

The Smud Khoi at the National Museum, Bangkok.

Looking thoughtful, Sunan—owned by Mrs Negus.

of danger by standing stiff-legged, facing the source, uttering a strange wailing cry interspersed with a sort of clicking sound. A certain Bangkok male was prized by his owner because in pitched battles with the neighbourhood dogs he was always victorious.

Korats are robust and adapt amazingly easily to their environment, seeming to expect, wherever they go, that love and admiration will be theirs just as it has been for hundreds of years in their native land. They form a curiously strong bond of affection with their owners and like to press close to them. Most responsive, they can be taught to perform small tricks, such as retrieving. They are gentle and watchful, and their breathtakingly beautiful eyes have a penetrating gaze. They are participators: whatever the activity in the home, the Korat owner can expect supervision, inspection, assistance.

Care must be taken to guard them from upper respiratory illness, and to keep them from any environment that will cause them to grow an uncharacteristically heavy coat, for which they will be penalized at shows. Even temperatures and frequent brushing keep the coat properly close-lying. Periodic bathing, especially just prior to showing, helps here. The Korat coat is perhaps not a truly single coat, but there is virtually no undercoat, just the new coat growing in. Although there is normal seasonal shedding, the hairs do not float off as do those of other cats when being stroked or petted. Many Korat males and some females pass through their adolescence as "ugly ducklings". As they mature sexually, their heads broaden, their eye-set takes on proper prominence and their bodies gain the right proportions.

Korats do well on a varied diet including fresh meats, egg yolks, cottage cheese, and a proprietary brand of cat kibble, but they do best when nutrients are added. They crave grass, and if this is not available, powdered alfalfa, chopped raw spinach or watercress, mixed in their food, may be substituted.

Many Korats enjoy a "pride" environment, and the males live happily with the queens throughout mating, gestation, parturition and the growing-up of the kittens. Because Korats dislike sudden loud noises, kittens which are to be shown should be raised in the midst of activity and noise, such as a raucous radio; they should be handled with love from birth. Korats do not flourish in large catteries with diverse breeds, where they are kept in cages. Another inheritance of their native social pattern is that some of them find irksome the company even of Korats if they are from other than their own bloodlines.

The Korat is silver-blue from birth to death: a cat of any other colour is not a Korat. It does indeed have smooth hair with roots like clouds and tips like silver. The silvering is highly favoured and is known as "sea-foam" by the Thais. Where the coat is short the sheen of the silver is intensified. White spots or lockets are a fault. Paw pads are dark blue, ranging to lavender with a pinkish tinge. Nose and lip leather is dark blue or lavender. There is a transition of eye-colour from the blue of kittenhood through the amber of early adolescence to the brilliant green-gold (the "dewdrops on a lotus-leaf") of maturity.

According to the Standards, the head, viewed from the front, is heart-shaped with breadth between and across the eyes, gently curving jungle villages they serve as "watchdogs", warning of the approach

Miss Kay Barclay's Dbl Ch Ma-Dee of Si-Kiu (female) and her three-week-old kittens. Bred by Mrs Suravadi.

See-la and her three kittens, owned by Mrs Saang Suravadi of Bangkok.

to a well-developed but not sharply-pointed muzzle. The forehead is large and flat. In the male an indentation in the centre of the forehead just above the brow ridge accentuates this heart-shaped appearance. Chin and jaw are strong. In profile there is a slight stop between forehead and nose, which is short with a slight downward curve. Ears are large with a rounded tip and a large flare at the base, giving an alert expression. Inside, the ears are sparsely furnished.

The Korat is medium in size with a strong, muscular, semi-cobby body and medium bone-structure. The back is carried in a curve. Legs are well proportioned to body; feet oval. The tail is medium in length, heavier at the base, tapering to a rounded tip.

The large and luminous eyes are particularly prominent, wide open, and oversized for the face. The eye aperture, which shows as well-rounded when fully open, has an Asian slant when closed or partially closed.

The Korat has a single coat: the hair is short to medium in length, glossy and fine, lying close to the body. The coat over the spine is inclined to break as the cat moves.

Manx

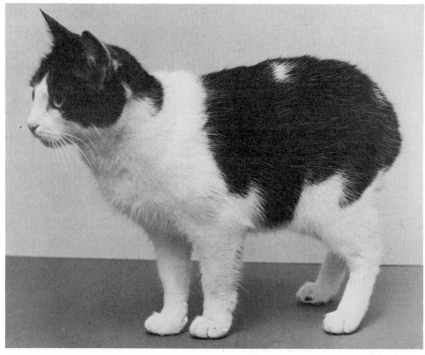

Above: Manxland Ann—her nose is longer than that of a Persian's and her ears, wide at the base, taper to a point.

The Mufti in profile, showing well-set ears, good head shape and a longish nose.

This breed has been known and written about for many years. It is one of the oldest known breeds, the "Mysterious Manx" whose origins are a mystery, whose name is wreathed in legend. Little of this legend can be traced to a basis in fact; the Phoenicians are said to have brought tailless cats back with them from one of their daring trading expeditions to Japan, not because there was a demand for the animals, as there is today, but for a more mundane purpose, the control of mice and rats on board ship. Perhaps such cats did exist in Japan at that time, they certainly do exist in parts of Asia today. Further evidence might exist in the fact that the peculiar "call" of the Manx is rather like that of the jungle cat of Malaya and elsewhere in the East, and some varieties have a very short, often knotted or kinked, tail.

Another tradition has it that tailless cats first came to the Isle of Man in 1588 from a ship of the Spanish Armada which was wrecked there. Two or three swam ashore near Spanish Point and lived to perpetuate the breed. The Manx has been with us from the time of the Flood, according to this old ballad:-

Noah sailing o'er the seas
Ran high and dry on Ararat.
His dog then made a spring and took
The tail from off a pussy cat.
Puss from a window quick did fly
And bravely through the waters swam
Nor ever stopped 'til high and dry
She landed on the Calf of Man.
This tailless puss earned Mona's thanks
And ever after was called Manx.

(The Calf of Man is a small islet off the south-west coast of Mona, the ancient Roman name for the Isle of Man.)

Manx cats are not prolific breeders, or "money makers", and more than most cat breeds have been subjected over the years to the whims of fashion. During the period between 1800 and 1910 the Manx was very popular in Britain and some excellent specimens appeared at early cat shows. At a show held at the Royal Botanical Gardens in London, attended by Queen Alexandra, then Princess of Wales, an award was made to a Silver Tabby named Bonhaki. Bonhaki was the first Manx champion in Britain. In 1901 a Manx Club was formed and the Standard of Points drawn up at that time has changed remarkably little since. It is mentioned in books printed during the reign of King Edward VIII that the King himself often visited cat shows when Prince of Wales, and had several Manx Cats, thus giving the breed a publicity boost and bringing it more into fashion. As a judge, Mr Gambier Bolton, the first secretary of the Governing Council of the Cat Fancy in Britain, specialized in the Manx.

Manx were again very popular from 1920 to 1930 and some notable animals were shown during this time. The 1930's saw a lessening in regard for the Manx and the numbers of breeders diminished. But the breed has always had its admirers and it survived through such quality specimens as Chs Bidye of Coryton, Kisser and Eubonuus; and Gloria Veen, White Clover of Runnymede and The Parson of Cademuir; and it was descendants of these cats who, surviving the war, were the basis of the post-war revival in the breed's popularity. Since the war the breed has prospered on the basis of such beautiful specimens as the handsome black and white male, Amego Winston, and the Stonor cats, Chs Teresiana, Miss Brown, Magnus and Black Maria – Stonor Kate was the first Manx to be Best Short-hair at Croydon, England, in 1948. The wave of popularity continues, and these names, and others who have descended from them (Chs No-end Marigold, Showman, Brumas, Bluewave Choirboy, Gold-dust, Bo Bo, Endless Stilts, Empire Maiden, Gay Sing, Ballaugh Express, and many more) figure on many a pedigree today. Until recently breeders obtained their breeding stock from the Isle of Man, but so great has been the demand for Manx kittens, particularly from America, that stock is in short supply.

The Manx cat has been known in America for well over a hundred years and appears early in American registries. There have been many outstanding Manx cats and cat breeders. But the deans of the Manx fancy in North America are the Carlson sisters, Ellen and Ruth of Illinois, who since 1933 have been raising and showing their Glen Orry Manx. Their Guthred of Manx of Glen Orry was the first American Manx Grand Champion, completed in 1951, and in 1971 their Grand Champion Glen Orry's Toshee was A.C.F.A.'s top cat of the year, and the Second Best All-American Cat of the Year. Guthred was a Red Tabby, Toshee is a Black.

Another great Black Manx male, Tra Mar's Sunny, owned by Mrs Marion Tracy (now Hall), was 1965 All-American Short-hair of the Year and A.C.F.A.'s highest scoring cat in 1966.

Manx also are now recognized in Australia, where a good strain has been developed in New South Wales.

Ch Katzenjammers Ghost, photographed here in 1930, had splendid type and was well-known in his day.

Brightwell Perseus, a "stumpy", has red tabby striping—his mother, shown also here, is a full Manx.

Individual breeders living on the Isle of Man are still breeding their own strains but the breed presents some unusual breeding problems. It is generally agreed that the Manx is not a breed in the normal genetic sense, but is the result of a genetic mutation, like the Rex. Further, it is unlikely that two tailless cats mated together produce all true kittens, and the litters are small in any case. A large proportion of the kittens born have tails or stumps, thus disqualifying them as true representatives of the breed and breeding first-class stock of Manx is thus a very slow process.

Little is known, even today, about the genetics of the Manx Cat; little more in fact than was known when the British magazine *Our Cats* in March 1900, published the findings from observations made in Germany:-

"The progeny of a tail-less cat of the Isle of Man – a cat (*felis catus anura*) brought in from the Isle of Man to S. Germain en Laye of which the pedigree is unknown, was mated with ordinary long-tailed cats, and among twenty-four kittens the following different kinds appeared :-

i.   Kittens with ordinary long tails.
ii. Kittens with short and stump tails.
iii. Kittens without tails, like the mother.
iv. Kittens without the least sign of tails."

Further observations from the six litters resulting from these matings indicate that the Manx mother was the dominant influence in fourteen of the twenty-four kittens involved.

Although some seventy years have elapsed since this piece of research was carried out, breeders today reach the same conclusion.

The Manx is a clever and curious little cat; the females are usually small but some of the males are large and handsome, especially those with Tabby coat patterns. A special feature of the breed has always been its double or rabbity coat, which however, is sometimes lacking today. The hind legs are longer than the front, thus the cat moves with a hopping gait, rather like a rabbit, and it can move very fast. The special feature which distinguishes the Manx from all other breeds of cat, is its lack of tail – it must be quite tailless, the rump as round as an orange; some have a small, soft tuft of fur where the tail would normally begin, but any suggestion of bone or gristle, however small, is a fault.

The Manx can be of any colour – tabby, bi-colour, tortie, any self colour, and white, and the Standard requires that the eye colour be in keeping with the coat colour, as with the British Short-hair varieties.

The Manx is a fascinating breed, well repaying the interest of owners with intelligence and faithfulness, but it is as well to make sure, when buying a Manx kitten, that it has no deformity and can move easily.

Gr Ch Tra-Mar's Sunny was Best All-American Short-hair in 1965 and Best A.C.F.A. Cat in 1966. Bred and owned by Marion Hall.

A brown tabby Manx, Gr Ch Blue Grass Tiger of Benton bred and owned by Judith D.K. Shaw of Vancouver. A cat with a highly successful show record.

Above: Brightwell Persephone, a mackerel brown tabby female at three months, illustrating the complete lack of tail, as required by the Standard. Bred by Mrs K. Butcher.

247

Rex, Cornish *Short-hair*

Ch Chah-Ming Encounter, a Blue-cream Cornish Rex female, owned by Mr and Mrs Goodwin.

The Rex cat originated as a spontaneous genetic mutation; examples have come to light in several widely-separated parts of the world. The first recorded Rex kitten was born in Bodmin Moor, Cornwall, England in 1950, and was given the name Kallibunker. The dam was a tortie and white farm cat; the father was unknown and the rest of the litter had normal straight coats. Fortunately, Kallibunker's owner, Mrs Nina Ennismore, had bred and shown Rex rabbits and recognised the characteristic Rexoid coat. She contacted the late Mr A. C. Jude, the geneticist, who realised that a new genetic mutation (i.e. a natural alteration of pattern of a pair of genes – *see* Genetics) had probably taken place, and advised test-mating the kitten back to his mother when he was old enough.

This mating took place several times and the litters produced were fifty per cent curly-coated – a mutation had indeed taken place, a rare event in feline history. The new breed was named Cornish Rex after its place of origin, and because of the likeness of its coat to that of the curly-coated Astrex rabbit.

The establishment of the breed was a slow process. Kallibunker died when still young, but his son, Poldhu, was kept as a stud. This in itself was unusual as he was a blue-cream, and cats of this coat pattern are almost invariably female or, if male, sterile. Poldhu, however, sired several litters before he, too, reverted to form and became sterile.

In the spring of 1957, Poldhu's daughter, Lamorna Cove, and her half-brother, Pendennis Castle, were imported into the United States by Mrs Frances Blancheri. Pendennis Castle never sired, but Lamorna Cove, who had been mated back to Poldhu before leaving Britain,

Kallibunker (male) with his son, Poldhu. Kallibunker was the first recorded Cornish Rex.

bore four kittens soon after she arrived in America. Two of them, Diamond Lil of Fan-T-Cee, owned by Mrs Peggy Galvin, and Marmaduke of Daz-Zling, owned by Mrs Helen Weiss, became the progenitors of the English Rex strain in the United States. Kittens from a mating between Diamond Lil and Marmaduke died at birth, but both these cats were mated to Siamese (for want of suitable "Domestic" mates), and in-breeding of the resulting progeny produced an abundance of healthy Rex breeding-stock in a wide variety of colours.

The American associations have only one Rex Standard, written apparently with the Cornish Rex in mind. There is also a German Rex strain in the United States, which can be traced back to a black female born some time before 1946 in East Berlin, and adopted in 1951 by Dr R. Scheuer-Karpin and named Lämmchen, because her coat resembled that of a lamb. From a breeding programme begun by Dr Scheuer-Karpin a number of "curlies" were born, and one of them, Christopher, was imported by Mrs Joan O'Shea of New York State early in 1961. Previously, in 1960, two non-curly hybrid females descended from Lämmchen were imported by Mrs Carl Muckenhoupt of Massachusetts. Mrs O'Shea, Mrs Muckenhoupt and others have since then imported several more curlies and curly-carriers from Germany, and the strain is well-established in North America.

Over the years, several native Rex mutations have appeared in North America too. Kinky Marcella, discovered by Mildred Stringham of Oregon on May 9th, 1959, was such a cat, the focus of an extensive breeding-programme. Although Mrs Stringham had little success in establishing a pure American strain of Rex, Marcella and her descendants seem to have blended into other lines, but with no definite proof that they are gene-compatible with any of them.

In 1970, however, two American breeders had apparent success in cross-breeding the German and Cornish strains. Mabel and Charles Tracy of Maryland had two curly-coated kittens born on May 16th from their Rodell's Rimski (Cornish) ex Paw Prints Schatz (German). Nine days later, five curly kittens were born to Una Bailey's New Moon Christina of the Willows (German), sired by Mrs Helen Weiss's Trinka's Icarus of Daz-Zling (Cornish). Subsequent crosses have also been successful, indicating that these two breeds may well be genetically identical.

Meanwhile in England, Champagne Chas, a cream and white half-brother of Lamorna Cove, was loaned to Mr Brian Stirling-Webb; he and a band of enthusiasts were able to proceed with the establishment of the Cornish strain of Rex in Britain. Champagne Chas was out-crossed, mainly to short-haired females; daughters were mated back to Chas, or brother to sister—a back-cross producing fifty per cent Rex, while sibling matings produced one Rex in three kittens, in accordance with Mendel's genetic theory.

After ten years, the Cornish Rex was well-established in Britain; and then in 1960 unforeseen complications were caused by the discovery in Devon by Miss Beryl Cox, of another curly kitten. After many test matings, this strain proved to be incompatible with the Cornish and was recognised as an entirely new mutation (see Rex, Devon).

Breeding of Cornish Rex was proceeding well but, after a time, the

Hi-Fi's Schwartz, a Rex of the German strain owned by Mrs W. O'Shea of New York.

Above: Two German Rex kittens living in America. In the foreground is Hi-Fi's Hilda, and behind her is Hi-Fi's Herman. Below: Products of the first German/Cornish Rex cross aged four months—Paw Prints Adam, owned by Mr and Mrs W. Bauer and Paw Prints Evan, owned by Mr and Mrs P. O'Brien. Both bred by Susan Tracy.

Great-great-great grandson of Kallibunker, Riovista Kismet, bred by Miss J. Jeffrey and now owned by Mrs Alison Ashford, was imported into Britain from Canada.

Robroy Blue Filou (left) and Robroy Apricot Brandy (right), bred by Miss A. Codrington.

Far right: Head study of Mrs A. Ashford's male, Ch Annelida Sundance Kid. The curly whiskers are characteristic of the Rex, although the ears are not quite as long as those of the Devon Rex.

Right: Ch Chah-Ming Encounter is an outstanding example of a female, with straight profile, good ears, and short, curly whiskers.

cats were beginning to look very "British" in type as a result of cross-breeding with short-hairs, and were unlike the original Kallibunker, whose type was "foreign" with a long body, long legs and tail, and a moderately long head with a straight profile. In 1965, Mrs Alison Ashford imported a blue male, Riovista Kismet, from Canada. He was a great-great-great-grandson of Kallibunker, to whom he and his offspring bore a great resemblance. Nowadays, Rex breeding is quite straightforward, with Cornish and Devon developing independently.

Rex are exported from Britain to many countries of the world; the Annelida cattery has provided many champions in the States and elsewhere. Mrs Nancy Hardy sent the first Rex stud to Australia and one of my own Watermills followed. More recently Mrs Ashford has sent two Annelida males and the breed is gradually gathering strength there and in New Zealand.

In Britain, the interests of the Rex have always been in the hands of the Colourpoint, Rex-Coated and Any Other Variety Club, founded by Mr Stirling-Webb in 1959. The club drew up the provisional Standards of Points for both the Cornish and Devon Rex, and later worked with the new Rex Cat Club to finalise them. Approval was granted by the G.C.C.F. in 1967. Both varieties are now eligible to enter championship classes at the shows. In America, the breed club for Rex is Rex Breeders United, formed by Mrs Mabel Tracy.

In my experience, Cornish Rex are hardy and not fussy about their food. In spite of having no guard hairs, they do not appear to feel the cold particularly, as do the Siamese for instance, and are equally happy in snow or summer sunshine. Being a new breed with mixed ancestry, they are healthy. The queens usually kitten easily and are devoted mothers. The litters are strong and the kittens very intelligent.

The coats are easy to groom and keep clean. I would recommend a warm bran bath before a show – wet baths are not normally necessary, but are endured philosophically if needs must. A hard brush should never be used and hand-grooming with silk or chamois leather gives the waves or curls a pleasing gleam. This is important as many Rex exhibits do not do themselves justice at shows owing to dull or greasy coats.

Rex make adaptable pets as they are very affectionate and enjoy the

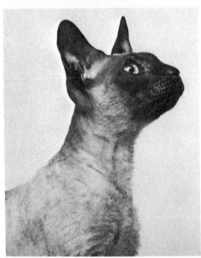

Mrs Ashford's queen, Ch Annelida Lucia, with excellent coat and tail and "foreign" body shape, with her promising kitten.

Head study of Ch Chah-Ming Encounter, showing a short, wide well-balanced head.

company of their humans, in and out of cars, on and off harness and leads. The queens alas! are rather enterprising and are apt to make assignations with attractive but non-patrician males. When they are calling no chances must be taken.

The Standard set in Britain says that the Cornish Rex coat should be short, thick and plushy, without guard hairs, and should curl, wave or ripple, particularly on back and tail. All colours are acceptable, but if there is any white it must be symmetrical, except in the Tortoise-shell and White.

The head should be a medium wedge in shape, with flat skull. In profile a straight line should be seen from the centre of the forehead to the end of the nose. The ears should be large, set high on the head, wide at the base, tapering to rounded tips and well-covered with fine fur. The oval-shaped eyes should be medium in size, the colour to be in keeping with the coat colour. The hard, muscular body should be slender, of medium length on long, straight legs, and the tail should be long, fine and tapering, well covered with curly fur.

Elan Ali Baba has a good, slender neck and large ears. Owned by Miss B. Stock.

Ch Annelida Sundance Kid; although a cream Rex, his coat is an unusual mushroom shade.

Rex, Devon

Rex, Devon *Short-hair*

Annelida Will o' the Wisp, a red Devon Rex male bred and owned by Mrs A. Ashford. A very useful stud of good type.

Head study of Annelida Will o' the Wisp.

In 1960, a new decade brought with it a new coat mutation in the cat. Several years before, cats with wavy coats had been born to ordinary domestic, non-pedigree cats in Cornwall, England and in East Berlin, Germany and in North America (*see* Rex, Cornish).

By 1960, kittens descended from the first curly-coated Cornish cat were being put on exhibition at leading London cat shows, and their photographs appeared in the national newspapers. One of these photographs caused particular interest to Miss Beryl Cox, who then lived quite close to a disused tin-mine in Buckfastleigh, Devon, England. It was known locally that a large cat with "masses of tight curls" lived in the old tin-mine. Miss Cox had befriended a stray tortie-and-white cat, which gave birth to a litter of kittens and, since one of these kittens had a curly coat, Miss Cox assumed that the strange tom in the tin-mine was the sire. She kept the curly-coated kitten as her personal pet, and when she saw the photographs of the Cornish Rex kittens, she contacted the late Mr Brian Stirling-Webb,

252

who was then conducting a breeding-programme for the Rex cats.

Miss Cox had named her curly-coated kitten Kirlee – a name that has since become world-famous. Kirlee had proved to be an exceptionally intelligent kitten, and Mr Stirling-Webb was convinced when he saw Kirlee that he must be a close relative of the original Cornish Rex cat, and Miss Cox allowed him to use Kirlee in his breeding experiments, as new Rex blood was obviously valuable. However, Kirlee proved even more unusual than was expected as, when he mated with a Cornish Rex female, only plain-coated kittens resulted! Numerous matings were made between Kirlee and Cornish Rex females, and always the resulting kittens were straight-coated! Thus it became plain that although all the cats used were curly-coated, Kirlee was genotypically different from the Cornish Rex cats.

At this time, the small group of Rex breeders working with Mr Stirling-Webb decided to call the Cornish cats "Gene 1 Rex" and the Devon cat, Kirlee, "Gene 2". Kirlee was mated with his plain-coated daughters from the experimental matings, and more Gene 2 kittens were born, and fifty per cent of these kittens proved to be Rex-coated. This showed that the Rex gene is recessive according to the Mendelian theory that a recessive gene is produced in a 1:1 ratio in a back-cross to the original recessive genotype (*see* Genetics). If, on the other hand, the plain-coated, first-generation kittens were mated interse (that is brother to sister) Rex kittens turned up in the expected 1:3 ratio.

Here a problem arose for the Rex breeders as it was only by test-mating that the second-generation curly-coated kittens were known to be of Gene 1 or Gene 2 genotype! A very few of this Rex generation proved to be homozygous for the other! Annelida Curly Coon was a famous example of this complex cat. In appearance she was obviously a Gene 1 Rex and, when mated to a Gene 1 male, she produced some Gene 2 Rex kittens *and* some plain-coated hybrids, carrying both genes! The study of genetics is not easy, and this surprise result caused some consternation in the cat fancy.

Kirlee, the first Devon Rex, was distinctly different in appearance from Kallibunker, the original Cornish Rex. Mole-grey in colour, he had the look of a pixie about him, with his wide-cheeked face, little short nose and huge ears like bat wings! The Cornish Rex had a long Roman nose. This was the chief difference between the two genotypes. Strangely enough, although all the Rex mutations come from ordinary domestic cats, they have all had body-type of distinctly "foreign" appearance.

Naturally, as a result of the first crosses between the Gene 1 (Cornish) and Gene 2 (Devon) cats, the two types became less distinct. However, the Colourpoint, Rex-Coated and A.O.V. Club in Britain undertook the breeding-programme of these two breeds and it was agreed that the two genotypes should never again be cross-bred. By careful selection of breeding cats, by 1966, the two distinct types were becoming easily recognisable.

In 1964, Mrs A. Watts (who had been Mr Stirling-Webb's chief helper in the Rex breeding programme) formed the Rex Cat Club, with Mrs Madge Shrouder (owner of the famous Hassan Rex cats) as the secretary. Thus Rex cats had two specialist clubs to cater for their needs and, with their help, the G.C.C.F. gave official recognition to

Mrs Fisher's three young kittens— showing the wrinkled foreheads; characteristic of the breed when young.

Kirlee—the first Devon Rex.

Right: An exceptionally tiny kitten with a long name and big future—Hephaestos Tropicana. Bred by Mrs G. Fisher.

Mrs Fisher's male Ch Sunbronzed Danny Boy, showing a break in the nose profile, one of the features distinguishing the breed from the Cornish Rex.

Mrs G. Fisher's Hephaestos Greek Goddess. She has very short, fine coat on the chest and stomach.

the two Rex breeds in February 1967. From this time, these cats have been known in Britain as Cornish Rex and Devon Rex, and they are eligible to compete for championships and to be elected as Best Cat in any show. The first Devon champion was Amharic Kurly Katie bred by Mrs Knight and owned by Mrs Genty.

Devon Rex cats and kittens are wonderfully healthy and hardy, despite their somewhat frail appearance, but they *do* need a warm place in which to sleep, and young kittens should be kept at an even temperature of 65°F - 70°F. However, as they grow up they love to play in the garden and will even venture out in the snow, patting at the snowflakes with mischievous enjoyment. They are essentially pets, wanting to be with humans all the time, and they do not thrive when large numbers are kept together. Devon dams seem to be excellent mothers and the kittens are usually born easily. Their eyes begin to open from about the sixth day after birth - watch must be kept that no stickiness appears. If it does, the eyes should be gently bathed with boracic lotion or eye drops. The average number in a Devon Rex litter is four and the dam can happily feed her family until it is four weeks old. Weaning should then be commenced.

A very important element in the Rex cat's diet is fat. Because the Rex coat lacks guard hairs, the cat loses body-heat more quickly, and therefore a higher intake of calorie-producing fat than usual is necessary. It is easiest to give in the form of shredded suet, a tea-spoon of which should be mixed with the kitten's food each day, and a dessert-spoon into the cat's food. By the age of eight weeks a Rex kitten should be having four meals a day plus plenty of fresh water.

Because the Devon Rex coat is so short, it is very easy to groom. Usually gentle hand-grooming is all that is necessary, although a soft natural-bristle brush can be used.

Special care should always be given to the Devon Rex ears. Due probably to their size, they easily become dirty and may also harbour ear-mite. The ears should be cleaned weekly with cotton-wool buds. Normally, the ear-wax is honey-coloured. If it becomes dark in colour, the cat should be taken to a veterinary surgeon, since this often indicates ear-mites, which will need special treatment before they can be eradicated.

Show preparation need be no different from normal grooming, except in the case of white Devon Rex. These really do look better if they are given a gentle bath using a cat shampoo and water that is slightly warmer than blood-heat.

The British Standard for the Devon Rex calls for a very short and fine coat, wavy and soft, and without guard hairs. It is perhaps interesting to note in this context that Mr Roy Robinson, M.I.O.B. has made a microscopic study of the hair from the various types of Rex coats, and concluded that while the Cornish, German and American Rex had coats devoid of all guard-hairs, the Devon Rex coat, which actually feels slightly harsher, does have a small number of guard-hairs. Bare patches are a fault in kittens, and all the more serious in adult cats, although many specimens have down on the underparts, which should not be interpreted as bareness. The Standard specifies crinkled whiskers and eyebrows, rather coarse and of medium length. A straight or shaggy coat is a fault.

All coat colours, other than bi-colours, are acceptable, although any white markings other than in Tortoiseshell-and-White are considered a fault on the show bench.

All Rex are of "foreign" rather than "British" type – the Standard for the Devon Rex calls for a wedge-shaped head with a full-cheeked face. The short muzzle has a strong chin and a whisker break, and the nose has a strongly marked stop, while the forehead curves back to a flat skull. A narrow, long or British-type head is a fault.

The eye colour should be in keeping with the colour of the coat; or, except in Si-Rex, chartreuse, green or yellow. Si-Rex is the name given to Cornish and Devon Rex cats with Siamese colouring. The ears of the Devon Rex are, apart from the curly coat, perhaps its most characteristic feature. They are large, set rather low, and very wide at the base, tapering to rounded tops and well covered with fine fur. There may or may not be ear muffs. Small or high-set ears are a fault in a show specimen.

One should look for firm muscular development in a Devon Rex; lack of it is a fault, and the body should be hard in feel, slender and of medium length, with a broad chest. The legs should be long and slim, with particular emphasis on the length of the hind-legs. The neck should be slender, and the paws small and oval. The long, fine, tapering tail should be well covered in short fur.

The Devon Rex is recognised as a separate Rex breed in all countries except the U.S.A., where it has been cross-bred with both American and German Rex. In these cases, however, the F1 generation of kittens have all been plain-coated. The American Standard allows for only one Rex type, which is close to the Cornish and German Rex types. Mrs Mabel Tracy in Maryland and Mrs Helen Weiss in Texas have carried out cross-breeding between Cornish Rex and German Rex, finding that the two breeds are genetically compatible, i.e. all Rex-coated kittens result from the F1 generation. Although a few breeders in North America have imported the Devon Rex, the breed has never achieved the popularity of the Cornish and the German Rex.

Above: A well-covered kitten bred by Mrs Fisher, showing a good profile, slender body and fine whipped tail.

Below: Another typical head of this specimen, showing a strongly marked stop to nose and very large well-positioned ears; Briarry White Heather (female), owned by Mrs Ashford.

Below: Head study of Hephaestos Greek Goddess, which is characteristic of the breed, with a fine pair of ears and short wedge head.

Russian Blue *Short-hair*

This breed, described by Marie Rochford as the "Cat for the Connoisseur", was, before 1900, known as the Archangel Blue; it is thought to have been brought to Great Britain for the first time in about 1860 by sailors trading from the Baltic port of Archangel. The Archangel Blues were distinguished by their long slender bodies, their small triangular heads, and long faces. Above all, they carried a strikingly beautiful coat, soft, short, very thick and silky and of varying shades of blue. All the early writers on cats are united in praising the exceptional beauty of the coat.

Although the original cats with blue fur and foreign type were said to have come from Archangel, they were also known by many other names, including Russian, Spanish, Maltese and Foreign. There was also confusion with the resident British cats with short blue coats. In the catalogues of cat shows in 1895, they were all classified as "Blue (self-colour)". It was realised, however, that there were two distinct types, one being called Russian by the owners of those with sleek shining fur and longish heads, and the other, British or English by those owning cats with plush-like coats and the broader heads. They were entered in the same classes at the shows, and to the great discontent of the "Russian" owners, the British invariably won. At the beginning of the century, there was still one class for Blues – Short-haired, and much cross-mating. Photographs of cats of this period showed comparatively small differences in type, although names indicated what their owners considered they were. Mrs E. Clark's Nicholaievitch, bred in 1910, whose sire was Peter the Great and dam was Ritza, and Mrs C. Carew-Cox's Meeshka, sired by Ivanovitch and whose mother was Mousmé, are examples.

By 1912, some agreement had been reached, and the classes became Blue British-type and Blue Foreign-type, sometimes even Blue Russian-type, with the above mentioned Meeshka doing well in the latter classes.

Mrs Carew-Cox of Saffron Walden, Essex, England continued to make a major contribution to the progress of the breed by keeping two well-known studs, Muchacho and Moscow, and several queens, of which two, Lingpopo and Yula, actually came from Archangel. Other important breeders of the day were Mrs MacLaren Morrison, Miss Wakeford, Miss Geach, Mrs Stevens, Miss Hill-Shaw and, later, Lady Coryton. They appeared to have been known as Blue Foreign right up to 1939, although their owners liked to refer to them as Russian. Although stated in many books that the name "Russian" came back into being in 1948, the Stud Books for 1939 definitely give the name as Russian. It was after the Second World War that Miss Marie Rochford began breeding her Dunloe Russian Blues; these were to become world-famous, many going to the United States where they were responsible for the establishment of the breed. The first American breeder to import them at that time was Mr C. A. Comhaire of Texas, who bought Dunloe Jan and Dunloe Blue Silk in 1947, although the very first Russian Blue American import was Lockehaven Royal Blue bred by Mr Towlerton Flansholme in England, and imported by Mrs Clinton Locke of Chicago around 1900. Other breeders followed, such as Howard and Blanche Warren of Casa Gatos Cattery, Mr Hoeller of Los Angeles, Florence Gates and Margaret Pusey of the Flo-Mar Cattery, and many more. Currently, perhaps, the most successful Russian Blue ever is Gr Ch Velva's Blue Viking, owned by Mrs Walter Seidel of Ohio.

An important date for the Russian Blue was 1944, when the Scandinavians became interested in the breed, starting with a little cat from Finland named Pierette. She was the only one they had and she was mated to a Siamese, Longfellow of Annam, who carried a factor for blue. News of this cross was brought to England and, rather unfortunately for the breed, prompted an outbreak of hybrid breeding. The consequence was that the British Standard of Points was rewritten in 1950 and the Foreign Blue was developed as a kind of all-blue Siamese, bearing little or no resemblance to the original Russian Blue.

This was the situation until 1965, when a group of British breeders, deploring the gradual disappearance of the original Russian Blue, attempted to re-establish the breed in its original form. To this end,

Mrs Foster's outstanding stud, Ch Hengist Bitochki, has a good, broad head with well-developed jowls, and correctly-positioned ears.

Ch Hengist Bitochki enjoying the sun.

Below: Khubsurat Platinum Puss, a well-developed male, with a good, sound, even coat. Owned by Miss Gamble.

A striking family group with Khubsurat Platinum Puss (sire), Anderida Gahina (dam) and their young son, Mansel Gronski.

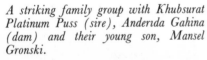

the Standard was rewritten, returning approximately to its pre-Second World War form, and a breeding programme embarked upon, involving the crossing of the English and Swedish lines. One of the first breeders to take this step was Mrs Aina Bjørnberg of Malmø, Sweden. Other breeders have followed, and the results have been so encouraging that there is now a breed association, the Russian Blue Association founded 1967, and there is a real hope that we shall see the original form of Russian Blue once again on the show bench.

Russians need no special care as they are very hardy little cats, used to all weathers. They should have a good mixed diet with plenty of raw meat and as much freedom as possible consistent with safety. They pine if kept indoors too much. The females are good, unfussing mothers who generally rear their kittens with the least possible human assistance. The chief difficulty is that they are very silent cats, so that it can be very difficult to know when a queen is on heat, unless you know your cats very well. Most male Russians are very good-tempered, and can usually be left quite safely with a litter of kittens or a queen, but they can be very aggressive with other males. Grooming is best done with a stiff brush against the lie of the coat, followed by a thorough combing; then a further brushing following the lie of the coat, and finally polish with a silk cloth. Powder is sometimes used to intensify the blue for show purposes, but must always be brushed right out, and should not be used to disguise a lack of colour. Too much powder can spoil the silvery effect.

American and British Standards are similar in their requirements. According to the current G.C.C.F. Standard of Points, the Russian's

coat should be a clear blue in colour, even throughout, and when mature, free from tabby markings or shading. A medium blue is the preferred shade. In the breeding process, Blue should be bred to Blue. Out-crosses already figure in the history of the breed perhaps more than is desirable, and should now be avoided. The Russian Blue is a very "seasonal" breed; that is, the coat shows variation with the time of year. The silver tipping, for instance, is most prominent in the winter months, and, in summer, the blue sometimes takes on a brownish tinge if the sun is very strong.

Father and son—Khubsurat Platinum Puss and Mansel Gronski. Note the well-developed jowls of Puss and excellent eye-shape. The kitten shows the desired ear placement and thinness of the skin to the ears.

The texture and appearance of the Russian Blue coat is the truest criterion of the breed – it is short, thick and very fine, standing up to give a soft and silky effect like sealskin. The coat is double, so that it has a distinct silvery sheen. I look for silver tipping on each hair. The Standard lays great stress on this thickness of fur – you can easily gauge what is required, for, ideally, it should be difficult to see the cat s skin, which should also be blue.

The current British Standard requires also a long body, graceful in outline and carriage, with a medium strong bone structure. The tail is fairly long and tapering. The head is a short wedge-shape with a flat skull; forehead and nose are straight, forming an angle. There is a verbal difference in the head Standard of the American C.F.A. and A.C.F.A. and the British G.C.C.F., but they all seem to aim at the same thing. Whisker pads are prominent. The vivid green eyes are almond-shaped, and set rather wide apart. The ears are long and pointed, wide at the base, and set vertically to the head. The skin of the ears should be thin and transparent, with very little inside furnishing.

Mansel Gronski at three months, still with his fluffy kitten coat and faint tabby markings, which will disappear with age.

259

Sphynx

Short-hair

A red hairless male—Dutchie's Ceza, bred and owned by Mrs Kees Tenhove of Ontario, Canada.

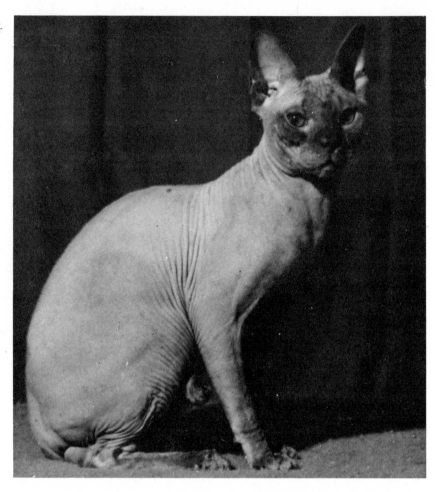

Early in 1966, in Ontario, Canada, a litter of kittens was born to a black and white house cat and amongst these kittens was a hairless male. A young general-science university student heard about the kitten, and, with his mother–a Siamese breeder at that time–obtained the kitten, plus the black and white mother, Elizabeth. It was not known at this time if this was a recessive gene, and if the hairless characteristics would be reproduced in subsequent generations.

In time, the hairless male was bred back to his "furry" mother and she produced both hairless and furry kittens. Later, hairless-to-hairless breedings from these kittens were attempted without success, and it was realized that out-crosses were needed. A programme was developed in which American Short-hair females were bred to existing hairless males. The furry female offspring from these litters were bred to hairless males from other hairless American Short-hair breedings. From this programme a strong start was made on a scientifically sound plan to produce good, sturdy stock. Contrary to some early beliefs, these cats are not more sensitive to cold than their furry cousins with normal coats.

Given the name "Sphynx", the cat is also known as the "Canadian Hairless". A hairless cat shows completely different type from the furry kittens born in the same litter, particularly in regard to the head.

Unlike other breeds, the Sphynx sweats and, because of the lack of hair, normal follicular secretions may accumulate on the skin and may turn a brownish colour. This may easily be removed by bathing or wiping off with a wash-cloth and mild soap, and is no problem. Believed at first to be the answer to the problems of "allergic-to-cats" cat lovers, the Sphynx unfortunately has proved not to be so in all cases, as the dander on the skin can produce allergic reactions.

The Sphynx is currently recognised by Crown Cat Fanciers Association and the Canadian Cat Association. (Provisional recognition by C.F.A. was withdrawn early in 1971.)

According to the Standard, the face is covered with a short, plush pile which should "look like velvet and feel like moss". The hair is longer on the backs of the ears, and plush around the lobes. Mask plush should be heaviest around the nose and sides of the mouth, distinctly breaking above the nose. There are no whiskers. Paws have fine down up to the "wrist" or "ankle". The testicles are encased in fine, long, fairly closely-packed hair, the longest on the cat's body. The tail-tip carries fine, flat-lying hair covering about an inch of the extremity. Kittens, on the other hand, are covered with fine, soft, short hair, which later restricts itself to the points. The back of the body should carry microscopic hair rather like that found on the mask-the finer the better. Absence of it suggests shaving and can lead to show disqualification!

Sphynx cats come in all colours-solid-coloured cats may carry a small pink neck locket; their colour should be uniform across the outer surfaces of the body, graded lighter over the inside parts. Breast points and the umbilical area are the only white spots acceptable on a solid, together with that part on the head covered by the ears folded down before the cat's birth. Parti-colour markings should be perfectly symmetrical.

The skin of the adult should be taut and wrinkle-free everywhere but on the head, although kittens "look lost, as if in a sweater far too large for them". Neither round nor wedge-shaped, the skull from the eyes back is oblong, flat between the eyes with a centre ridge. There is a slight break before the nosebreak, and due to the mask, the nose appears to taper slightly. The eyes tend to be set back into the face, and the snout is short in relation to the whole, tapering slightly. The jowls must not sag, and the chin should be square, giving an impression of firmness. A rounded or horse-like head is a fault. The round eyes have a slight slant, and are golden in colour, the deeper the better, and there should be no green around the pupil. The ear-set is large with a wide base, the ear sweep breaking at the lobes before meeting the head.

The body should be fine-boned but powerful, the chest short and barrel-shaped, Burmese-like but appearing smaller because of the lack of hair. The front of the cat is compared to a Boston Bull Terrier, a more pronounced likeness in kittens, which are bow-legged. Front legs are long and fine-boned, with small round paws. Hind legs are slightly longer, firm with soled haunches-they appear to curve in slightly under the cat, reminiscent of the kitten stage. When standing, the body stands slightly higher on the back legs, with a slight tuck. The tail should be long, thin and hard, and without kinks.

Any Other Variety

A Short-hair Smoke kitten, recognized in the U.S.A. but not in Britain. This young kitten is only just beginning to show the silver roots to the hair. Bred by Mrs Betts.

In Britain a breed number is given for Any Other Variety, i.e. for a breed or variety whose characteristics do not conform to any standard already recognized. Many breeders look askance at some of the cats registered under this heading, produced in some cases by experimental breeding, probably fearing that existing breeds may be harmed by crossing with these new ones. It should be remembered, however, that many of today's very popular varieties made their debut at the early cat shows under this heading, as the recognized varieties were very few indeed.

Many of the cats seen in this class at the shows are the result of many years of work and careful planning, often at considerable expense and with no immediate reward, but very necessary in the formation of a new variety. Were it not for the determination and single-minded endeavours of such fanciers, many lovely varieties now seen today would not in fact exist.

Not all the cats and kittens entered in these classes are experimentally bred, they may just have happened as the result of mis-matings, or may

be varieties recognized in, or native to other countries; some are naturally-developed colour dilutions and coat pattern variations of already-established varieties. Any new variety has to be tested and tried, and bred for a required number of generations successfully before recognition is even given consideration.

In the past, the now recognized Bi-Colours and the Devon and Cornish Rex appeared under this heading, and at the present time, in Britain, there are Lilac Foreign Short-hairs, Foreign Whites, White Russians, Egyptian Maus and the British Blue Tortie-and-White all registered as A.O.V. as such. The type for Any Other Variety may be "British" or "foreign", but does not include Siamese with points-colouring different from that already recognized. These may be registered as Any Other Colour Siamese.

At Shows, the Any Other Variety cats and kittens may only enter in classes specially for them, and may not compete against the recognized varieties. Naturally no challenge certificates are given.

Frequently after many years spent in establishing a new variety, a provisional Standard may be granted which is a great help to the judges, but no challenge certificates can be given to the winners. It is expected that several new varieties will achieve the desired Standards and apply for official recognition during the 1970's, and many more will do so in the future, as there are countless permutations of gene patterns present in the cat.

In Britain, the Governing Council of the Cat Fancy ensure that while colours and coat patterns may be changed without limit, no animals showing weaknesses or deformities as part of their new standards will ever be allowed full status and recognition.

In the United States there is no breed number for Any Other Variety, but cats may take their debut as Non-Championship Provisional breeds, e.g. the Bombay, but each Association makes its own decision regarding full recognition of any specific variety, not all necessarily recognizing the same.

Shawnee Silhouette of Dulac—a Bombay owned by Norman and Ruth Cukras of Ohio.

263

Pet Cats (non-pedigree)

Three little household pets on show; they were all rescued by Miss M. Frank. The non-pedigree cat makes a delightful pet and must be cared for just as much as any pedigree animal.

The history of the domestic cat is a long one, dating from the time when it was worshipped in the temples of the ancient Egyptians, and down through the days of witchcraft and superstitions in the Middle Ages until the present day, when it has become a domestic pet in countless homes over the world. Alas, it is also very often the innocent victim of cruel and thoughtless neglect by its so-called human "friends".

These household pets have no traceable pedigrees, and do not conform to Standards for pedigree cats, but the combinations of coat colour are endless. Tortoiseshells, always female, show lovely mixtures of ginger, black and white, plain or with stripes, or just black mottled with ginger. The tiger-stripes of the tabbies vary from silver and black, or fawn and black, or brown. Coats often show smart white "shirt fronts" and paws. There are smooth short-haired cats, cats with dense, woolly fur, and the long-haired semi-Persians.

The household cat should always be "doctored" or "neutered". If this is not done a tom cat will not only cause a horrible smell in the house, but he will go off for days on end in search of suitable lady friends, and it is then he can so often become the target for water, or stones, etc. thrown by irate householders; he will get involved in fights and also run the risk of injury or death on the roads. If the female is not treated she will produce a succession of unwanted kittens, which in their turn will add to the cat population – unless the owner is prepared to cope with the situation and finds suitable homes for the kittens, then the female cat must be spayed. This can be done at any age after six months, and even after having many litters of kittens – it is never too late to have a female cat spayed. A male can be castrated at any age up to five years, but preferably after nine months. Happily for the many abandoned and unwanted cats and kittens, there are in Britain, the U.S.A. and many other countries, several societies and many small voluntary Rescue Centres working hard to help these little creatures, not only by giving food and shelter, but by having them neutered and placing them in kind and loving homes. In doing this work great care has to be taken that each cat or kitten is placed in a home suitable to its own particular temperament and special need, and preferably where there are no very small children. To illustrate this briefly, a blind cat and a spastic kitten were found wonderful homes, where their devoted new owners took great care of them; the blind cat becoming the inseparable companion of a large neutered ginger cat living next door who guided the blind cat everywhere and taught her to play. The spastic kitten was much loved by its owners, but not more so than by the old spaniel which "mothered" it. These are only two of many instances where care was taken in the placing of these animals and this is always the first essential – the human being and the animal must be compatible; if not it is a strict rule of every good cattery that the cat or kitten is returned and a more suitable home found.

The ordinary little domestic cat must be loved and cared for in just the same way as its more high-born brothers and sisters.

Other Matters Relating to Cats

Anatomy

This is a description of the main anatomical features of the cat, along with a brief explanation of their function.

Skeleton: Owing to selective breeding, the dog's skeleton shows a great range of variations in the size and shape of many of its bones. In the cat, the original shape of the skeleton has been retained with only relatively minor changes affecting some of the bones; compare for example the cobby shape and heavier bone of the "British" long-hairs and short-hairs with the long, fine bones of the Siamese and other "foreign" types.

The functions of the skeleton are: to dictate the shape of the animal; to give protection to vital organs; to provide a foundation to which the other parts of the body are attached. The cat is a quadruped and its skeleton is adapted for walking on all-fours. It walks on its digits or toes, whereas hooved animals walk on the tip of the toes and man walks on the hind limb from the hock downwards.

The skeleton can roughly be divided into:

1. The skull.
2. Vertebral or spinal column consisting of – seven cervical (neck) vertebrae, thirteen thoracic vertebrae, seven lumbar vertebrae, three sacral vertebrae fused to form the sacrum, and a variable number of caudal (tail) vertebrae.
3. The ribs – thirteen pairs which articulate with the thoracic vertebrae. The first eight pairs also articulate with –
4. The sternum (breast bone), to form the rib cage.
5. The two forelimbs, which have only muscular attachments to the spinal column. Each limb consists of a scapula or shoulder blade; a small clavicle or collar bone (the cat is the only domestic animal possessing a clavicle); a humerus or upper arm; a radius and ulna or forearm; and a number of small bones forming the carpus (wrist), metacarpus and digits.
6. The pelvis, consisting of three pairs of bones fused to form a girdle which articulates with the sacrum.
7. The two pelvic limbs, which are joined to the pelvis at the hip joint. Each limb consists of a femur, a tibia and fibula and, in front of the joint between the femur and tibia, the patella or kneecap; a number of small bones forming the tarsus (hock), metatarsus, and digits.

The claws correspond to the end bones of each digit. They are five in number on each forepaw. The inner claw is shorter than the other four and is called the dew claw. There are four claws on each hind paw, the dew claw being absent.

The bones of the skeleton are connected to each other by ligaments to form joints, the ends of the bones being cushioned by cartilages. There are three main types of joints classified according to their movement:

1. Ball and socket joints, e.g., the hip.
2. Hinge joints, e.g., the elbow.
3. Gliding joints, e.g., the small joints in the hock.

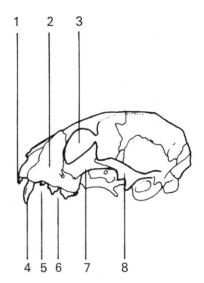

Skull (lateral view)
1. incisors
2. maxilla
3. orbita
4. canines
5. pre-molars
6. molars
7. os zygomaticum
8. Arcus zygomaticus

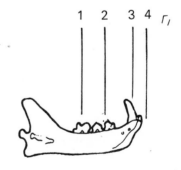

Mandible
1. Molar
2. Premolars
3. Canine
4. Incisors

Skull (dorsal)

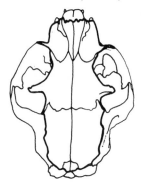

Skull (ventral view)

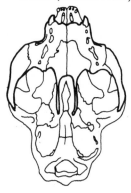

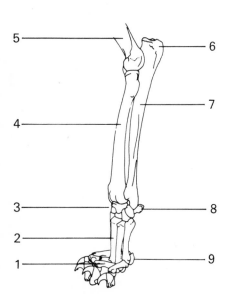

Bones of the front leg
1. Phalanx prima
2. Metacarpus
3. Carpus
4. Radius
5. Humerus
6. Olecranon
7. Ulna
8. Os pisforme
9. Sesamoid bones

Muscular System: Cats are carnivorous animals and before domestication, lived by hunting. Their muscles are therefore adapted for great freedom of rapid movement, making their bodies extremely supple. There are two main groups of muscles:

1. Voluntary – which act under the control of the will, e.g., muscles of the limbs.
2. Involuntary – which act automatically, e.g., muscles of the bowel wall.

Muscles are attached to bone either directly or by means of fibrous tissue in the form of tendons. They act by contracting, thereby flexing or extending the limb, turning the head, etc.

Digestive System: This consists of the mouth, with lips, tongue, and teeth, the oesophagus, stomach, small intestine, caecum, large intestine, rectum, liver and pancreas.

Food passes into the mouth via the lips which help to pick up the food and retain it in the mouth. The tongue is used to lap up liquids and also bears taste buds; the surface is covered with papillae, which point backwards – their purpose is to comb the coat during grooming. The cat has two sets of teeth. The milk teeth appear at three to four weeks old. These are shed at five to six months of age and are replaced by permanent teeth, usually thirty in number but there can be slight variations. When food is swallowed it passes into the oesophagus, a tube which leads from the pharynx down the neck, through the chest and diaphragm into the stomach. This lies in the abdominal cavity towards the left side of the body. It is an elastic sack, which varies in size according to the amount of food it contains. It secretes acid which starts off the process of digestion. The cat is a carnivore, and so its gastric juices are about four times more potent than those of the human. The partly digested food now passes out of the stomach through a sphincter known as the pylorus into the small intestine. This consists of three parts – duodenum, jejunum and ileum – and here digestion continues.

The pancreas lies alongside the duodenum and secretes an enzyme, which flows into the duodenum by a duct and aids digestion. The bile duct from the gall bladder in the liver also enters the duodenum and down this duct bile flows to help in the breaking down of fats. The small intestine also secretes substances which convert carbohydrates into sugars and glycogen and converts fats and proteins into fatty acids and amino-acids. These are then absorbed by the small intestine and are carried by the blood throughout the body. The waste material now passes through the ileocaecal valve into the large intestine which consists of the caecum, the colon and the rectum. Fluid is absorbed from the waste material in the large intestine, and there is heavy bacterial activity here which further breaks down the waste which then passes through the rectum and is expelled through the anus. The liver is the largest gland in the body and lies just behind the diaphragm in proximity to the stomach. Its functions include the storage of glycogen, secretion of bile, the breakdown of old red blood cells, and the formation of urea from broken-down body tissues.

Respiratory System: The respiratory system consists of the nose, containing the paired nasal cavities; pharynx; larynx; trachea;

bronchi, continually dividing into smaller and smaller bronchioles and terminating in the air sacs where the gaseous exchange takes place. This mass of bronchi, bronchioles with their many divisions, and air sacs, is known as the lung, of which there are two. The lungs are contained in the chest or thoracic cavity which is formed by the thoracic vertebrae, the ribs and the sternum. The thoracic cavity is separated from the abdominal cavity by a muscular curtain – the diaphragm.

The diaphragm, along with the muscles attached to the ribs and vertebrae, forces air in and out of the lungs at a normal rate of between twenty and thirty times per minute.

Urinary System: There are two kidneys, which are situated in the abdominal cavity under the lumbar vertebrae, and one on each side of the spinal column. They act as filters to the blood by removing the waste products. These are passed from the kidneys as urine down the ureters to the bladder, which also lies in the abdominal cavity. In the female the urine passes from the bladder by the urethra to the vagina and is expelled through the vulva. In the male, the urine passes down the urethra and is expelled through the penis.

Reproductive System: *Male.* The two testicles in the male are enclosed in a bag, the scrotum, which is situated outside the abdominal cavity below the anus. They produce spermatozoa, for whose production the temperature *inside* the cat's body is too high. The prostate gland around the neck of the bladder produces seminal fluid. The spermatic cord carries the spermatozoa to the urethra from which they are discharged through the penis at copulation.

Female. The ovaries are situated in the abdomen – one behind each kidney. These produce the eggs, or ova. When the female is mated, these eggs are shed and pass down the Fallopian tubes into the horns of the uterus where fertilization takes place. The fertilized egg becomes attached to the lining of the uterus where it develops. At birth the foetus passes from the horn into the body of the uterus, through the cervix, into the vagina and out through the vulva.

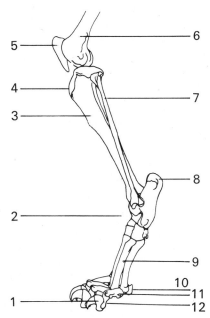

Bones of the rear leg
1. Phalanx tertia
2. Tarsus
3. Tibia
4. Tibia swelling
5. Patella
6. Os femoris
7. Fibula
8. Tuber calanei
9. Metatarsus
10. Sesamoid bones
11. Phalanx prima
12. Phalanx tertia

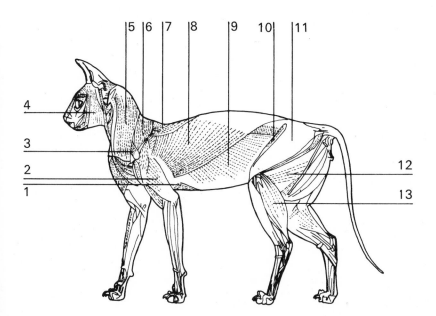

Superficial muscles
1. M. pectoralis minor (posterior section)
2. M. triceps brachii
3. M. deltoidens
4. M. sternomastoidens
5. M. cleidomastoidens
6. M. trapezius
7. M. trapezius
8. M. latissimus dorsi
9. Aponeurosis
10. M. sartorius (anterior belly)
11. M. glutaeus maximus
12. M. biceps femoris
13. M. gastrocnemius

Circulatory System: The body is composed of millions of tiny cells. These cells have to be nourished and it is the function of the blood to carry out this task and also to remove the waste products of the cells.

Blood contains red blood cells and white blood corpuscles, which are suspended in a fluid called blood plasma; the red cells contain a compound, haemoglobin, which carries the oxygen to the body cells. The white corpuscles get rid of impurities and bacteria which have entered the body. The plasma also contains blood platelets which help to make the blood clot on leaving the body, thus preventing fatal haemorrhage from small cuts.

The heart is the organ which is responsible for the circulation of the blood. It is really a muscular pump containing four chambers, two auricles above and two ventricles below. The left ventricle contracts and drives the blood out through a large artery – the aorta – which divides and subdivides into arteries, arterioles, and capillaries throughout the body. The blood takes oxygen and nutrients to all the cells by this network. In exchange, it picks up their waste materials, travels back to the heart by means of various capillaries, venioles, and veins reaching the right auricle by means of a large vein – the vena cava. From here it passes through a valve to the right ventricle, which drives it to the lungs by an artery. In the lungs, carbon dioxide is given off and oxygen picked up. The blood now returns to the left auricle, then passes through a valve to the left ventricle to start its circulation again. The cat's pulse rate is approximately one hundred beats per minute.

Skeleton
1. Atlas
2. Axis
3. Clavicle
4. Cervical vertebrae
5. Scapula
6. Humerus
7. Thoracic vertebrae
8. Sternum
9. Ribs
10. Lumbar vertebrae
11. Femur
12. Hip bone
13. Caudal vertebrae
14. Patella
15. Sesamoids
16. Tibia
17. Fibula
18. Tarsus
19. Metatarsus
20. Phalanges
21. Phalanges
22. Metacarpus
23. Carpus
24. Ulna
25. Radius
26. Hyoid
27. Skull

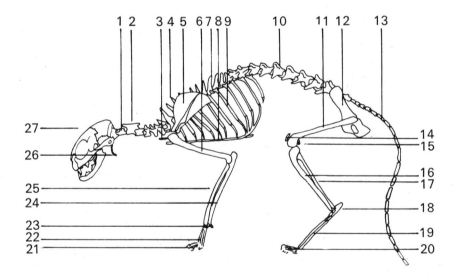

Nervous System: The cat has a highly developed and efficient nervous system. It consists of the central nervous system and the peripheral nervous system.

The central nervous system is made up of the brain and the spinal cord, which lie within the skull and the spinal column for protection. There are two main parts of the brain – the cerebrum and the cerebellum. The cerebrum is mainly concerned with the senses and is the receiving area for messages from the sense organs. The cerebellum, which is highly developed in the cat, co-ordinates muscular movement, controls the balance of the body and governs direction. Because of this development, the cat has fast reflex action and great speed of movement as well as a fine sense of balance.

The peripheral nervous system is made up of sensory and motor nerves distributed throughout the body. They transmit impulses to and from the brain, the sensory nerves conveying sensation and the motor nerves activating the muscles.

Eyes: The cat has excellent eyesight, and it relies mainly on this for hunting. It has the faculty of seeing in subdued light which is partly due to the great powers of dilation of the pupil, and a light reflecting mechanism at the back of the eye – the tapetum lucidum. The eye is a globe set in the orbital cavity of the skull. There are upper and lower eyelids and, at the inner corner, a third eyelid, the membrana nictitans, or haw, which acts as an extra protection to the eye. The lids are lined by the conjunctiva which is continued on to the surface of the eyeball. The front of the eye is covered by a transparent layer, the cornea.

The eyeball is divided into two fluid-containing chambers by the iris, a curtain which acts as a shutter controlling the size of the pupil, according to the light entering the eye. In bright sunshine the pupil appears as a narrow vertical slit, while in subdued light, it is a large round opening. The lens, whose function is to focus the images, is situated in the posterior chamber behind the iris. From it the images are projected on to the retina at the back of the chamber, activating impulses to the brain via the optic nerve.

Ears: The cat has very acute hearing and partly depends on this for hunting. Sound waves are gathered by the outer ear and pass down the ear canal until they reach the drum. This is a thin membrane which separates the outer ear from the middle ear. This ear contains three small bones called the hammer, anvil, and stirrup bones, which vibrate and transmit the waves to the cochlea in the inner ear, from which they are communicated to the brain by the auditory nerve. The balance mechanism, or semi-circular canals, is also situated in the inner ear, as is the Eustachian tube which connects the ear to the throat, and acts by equalizing pressure in the ear to prevent rupture of the drum.

Skin and hair: The skin envelopes the body and is continuous with the lining of the various orifices. Its functions are to protect the body from bacterial invasion; to regulate the temperature of the body; to prevent excessive loss of fluid from the body by reason of its waterproof qualities; to help the cat adapt to its surroundings through its extremely sensitive nerve supply transmitting sensations of heat, cold, touch and pain to the brain.

The skin also contains follicles from which the hair grows. The cat has three kinds of hair – guard hair; wool hair or undercoat; tactile hairs or whiskers. Some authorities have it that there are three kinds of *coat* hair, additional to the whiskers – the guard coat; the outer hairs, which are thicker than the guard hairs, and the wool hairs or down coat.

The main function of hair is to insulate the body and protect it from injury. A secondary function is to intimidate an enemy by being caused to stand erect, thus increasing the apparent size of the cat.

Establishing the sex of a kitten. The male is on the right and the female is on the left.

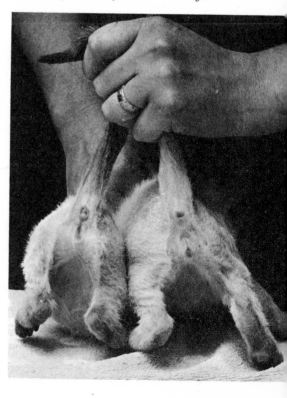

Boarding

In America, there are no nationwide standards for cat-boarding establishments, nor are there many local ones. Licensing programmes are in existence in only a few municipalities. However, most boarding catteries maintain their own standards and have excellent reputations. In 1963, the British Parliament passed the Animals Boarding Establishments Act, which has helped in some degree to improve the general standard of boarding catteries in the United Kingdom. The Act does, unfortunately, leave many loop-holes for the unscrupulous person who wants to board cats with the sole object of gaining a quick monetary return for the least possible amount of effort and capital outlay.

The Act requires that all boarding kennels and catteries are licensed by the Local Authority, who send their Inspector to examine the premises, and to satisfy himself that the licensee, accommodation and facilities conform to the requirements laid down by the Act. The licence is renewable each year and the premises are regularly inspected. Any person, who runs a boarding cattery without a licence, is liable to a fine of £25 ($60) or three months imprisonment, or even both! This still has not eliminated some unlicensed places, and it is up to the individual client to ensure that the premises at which his cat is to stay has a current certificate of licence.

The licence lays down, among other things, that animals should not be exposed to interference from any other animal or person. They should be kept in suitable and clean accommodation with adequate space, lighting and heating, and supplied with adequate suitable food, drink, bedding; they should be given adequate exercise. They should be easily accessible in case of fire or other emergency. Responsible persons within reasonable reach of the premises should be on hand in case of emergency. Water and/or an efficient fire extinguisher should be kept on the premises. An animal must be isolated if suffering from an infectious disease. Water, food etc. should be prevented from dropping on to animals in cages situated below other cages. Each animal should be registered on reception and this register must be available for inspection at any time by an authorized person.

The problem is that anyone, without any knowledge of the comprehensive care of the cat, can open a boarding cattery, and the cats can be housed in anything, from a small hutch in a vast row of other hutches, to a converted greenhouse! As holidays abroad become cheaper each year, and more people take advantage of them, more and more cat owners are finding it necessary to board their pets. Many new catteries have opened and some small catteries have extended their facilities. The best ones are constructed in the open air and consist of a hut and a wired-in run for each cat or cats from the same family.

The huts can obviously be as large and roomy as space and finances will allow, but too large a hut proves difficult to heat adequately, and does not provide the privacy and cosy quarters that most cats enjoy. Cedar-wood huts can be obtained from several manufacturers in England; 4 ft. wide by 3 ft. deep is adequate with a height of 4 ft. or 6 ft. If the 4 ft. high hut is used, this can be raised some 2 ft. off the ground so that the interior floor is at a convenient working height for cleansing purposes. A wired-in run, 6 ft. high for access and 4 ft. wide with a minimum length of 6 ft. is adequate. Too large a run will cause some cats to lose their confidence, and too small a run will make cleaning and attending to the cats' needs difficult. The huts should be wooden as this is a warm material and, if of cedar-wood, will last years without rotting. The interior should be insulated against excessive heat or cold, and chipboard, hardboard or plywood is then fitted over the insulation and the edges carefully sealed. The whole interior, including ceiling and floor is then painted with a sealing compound, and given two or three coats of scrubbable paint. The floor may have a sheet of vinyl cut to fit for ease of cleaning. The hut should have a service door about half the width of the front, and a large window. A cat door with a closing hatch should be provided for access to the run. The run should be made of substantial timber, treated with a water-proofing agent, and the bottom timbers raised $1-1\frac{1}{2}$ inches above the smooth concrete base on brackets; this enables water to run away under the timber, prevents it from rotting and makes it possible for the concrete to be hosed down when necessary.

The run must be entirely wired in and staples placed a maximum of 4 inches apart to hold the wire in place. Welded mesh is better than chicken wire which cats are liable to bite through, and easier to handle than chain link fencing. If huts are built in a "terraced" fashion with common walls between, the common run walls should be of solid construction to prevent the cats touching nose-to-nose and possibly passing infection, or fighting through the wire which may result in badly bitten and abscessed paws. Fibreglass or heavy duty polythene sheet can be used, commercial glass, or the wire mesh may be obtained with heavy plastic already fitted. The run doors must fit well and be fitted with a bolt inside as well as outside. All the runs should open into a wired safety area, so that a nervous cat bolting past the attendant at feeding time would be unable to escape completely.

If the cattery boards during the winter, heating is a necessity in the huts. Electric heating is the only feasible form, and should be installed by an expert, bearing in mind the risk of fire. The type and wattage of heater will depend on the size and layout of the hut. Tubular heating is excellent, but cats love the comfort and glow of infra-red bulb heaters. Control switches should not be in the individual huts, but operated from a remote-control board. A stool or log for the cat to sit on can be placed in each run, but it must be remembered that all furnishings have to be easily sterilized between boarders. Equipment in each hut should consist of non-spill drinking bowl, feeding bowl, bed and toilet pan. A hand-brush on a hook inside each house will also help to cut down the risk of cross-infection. Beds may be of fibreglass and easily washed, or of new cardboard boxes, burnt after each occupant. Toilet trays should be of plastic and sterilized after use, or of disposable fibre and burnt daily. Feeding dishes can also be obtained in fibre and discarded after use. Litter used in the toilet trays should be of an easily disposable nature. Soft wood shavings are best, as these can be burnt daily, and cut down infection risks, and prevent the formation of fly-breeding grounds.

The whole cattery should have an uncluttered and pleasantly clean

Typical "holiday" accommodation.

appearance, with bins for waste disposal, plenty of cleaning equipment, and an adequate fire-extinguisher to hand. When visiting a cattery with a view to boarding one's cat, the visit should be planned within normal working hours, when it should not be necessary to have an appointment. One should look for an air of organization about the place, and no signs of clutter or waste. The huts and runs should be spotlessly clean and there should be no strong smell of "cat". The cats should appear happy and contented, and the surroundings should be light and airy. There should be some form of safety passage to prevent escape, and the runs should be of concrete or paving.

It is usually necessary to book well ahead at peak periods; some catteries book for Christmas when the cats are collected from their Easter Board! Charges vary considerably, and are usually in line with the facilities offered; heating and special dietary requirements usually cost extra, so a full quotation in advance is advisable if in doubt. In a good cattery, it will be necessary to give name and address, name of cat, age, sex, description and vaccination details. An emergency address may be given also, and some catteries will ask for details of the cat's favourite diet and any fads or fancies he may have. Owners of cats to be boarded should ensure that their pets are in good health, and that their vaccination programme is up to date. Any booster doses necessary should be given in good time in order to take effect. He should be carefully checked for fleas, and his ears should be spotlessly clean with no trace of canker. Some catteries participate in an insurance scheme and details will usually be given to the cat owner at the time the reservation is made. When the cat arrives at the cattery, he will be inspected for any signs of parasites or illness (of which the cat owner is often unaware) before being allowed to take up residence in his chalet. This is done to protect the other boarders and is no reflection on the integrity of the cat-owner. Ear mites and fleas can be dealt with quickly and effectively by most cattery proprietors, but if the animal has a skin disease, which is unspecified, or is suspected of being in the incubation or infectious stage of any illness, he will be refused admission for the sake of the other boarders present. Most catteries, however, do have a working arrangement with their veterinary surgeons who will take a suspect cat in to board or under observation, in order to allow the owner to keep to his holiday plans without delay. It is usual for a form of indemnity to be signed by the owner, so that while every care and attention will be afforded his cat, the cattery owner will not be held liable in law should an accident occur. Cats should be taken to, and collected from, the cattery by their owners, and should be transported in a suitable container, either a travelling box or basket or even a zipped-top bag. Baskets should not be hired or borrowed as they are difficult to clean properly and may be infectious or harbouring parasites. Disposable cardboard carriers are ideal for use to and from the cattery. Some catteries allow the cat's own bed to be taken along, and a few toys. All grooming equipment and blankets, however, should be carefully labelled as they may be lost during washing or cleaning operations.

The cat, when boarding, can undergo a complete change of personality. Most cats, after a couple of days, accept their confinement with a degree of resignation. Some take to cattery life and have a good time; others become "touch-me-and-I'll-bite-you" characters. Then there are the neurotic cats who wet their beds, are sick in the run and quietly work away at the wire when no one is looking. Obviously, all these cats need an individual approach, and this is where the difference is marked between an experienced and inexperienced cattery owner.

The experienced proprietor will also come off better should the real problem, which besets boarding catteries, rear its ugly head. This is the problem of upper respiratory infection (*see*. Diseases) where prevention is better than cure; if caught early enough it may be controlled, but if neglected may prove fatal. Cases have been known where every occupant of a cattery has died from upper respiratory virus disease during epidemics; one of these catteries was owned and run by a veterinary surgeon, but even his skilled attention could not save his boarders once the disease was rife. These cases were all in indoor catteries, and it is known that outdoor catteries with a good fresh air-flow can help to minimize the risk of infection, even if a carrier animal is admitted unknowingly. It is an ever-present fear in the mind of any conscientious boarding cattery proprietor that at any time one of his charges may go down with a virus disease, and he will always be on the alert for any sign that anything is the slightest amiss in any of his paying guests. Indoor catteries should be fitted with extractor fans to keep the air inside constantly changing, and air sprays can be used with care and in moderation. Animals suspected of succumbing to any infection should be immediately removed from the cattery into the isolation accommodation, and a close watch kept on his neighbours. His temperature should be checked and, if abnormal, or if his throat is inflamed, veterinary advice should be sought. The main weapon in disease control in the boarding cattery is hygiene; this, coupled with adequate ventilation and the insistence on up-to-date vaccination for all boarders, will help to keep infectious illness at bay. Daily and weekly routines should be drawn up and strictly adhered to, and each hut and run and its entire contents should be rigorously scrubbed, then sterilized when each boarder vacates the accommodation. The highest accolade the genuine cat-loving cattery proprietor can receive, is the whole-hearted thanks of the grateful owner who returns to find his cat waiting, happy and well-fed, and in glowing health.

Cattery management is not to be undertaken lightly. A degree of good health and stamina is necessary, with a temperament that can stand up to the incessant ringing of the telephone all through the spring months, a possible fourteen-hour day all through the summer months, and the repainting and maintenance in the autumn and winter. The owner must have forcefulness of character to refuse to squeeze "just one more" in at holiday times. A businesslike mind and the ability to keep the records, register and accounts in good order is very necessary and, above all, the sort of regard for cats which enables one to perform any and every task for their complete comfort, no matter how distasteful some of these may be.

The reputation of a good boarding cattery is only achieved by the combination of well-designed and carefully built accommodation, run and maintained by an intelligent and knowledgeable person with a genuine love of cats. Cattery standards will only be as high as the general public demands; with more and more publicity given to the good catteries, and open invitations offered to visit before bookings are made, poorer catteries will have to improve their general standards or go out of business, so the average standard must progressively improve.

Breeding

If you are thinking of taking up breeding, it is really best to buy a young female from five to ten months old, as by this time you can see how she is going to turn out as an adult. If possible, before buying, go to the cat shows and meet the breeders. Visit them in their homes to see the conditions under which the stock is kept, and ask them to be honest with you, as to which female kitten they consider would make the best breeding queen. Only choose a kitten that looks strong, healthy and lively. Pedigree too is very important from a breeding point of view. If it can be avoided, never buy a future breeding queen without seeing her, unless a judge or some knowledgeable person has seen and can recommend her. Buy the best you can afford from a reliable breeder. Your female should already have been inoculated against feline infectious enteritis. As the term "queen" implies, any female chosen to breed from must be of the highest quality. Look for a female with no glaring faults and, in long-hairs, a short nose, small ears and sound eye-colour for the breed chosen – two of the most difficult faults to "breed out" are large ears and poor eye colour.

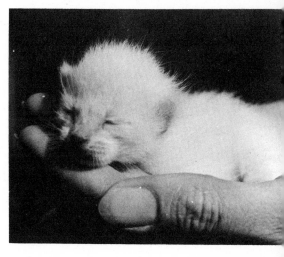

A new-born kitten.

Quality means more than beauty when choosing your female, so do not go for type (*see* Glossary) only. Good physique is most important, as health and strength are essential to producing sound healthy stock. A sweet nature is an important asset, as a cat with an even temperament and a companionable disposition is easy to handle, especially in times of kittening or illness. It is very important to make great pets of your cats. Give your cat as much freedom and as much home life as possible. In the end, however, correct feeding is really the most important factor of all, as a well-fed cat is a strong cat (*see* Nutrition).

Cats must also be kept spotlessly clean, as must their sleeping-boxes and general surroundings; twice yearly a safe worm-dose, obtainable from a veterinary surgeon, should be used but *never* during pregnancy,

Females should be mated from ten months of age. It is a great mistake to keep them back to the second year, as they may become frustrated and be poor breeders, and in any case, it serves no useful purpose. Do not allow your cat to become fat or she will not breed well. In the month before you have your cat mated, make arrangements with the owner of the stud you want to send her to. Then, when she starts to call, contact the owner at once, and send your queen away not later than the end of the first day. The first visit is not always a success, so arrange to return her as soon as she calls again. After any visit to a stud, keep your cat in until she has completely stopped calling, otherwise she may get out, and a dual mating result. Keep note of the mating dates, so that you know when to expect the kittens. The average gestation period is 64–65 days but may vary by a few days. Begin about a week before the expected birth date to add to her milk-food a pinch of bicarbonate of potash to prevent acid milk which can cause fatalities among the kittens. During pregnancy vitamins are necessary, and nothing is better than vitamin E tablets, 3 mg. per day, and extra supplies of vitamins A, D and calcium. If taken as directed, these additives will supply the requirements in the correct proportions.

Cats usually have their first litter on time, to the day, so a week or

Top: Ten-day-old kittens—three Abyssinians and one Red Abyssinian.

Centre: Taishun litter of Abyssinian kittens at six weeks.

Bottom: Abyssinian and Siamese kittens three to four weeks old. All the kittens on this page were bred by Mrs Menezes.

even a fortnight beforehand prepare a comfortable bed for the great event. If at all worried, inform your vet beforehand as to the probable date and telephone him should there be any difficulty. Most cats have their kittens with no trouble at all. If you have a quiet corner out of draughts and free from traffic, in the house and not isolated, put the cat's box there, and let her get thoroughly used to it before the day arrives. The box should not be exposed to direct light, as kittens' eyes must be shielded from light. When the kittens are about to arrive, it is best to put in the box a clean newspaper for the cat to have her kittens on; and keep a warm smooth blanket handy to slip under the mother when all are born.

When you think the birth is imminent – this you will easily detect as the mother will lie down in her box and show disinclination to come out – get a cloth and wring it out in hot water, as hot as you can bear. Shake out the steam and lay it along the mother's nipples, repeating this several times. The warmth is comforting and encourages the milk to flow freely. As each kitten arrives see that the mother severs the umbilical cord. If she does not do this, do it yourself with a pair of sterilized scissors, cutting about an inch distant from the kitten's body. Have ready a hot water bottle well wrapped in blanket, and as each kitten arrives and has been attended to, place it on the blanket in a fairly deep cardboard box. When all the kittens are born, change the newspaper and place the blanket on it; and return the kittens to the mother. Give the mother a saucer of warm milkfood, with a pinch of bicarbonate of potash, as mentioned above, and one crushed vitamin E tablet. After all the kittens are settled in, try to resist the temptation to keep looking at them and, particularly, handling them. Keep an eye on the cord, and wipe the severed end with cottonwool dampened with glyco-thymoline or mild, diluted disinfectant, which helps it to heal satisfactorily. If the family is a large one, keep a lookout for hungry kittens or any that might get pushed out at feeding-time. Give a few drops of glucose (corn syrup in America) and warm water to help it along, using a teaspoon and giving very little at a time, as it is very easy to upset the digestion of a young kitten.

At eight weeks, kittens can be given a quarter of a worm tablet, obtainable only from the vet, and given immediately after a light breakfast, the mother having been dosed when the family was six weeks old. At ten weeks they should be inoculated against infectious enteritis – there are several vaccines on the market and some breeders have a preference for one or the other. At about four months the baby teeth begin to fall out, and the second teeth begin to appear. Some kittens do not react at all; others get a little upset until their teeth are through. All this disappears when teething is complete. This can take from a month to six weeks.

The ideal nesting box is one where half the front lifts off and fastens with a wooden button. It should be void of draughts and sheltered, thus keeping the kittens' eyes from strong light. Provide plenty of room for the kittens to romp and play, as exercise is so good for them. When the family gets bigger, a tea chest turned on its side is ideal, as this gives ample room for mother and children. Give the kittens plenty of love and caressing, as they are very affectionate by nature. If eyes get sore or inflamed for any reason, bathe with boracic (boric acid in

America) and warm water, taking care that none goes up the nose and, after drying with cottonwool, insert a very little petroleum jelly. All in all, there are a few salient points to bear in mind in breeding kittens.

1. The parents should be strong and healthy.
2. You must pay attention to detail and be very observant at all times.
3. Maintain scrupulous cleanliness in all you do.
4. No coddling or heating are necessary, but care must be taken to provide weatherproof and draughtproof houses if the animals are to be kept out of doors.
5. Good sensible foods is essential.
6. Give your cat and kittens plenty of home life and affection; you must have, above all, a real love of animals.

Should you have the misfortune to lose the kittens either before or after birth, it is best to re-mate your cat as soon as she calls, the only exception being if the mother has been ill.

Avoid too-close in-breeding, although a certain amount of line-breeding is necessary to produce prize-winning kittens of the first order. Always remember that first class show conditions means first class health condition, and that this starts from birth with good management.

Kittens should not be sold until they are at least ten weeks old. Advertisements can be put in the National or local newspapers, in *Fur and Feather* in Britain, in *Cats Magazine*, or *Cat Fancy* in the United States, and the various cat publications in other countries. It is inadvisable to sell a kitten unless you meet the would-be owners and learn something about them. If you exhibit at the shows and the kittens do well, people will be anxious to buy them. If intending to go in for breeding seriously, it is advisable to register a cattery name, i.e. a prefix. This distinguishing name may only be used by the breeder registering it, and it will appear on the kittens' pedigree, and is an excellent form of advertising. In both America and Britain, a prefix may be registered on application to the governing bodies. On payment of the required fee, it becomes the property of the breeder for life.

Keeping a Stud

The same rules apply about buying a male kitten for a future stud as for buying a breed queen. Choose one that is as near the required standard as possible, and if you are able to exhibit and eventually make him a champion, his services as a stud will be more in demand, although he should never be over-used.

It should be realized that it is practically impossible to keep a full male in the house as a pet, as undoubtedly he will spray, leaving his pungent smell around. It is essential to provide light and airy quarters with a good sized run safely closed in. The inside of the house should be lined with a material that can be washed down, as should any shelves and boxes. Separate accommodation for visiting queens must be provided in his house if it is intended to place him at public stud. A young male should be a year old, or more, before being used as a stud, and his first queen must be a placid experienced one. He should only be used once or twice for the first few months.

There should be ample room to stand up inside with a wired-off large

"Just arrived"—British Blue babies, bred by Mrs J. Richards.

Stud quarters.

compartment for visiting females, and a communicating door. Visitors must be kept separate except when mating, and must be introduced to the stud gradually. It is important to have a good-tempered male who will be gentle with the females. A strong, healthy, well-built cat of the best quality, and fully developed physically, will give good results and sire good healthy kittens.

Never leave the two cats together alone, but always return the visitor to her quarters after mating. These must be arranged so that the cats can see each other and so become acquainted. Stud cats have a lonely life if not provided with a companion, so an older female, no longer breeding, can be with your male for a few hours a day when it is not the breeding season.

If living in the country, it is usually possible to allow a stud cat his freedom for some hours during the day, which is all-important as lots of exercise keeps him fit. It this is not possible, he must have a very large run. A large helping of raw meat, up to six ounces a day, is essential, with vitamins in the breeding season, and a good breakfast of cooked fish or meat and biscuit in the morning. Clean cold water must always be available – also fresh grass. Give your stud a lot of love and attention, and he will reward you by being easy to manage.

Gestation Periods

On the left of each column are the mating dates, on the right the corresponding dates on which kittens may be expected; a gestation period of 64 days has been assumed, although in practice, the time may vary by several days either way.

Jan	Mar	Feb	Apr	Mar	May	Apr	Jun	May	Jul	Jun	Aug	Jul	Sep	Aug	Oct	Sep	Nov	Oct	Dec	Nov	Jan	Dec	Feb
1	6	1	6	1	4	1	4	1	4	1	4	1	3	1	4	1	4	1	4	1	4	1	3
2	7	2	7	2	5	2	5	2	5	2	5	2	4	2	5	2	5	2	5	2	5	2	4
3	8	3	8	3	6	3	6	3	6	3	6	3	5	3	6	3	6	3	6	3	6	3	5
4	9	4	9	4	7	4	7	4	7	4	7	4	6	4	7	4	7	4	7	4	7	4	6
5	10	5	10	5	8	5	8	5	8	5	8	5	7	5	8	5	8	5	8	5	8	5	7
6	11	6	11	6	9	6	9	6	9	6	9	6	8	6	9	6	9	6	9	6	9	6	8
7	12	7	12	7	10	7	10	7	10	7	10	7	9	7	10	7	10	7	10	7	10	7	9
8	13	8	13	8	11	8	11	8	11	8	11	8	10	8	11	8	11	8	11	8	11	8	10
9	14	9	14	9	12	9	12	9	12	9	12	9	11	9	12	9	12	9	12	9	12	9	11
10	15	10	15	10	13	10	13	10	13	10	13	10	12	10	13	10	13	10	13	10	13	10	12
11	16	11	16	11	14	11	14	11	14	11	14	11	13	11	14	11	14	11	14	11	14	11	13
12	17	12	17	12	15	12	15	12	15	12	15	12	14	12	15	12	15	12	15	12	15	12	14
13	18	13	18	13	16	13	16	13	16	13	16	13	15	13	16	13	16	13	16	13	16	13	15
14	19	14	19	14	17	14	17	14	17	14	17	14	16	14	17	14	17	14	17	14	17	14	16
15	20	15	20	15	18	15	18	15	18	15	18	15	17	15	18	15	18	15	18	15	18	15	17
16	21	16	21	16	19	16	19	16	19	16	19	16	18	16	19	16	19	16	19	16	19	16	18
17	22	17	22	17	20	17	20	17	20	17	20	17	19	17	20	17	20	17	20	17	20	17	19
18	23	18	23	18	21	18	21	18	21	18	21	18	20	18	21	18	21	18	21	18	21	18	20
19	24	19	24	19	22	19	22	19	22	19	22	19	21	19	22	19	22	19	22	19	22	19	21
20	25	20	25	20	23	20	23	20	23	20	23	20	22	20	23	20	23	20	23	20	23	20	22
21	26	21	26	21	24	21	24	21	24	21	24	21	23	21	24	21	24	21	24	21	24	21	23
22	27	22	27	22	25	22	25	22	25	22	25	22	24	22	25	22	25	22	25	22	25	22	24
23	28	23	28	23	26	23	26	23	26	23	26	23	25	23	26	23	26	23	26	23	26	23	25
24	29	24	29	24	27	24	27	24	27	24	27	24	26	24	27	24	27	24	27	24	27	24	26
25	30	25	30	25	28	25	28	25	28	25	28	25	27	25	28	25	28	25	28	25	28	25	27
26	31	26	May 1	26	29	26	29	26	29	26	29	26	28	26	29	26	29	26	29	26	29	26	28
27	Apr 1	27	2	27	30	27	30	27	30	27	30	27	29	27	30	27	30	27	30	27	30	27	Mar 1
28	2	28	3	28	31	28	Jul 1	28	31	28	31	28	30	28	31	28	Dec 1	28	31	28	31	28	2
29	3			29	Jun 1	29	2	29	Aug 1	29	Sep 1	29	Oct 1	29	Nov 1	29	2	29	Jan 1	29	Feb 1	29	3
30	4			30	2	30	3	30	2	30	2	30	2	30	2	30	3	30	2	30	2	30	4
31	5			31	3			31	3			31	3	31	3			31	3			31	5

The Cat Fancy
The Cat Fancy in Britain

The Governing Council

The world's first cat show was staged at the Crystal Palace on July 13th 1871, and received an enthusiastic coverage in the British press. One hundred and seventy cats were penned and judged by the organizer, the noted naturalist and animal painter Harrison Weir, by his brother, Jenner Weir, and by the Reverend Cumming Macdona. There is no doubt that an event of such magnitude could only have been contrived after a great deal of organizational effort, which suggests that even at that time, a feline organization of some scope and complexity was already in existence; and it was not until sixteen years later that it was replaced by the first major cat club which systematically brought into being, and operated, a Stud Book and Register of Cats. Its name was the National Cat Club; and it was founded in 1887. The Cat Club, a rival body, was founded eleven years later by Lady Marcus Beresford and it also maintained its own Register of Cats.

These two clubs co-existed in more or less friendly rivalry for a number of years but, in 1910, both managements realised the waste and futility of maintaining two registers. Very sensibly, they agreed to combine into one governing body to which they gave the name: The Governing Council of the Cat Fancy. As part of the terms of association, the older and larger of the two clubs received in perpetuity the privilege of being represented by four delegates on the new governing body. This privilege has never been revoked and is honoured to this day.

Almost immediately following the establishment of the Governing Council a number of other specialist cat clubs were formed. These clubs duly became affiliated to the Council; and, in return, were given the privilege of sending a voting delegate to its meetings. More and more cat clubs were formed and the most successful of them were granted affiliation, until today, more than sixty cat clubs, some of them dealing with all breeds of cat and others concerned with only one variety, are represented on the Council which now rules over the feline destinies of something like eight thousand people all over the British Isles.

The Council operates in accordance with its constitution, which clearly defines its powers and its obligations towards member clubs. Annually, the Council elects a chairman, a vice-chairman and a treasurer from among the delegates. The first two officers retire annually but may stand for re-election for a maximum period of three consecutive years. In addition, the Council employs a secretary and enjoys the services of an honorary solicitor who advises it on legal matters.

The members of the Council are the delegates elected by each affiliated club having the right of representation, this right being dependent upon the possession of more than one hundred members. Clubs with over 150 members may have two delegates; and no club may be affiliated until it has been in existence for at least three years and possesses fifty members.

The day-to-day business of the Council and of the cat fancy is carried out by an executive committee of sixteen members elected annually from the body of delegates. Other special duties are performed by the Disciplinary Committee, the Genetics Committee, the Finance Committee and by other specialist committees, which meet at regular intervals. The Council itself meets at least four times a year and may be convened for additional meetings by the chairman. Special meetings, held to decide on specified and restricted issues, may be requested by a prescribed body of delegates in an emergency. The officers of the Council are ex-officio members of all the committees and the Council chairman presides at all committee meetings other than that of the Disciplinary Committee and the Genetics Committee, both of which elect their own chairman. Apart from the National Cat Club, which has a right to four delegates, no matter what its membership might be, seven other clubs have been granted permanent representation because of their historic association with the Council.

The powers of the Council are extensive and far-reaching. These powers are exercised not only over affiliated clubs, but also over their individual members; and as one of the conditions of affiliation, the rules of every club must acknowledge its submission to the disciplinary powers of the Council, which has the right to impose upon such clubs or members who offend against its constitution or rules; penalties ranging from a warning or fine to permanent suspension, or, in the case of a club, to disaffiliation.

A suspended person is cut off from all the activities of the fancy. He may not register his cats or exhibit them at any show, nor may he remain a member of any affiliated club. The Disciplinary Committee deals with all complaints arising from alleged breaches of the rules or constitution and consists of nine elected members. Persons found guilty of an offence by the Disciplinary Committee have a right of appeal to the Council either on points of law or upon points of procedure. No appeal may be lodged on the grounds of fact. Persons charged with an offence have the right to be represented and to call witnesses; and the Council has taken great care to ensure that all disciplinary hearings are conducted strictly in accordance with the principles of natural justice.

Among the other principal powers of the Council is the right to grant show licences, to appoint judges nominated by the specialist clubs, to keep a register of cat and kitten pedigrees and to issue pedigree certificates. The Council may also publish stud books, award challenge certificates at licensed shows, deal with the property and finances of the Council and make and amend rules for the registration and exhibition of cats. It may recognize new breeds or varieties of cat and allot breed numbers. As already stated, it may exercise disciplinary powers over clubs and members in accordance with the constitution and it may sit as a court of appeal.

The chairman is elected from among the delegates and ceases to be a delegate on election. His duties are to convene and conduct meetings of the Council and to issue directives on all matters of procedure in accordance with the constitution. He may guide and advise the Council on all matters, but the power to make decisions other than in the special field of procedure is vested in the delegates alone. Once a chairman has gained the trust and respect of the Council his influence for good can be enormous. Outside the Council chamber the chairman is the accredited representative of the British cat fancy. Having no personal powers, he reflects the delegated authority of the Council, and for this reason, he must consider himself to be "on duty" during his entire term of office. It is a duty which is both emotionally and intellectually demanding; and yet, infinitely rewarding and not one to be lightly undertaken.

The stability of the Council and of its relationship with the cat fancy may be judged from the fact that never since its formation in 1910 has any serious attempt been made to set up a rival governing body. The Council governs the fancy strictly, but justly and compassionately; and it deserves and receives the respect and loyalty of every affiliated club.

The Registrars

The greater part of a registrar's work is the issuing of Registration and Transfer Certificates for pedigree cats. The number of applications received by the registrar in a day can vary from, say, twenty-five to nearly two hundred at the height of the show season. It is a major task, therefore, and in addition letters are received on every other aspect of the cat fancy, requiring a good deal of research.

Registration Certificates
The application form for a registration certificate will contain details of the sire, dam and grandparents of the kitten concerned. The registrar checks the entered information against that recorded in the registration files, and corrects any spelling or numerical error on the application form. The names submitted for registration are then checked against names previously registered by both prefix-holders and non-prefix holders to avoid repetition of a name or part of a name. Generally, this checking takes up to fifteen minutes for each application, provided all the details on the application form are correct. Certificates are made out, and a file card completed for the litter giving details of sire, dam, dates of birth and registration, names of breeder and/or owner, and the names and registered numbers allocated. Prefix and non-prefix registrations are filed separately. Certificates are sent to the applicant, together with replacement registration forms and a transfer application form for each kitten.

Transfer Certificates
Transfer certificates record the transfer of a previously-registered cat or kitten from the ownership of one person to another. The application form gives details of the cat concerned, as well as of the sire and dam; it shows the signature and address of the new owner (in the case of an export transfer the present owner can sign on the new owner's behalf to avoid delay), and also of the transferer, who must be the person recorded previously as the owner on the registrar's card. Details are checked and the certificate written. All the information about the transfer of ownership is then entered on the cat's file card. The number

of a transfer certificate applies only to the change of ownership, and should never be given as the cat's registered number. A blank registration form for future use is sent with the certificate for every transferred female, unless she is known to be spayed, or not to be used for breeding.

Export Pedigree Certificates

When a cat is exported, an official pedigree issued by the registrar is usually required by the registering authority in the country concerned if the cat is to be eligible for registration there. Certificates covering up to five generations can be supplied, although three generations are usually sufficient. No export pedigree certificate can be supplied for a cat that has not already been transferred to the new owner; in the case of an adult male, the registrar must also be sent a Veterinary Certificate of Entirety, to certify that it is fully developed.

Certified Pedigrees

These are applied for by breeders and owners in Great Britain, who simply wish for an official pedigree made out, on payment of a fee, from the G.C.C.F. registration files.

Prefix Registration

Although the Secretary and Executive Committee of the G.C.C.F. are responsible for the applications for, and granting of, registered prefixes, the secretary passes all proposed prefixes to the registrar, who checks them against the cards in the Registered Prefix files – about 10,000 in number! Well-known geographical names, colours, titles, names already registered or bearing too close a resemblance to an existing prefix, particularly if carelessly written, are not eligible.

Show Catalogues

After every cat show, the show manager sends to the registrar, through the Secretary of the G.C.C.F., a marked catalogue showing the placings of the exhibits in the classes. The registrar checks each open class prize-winner and reserve winner against their respective file cards and lists any discrepancies. The secretary of the G.C.C.F. can then check from the show entry form whether the error was made by the exhibitor. A catalogue check of this kind normally takes some five hours, although in the case of the National Cat Club show, with its thousands of entries, it takes more than twice as long.

The Cat Fancy in the U.S.A.

The cat fancy in the United States has been compared to the Protestant church with its many sects and denominations, in contrast with the fancies of most other countries or continents where all believers worship under the benevolent shepherding of one organization. The nine North American registering bodies give us a wide choice politically and in standards and procedures, but they provide an extraordinary amount of confusion, rivalry, paperwork, duplication and expense as well.

American interest in showing cats dates back to about the middle of the nineteenth century. The first really professional show was inspired by the Crystal Palace exhibitions in England, and was held in New York City in 1895, but the generally accepted date for the beginning of the organized fancy is the formation of the Beresford Cat Club in Chicago in 1899. With this nucleus, the American Cat Association was founded in 1901 as a continent-wide registering and show-sponsoring body.

From this beginning have branched off: the Cat Fanciers Association (1906), the Cat Fanciers Federation (1919), the United Cat Fanciers (1946), the American Cat Fanciers Association (1955), the National Cat Fanciers Association (1960), the Crown Cat Fanciers Federation (1965) and the Independent Cat Federation (1969) – all commonly designated by their initials.

C.F.A. has long been the largest association, and now has about half the cat fancy membership and half the shows. A.C.F.A. is in solid second place, and the others follow. The Canadian Cat Association (founded in 1961) is an exclusively Canadian organization (*see* The Cat Fancy in Canada); A.C.F.A., A.C.A. and C.F.A. have shows and member clubs in both the United States and Canada, with C.F.A. also having Japanese affiliates; the others presently confine their activities to the United States. Only A.C.F.A. and C.F.A., however, can be said to be continent-wide organizations.

Most of C.F.F.'s shows are in the East, most of N.C.F.A.'s in the mid-West, all of U.C.F.'s are in the West, and both of I.C.F.'s in the East. A.C.A. has shows only in the East and West sections of the continent, Crown in the mid-West, West and South. Standards for the several organizations vary in only minor respects, but there are major differences in philosophy among them. The smaller groups seem to be more liberal in accepting new breeds and colours – Blue and Champagne Burmese, Maine Coons, Lavender (Lilac) Short-hairs, and the multitude of new Siamese colours, for example, are being accepted for showing by many of the associations, but not the C.F.A. The Himalayan is registered and shown in N.C.F.A. and Crown as a colour of Persian, but in C.F.A. and most other associations it is classified as a separate breed.

In organization, A.C.F.A. and Crown lean toward a one-man/one-vote direct democracy, and their individual memberships are with the central association as well as with member clubs. Mail votes of members for officers and on major issues are a fundamental part of their operation. The remaining associations may be classified as "republican"

Blanche Smith's Gr Ch Gallahad's Heritage—a Blue-eyed White Persian male.

in philosophy. There, individual memberships are with clubs only, and it is the representatives of the clubs who vote on policy and on national officers. In all cases, of course, the day-to-day work is carried on by boards of directors, salaried or commissioned registrars, and, in the cases of the two major associations, by sizeable staffs of paid employees.

In addition to those giving shows, there are one or more clubs for almost every breed, and at least one for a particular colour – the White Persian Society International. Some of these clubs are completely independent, belonging to no national association; many belong to C.F.A., and a few to other associations. They exist to promote the advantages of their own breeds, to advise their members on successful breeding methods, to form clearing-houses of information, and often to devise standards for their breeds. Such standards have no official effect, but tend to be adopted by the governing organizations either exactly, or with minor modifications.

The cat fancy as it has developed in the United States is a triumph of diversity – among all the associations, one can find almost any type of club, show and thinking one desires. But the costs are high. To win championships in most of the associations – and even to show, in many – cats must be registered in the stud book of the association sanctioning the show in which they are entered. Thus, to participate fully should one live in an area where all associations have clubs, one's cats must be registered in all the associations – a financial and paperwork burden that most exhibitors find excessive. Ever since the first split in the fancy in 1906, there have been efforts to re-unite it, but none of them have met with great success. Currently, all of the independent associations – those other than C.F.A. – co-operate loosely, most of them choosing to do so under the designations of the Independent Cat Associations – I.C.A. They have working agreements on the interchange of judges and occasionally have round-table meetings to consult on other matters; but the problem of the redundancy of registrations shows no immediate signs of diminishing.

All of the independent associations co-operate with *Cats Magazine*, the American journal of the fancy, in the selection of the All-American cats – the best cats of each breed and colour, computed mathematically on the basis of their show records in all shows of the independent associations. C.F.A. has similar awards for its own shows, and most of the other associations also have their year-long competitions in addition to the All-Americans.

Such awards are based solely on the number of other cats defeated during the course of a season, and are independent of any championship rating. They keep show interest high throughout the season, and have been credited with much of the recent growth of the American fancy (from 5,000 to 50,000 show entries per year since the All-Americans were devised in 1947), but they also have been blamed for encouraging the growth in number of associations from three to nine in the same period.

A few names which stand out in the nearly seventy-five years of the American fancy start with Mrs Clinton Locke who, as founder of the Beresford Cat Club, can perhaps be designated as Mother of the American Cat Fancy. Mrs F. Champion and her daughters, Dorothy and Ethel, were responsible through their writings and breeding pro-grammes for many advances in the first decade of the twentieth century. C. H. Jones and his *Cat Journal*, and Laura Dosche of the *Cat Review* were important influences during the same period. The *Cat Courier* under the successive editorship of Elizabeth Brace and Gertrude Taylor was the communications medium from 1912 to 1938. Currently, in addition to the more fancy-directed monthly, *Cats Magazine*, founded in 1945, cat lovers are also served by *Cat Fancy*, published six times a year.

Recent leaders, who have accomplished important advances in the fancy, have been the late Robert H. Winn, C.F.A. attorney from 1938 to 1971, Russell Middletown who founded A.C.F.A. in 1955, and Richard Orman who was mainly responsible for the 1967 formation of I.C.A. – under which has occurred the first inter-association co-opera-tion among all the independent organizations

For the future, we can look forward in the United States to continued growth in interest in pure-bred cats and the cat fancy. Shows will certainly increase in number and in average size, but we are still many years from entries in the thousands which are so common in England. There are strong indications that the trend toward proliferation of associations is at an end and that future growth will be within the present association structure. C.F.A. will, without doubt, maintain its position as the strongest single association, but the other registering bodies, A.C.F.A. in particular, because of its size and philosophy, will continue to present the cat breeder with most attractive alternatives. If, as appears possible, the I.C.A. concept can be put into effective operation, we can look forward to a fancy in which two evenly-matched groups will be competing in service to the fancier and exhibitor, to the benefit of all.

The Cat Fancy in Canada

The first three decades of the twentieth century saw the gradual development and growing interest in the cat fancy in Canada, with shows being held in Toronto, Hamilton, Windsor and London, Ontario. The first recorded show was in 1906 – a two-day show held in Toronto with one judge officiating. There were 124 entries, including Blue, Red Tabby, Silver and Black Persians, various colours of Domestic Short-hairs (now known in most associations as American Short-hairs) and a good sprinkling of household pets. Cats did not have to be registered to enter in those days and anyone owning what they considered to be a good cat could enter it, for it was an All-Breed show. It was not until a few years later that the first Siamese Seal-points started to appear and then only in very small numbers.

Amongst the early breeders there were some who showed fine Persians, most of their original stock being imported from England. Mr and Mrs Fessenden specialized in Silvers and Blacks, Mrs T. Fortescue and Mrs S. Pugh imported fine Blues and Mr David Deans Henderson showed Smokes. Miss Grace Hinchcliffe bred magnificent short-haired Silver Tabbies and all these breeders were well known for their prize-winning cats.

During the war years of 1939–1945, most activities in the cat fancy were greatly curtailed and interest in breeding pure-bred cats dropped alarmingly. Fortunately, a few of the well-established breeders maintained their stock during these difficult years and were responsible for rekindling the interest when, after the war, conditions gradually returned to normal.

The Canadian National Cat Club, one of the oldest and most active Clubs, once again sponsored shows at the annual Canadian National Exhibition – for which it was named. The C.N.E. – as it was affectionately known – is the largest annual exhibition in the world and has live exhibits of every kind of animal, and competitions. For many years, the C.N.E. Cat Show was one of the biggest prestige shows in North America, drawing exhibitors from many parts of Canada and the United States.

In 1968, the old Canadian National Cat Club disbanded and the sponsorship for the C.N.E. show was passed to the Royal Canadian Cat Club that was by now affiliated with the Canadian Cat Association.

Up until 1960, there was no registering body for cats in Canada and all cat registrations were sent to one of the several American Associations. However, in 1960, the Canadian Cat Association was founded, finally being incorporated in May 1964. Progress was slow and uncertain during the first few years of its existence, but, finally, under the guidance of Mr Kenneth McGill, Mr David Deans-Henderson, Mr and Mrs Garnet Lamb and Mrs Mary Maling, the association was put on the right tracks and started to expand. Wisely incorporating some of the well-tried practices of the larger and long-established American Associations, the Canadian Cat Association now has twelve directors – six from Ontario and Quebec and six from other parts of Canada.

The first C.C.A. show was held – appropriately enough – in Canada's capital city of Ottawa, in October 1963. There are now twelve active clubs across Canada, from Vancouver in the extreme west to Halifax on the east coast. All the clubs sponsor at least one show per year and, reportedly, new clubs are being formed.

There are over five hundred catteries registered with C.C.A. from all parts of Canada and the U.S.A. and more than 10,000 cats are registered.

In addition to offering Championships and Grand Championships, C.C.A. offers International Championships and International Grand Championships. To win these coveted awards, a cat must first have completed a Championship or Grand Championship under C.C.A. rules and must then repeat the feat under one of the American association's rules. Canadians are offered special "All-Canadian" awards for cats that are shown in C.C.A. shows between May 1st and April 30th each year. The wins are computed at the end of each season and awards made annually to the top ten cats, top five kittens and top five alters (neuters). Also very active in Canada are twelve clubs affiliated with the Cat Fanciers' Association Inc., the largest cat organization in the world and international in every sense of the word. These C.F.A. clubs are also very active, busy planning shows, sponsoring Clerking Schools (for the instruction of assistants in the judging ring) or holding pure-bred cat exhibitions for the general education of the public who are not familar with the rarer type of cat.

There are several clubs affiliated to the American Cat Fanciers Association, which hold well-supported shows.

In the last decade, most breeds have been developed to high show quality and Canadian breeders have produced top winners, establishing good reputations for raising some of the finest cats in North America. Included in some of the cats in great demand from all parts of North America are Lois Weston's Simbelair White Persians, Ben and Ann Borrett's Chestermere Himalayans, Joan and Frank Jeffries' Wineta Blue and Cream Persians. In the short-hair breeds are Sally Bray's Silkwood, Jeanne Jeffrey's Rio Vista Burmese and Mrs E. Field's Chota-Li Abyssinians. In Siamese, Marjorie Buckner's Queen's Canada and Marjorie Elliott's Shan Ling are noted for fine type; also Siamese from two other catteries, Joan McDonald's Tien Ming and Pat Brown's Wila-way, have won top wins. Mary Carroll was one of Canada's first breeders of Rex, importing most of her stock from England, and her cattery name of Karl-Katz soon became known for Rex quality. All of the above mentioned breeders produced Grand Champions of their own breeding. In the newer breeds, the Sphynx (or Hairless) Cat was developed in Canada by Riyadh and Yanya Bawa and Mr and Mrs Kees Tenhove.

In addition to the C.F.A. and C.C.A. clubs in Canada, there is also a club in Montreal affiliated with A.C.A. (American Cat Association) and this club holds an annual show drawing great crowds of people.

Interest in cats increases each year and the C.F.A. show in Hamilton, and the C.C.A. show in Toronto each draw more than 350 entries. Each season sees more young people interested in cats and, with this encouraging sign, the cat fancy in Canada looks forward eagerly to a great and growing future.

Part of a showroom at the Centennial Cat Club's show at the King Edward Hotel, Toronto, Canada.

The Cat Fancy in Europe

The fundamental difference between the British and the European Cat Fancies is that, whereas the former is solidly united under its Governing Council, the latter is divided into a considerable number of independent bodies, of which the largest, the Fédération Internationale Féline de l'Europe, generally known as F.I.F.E., controls a total of about fifteen cat clubs operating in twelve different countries: Austria, Belgium, Czechoslovakia, Denmark, Finland, France, Germany, Holland, Italy, Norway, Sweden and Switzerland. Each of the F.I.F.E. clubs is entitled to send a delegate to the Annual General Meeting, which determines the overall policy of the organization and establishes basic rules of conduct. The member clubs in each country maintain their own register of cats and issue their own pedigree certificates, deriving a steady income from this activity; and all registration data is available to other F.I.F.E. clubs.

In addition, in Europe, there are a number of independent cat bodies, which for some reason or another have not seen eye to eye with the Fédération Internationale Féline de l'Europe, and have formed their own registering bodies and clubs, holding their own shows.

New clubs constantly arise in Britain; but on reaching maturity invariably apply for affiliation to the Governing Council one of the rules of which is that such affiliation may not unreasonably be withheld. Because of this, the British fancy is able to grow and develop under one leadership which has not been seriously challenged since the formation of the Governing Council in 1910.

The cat shows staged by the European fancy differ from the British in that they are invariably two-day affairs whilst shows in Britain are completed in one day. The principal reason for this difference is that in Europe, as in America, exhibitors often have to bring their cats over great distances to attend these events; and any attempt to compress a show into one day would inevitably impose great hardship and fatigue upon managements, exhibitors and cats alike.

Central to the well-being of every cat fancy is the degree of skill possessed by its judges. In Britain judges are appointed by the specialist clubs and their appointment is submitted to the Council for confirmation. The basis of selection is essentially breeding and stewarding experience coupled with an assessment by the specialist club committee of the candidate's temperamental suitability. The European fancy, like the American, adopts a different system for appointing judges. To begin with, all cats are divided into only two basic categories, the long-hairs and the short-hairs (including Siamese). To become a long-hair or a short-hair judge, one must not only possess a high degree of breeding and administrative experience but, in addition, successfully pass one or more stringent examinations in which the candidate is required to judge various classes of cat, and also answer a number of questions regarding the different varieties.

The Cat Fancy in Australia and New Zealand

Australia is a large, sparsely populated country and the cat fancy is somewhat scattered and widely distributed. A single fancy under the control of one central governing body, such as is known in England, does not exist; but rather a number of separate fancies, one at least, and in some cases more, to each state of the dominion, form a loosely-linked structure which represents the Australian world of pedigree cats.

Australia's cat fancy has developed over a long period and, because of isolation due to the great distances involved, has progressed in separate stages rather than as one unified whole. There are seven distinct areas – Queensland, New South Wales, Victoria, South Australia, West Australia and the Northern Territory, plus the island of Tasmania, each with a separate cat fancy and its own separate Cat Register, and ruled autonomously by its own separately constituted governing body. The only connection between each one is that of agreement and recognition. Despite the situation, the system of registration, show organization and judging are remarkably uniform, due no doubt to the fact that they have been based on the English systems from the beginning. The organizations linked under these arrangements are: R.A.S. Consultative Committee of New South Wales, R.A.S. Feline Control Council of Victoria, The Consultative Committee of the Cat Fancy of South Australia, R.A.S. Feline Control Council of West Australia, The Cat Association of the Northern Territory, Council of Federated Cat Clubs of Queensland and R.A.S. Cat Control Council of Tasmania.

In New South Wales, Victoria, West Australia and Tasmania, the Royal Agricultural Society governs the Cat Fancies, but in Queensland, Northern Territory and South Australia, the fancies are still under the control of privately operated councils, selection of representation being by election, nomination or appointment.

Warana Silver Nutmeg was a Tabby-point Siamese well known to all Tabby-point fanciers. He was bred and owned by Mrs Batten and Mrs Gillingham of Queensland.

Cat clubs flourish in each state and are affiliated to or controlled by their particular governing body. The show scene is a busy one which, in some cases, extends over the full twelve months, and many clubs hold two or even three championship shows in a season. The shows are run in accordance with the rules laid down by the controlling body in each state, but in fact differ in only very slight degrees from state to state. The size of an average Australian cat show would vary from between 200 to 300 cats, although one annual show in Sydney, N.S.W. benches close on 1,000 cats.

All cats must be examined by a qualified veterinary surgeon before benching and each cat is exhibited in a numbered cage. The judges, attended by one or more stewards, must remove each cat from its cage in order to judge it, and the decision of the judge is final. Challenge certificates are awarded to open class winners and, in most states, the winner of three Challenges, awarded by three different judges, becomes a Champion. New South Wales awards Challenges, but calculates its Champions on a point system. The English Standard of Points for judging is used in the majority of states, in some cases a minor adjustment being made to suit the particular circumstances. No sub-register exhibit (i.e. an experimentally bred variety which has not yet achieved four generations of registered breeding) may compete in the fully-registered classes or for Best in Show, special sub-register classes being provided. Challenges are not awarded to sub-register cats.

Australian judges must attend a definite training course and pass a stringent examination on all aspects of judging before being appointed to a judges' panel. Each state provides a panel of accredited judges who, on the whole, are recognized interstate and who, on occasion, are invited to officiate at shows conducted in states other than their own. The interchange of judges between states, considering the distance involved, the time consumed and expenses incurred, is fairly regular. This, more than anything else, is helping to establish a uniform standard of breeding and judging on an overall Australian basis. The difficulties of communication, which were most apparent thirty or forty years ago, are now no longer of such importance. Air travel has reduced distance to a minimum and it is not unusual for a judge to travel the 2,500-odd miles from Melbourne in the south to Darwin in the north, or from Brisbane in the east to Perth in the west, just to officiate at a one-day show. Similarly, cats are flown thousands of miles to be mated to chosen studs, and the interstate entries at every show are on the increase. Distance no longer holds our cat fancy back, but it must be admitted that it does still slow it down.

The pedigree cat fancy embraces a wide range of varieties. As far as long-hair and "foreign" short-hair breeds are concerned, all those recognized in England, with the exception of the Van cat, are represented somewhere on the Australian scene. The British Short-hair, however, is sadly lacking representation.

Despite a varied climate, Australia is an ideal place in which to breed cats. Of course, one does not expect the long-hairs to be "in coat" for extensive periods, especially in the north, where the Siamese point-colour development is also affected by the tropical climate. However, in most parts of the continent, the cat thrives in natural conditions. Long-hairs were the first to make their appearance in this country, followed considerably later by the Siamese which have been gaining in numbers and popularity ever since. Over the last thirteen or fourteen years, the other "foreign" short-hairs have been gradually introduced, the Burmese especially proving a very popular variety.

Today, Seal-point Siamese easily predominate over all other breeds. Blue-points, Chocolate- and Lilac-points share practically equal honours, with the delightful Tabby-points gaining ground rapidly. The Red- and Tortie-points appear only in small numbers. Tabby-point Siamese were first developed by experimental breeding in Australia in early 1962, and six generations of purely Australian breeding have now been produced. Good type is not limited to any one colour. There are some outstanding specimens amongst Seal- and Blue-points and, quite often, one comes across a noteworthy Chocolate- or Lilac-point exhibit. The new colours, Tabby-, Red- and Tortie-point on occasion also excel in startlingly beautiful type and colour. The standard of Brown and Blue Burmese is very high in most states, while the Abyssinians are improving in type and colour as their numbers increase. Russian Blues, though few in number, are of very attractive appearance, and the few Rex on the benches are proving to be most attractive to the public. The Korats are an interesting breed, while the few Havana Browns to be found are of fine type.

Among the long-hair breeds, the Blues and Creams are outstanding for their excellent type, while some very good Orange-eyed Whites and Torties are also making their appearance. Blue-creams are mostly of good type, though failing in colour, and the Chinchillas, though not achieving the head type of the Blues, are of good substance and delightful colour on the whole. There is little interest today in the Blacks and the Smokes, and Brown Tabbies are equally rare. There are a few well-marked, richly coloured Red Tabbies shown and, on occasion, one comes across a very pleasing Self Red. Shaded Silvers are accepted in Australia, and Cameos are being developed. Colour-points and Birmans are only represented in a small way as yet. It would be useless and unfair to attempt to deal with the qualities of individual cats in Australia. Though interstate competition is increasing, some of our best exhibits only compete within the boundaries of their own particular fancy, and so never come into competition with one another.

Australia's pedigreed cats have been developed from the English bloodlines imported direct from the U.K., or by way of New Zealand. Australian quarantine laws are very rigid and only permit the importation of stock from these two regions. Our best long-hairs still come almost directly from imported stock, while many Siamese and some Burmese and Abyssinians of outstanding quality can now count many generations of Australian breeding in their pedigrees. With the rarer breeds, there are not yet enough bloodlines available for any extensive self-contained breeding programmes, the importation of out-cross lines still being necessary, but as far as the Siamese are concerned, used wisely, these Australian bloodlines should continue to produce cats of high quality and stamina. Over the last ten years, cat breeding in this country has taken on a new aspect. With the increasing spread of information on cat genetics, fanciers have become more aware of the various factors involved, and so are approaching their problems with a greater amount of knowledge of the subject. They are finding that, sometimes, the solutions can and do lie in their own hands, and that it is he who plans, investigates and anticipates who produces the most satisfactory results. Hence the pronounced upsurge of interest in scientific and selective breeding, and this can only be of advantage to the future of Australia's growing cat fancy.

Both islands of New Zealand support a very active cat fancy, coming under the control of one central council; the Governing Council of the Cat Fancy of New Zealand. The rules of registration, breeding and showing are broadly similar to those of Australia.

The largest show to be held in New Zealand is the National Cat Show, which is sponsored by a pet foods firm and is conducted by a different club in a different city each year. Here the cream of New Zealand's cats are benched, resulting in an entry of well over 600 exhibits of all breeds.

New Zealand's long-hair cats easily excel in type and colour and she can boast of some magnificent Creams, Blue-creams, Blues, Orange-eyed Whites, Chinchillas and Torties, mostly from bloodlines imported from the U.K. Some have been exported to Australia to enhance that country's long-hair fancy.

There are no quarantine restrictions governing the export of New Zealand cats to Australia nor cats from the southern states of Australia to New Zealand. Hence there is a very free exchange of cats, mostly by air, across the Tasman Sea which separates the two countries. Most of the short-hair varieties are to be found on the New Zealand show benches; some of outstanding excellence and some, as with most other fancies, of moderate quality. Some particularly impressive Foreign Whites are being developed in this country at the moment.

A contemporary New Zealand-bred Foreign White Short-hair, Ourlynn Apollo, owned and bred by Miss L. Moran.

The Cat Fancy in South Africa

The cat fancy in South Africa is now very well established with most of the accepted breeds represented and of good type. Over the past few years, many animals have been imported from England, America and the Continent of Europe, and these have helped to up-grade the stock previously imported when the fancy got into its stride in the early 1950's. Most of the earlier imports came from England and were chiefly Siamese and Burmese, but from 1960 onwards, other breeds came to the fore, including Abyssinians, various coloured long-hairs, Russian Blues and, from the United States, the Korats. The increased interest in cats has been most noticeable since 1964 when the number of registrations, transfers and entries in shows showed a considerable upward trend, which has been maintained and increased annually.

The Standard of Points used in South Africa is that in use in England, and the show rules have been based on the English show rules, with modifications, additions and amendments to suit South African conditions and requirements.

There are five clubs in South Africa, the Eastern Province Cat Club in Port Elizabeth, the Natal Cat Club in Durban, the Rand Cat Club and the Siamese Cat Society in Johannesburg, and the Western Province Cat Club in Cape Town. These five clubs formed the Governing Council of the Associated Cat Clubs of South Africa early in 1970. One delegate from each club and the registrar meet annually to discuss points, which effect show and registration rules chiefly, and to make any alterations to these which might be thought necessary. The clubs operate autonomously and the Governing Council is primarily a liaison body, the delegates carrying mandates only from their respective clubs for all matters except show rules; no resolutions can be carried without reference to all the clubs, and a majority agreement.

The South African Cat Register deals with all registrations and transfers in South Africa. A second register operated in Cape Town some years ago, under the title of the South African Cat Union, but it was ultimately agreed that with such a relatively small community interested in feline affairs, one register would be more workable and the present one came into being.

South African judges undergo a long and very thorough training course before being accepted. Lectures extend over long periods and oral and practical examinations terminate a course, with judges' reports being written. Newly-appointed judges only judge kitten and Any Other Variety classes for at least three shows; if, after this, they are considered suitable, they are permitted to judge the challenge classes. Specialist judges are not practical, because of the small number of people who are considered suitable for training as judges, so the course has to be very comprehensive.

Any newly-formed club wishing to become affiliated to the Associated Cat Clubs of South Africa has to conform to some very rigid rules before being accepted; for example, it must have organized three "match" meetings under Associated Cat Club show rules, using judges acceptable to that association. The membership figure must reach a specified number and the balance sheet must confirm that the club in question is in a financial position to be able to run a championship show.

As in most countries, the Siamese is by far the most popular breed in South Africa and, in that group, the Seal-point holds pride of place. All the other colours are seen in the shows, including the Tabby-point, which came to the fore very quickly and has been Best Siamese on Show. Other very popular breeds are the Brown Burmese (which seems to have the edge on its blue brother), the normal and Red Abyssinian, which increase in number consistently, and Russian Blue, which is having a difficult journey towards popularity. Long-hairs of all colours are here, but their numbers are limited, as are the numbers of their breeders. Few people have the time now to devote to a breed which needs considerable care and attention. A pair of Birman arrived from the States in 1968, and have made their mark with their offspring. Colourpoints were lagging behind, but the 1970 show season produced several. Tabbies, both long- and short-haired, are few and far between, but a few long-haired tabbies have been seen, as have some long-haired Torties and Tortie-and-Whites. Bi-coloured and Turkish Van Cats have yet to make their appearance. Korats have been in South Africa for several years, but have been dogged by misfortune. New stock has now been imported from America and is stimulating interest again in this very lovely breed. A South African breed number was given to the Korat soon after its original importation.

The Rex has also had a very slow start here, chiefly due to few being imported after the first two arrived, but this has also been overcome and, as with the Korat, it is hoped to see increasing exhibits of this breed in the future. Havanas have recently appeared, an import from Rhodesia assisting here, together with a pair from England. Experimental breeding has been carried out with Self-Lilacs and these usually constitute the majority of the exhibits in the A.O.V. classes.

The cat fancy in South Africa is still very much of a hobby. Club membership subscriptions are very reasonable and all jobs connected with running the clubs and shows are carried out entirely voluntarily by club members. Show managers and judges are usually members of the club organizing the show, with visiting judges sometimes invited from other provinces. The clubs all own their own cages, trollies etc. and do all the physical work involved in setting up a show. Exhibits from long distances are met at airports, boarded, benched and returned to their owners by members of the club concerned. Distances between the venues are long, from 370 to 1,000 miles, and air transport is the order of the day for exhibits and owners alike in most instances. Six Championship shows are held annually, two in Cape Town, two in Johannesburg, one in Durban and one in Port Elizabeth. It is possible for South African cats to be shown on the Rhodesian shows and vice versa, but, as rabies regulations do not make this easy, it does not happen very frequently.

Cat Shows
Cat Shows in Britain
Organization

Although cat shows in Britain are one-day events, running one involves work spread over a period of more than a year.

The Governing Council of the Cat Fancy has ruled that no cat shall be shown twice within fourteen days, which means that clubs are anxious not to stage their annual show within fourteen days of another, particularly if the location is not far distant. Application for a licence must be lodged with the G.C.C.F. in September of each year for the season starting the following June, giving the name of the show manager, who must have had some previous experience, either by running a show or by acting as assistant show manager.

Prior to application for a licence, a suitable hall and the show-pens should be provisionally booked. Failure to do this may result in a date being granted and the hall and/or pens being unavailable. It is also wise to engage judges beforehand, depending on how early in the show season the show is to be held. Although not a G.C.C.F. rule, it is generally accepted that judges should not judge the same breed more than once during the season, except as an emergency when one judge is unable to fulfil an engagement, or if the two shows concerned are widely spaced in time and geographical position. Engaging judges for an all-breed show can be rather like doing a jig-saw puzzle by post. Each judge should be able to handle about eighty cats during the day, but a lower number is preferable if finances will allow. One has to estimate very roughly the number of judges required, bearing in mind that each exhibit may be entered in up to twelve classes, although the average is probably about five or six. A number of veterinary surgeons must be engaged to examine the cats on arrival, and one to be "on call" in the hall throughout the day. One vet for every hundred cats is reasonable.

The show manager then prepares a "support" letter for circulation to all club members, secretaries of all the cat clubs, possible advertisers and anyone likely to support the show. This letter invites other clubs to guarantee classes for their members, which are included in the schedule, and which only members of that club may enter. In the event of these classes involving the show management in financial loss, the club concerned pays the difference between entry fees received and prize money paid. Other means of support are special prizes, advertising in the show catalogue, etc.

In compiling the schedule, much thought goes into allocating the various miscellaneous and club classes to the judges already engaged for the important breed or "open" classes, to ensure that the same cat is not judged by the same judge in too many classes. In the front of the schedule will appear such details as the list of judges, veterinary surgeons, various rules and regulations together with abbreviations used and definition of classes. Club classes should, if possible, be in alphabetical order, preceded by the club sponsoring the show.

At the end of the actual schedule of classes, are listed the "club specials" and "open specials". The former are usually trophies and/or rosettes offered by clubs to their members for outstanding successes, or points trophies to be competed for at all shows throughout the season. The open specials are those given by individuals, or firms, for a specific win.

Copy having been despatched to the printer, together with an order for entry forms and copies of the G.C.C.F. rules, envelopes will be prepared for the schedules. At this point, the show should be advertised so that intending exhibitors may apply for a copy of the schedule. It is usual to send one to all club members, all exhibitors at the previous year's show and all club secretaries supporting the show. They should be sent out about two months before the show, closing date for entries being about five to six weeks before the day.

The wise show manager will have been attending to as many arrangements as possible beforehand. Judges must have a copy of the schedule, together with a note for them to return, stating whether or not they will require overnight hotel accommodation, who will be acting as steward for them, or whether they wish the show manager to engage someone. Catering arrangements can be put in hand. Some of the work can be delegated to members of the club's show committee, but it is wise to remember that it is the show manager who will be held responsible for the smooth running of the show.

A certain amount of knowledge of book-keeping is most useful. Accounts must be carefully kept, entering each item under appropriate headings – advertisements, entry fees, benching fees, donations, club subscriptions, etc., ending with Total and Bank. A petty cash and post book is also required.

Quite a number of exhibitors make mistakes when completing entry forms, so each must be checked for errors and omissions, the exhibitor concerned advised, and the entry form put on one side until the correct information is received.

Probably each show manager has his or her own way of compiling the catalogue, possibly evolved over many years' experience. A large book for this purpose can be obtained from the printer specializing in cat fancy printing if it is preferred to do the work by hand. However, if the show manager is a reasonably efficient typist, the work can be done much quicker. The entry forms should now be arranged in numerical order of classes, where several cats are entered, treating the lowest class number as the index. The open classes can now be typed, with a carbon copy for the printer, using a separate sheet of paper for each class so that further entries may be added if required. The miscellaneous and club classes can also be drafted at this point, either by card index system, or by entering by hand on a "loose leaf" system to be typed later. The latter system works very efficiently and avoids the necessity of a large number of cards. If care is taken to leave sufficient space between each group in relation to the open class numbers, so that more may be added in the appropriate position if necessary, the exhibit numbers will automatically be in the right order.

Once entries have finally closed, the exhibits can be numbered. Side classes can now be typed, referring back to the open classes for exhibit numbers and any side classes which are too large may be split, by age, sex or colour.

Having completed the actual catalogue of cats, the names and

This is the ideal way to take your exhibits to a show.

298

The National Cat Club's annual show at Olympia, London; this is Britain's largest show, attracting entries of some 2,000 cats.

addresses, with exhibit numbers, of all exhibitors must be prepared for the alphabetical index at the back of the catalogue.

When the catalogue copy has been despatched to the printer, the next task is to prepare vetting-in slips, pass-out slips and tallies to be sent to each exhibitor. A list of the pens required, and, if necessary, a detailed plan of the hall showing the layout required, not forgetting double pens, must be sent to the firm engaged for penning. Best-in-Show pens and a sick bay of about six pens must not be forgotten.

Judging books must also be prepared, preferably in good time so that time and care can be taken over this important task. The number of each exhibit is entered in triplicate, well spaced to allow the judge plenty of space for notes. After the open classes are entered, side class numbers must be checked for repeats, which are bracketed on the section retained by the judge, so that she knows immediately that this cat has already been judged in a previous class. At the back of the book the numbers of any special prizes which must be awarded by the judge are entered, again in triplicate.

In the weeks immediately preceding the show, there will be many small details to be dealt with which add to the smooth running of the show. Small items for use of judges, stewards and workers, such as Best-in-Show nomination cards, staplers, drawing pins, etc., should be collected and the sundry helpers for the day appointed. Publicity is well in mind at this time; a good "gate" can make the difference between a profit and loss. Although cat shows are not organized with a view to making money, it is encouraging to everyone concerned if there is a small margin of profit. Contacts in the world of radio, television and the local press are most useful.

The day before the show is a busy one for the show committee and all the helpers one can muster. The hall has to be prepared, all the equipment transported and everything arranged for an early start the next day. The general appearance of the show will be much improved if the benches are draped with material to hide the exhibitors' miscellanea stored under the pens. Any last minute emergencies have to be dealt with – the one most dreaded by show managers is having to find a replacement for a judge, not always easy at short notice and often entailing long and frustrating telephone calls.

At last the day dawns. Exhibitors start to queue, waiting for the veterinary surgeons' arrival and the doors to open. Inevitably, there will be queries to answer, tallies to be provided for exhibitors who have left theirs at home and a hundred and one calls upon the show manager's time. The vets and their stewards cope with the chattering exhibitors and their cats, two helpers checking the numbers of the exhibits as they arrive and noting any absentees. Judges arrive and are shown to the room allocated to them, stewards prepare the judges' tables, etc., and the exhibitors settle their cats in the pens.

At around ten o'clock, when judging is scheduled to begin, the show manager asks all exhibitors to leave the hall and for about two hours, peace reigns, while the judges concentrate on the important task of judging the open classes. The team of volunteers start the work of recording the results, marking prize cards and catalogues and fixing results on the award board, which will go on all day. At midday the show is opened to the public; the crowds in the aisles make the judging much more difficult, but judges and stewards cheerfully battle their way through to the exhibits.

The highlight of the day is the "Best in Show" judging. Each judge nominates his or her best cat, kitten and neuter, which must be an open class winner. These cats are taken up to the platform to be judged by a panel of three or five judges who decide, by vote, which is the best of each section. Senior judges are usually chosen for this and there are separate panels for long-haired, short-haired and Siamese. The winning cats are then placed in the Best in Show pens, usually suitably decorated with coloured-curtains and cushion and a rosette. These are the cats the press are usually most interested in and proud owners pose with their, usually, nonchalant exhibits. At last the exhibitors pack their cats and prize cards. The hardworking show committee and helpers survey the chaos. The show is over – but not the work; there is money to be checked and banked, wet towels and drapes to be laundered, bowls to be washed, a conglomeration of things thrown together in boxes to be sorted. Marked catalogues have to be sent to the G.C.C.F. for the registrars to check the details of the winning cats with their registration details. A list of cats winning challenge certificates, together with the names of their owners and the judges awarding the certificates, must also be sent to the G.C.C.F.

Catalogues must now be marked for the secretaries of the various clubs supporting the show and accounts for losses on guaranteed classes sent to them. Accounts to advertisers, and stallholders must be sent, judges' expenses and other outgoings paid. Once the registrars have checked the catalogue, prize money may be paid out, working systematically through the catalogue checking each cat in all its classes. Details must be entered in the show accounts, cheques made out and posted. By the time this is finished it is probably eight weeks after the show and the final work of collecting outstanding accounts and paying the last bills must be done. At last the accounts can be balanced and handed to the auditors – and the show manager can start the preliminary work on the next year's show!

Judging

To be a judge is a great responsibility; you have to be fearless and honest at all times; all breeds are beautiful and, in mixed classes, always try to place the exhibits in order of merit, whatever breed they are; do not think that your speciality is automatically the best in the class. No matter how conversant with the various breeds, a judge should, at all times, carry her *Standards of Points*.

Having arrived at the show hall and collected the judging book or books from the steward, it is advisable for the judge to check these against the classes which have been allocated to her in the schedule. Go carefully through the book and make sure that all repeats have been ringed and that, at the bottom of each page, it says either "end of class" or "continued over". Look and see how many prizes you are allowed to award – in some large classes the show manager may grant as many as five or six prizes. If you feel that some exhibits are so even in quality you wish to award, say, an extra third, never do so until you have contacted the show manager. A judge must be absolutely conversant with the rules.

Before handling each exhibit a judge should always cleanse her hands; this is most important as not only can a germ be passed from one cat to another, but when handling the males, a certain smell can be detected which, in some cases, makes the next exhibit very difficult to handle. The first thing to do, when the steward hands you an exhibit, is to run the fingers carefully down the tail to see if there is a kink or defect; if a defect is found, the exhibit will be downgraded. Check also for good grooming, cleanliness, absence of powder in coat,

Smoke and Brown Tabby kittens on exhibition. Bred and owned by Miss V. Rolls.

etc., before going on to assess type, body shape, coat colour, texture, pattern and so on.

You must be extremely careful, having dealt with one class and made your awards, to see that in following classes you do not cross-judge: if, say, you place exhibit number six over exhibit number twelve in one class, do not place exhibit number twelve over exhibit number six if they meet again in another class. The steward should also watch out for this.

When all the open classes have been judged it is a good idea to go through them to see which of the winners you wish to nominate for Best in Show awards; each judge is only allowed to nominate one adult, one kitten and one neuter. Enter the numbers of your selections at the back of your judging book and when you have finished all your classes go round and make sure that the numbers you have earmarked are the ones you finally wish to nominate. Sometimes it happens that none of the exhibits you have judged in the open classes are worthy of nomination; you may have had an outstanding cat or kitten in a side or club class; if it has won in its open class and has not been nominated by the open class judge of that breed, you may nominate it instead. Some clubs are now awarding "Best of Breed" instead of "Best in Show".

When all the individual classes have been judged, there is the Best in Show to be dealt with. The ideal Best in Show panel consists of five judges all of whom should be on more than one judging list and should have been judging frequently; the selection of judges to be included on the Best in Show panel is, of course, in the hands of the show committee. If you should be selected for such a panel, always remember that this judging should be conducted in silence, as any comments made by one judge may influence the decision of the others. The voting is carried out by a secret paper ballot, the winner being selected by a simple majority. Should there be a tie, the Referee Judge is called in and her decision is final.

When you accept an invitation to judge it is acknowledged that you also accept the responsibility of sending in to *Fur and Feather* a report on the 1st, 2nd and 3rd and Reserve winners in all your open and side classes; it behoves a judge, therefore, to make sure that the notes she makes in her judging book are understandable enough for her to do this. It also helps her to give a logical reason to any exhibitor who may approach to find out why an exhibit was placed, say, third in the class instead of first or second.

Becoming a Judge

It takes years of experience in stewarding, breeding and exhibiting before one is qualified to become a judge; even then, one either has an eye for a cat or one has not. Nevertheless you can learn a lot by making your own assessments as though actually judging, and comparing these with the official results. Do not worry if your conclusions are different, as it is really impossible to assess a cat without handling it.

The most important first step is to get as much stewarding in as possible. Some judges are not very communicative with their stewards but most will readily explain their placings. When handling the cats place them in your own mind and see how you compare with the judge's placings. Breeding and exhibiting your own line of any particular breed is, of course, very instructive, as you naturally study the good points of your own exhibits before deciding in which classes to enter them. Obtain a G.C.C.F. *Standard of Points* and study it very carefully as, when you are going through your training, you will find in the side and club classes that you will have many different breeds to judge; you must be conversant not only with your own breed of cats, but all the other varieties as well.

People are officially put forward for appointment as a judge by the specialist breed clubs, which all have their own rules and methods. The various Siamese clubs, for instance, have formed a central committee to deal with Siamese judges as a whole, so that a person when appointed can judge all varieties. In other cases details of stewarding and breeding experience are submitted; sometimes names are voted on in a paper ballot by the club's committee; names always require a proposer and seconder.

The name of a person thus selected is then submitted by the club to a full meeting of the G.C.C.F. for approval.

Many clubs require a person to serve a probationary period before becoming a fully-fledged judge, which involves the judging of kitten classes at three different shows.

Stewarding

A steward's duties are all-important to a judge. First of all, the steward must get to the show hall well before the judge, to collect the judging book or books from the show manager together with the judge's and steward's badges, and see that lunch tickets for the judge and herself are provided. She must also see that a table, bowl, towel and disinfectant are available for the judge. She must at all times keep with the judge and see that her judge's classes are drawn up on a card showing each class number; as the judge makes her awards, the numbers of the winners – 1st, 2nd, 3rd, Reserve etc. – must be entered against each class. This is very important, as when the judge has to place the same exhibits in various classes, the steward can make sure there is no cross-judging (*see* Judging). It is also helpful to enter the numbers of any absentees on this card, so that if the judge has this number in a subsequent class, she can see at a glance that the exhibit in question is absent without having to go back to the pen.

When the hall is cleared and judging is ready to commence, the steward must take the judge's table and other paraphernalia to the pen of the first exhibit to be judged. She must remove the exhibit from its pen and either hand it to the judge or place it on the table for the judge to examine it; when the judge has finished, the steward then returns it to its pen. Do not get the next exhibit out until the judge has finished making her notes; wait until she asks for the next number to be taken out of its pen before doing so. When the judge has finished that class and marked her placings in her book she will sign the two slips, tear them out and hand them to the steward, who should then mark the awards on the card referred to above and then take the two slips up to the secretary's table; one slip will be fixed to the award board and the other to the master catalogue.

Another very important thing for a steward to learn is the handling

A steward holds a cat ready for inspection by a judge.

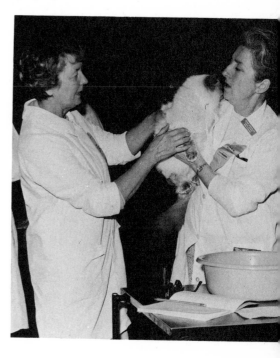

of the exhibits; if a steward is gentle with the cats and takes them out of the pen rear-end-first there should be no problem. Never drag a cat out of its pen head-first; it will only cling to its blanket and bring blanket and possibly sanitary tray out with it. The correct method is to put one hand under the cat's tummy and one hand on its back, turn it round and gently bring it from its pen. If you should be unfortunate enough to get an exhibit which, either through fright or plain bad temper, cannot be handled, do not try to drag it out of its pen by brute force. It is not fair to judge, steward or cat to force the issue; in fact the judge would undoubtedly mark in her book "c/n/h" (could not handle) and not let the steward make the attempt.

Remember the bowl and disinfectant; always see that the hands are washed and dried before each exhibit is taken from its pen – not only to safeguard each cat, but disinfecting the hands does take away any smell from another cat; they are very discerning where smells are concerned and this can make all the difference to an exhibit's temperament.

When the last class in the judge's book has been dealt with, the steward must make sure that the bowl, towel, disinfectant and table are taken back to the show manager, from whom she will collect a catalogue for her judge and one for herself. From this catalogue the judge will be able to mark off any special prizes appearing in her book.

A steward's duties are not by any means finished when the actual judging is over, as the Best in Show awards have still to be dealt with. Each steward is responsible for the exhibits nominated by her own particular judge; she must be on hand to bring them up to the Best in Show table when called upon to do so and wait to take them back to their pens when they have been judged. The cat in question should be taken out of its pen and placed in a basket for transport to the table; it is most unwise to attempt to carry the cat in one's arms, as there is usually a little delay when each exhibit has to be passed along for five judges to inspect it and a nervous cat could easily escape.

A steward should never speak to her judge or pass any comment about the judge's placings unless the judge invites her to do so. Many judges like to talk to their stewards to explain placings and this is very much to be commended; it must be very disheartening for a steward not to be spoken to, as one of the main reasons for anyone to take on a steward's arduous duties is to learn.

Although stewards are not prohibited from exhibiting at shows where they are stewarding, it is not very satisfactory for them to do so, as it is difficult for a steward to concentrate on the job in hand and not let attention wander to the award board to see how her own exhibit has fared. She is, however, not permitted to enter a cat in the open class judged by the judge for whom she is stewarding. Cat shows are getting larger and more exacting year by year and it is therefore most important that a judge has her steward's undivided attention throughout the day.

Good stewards are worth their weight in gold; their day is a long and arduous one with a lot of running about to do, but nevertheless very rewarding if one wants to learn. A judge will always ask a good and conscientious steward to help her again; word quickly gets around of a really first-class steward, who need never be short of engagements.

*Olde Calico's Chica-Boom, a Calico
Persian bred and owned by Mrs B.
Prendergast of Arkansas, U.S.A. The
variety known to most American fanciers
as the Calico is called Tortoiseshell and
White in Britain.*

*Below: Pathfinders Tangled Skein, Tor-
toiseshell and White Long-hair female,
bred and owned by Miss N. Woodifield.*

Above: Gr Ch Simbelair Felicia, an Odd-eyed White Persian, or Long-hair, female. Bred and owned in Canada by Mrs Lois Weston.

Opposite: Mrs M. Howes's female Orange-eyed White Long-hair, Honeymist Snowdream, aged seven months.

Left: Ch Bruton Snokat, a male Blue-eyed White Long-hair bred and owned by Mrs N. Rosell.

*Above: A Black male British Short-hair;
Mrs I. Johnson's Jezreel Murrey.*

*A Pensylva Blue queen and kitten, bred
and owned by Mrs J. Richards.*

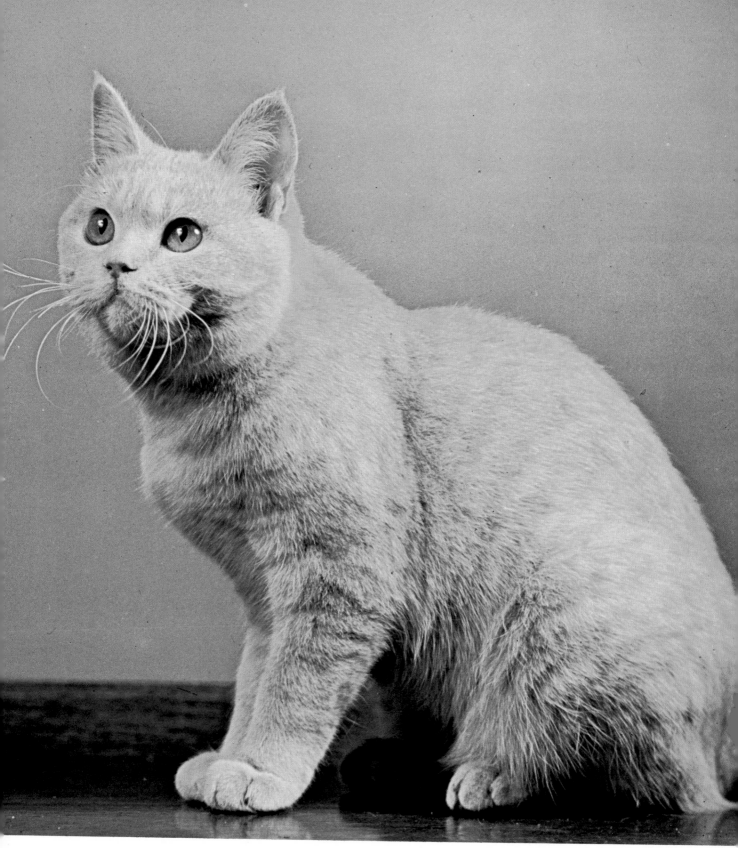

*Pensylva Fairy, a Cream British Short-
hair bred and owned by Mrs J. Richards.*

Pathfinders Mary (female) is a Short-haired Tortie and White. Owner and breeder: Miss N. Woodifield.

Opposite: A female Odd-eyed White British Short-hair—Mrs K. Butcher's Pansy Potter.

Left: Blue-pointed Siamese—Mrs H. Buttery's male, Taurus Kock-A-Leekie.

Opposite: Gr Ch Karnak Zapata, Seal-pointed Siamese male, bred and owned by Dr and Mrs Steven Karr of New York City.

Below: Craigiehilloch Chomarcus, a male Chocolate-point Siamese bred by Mrs D. Clarke and owned by Mrs N. Halliday.

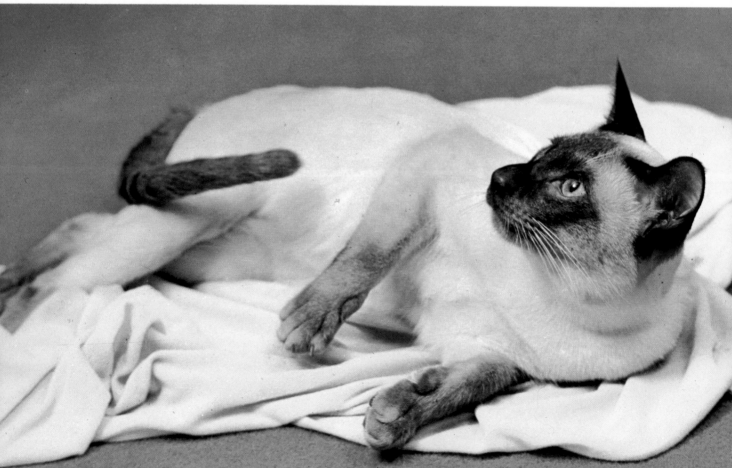

Lu-Chu Coppelia, a Seal-pointed female Siamese kitten bred by Mrs Y. Kite.

An American Lilac-point (or Frost-point) Siamese female, Double Gr Ch Li-Gon's Dacqueri, bred and owned by Fred and Charlotte Ligon.

Above: Catherston Caesar, a Red-point male Siamese kitten bred and owned by Mrs D. White.

A male Tabby-point Siamese, Gr Ch Seremban Liger, bred by Mrs A. Aslin. The Tabby-point is known as the Lynx-point in North America.

An American Short-hair, a Blue-eyed
White male owned by Muriel Slodden.

Opposite: Contented Bambino, a male
Abyssinian bred by Miss I. Wiseman.

Gr Ch Richmar Eric the Red, a Classic
Red Tabby American Short-hair male,
owned by Jim Shinkle of San Francisco.

Below: Contented Ras (male), Red
Abyssinian, bred by Miss I. Wiseman.

Mrs A. Ashford's male Cornish Rex, Ch Annelida Sundance Kid.

Below: Two Brown Burmese; Mrs P. A. Lloyd's "Gossip" (female), and Puss-in-Boots Willowisp (neutered female), bred by Mrs R. M. Pocock and owned by Mrs Lloyd.

Vetting-in

At shows held in Great Britain under the rules of the Governing Council of the Cat Fancy, all exhibits must be examined by a veterinary surgeon before being admitted to the show hall, as under G.C.C.F. rules, the veterinary surgeon must reject any exhibit which, in his opinion, is not fit to enter the show, whether on account of suspected infectious or contagious disease, which could be passed on to other exhibits, or because of any debilitating conditions. The veterinary surgeon must also disqualify any queen obviously in kitten, and any male adult which is either a monorchid or a crytorchid, i.e. with one or both testicles absent from the scrotum. (In North America, however, monorchids are accepted for showing.)

There are usually several veterinary surgeons on duty at the vetting-in, each having the assistance of a steward. The steward helps to take the cat out of the basket, holds it for veterinary examination, and deals with the vetting-in card, which will have been sent to the exhibitor about a week before the show. It shows the pen numbers and names of all the cats or kittens belonging to the exhibitor. At the vetting-in it must be handed to the steward who will tick the numbers, showing that the cat is present and has been passed by the veterinary surgeon. The exhibitor should present the cat in a suitable basket or container with simple but secure fastenings. Baskets tied up with string or boxes with padlocks take too long to open, and so hold up the queue of waiting exhibitors.

The veterinary surgeon examines the cat as thoroughly as possible, and is particularly looking for any symptoms of infectious or contagious disease. While the steward holds the cat, the veterinary surgeon examines firstly the head; looking at the eyes for conjunctivitus, weepiness or even a discharge of pus; any nasal discharge; the mouth, looking at gums, tongue and throat for any inflammation or ulcer formation. Next he feels the glands under the jaw and below the ears for signs of enlargement indicating an ear, nose or throat infection. Should the veterinary surgeon suspect a bacterial infection, he will take the cat's temperature and if this should be significantly raised, he will exclude the cat, and probably all others belonging to the exhibitor, from the show. The ears are then examined for any evidence of otodectic mange (ear canker). The coat is looked over for evidence of fleas, lice, mange or ringworm. While searching the coat, the veterinary surgeon is also running his hands gently over the cat's body, legs and tail, feeling for any abnormalities – such as a swelling indicating abscess formation.

If the exhibit is male then the scrotum must be felt to make sure that both testicles are present. If the abdomen of a female looks at all enlarged it must be palpated for pregnancy diagnosis, as pregnant queens may not be exhibited. The underside of the body is also looked at, particularly round the anus for signs of diarrhoea.

When all cats belonging to an exhibitor have been passed by the veterinary surgeon, they may then enter the show hall. If an exhibit fails to pass the veterinary inspection then it is disqualified from exhibition and must leave the hall immediately. If it is desirable in the opinion of the veterinary surgeon, all other exhibits from the same cattery and their owner shall be prohibited from entering the show.

Opposite: This little marmalade kitten has no pedigree, but makes a charming household pet.

Vetting-in: All exhibits must be examined before admission to the show.

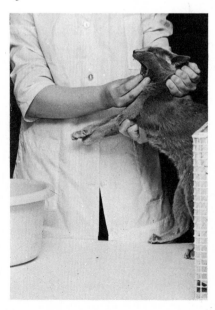

The veterinary surgeon must then give the reason for disqualification in writing to the show secretary as soon as possible.

During the show, the veterinary surgeon can be called to examine any exhibit which is suspected to be suffering from infectious or contagious disease, or which is unwell, for example suffering from heatstroke, exhibiting stress symptoms, or showing signs of having been given a sedative prior to the show. If necessary, he is empowered to have the cat removed from the show, either to be taken home or to be placed in the show's isolation pens. He may also be called to look at a cat whose coat has been improperly prepared for show. This includes cutting, dyeing or plucking the coat (apart from dead hairs), or leaving a substance such as powder in the coat.

A veterinary surgeon must, of course, also render first-aid to any cat in trouble, and frequently to the judges and stewards also!

The mere fact that there is a veterinary surgeon at shows is enough to deter an unscrupulous person from deliberately showing an infected cat. The argument against it is that there are practically always long queues at the vetting-in with the exhibits in close contact while waiting for their turn, and a sneezing cat could be spreading infection around before entry to the show. It may be that the cat world in Britain will follow the example of the Kennel Club and abolish vetting-in. If this were to happen, then I think it would be essential, in view of the highly infective nature of some cat diseases, for one or more veterinary surgeons to be present at the show at least until after all the open classes have been judged, so that each exhibit will have been seen by a judge who would report any suspicious cases. In North America, however, there are no thoughts of abolition at the present time. Although it is very disappointing to be barred from the show, exhibitors must remember that no veterinary surgeon likes to turn anyone out and will not do so unless circumstances warrant it. After all, it is easier to pass a cat than face an angry exhibitor!

If disqualification should turn out to be unfounded then the exhibitor must send a clearance certificate from his veterinary surgeon to the G.C.C.F. within fourteen days of the show. It quite often happens that the stress of a long journey produces symptoms such as inflamed eyes and a rise in temperature, which will cause a veterinary surgeon to debar the cat. Just being shut in a basket makes some cats sneeze, and miaowing all the way can cause an inflamed throat. Again, a cat may have been perfectly well when it left home and have developed an illness on the journey. In these cases, there is nothing for the honest exhibitor to be ashamed of in being rejected at a show.

Cat Shows in the U.S.A.

Organization

In the United States and Canada there are nine different show-sponsoring organizations, but with few exceptions (which we will mention later), all shows are conducted along much the same general lines. So, let me take you to a typical show, along with the cat which you would have "entered" by mail a month or two earlier.

At the showroom door, you'll be handed a card with your name, your cat's name and your cage number. With it will probably be a

Judging of Household Pets at a Houston, Texas, C.F.A. show in January 1972.

schedule showing the times your cat's various classes will be handled by each of the four judges. You will also buy a show catalogue, so you will know who else is there and who your neighbours are, and glance at it between chats with other cat people who are standing in line with you waiting to have their cats examined by the show veterinarian.

For its safety and your own comfort, your cat will be in the carrier in which you brought it from home. You will have arranged for your cat to have had its permanent feline enteritis (feline panleukopenia) shots at least two weeks before the show date. You'll have carefully clipped its claws, checked its ears for mites and its fur for fleas and fungus. If it's a girl, you'll be sure that she's not visibly pregnant. And, of course, you'll be absolutely certain that the cat is not sick and that there is no communicable disease of any kind in your cattery. For, if the veterinarian sees, or suspects, that any of these mentioned conditions exists, your little pride and joy will not be allowed beyond the examination table.

You passed! So now down to the cage that's been assigned to you. It's been steamed clean before being erected, but you'll give it another good cleaning before putting up the decorations you've brought with you. Some weeks before the show date, you bought yourself several yards of the material which most flatters your cat, and made it up into curtains to fit the back and sides of the 27 × 27 × 22-inch cage. You'll have a plush pile rug or thick Turkish towel to use in the bottom of the cage, and perhaps a favourite bed or cushion for your pet to rest on. You'll have given some thought to the colour of your decorations. They should be planned to bring out the full beauty of your cat. A Chinchilla or Shaded Silver, for instance, will have an emerald-green background; a Blue-eyed White, teal-blue; a Siamese, deeper blue. Cats are not judged in the pens, so decoration will have no effect on the results. The show committee will furnish you with litter pan, food, and water, but if you prefer to bring your own, that is perfectly acceptable.

Now that you're all set up, it won't be long before you'll notice activity at one or all the judging areas (there are usually four of them in various parts of the showroom). They consist of a table for the judge who will examine the cats there, one at a time. There are chairs for the judge and her clerk, and ten empty cages. Numbers will be put on these cages behind the judge's table, and the announcer will start calling out the numbers over the public address system.

When your cage number is called, you take your cat up to the judge's ring, put it in its cage as unobtrusively as possible, then join the other hopeful owners who are standing or sitting in front of the judge's stand. Watch how the judge carefully examines each cat and weighs every point, then marks up her sheet and begins placing the ribbons on the cages. This is the first judging – for colour wins against all the cats of its colour in the show, and if your cat doesn't get a blue ribbon of some kind, your troubles are over. You can sit down with the other spectators and enjoy the rest of the show. (Exception: once in a cat's age, a red ribbon winner does become Second Best in Show, but don't count on it).

If you do get Best of Colour, though, or Best Opposite Sex of Colour, or a first in your class, then you won't rest easy for quite a while. Your cat will be called up – if, as I'm assuming, it's a long-hair novice – for

Best or Best Opposite Sex Cat in Show, for Best and Best Opposite Sex in its colour division (its breed, if it's a short-hair), perhaps and, finally, if the judge rates it high enough, for Best, Second Best or Best Opposite Sex Cat in Show. For the novice, I should explain that if the best of classes being judged is a male, then the best of the females will be named "Best Opposite Sex". Often there are only two, instead of three, top cats, since it frequently happens that the judge decides that the second best cat in show is a cat of the opposite sex from the best cat. In this case, Second Best and Best Opposite Sex Cat are the same cat.

To try to simplify things, let us follow one judge and one ring as if it were one show unto itself. Actually, while this one show has been going on, five others (three applicable to your cat) have also been in progress, all more or less alike, and your cat has been called to appear in all of them on a time schedule which interweaves its four shows. Shortly after you've been turned down for a colour win in ring one, it's quite possible for you to go Best Cat in Show in ring two, and to make any wins the other judges decide on in the other two rings. The shows are completely independent of each other, and judges are not allowed to consult, or even to know what the other judges are doing. It has happened that cats have earned four Best Cat awards in one show; at others, every ring has had a different Best Cat – there's no telling. Except in the rare cases of a "sweep", it's only in the "Best of the Bests" shows, discussed later, that there is ever *one Really Best Cat*.

As you have gathered, cat shows are different in the United States and Canada from those in most other countries. They have been that way since they started in roughly the same form in 1899 at Chicago. In those early days of the fancy, cats of all breeds (but long-hairs mostly) were examined by one judge for bests of colour, breed, division and, finally, for Best of Show.

By about 1910, however, a long-hair division specialty show, such as Silver or Solid Colour, would occasionally be staged at the same time as an all-breed. They added interest, and in the late 1940's, when the short-hair breeds had grown in popularity in all associations, the most common type of show consisted of three rings; an all-breed under one judge, and a long-hair and a short-hair specialty under one different judge. This gave three possible titular "Best Cats", but the all-breed winner was usually considered to have earned the highest award. The formation of the American Cat Fanciers Association in 1955 changed all this. It introduced a two-all-breed/four-specialty arrangement under the name "quadruple show" (referring to the use of four judges – one for each all-breed, one for each pair of a long-hair and a short-hair specialty). Among the results were easier championships, more All-American and other seasonally awarded points – and *six* Best Cat trophies per show.

The "quad" show still reigns supreme in America. Once in a while there is a "double" show – the old-fashioned one-all-breed/two-specialty variety – and increasingly, especially in the Cat Fanciers Association, a new type of show called a Congress of Specialties is being scheduled by the larger-entry shows.

In the typical Congress, there are three long-hair specialties under three different judges and, under a separate judge, a series of specialties

View of one section of cage layout at the Houston C.F.A. show in January 1972— the largest-entry show ever held in America—756 entries.

325

for each long-hair breed and each Persian division. For short-hairs, there is the same show set-up under four other judges. Then a new judge is brought in to choose, from the Best Cats of all these shows, the best cat of all – the Best of the Bests – and its four runners-up. Recently, too, the American Cat Fanciers Association (despite the similarity in association names, there is no connection between them) has adopted a modified form of the "Congress", scheduling four all-short-hair and four all-long-hair specialties under eight judges, with a ninth judge choosing the Best of the Bests.

To return to the individual show rings, judging in America is still being handled in most shows almost as it has been for the past seventy years. Of the six sub-shows in the typical show, each has classes for adult whole cats labelled Novice, Open, Champion and Grand Champion, divided by sex, for each colour class. Cats who have never made an adult win of any kind are entered as Novices. Any who have made wins, but have not become Champions, are entered in the Open Class.

The Champion classes consist of cats who have earned four or more "winners" ribbons (for being the best cat of their own sex in the combined open and novice competition of their own colour).

Grand Champions earn their titles through mathematical systems varying with the association, but in most cases depending upon the number of other Champions defeated, and the earning of at least one "Best Cat" award.

Any whole registered cat of a recognized breed is eligible to earn credit toward these titles, and to go on to become Best Cat in Show, or to win the other high awards such as Second Best Cat, Best Opposite Sex Cat, Best or Opposite Sex Champion, Grand Champion or Novice.

There are usually completely separate shows for neutered and spayed cats (called "Alters" in America) along the same lines as those for whole cats. Household pet shows – for non-pedigreed cats judged solely on beauty and disposition – are popular in connection with championship shows, and there is almost always a series of kitten shows wherein Best of Colour, Best Opposite Sex of Colour, Best Kitten in the Show and Best Opposite Sex Kitten in Show are named.

In May 1972, the Cat Fanciers Association put into effect the provision that six winner's ribbons rather than four would be required for championships, and made mandatory a type of show they had been testing in which, instead of the previous Best and Best Opposite Sex Cats in all categories, there would be Bests and Second Bests only – sex would no longer be a factor at any point, except in the awarding of winners' ribbons, which is unchanged.

Some years ago, C.F.A. replaced the rather clumsy Best Cat, Second Best Cat, and Best Opposite Sex Cat in Show procedure by choosing instead five top cats from Best to Fifth Best with no regard for sex. Although none of the other associations have followed their lead, the non-sex arrangement has worked so well for C.F.A. that it now applies throughout and has become their only authorized form of show.

These recent changes seem to indicate that after seven decades of more-or-less mindless development aimed at providing bigger and better wins for the exhibitor, the American show may now be developing a disciplined approach toward the selection of a lesser number of top prize-winners per show, so that the judges can offer the exhibitor a clearer indication of the quality necessary to earn a truly meaningful Best Cat title.

Judging

One might think that with nine show-sanctioning bodies there would be nine different methods of judging and nine different standards of perfection for each breed of cat in North America. This, fortunately, is so only to a slight degree. Over the years cats which win in the shows of one association tend to win in others as well. Good cats are good cats, bad ones bad, regardless of where shown. The basic reason for this uniformity of results is that the nine standards, although they have some differences in terminology, are with only a few exceptions effectively identical. Procedures in judging cats, and methods of choosing judges do vary from association to association in some respects, but even here, the similarities are in most cases far more in evidence than the differences. Almost all associations, for example, require some basic qualifications and fairly extensive training from a candidate judge. In the Cat Fanciers Association, the largest organization, candidates must have had a cattery name registered with that association for five years, have been a club member active in the fancy for five years, and have bred at least one cat which has finished in the top five of a C.F.A. show. Training must have included successful experience as a clerk and several test sessions of handling cats in the ring under the guidance of approved judges. The applicant's advancement from trainee to apprentice, to approval-pending judge, to fully approved judge depends on the ratings given by her supervisors, and by the clubs where she has undergone her trials, and by her passing of a judging questionnaire, and is always subject to final approval by the Judging Chairman and the Executive Board of C.F.A.

The *American* Cat Fanciers Association (distinct from C.F.A.) the second largest association, has a somewhat similar system requiring five years of breeding, and the breeding of three champions. Their candidates must successfully attend a course at an A.C.F.A. judging school, and must satisfactorily complete a written judging examination. Their test judgings must cover every colour class and breed. Final approval is given by the Executive Board on the recommendation of the Judging Co-ordinator. In both associations, the normal procedure is first to earn approval as a specialty judge, then work – if the applicant desires – towards all-breed judge status.

Most of the other associations choose their judges under somewhat similar training patterns, modified in some cases to fit the fewer number of shows sponsored.

There are at present in America two judging methods: the written point-scoring system of A.C.F.A. wherein the judge furnishes the exhibitor a written report showing a point-evaluation of each show-significant quality of every cat; and the informal evaluation system used by all other associations whereby computations are made in the mind of the judge only. Results vary little, however, and although over the years a number of judges have changed from one association to another, few of them have found it necessary to make substantial adjustments.

There are also two different award systems: that of most associations in which Best and Best Opposite Sex cats are chosen for all colours and all class and division wins (Novice, Open, Champion, Grand Champion, Breed, Pattern, etc.); and that which became effective with C.F.A. on May 1st 1972 whereby the Opposite Sex Cat is disregarded, and only Best and Second Best are chosen in each category throughout the show.

Now, let's project ourselves, if we can, into the mind of a typical judge as she goes about her job in America. If she's an A.C.F.A. judge, her mechanics will be simplified by the fact that she has a total point-score written down for each cat as she's judged it, and comparisons will be used only to break ties. If she's a C.F.A. judge, sex will not concern her, except in awarding "winner's ribbons", but these two variations will not influence the general procedure which is the same throughout the American cat fancy. "Goodness", the judge might think as she takes a look at her first championship class which has been benched in the cages behind her, "there are certainly some fine Blue-eyed White Persians here. What good weight for its size, what fine muscle tone," she might reflect as she takes Number 27 from its cage and moves it to her table. "Is its skull just a bit too narrow, its body too rangy?" she might wonder as she feels its head and its bone structure. "Are the eyes round and widely spaced; are they clear and completely blue; are the ears small and well-positioned – towards the sides of the head rather than the top; is the fur clean and of good texture, standing away from the body; is the tail pure white and of proper medium length?"

These and dozens of similar questions will be intuitively asked of her fingers and eyes, and answered with – in an experienced judge – almost no indication to the observer of all that is going on. Many judges will show the audience, though, either by action or word, the better points of each cat, and, where it would serve a purpose to do so, some of the defects, but few in the audience will realise how much deft touches and sharp glances have told the judge. From all these first entries, the judge will choose her two top Blue-eyed White Persian Novices, and will have them remain in their judging cages. The others will be sent back to their own cages in the main area. Then the Blue-eyed White Opens will be brought up, and they will be judged exactly as the Novices. The two winning Opens will compete with the two winning Novices, and from these the judge will select the two cats to get "winner's ribbons" – the awards on which championships are based.

These two winners will remain on the stage while the Champions are judged for their two best, who stay also; then the Grand Champions – and from the six cats who remain, the judge will pick her two best cats of the Blue-eyed Whites. For every colour of every breed this same procedure will be followed.

On a "score sheet" the A.C.F.A. judges will maintain a mathematical record to show them which of their cats will be in the running for higher awards; and judges for the other associations will have accomplished much the same result by marking which of their cats (even, occasionally, some of which have been defeated for Best of Colour) should be considered for higher wins.

Then, using the score sheet, the judge will call up all those entries she considers in the running for Best Novice (and Second Best or Best Opposite Sex, as the case may be), and will choose the two she considers best. The same will happen for Best in Breed, pattern division, long-hair and short-hair divisions, the Novices, Opens, Champions, and Grand Champions; and then from these winners, the Best, and the Second Best, and (except in C.F.A.) the Best Opposite Sex Cat in Show are named. Although usually these awards go to a cat who was Best of Colour, this is not necessarily so except in the case of the Best Cat in Show. So long as a cat has been defeated only by the Best Cat it may aspire to some "final" honours. A Blue Persian Champion, for example, who was second in its colour class to the champion who became Best in Show, might now be named Second Best in Show if the judge believed him to be better than all but the Best Cat.

In most associations, the judge will award second and third ribbons in the colour classes, and will judge kitten classes and make awards much as she does for adults. There will also be a show (identical in form to the championship competition) for altered pure-bred cats, called, depending upon the association, alters, premiers, or neuters. And there will be in most shows a household-pet judging with awards going to the most beautiful cats regardless of their conformity to the show standards, and a show for pure-bred kittens.

There will be at least one clerk to assist the judge in scheduling her cats and in keeping her records. The title of "clerk" is given to the person handling most of the record keeping assigned to the steward in Great Britain. The judge in America, once a cat has been placed in the judging cage, is required to handle the cats without help from anyone unless the cat is particularly unruly, in which case the owner may be called. "Stewards" in America refers only to those who keep the judging areas and cages clean. The judge will work from a specially prepared book in which cats are identified by number only, and she will not see a catalogue nor will she converse with an exhibitor until the show is over. She will handle – depending on association – not more than 150 to 200 cats in one day, or from 300 to 400 in two. In most well-managed shows, her day will run from ten in the morning to six or seven in the evening, but, on occasion, shows have lasted well into the night, with twelve or even fourteen-hour days for the judges. Fortunately, such shows are becoming infrequent as methods of judging and of show management are being tightened up.

A judge may be called upon to handle only a short-hair show or a long-hair show, or a group of breed or colour specialty shows, but the usual assignment is either a complete all-breed show or one complete long-hair and one complete short-hair specialty show. Typically, four judges will have assignments at one show – two handling all-breed shows, two handling two specialties each – giving every cat there four chances for all awards open to it. Seldom do judges see identically, hence there may be as many as four or six *Best* Cats at one show. Confusing, but it does mean that few cats will go home without awards of some kind. And while each judge's authority is thus somewhat diluted, most Americans find that the four-judge system with its something for everyone, almost, and with no intense pressure on anyone, a highly workable and very pleasant arrangement.

Cat Shows in Europe

At the cat shows on the Continent of Europe, judging is carried on slightly differently from that at British shows, although a few are now adopting the procedure followed in Britain, whereby judges go to the pens. The shows range over one, two, or sometimes three days. As exhibitors travel long distances from all over Europe to attend these shows, it would be physically impossible for them to get to the show and back home in one day. None of the European shows have club classes, and only one or two have side classes, so the judges have far less work to do, although they probably handle more cats. As the exhibits emanate from many different countries, there are two kinds of honours to be won; firstly, the C.A.C. (Certificat d'Aptitude de Championnat) – three challenge certificates to be awarded by three different Judges, as in Britain; and secondly, the C.A.C.I.B. (Certificat d'Aptitude de Championnat International de Beauté – three challenge certificates to be awarded in three different countries, to make an International Champion – these classes are of course open only to full Champions.

As the judges, like the exhibits, come from many different countries, each judge has an interpreter at hand throughout the day, as well as a secretary and a steward. The method of judging varies slightly in each individual country, but in the main is as follows.

The judge is in a separate part of the hall, where a row of empty pens has been erected. The steward brings each exhibit to the judge who assesses its quality, makes notes and places it in one of the pens. When the class is finished, all the cats in that class can be seen at a glance and the judge can make her awards. The exhibits are then returned to the body of the hall and the pens disinfected ready for the next class.

At some shows the exhibits are brought to a judge in a separate part of the hall, but instead of making notes and remarks in a book, the judge has to write these out in triplicate on separate cards for each exhibit. One copy is attached to the pen, one copy goes to the club secretary, and one copy is retained by the judge. It behoves the judge, therefore, to be discreet in her comments as they are of course seen by the owners of the cats.

At all European shows, if possible, the judging is finished on the first day of the show, and on the second day the Best in Show is chosen and ALL award cards have to be checked and signed by the judge before they are attached to the cats' pens.

As the judges do not see the exhibits in their own pens it is permissible for these pens to be decorated; it is very interesting and attractive to see the exhibitors taking advantage of this concession, draping the pens with all the international rosettes, streamers and ribbons they have won at other shows.

The Cat in the Home

If you are thinking of buying a kitten for a pet, or for breeding, make your choice carefully, bearing in mind that ownership carries with it responsibility. Decide whether to have a pedigree or mongrel pet – if the former, allowing a female to have one or two litters a year can give a great deal of pleasure, as well as helping to cover expenses, as there is, these days, a steady demand for pedigree kittens. In addition, there is all the pleasure of having kittens in the house. Whatever your choice, get the best you can afford. If you are going to breed, pedigree stock is desirable, as non-pedigree kittens are not always easy to find a home for. Too many are abandoned as strays. If you just want a pet, one that is not technically up to show standard will be less expensive than a near-perfect, likely future champion. If you are not interested in breeding, bear in mind that your kittens should be neutered, if a male, or spayed if a female. You may be given a non-pedigree cat, or see a kitten you take a fancy to in a pet shop, in which case ensure that the shop has a good reputation and the animals for sale seem lively and well cared for.

The different pedigree breeds have different characteristics, which should be born in mind when you are choosing your pet. For example, the Abyssinian is very active, disliking being confined to rooms and should be allowed plenty of exercise. They do best in the country, although because of their coat colouring they face a real hazard of being shot in mistake for rabbits! Rex make excellent pets; they give their owners a dog-like devotion and have a "small" voice, which may be important if you live in an apartment with neighbours close by. The Cornish type usually have thicker coats, but the Devon has the

Below left: How to hold a pregnant queen.

Below right: Holding a "difficult" cat.

Using a toilet-tray. A kitten must have a tray small enough for it to use easily.

Better than your furniture—a scratching post made of rough, but unsplintery wood.

cute pixie-like expression which appeals to many people. All cats, however, need as much space as possible, and should not be over-crowded or they will not do well; unlike dogs, they do not have the herd instinct, and unless brought up together, may really dislike one another. If you already have adults, and wish to introduce another cat, try a kitten; after a short time adult cats will accept it, but it is a difficult and tiring job to fit in an adult cat. In fact, it may never settle in at all; although there are exceptions, they are rare. When you are introducing the new arrival, take care not to make an older pet jealous by making too much of a fuss over the newcomer in front of it; do not leave a lively puppy and a kitten alone together, as they may injure one another in play. Do not keep picking up your new kitten, despite the temptation to do so, as cats do not like being fussed excessively. If you do pick it up, be sure to hold it correctly – not by the nape of the neck (mother cats only pick up their kittens in this way when they are still very small), but in the way shown in the illustration. Be careful not to squeeze young kittens, or to allow children to do so, as its bones will still be rather soft, and permanent damage is easily caused.

Your kitten should be house-trained when it arrives, and so it will probably be used to the idea of an indoor toilet-tray. But in due course, it will be able to go into the garden by itself when the need arises, unless you live in a flat, in which case an indoor tray will always have to be provided. Be firm with your kitten, but do not smack it if it has an accident on the carpet, this will simply make it frightened of you. Always provide more than one sanitary tray for kittens; as they will need to use them frequently they must be cleaned often as cats and kittens will not use dirty trays and will find other places. The tray must be of a size easy for a small kitten to get in and out. Newspaper can be used in a tray, or cat litter which can be bought at pet shops. It is better to have a special bin for used litter; put it in a plastic bag and seal it up, and it can then be put in the dustbin. If peat is used, this can be put on the compost heap; treated with a little of the chemical used to break down the compost, it will be very good for the garden. Do not burn the used litter as the smell is very unpleasant and you will be very unpopular with the neighbours. House-training is generally quite straightforward with cats in the country – if the cat is let outdoors at intervals, it will soon learn not to misbehave in the house.

A scratching post is a necessity and will save your furniture – use a piece of rough but not splintery wood, or purchase a ready-made one from a pet shop. Energetic play will give your cat exercise, but do not give it soft rubber toys, or anything made of plastic, paper, chicken, rabbit or chop bones, as these materials can be very dangerous if swallowed.

If your cat has to spend its time indoors, arrange to have a wire-netting window frame or frames made, so that the windows can be opened in good weather, especially in a sunny room. If your pet can have the use of a garden, wire a part of it in if possible. Cats and kittens are inquisitive by nature, and will stray. Too many cats are killed on the roads, and in many areas the number of stolen cats is increasing – so safeguard your pet.

If you are out all day, it is a good idea to have two kittens; they will be company for one another and will thrive better if not bored or lonely. It is better not to take kittens until at least ten weeks old, unless you can be around all the time to see that they get at least four small meals daily. It is not a good plan to leave a plateful of food in the morning to last until the evening, as the kittens will invariably eat it up at once, and will be very hungry by the end of the day. They will then bolt their evening meal, setting up indigestion and probably sickness, and they can become quite ill very quickly.

Brush and comb your kitten or cat daily; this is particularly important with long-hairs. It is not only necessary in order to keep the coat free from fleas, but cats really enjoy their grooming. As they are fundamentally very clean, they can become anaemic and miserable if kept in dirty or overcrowded conditions. With long-haired kittens, also, an early start is desirable to train the coat to lie the right way, as well as to get the animal used to being handled. Use a bristle brush, as anything stiffer, such as wire or plastic, will tend to pull out the hairs. A wide-toothed steel comb is useful for general grooming of long-haired cats, as well as a closer-toothed flea comb. It does no harm to give short-haired cats a daily brush and hard stroking with the hand. Remember to wipe any dust from your cat's ears, and dirt from the corners of the eyes. Make sure there are no fleas or any sign of worms.

Some owners believe in bathing their cats – and sometimes this is the only way to get a cat clean, particularly if it has oil or grease on its coat. There are special shampoos available; detergents and medicated soap should be avoided. Cats do not normally enjoy being bathed;

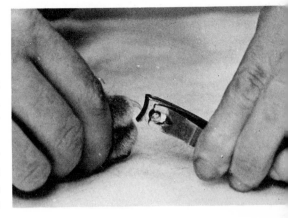

Clipping claws.

Grooming is important. Processes involved —below left: Grooming a long-haired cat; below: Grooming a short-haired cat; bottom: Using a fine-tooth comb.

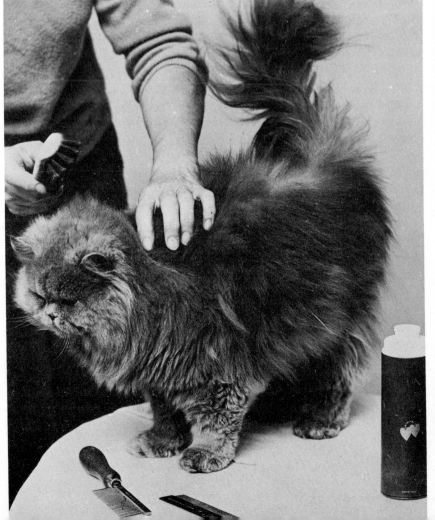

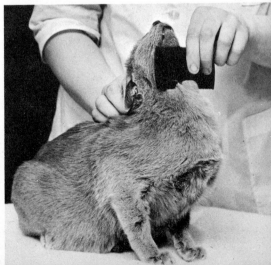

care must be taken not to alarm them. The kitchen sink is the best place, with an inch or two of warm water. After the cat is dampened all over, gently rub in the shampoo, taking care to avoid the eyes and ears. Rinse several times until the fur is quite free of lather, and then give a quick rub with a rough towel. A hair-dryer can be useful for the final drying if the cat is not frightened by it. In any case, keep your cat out of draughts, and do not let it out of doors, until its fur is quite dry; in this way it should suffer no ill effects.

Combining firmness with affection will cure your cat of most of the bad habits it may acquire. Many cats will jump up on to the table when food is being prepared, and it may be necessary to keep it in the next room at meal times. It may like to leap into bed with babies and children; a baby could be harmed in this way, and, in addition, the cat may carry insects and germs.

A little care can prevent your cat from being harmed in accidents – for example, it may get its head jammed in an empty can while looking for food, so confine empty cans to the dustbins. Keep insecticides, etc., out of reach of your pet, and make sure it does not chew on electric wires. If it does get a shock, pull out the plug before touching the cat.

Careful attention to the eyes removes any discharge.

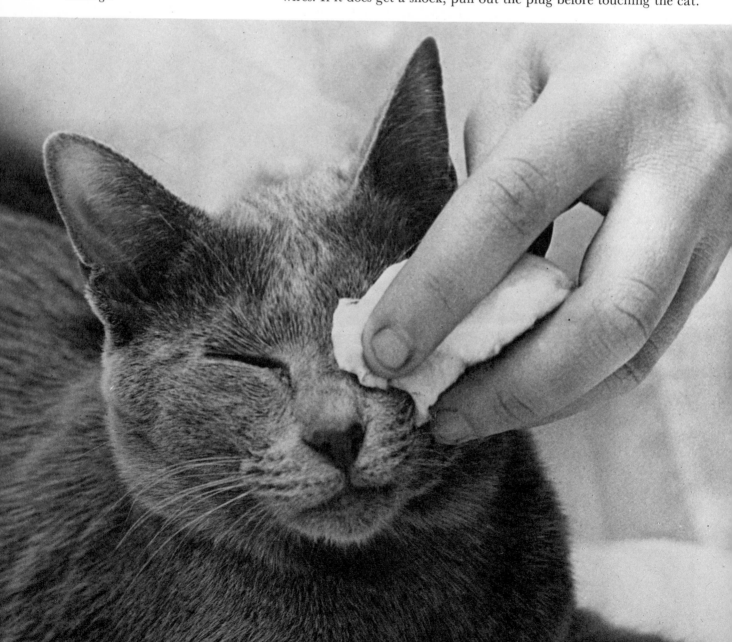

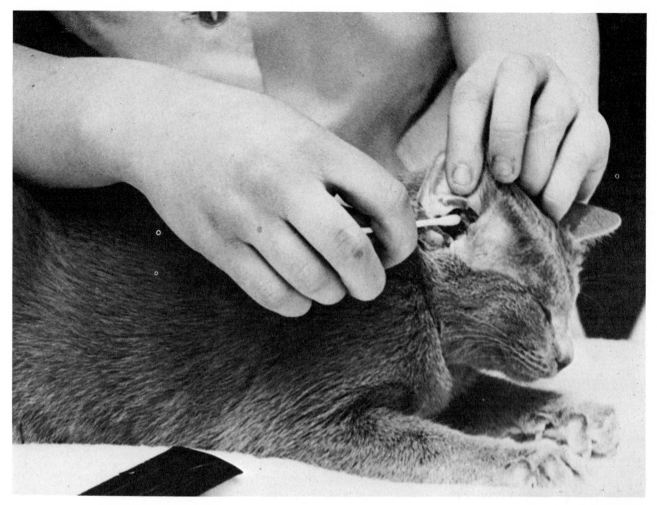

Cleaning ears with cotton-wool—the greatest care is necessary, so as not to cause any damage. Do not go in too far.

For your own sake as well as the cat's, be sure not to trip over the cat while carrying heavy objects or hot foods around the home.

Treat your cat with care, attention and affection, bearing in mind that cats are by nature independent, and dislike being fussed over too much. As you get to know your cat, you will come to recognize the various ways in which it registers its feelings, perhaps by a shake of the head or a twitch of the tail. A cat can express much by the way in which it "mews". Some cats even growl like a dog when a stranger is in the offing. Purring is its best known sign of pleasure, although it is not known exactly how this sound is produced. You will be surprised by the way your cat will respond, in time, when talked to – a young kitten soon learns to react to its own name. A cat dislikes loud noises. Its sense of hearing is very sensitive, and the slightest sound will often attract attention. It is often said that cats can see in the dark – this is not strictly true, although they do see much more than we do in a very dim light. Its whiskers are also very sensitive, and are used by the cat for feeling its way in confined spaces.

Properly cared for, a cat is a graceful asset to any household, a source of pleasure for adults and children alike. It is sad to reflect that, owing to urban housing-conditions, many children can never have a four-footed friend and have to be content with a gold-fish or budgerigar; however interesting, this is not quite the same as owning your own cat or dog.

Nutrition

The saying "a cat needs a good mixed diet" may be a cliché, but is none the less true. Too much of one particular food and too little of others will result in the deficiency of some essential nutritional requirements. This is of greater significance in cats which are kept in a cattery, and who are therefore unable to make good by hunting the elements that a restricted diet may lack.

The essential constituents of a diet are:

Water: In common with all mammals, the cat needs a large fluid intake. This is in the main supplied by the food of a mixed diet which will be made up of about seventy per cent water. Further fluid requirement is met by drinking water, milk, etc. The sick cat very quickly becomes dehydrated when the fluid balance of the tissues is disturbed, e.g. when fluid loss is excessive due to vomiting or diarrhoea with no fluid intake. On the other hand, healthy cats have been known to survive for long periods without food or water if they have been inadvertantly shut in a shed. Aged cats, especially those with impaired kidneys, need more water to keep their fluid balance correct.

Protein: The cat has a large protein requirement compared with other animals. An adult cat weighing 8–10 lb. should have around 6 oz. of protein-rich food per day. Proteins are found in meat, offal, rabbit, fish and chicken.

Carbohydrates: The cat does not require much carbohydrate, although it can be useful as roughage, adding bulk to the diet to promote intestinal movements. Carbohydrates should only be fed cooked. Useful sources are rice, barley, brown bread and cornflakes.

Fats: Fat is an excellent source of heat and energy and can be digested by the cat. The problem lies in getting most cats to eat it in any form, although probably a little will be taken with meat.

Minerals: Calcium and phosphorus in the correct proportions are essential to the cat for bone formation. The calcium and phosphorus ratio should be in the region of 1:1. A deficiency of calcium produces the bone condition known as osteogenesis imperfecta (*see* Diseases). A high calcium and low phosphorus ratio together with an absence of vitamin D, can produce rickets. Phosphorus is found in meat and calcium in milk. It is most important that pregnant and nursing queens and kittens should be given calcium as a supplement to their diet in view of their high requirement.

Sodium and potassium salts are important in the control of the fluid balance of the body. They are found in sufficient quantity in adequate protein diets.

Small amounts of other minerals known as trace elements are required, and will be sufficiently supplied in a mixed diet.

Vitamins: are substances which are present in natural foods and are essential to good health.

Vitamin A: Deficiency of vitamin A leads to loss of condition, lack of appetite, corneal ulcers and weakness of the hind legs. Breeding queens may abort or produce malformed kittens. Vitamin A is mainly found in liver or cod liver oil. Pregnant and nursing queens and kittens must have vitamin A added to their diet.

All cats need water—this mackerel tabby shows splendid co-ordination.

Vitamin B₁ (thiamine): Lack of vitamin B_1 causes loss of appetite and peripheral neuritis. It is found in yeast and, to a lesser extent, in meat.

Vitamin B₂ (riboflavin): Deficiency of this vitamin rarely occurs as cats are thought to synthesize it in the intestinal tract from carbohydrates.

Vitamin B₆ (pyridoxine): Deficiency causes anaemia and lack of growth. It is found in yeast and liver.

Vitamin C (ascorbic acid): This is the anti-scurvy vitamin. It is found in vegetables and grass.

Vitamin D: is necessary for the body to utilize calcium in the formation of bone. It is important that kittens and pregnant queens have a sufficient supply but care must be taken to avoid over-dosage. Found in cod-liver oil.

Vitamin E: This is the anti-sterility vitamin. It is found in meat and wheat germ.

Nicotinic Acid: Deficiency causes gingivitis and ulceration of the mouth. It is found in meat.

Cats are individualists, and in nothing more so than their feeding habits. Given the basic requirements, the diet can be varied to suit individual tastes. There is usually more than one source of each nutrient. For instance, if a cat really dislikes meat then his protein can be supplied in liver, offal, fish, chicken or rabbit. As hare and rabbit are virtually unknown now in America, processed food (dry or canned) and, perhaps, fresh frozen horsemeat would act as a substitute for these. Adult cats do best on two main meals per day, morning and evening. For those who can take it, some milk may be given at mid-day, as few cats digest cows' milk properly. This is better in the form of evaporated or dried milk as supplied for babies, with only two-thirds of the recommended water added; or this milk snack may be given last thing at night to encourage free-ranging cats to come indoors. If milk is not included in the diet in any form, a supplement of calcium is necessary.

Given below is a list of some foods particularly suitable for the cat, divided into those rich mainly in proteins, and those rich mainly in carbohydrates. Suitable combinations of these foods in a good mixed diet will provide not only proteins and carbohydrates but many of the other nutrients mentioned in this article.

Rich in protein:
Cow beef, raw or cooked, minced or cut in small pieces (horse meat is too acid for some cats).

Liver, raw or cooked 2–3 times weekly – fed too often it can produce diarrhoea.

Spleen (melts) 2–3 times weekly – fed too often it can produce diarrhoea.

Heart, raw or cooked.

Tongues, cooked – too tough to be eaten raw.

Fish – cooked white fish such as cod and coley; herrings; tinned pilchards occasionally.

Rabbit, cooked.

Hare, cooked.

Chicken and giblets, cooked.

Food containing bones, e.g. chicken necks, can be pressure-cooked with a small amount of water, until the bones can be crushed easily between finger and thumb. This makes a useful source of calcium.

Eggs, may be given occasionally especially to nursing queens and kittens, hard-boiled or beaten up in milk.

Rich in carbohydrate (These should always be cooked as the cat is unable to digest raw carbohydrate):

Rice or barley, preferably cooked in meat or rabbit stock to add flavour.

Wholemeal bread.

Cornflakes.

Suggested feeding of an 8–10 lb. cat: For breakfast give 2–3 oz. rabbit, fish or chicken giblets, together with a tablespoonful of cornflakes or brown bread.

For supper, give 2–3 oz. meat, liver, etc., plus a tablespoonful of rice or barley.

In addition a milky snack may be given at mid-day or at night.

Drinking water should always be available, and the cat should have access to grass to nibble at as it wishes. These feeds can be varied to suit the individual both in content and quantity. Feed as much of the liquor from cooking any food as possible, as it contains the water-soluble vitamins from the food. Do not give highly-seasoned food, but add a small amount of salt when cooking. Good-quality tinned foods can be substituted for one meal for convenience.

Feeding of pregnant and nursing queens: Pregnant and nursing queens require extra supplies of vitamins A and D and calcium, which can be obtained in the form of many proprietary brands available in Great Britain and America, all of which are satisfactory. Taken as directed, these additives will supply the requirements in the correct proportions. The queen should not need extra food until the 4th–5th week of pregnancy and the amount should thereafter be increased gradually. Do not over-feed; the daily intake should not exceed a 50 per cent increase over normal. The extra food should be given as a mid-day meal, rather than increasing the size of existing feeds. If the queen is carrying a large litter, she may prefer to have her meals divided into four each day to avoid the discomfort of an over-full abdomen. A small teaspoonful of liquid paraffin (mineral oil in the United States) or salad oil may be given twice weekly during the last two weeks of pregnancy to ensure that the queen is not constipated during kittening, a condition which can lead to delayed parturition owing to mechanical blockage of the pelvis with hard faeces.

After kittening, and depending on the size of the litter, the queen should be encouraged to take as much fluid as her digestive system can handle, in order to produce and maintain an adequate supply of milk for the kittens. This can be in the form of gravy, beaten-up egg and milk, evaporated milk (which contains twice as much protein as cows' milk), or dried milk reconstituted with one-third less water than for babies. As the kittens grow, she will require plenty of high-protein food. The extra amount given is really a matter of common sense and giving the queen as much as she can eat to maintain herself and produce milk, without causing sickness or diarrhoea. Most queens lose some weight while feeding kittens, but very soon regain it when the kittens are weaned. While the kittens are being weaned, the queen's food and fluid should slowly be decreased to reduce her milk supply. When the last kitten has been weaned, reduce the fluid intake sharply for a few days until her milk has dried up. Feed fairly dry foods and do not feed milk. However, if the queen is being fed the commercial dried foods, an adequate amount of water must still be provided. After her milk has dried off completely, she may then be put back on a normal diet. If she has lost weight, she must be given extra rations until her weight and condition are normal.

Feeding of kittens: There is no hard and fast rule for the age at which kittens should be weaned. It will depend on the size of the litter, the condition of the queen, and the amount of milk she can produce. On average, feeding of kittens can be started about 3–4 weeks old. The first attempts at feeding should be made when the kittens have not recently been suckling – probably after sleeping. A few drops of the milk which has been made up for the queen with the addition of a little glucose (corn syrup in the United States) is suitable. It should be at blood heat. When this is being taken readily, some baby cereal should be added. Gradually increase the quantity and number of feeds per day. When the teeth have erupted, the kitten is ready for some solid food, usually at 4–5 weeks. Cooked rabbit or cooked white fish can be given. Some kittens, especially Siamese, can digest scraped raw meat from about five weeks old but, in others, it may cause diarrhoea if given before 7–8 weeks. Vitamins A, D and calcium should be added to the kittens' diet as they become less dependent on their mother's milk.

Kittens should be completely weaned by eight weeks old, and at this stage they should receive five small meals per day, three of protein foods and two of milk food and baby cereal. Kittens grow very rapidly and therefore require a high protein diet. The amount given at each meal will be governed mainly by the kitten's appetite, usually about $1\frac{1}{2}$–2 tablespoonfuls of solid food, but in any case not more than it readily clears up; and about 2 oz. of milky food per meal. From now on, foods suitable for adults may gradually be incorporated in the diet. At around 9–10 weeks, the number of meals should be reduced to four per day, but with no reduction in quantity of food. Over the next few months, the number of meals is reduced and the quantity of food increased until at 9–12 months, the kitten is receiving the adult diet.

A Short-hair Silver Tabby queen feeding her kittens.

Bottle-feeding a new-born kitten.

Diseases

Cats are remarkably healthy animals, but are sure to need veterinary attention at some time in their lives; for inoculation and neutering if not for actual illness. So one of the first things to do when you get a kitten is to contact a veterinary surgeon, if you do not already have one, and arrange for your kitten to become his patient. Do not wait until an emergency arises.

You must study your cat's appearance and behaviour in health so that you may know when it is off-colour. A healthy cat should look alert; take an interest in surroundings; be hungry for its food; sleep normally; and spend a fair amount of time grooming itself. An observant owner can very soon tell, just as one can with human beings, simply by the expression on the cat's face if it is feeling unwell.

Among the signs of illness are the following: lassitude; refusing one or at most two meals; dull, staring coat; vomiting; diarrhoea; sneezing and coughing; excessive scratching and head shaking; lameness; abnormal swellings on the body; constantly squatting in the sanitary tray without passing faeces or urine.

If in doubt whether your cat is really ill, do not hesitate to telephone your veterinary surgeon who will advise you, and who would always rather be called too early than too late.

Respiratory Diseases

"Cat 'Flu": The illnesses which used to be known in Britain collectively as "cat 'flu" and in the U.S.A. as pneumonitis are, without doubt, the most troublesome to the cat breeder, cattery owner and veterinary surgeon. They are caused by viruses and are highly infectious and contagious. As in the common cold in people, there are many viruses or variations of the same virus involved, making vaccination difficult if not impossible.

In the disease known as viral rhinotracheitis, the nose, mouth and throat are mainly affected; other viruses affect the lung.

Symptoms: The incubation period varies from 2–10 days. The first symptom is nearly always sneezing, and this usually continues throughout the illness. This is followed by a clear discharge from the eyes and nostrils and a rise in temperature. The discharges may become thick and purulent due to secondary bacterial infection, and in chronic cases the sinuses of the head become affected, a condition which tends to become permanent. The cat may drool ropy saliva, and it will then be seen that there are ulcers in the mouth – on the tongue, hard palate, gums and throat. At this stage, if not before, the cat loses its appetite due to loss of taste and smell. Coughing may also occur, more especially if the lungs are affected.

The course and duration of viral respiratory diseases vary enormously, but it is usually some weeks before a cat returns to normal. Death may occur, especially when the lungs become involved. There may be several relapses during the illness. Recovered cats can become carriers, and may have recurrences of the illness when off-colour or under stress, e.g. when taken to shows or sent from home to a boarding cattery. During this time, they are infective to other cats, whether they show symptoms themselves or not.

340

Treatment: Do not take your cat to a surgery, where it may contact other cats, without first telephoning your veterinary surgeon to ask if he wants you to bring the cat in or if he prefers to call. The affected cat should be isolated immediately and strict quarantine imposed. Where possible, one person should attend to this cat and another to the in-contact cats. The attendants must not attend cat shows or indeed come in contact with any other cats, nor allow cats to be brought to the premises. The dishes and all feeding arrangements must be kept separate and the attendant should keep an overall and shoes to be worn when handling the cat. Disinfection of the premises must be thoroughly and frequently carried out. In spite of all precautions, these diseases are likely to spread through a cattery because of their highly infectious nature. Apart from the treatment carried out by the veterinary surgeon, nursing is most important in respiratory diseases. It is desirable that a bond should be established between the sick cat and its attendant, by means of affection, care and petting.

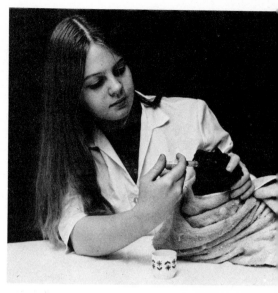

Syringe-feeding a sick cat.

The patient should be in a dry, warm atmosphere, out of draughts, but with plenty of fresh air, and sunshine when possible. If the eyes are affected, avoid strong sunlight. If the cat's temperature is normal, subject to your veterinary surgeon's approval, it should be allowed to go outdoors (of course not in contact with or near other cats) when the weather is suitable, and under supervision. Do not turn it loose in the garden. Exercise outside seems to boost the cat's morale.

The eyes, nose and mouth must be wiped clean with damp cotton wool at frequent intervals to prevent the formation of hard crusts around the eyes and nostrils. In severe cases, the nostrils can become completely blocked, causing breathing difficulties. Unlike dogs, cats are averse to mouth breathing, and will only pant if in a fair amount of distress. The cat must be encouraged by all possible means to eat and drink.

If necessary, fluids such as essence of beef, protein hydrolysate, or glucose and water may be forcibly fed. Great care must be taken when doing so. The cat should be wrapped in a blanket with only its head free. The head is then grasped in the left hand with thumb and fore-finger under the cheekbones and tilted slightly backwards and upwards, when the lower jaw will be relaxed. The fluid should then be dropped in the mouth through the slightly opened teeth. Give the cat time to swallow, and release the head at the smallest sign of choking. All sorts of tempting and strong smelling tit-bits should be offered, such as liver sausage and sardines. They should be removed fairly soon if not eaten. The exception to this is that some sick cats will eat at night and some food can be left with the patient during darkness. Water should always be available.

Pneumonia and Pleurisy: These occur mainly during and secondary to viral respiratory diseases and require veterinary attention.

Asthma: This is largely caused by the cat being allergic to various substances. The cat wheezes and has prolonged bouts of coughing. Treatment consists of removing the cause if it can be traced, and the administration of prescribed drugs. If the cat is distressed by wheezing or coughing, medicated inhalation may help it. A small teaspoonful of compound tincture of benzoin should be put in a jam-jar, which is then placed in a safe container such as a washing-up bowl, and the jar filled with boiling water. The cat should be held as near the steam as is comfortable.

Tumours: A malignant type of tumour appears around the nostrils of cats, which gradually erodes the tissues. In the bronchi and lungs, cancer is sometimes found in older cats. Breathing becomes laboured and the cat loses weight and condition.

Diseases of the Digestive System

The Mouth: Ulceration of the tongue, gums and palate occurs in viral respiratory diseases, and also when the cat has licked an irritant substance, probably when grooming itself. It may be seen in nephritis. The cat has long strings of saliva hanging from its mouth, and is unable or unwilling to eat. Examination of the mouth shows red circular areas, sometimes covered by a white membrane.

The tongue may be torn in road accidents by getting caught between the cat's teeth. Another cause of a cut on the tongue is a cat licking a sharp-edged can. It may require stitching, depending on the extent of the wound. Punctured wounds and small cuts, where there is no loose flap, heal very well on their own.

Teeth: Caries (decay) of the teeth, which is common in man, is rarely seen in the cat. What is common is a deposit of tartar on the canine and molar teeth. This often grows to such an extent that it prevents the cat from eating and the cat will be seen clawing at its mouth in an attempt to remove the obstruction. The tartar must be removed and this is best done by the veterinarian using general anaesthesia. If allowed to remain, it presses on the gums exposing the roots of the teeth which become infected by the entrance of bacteria. Cats affected with chronic nephritis also accumulate tartar on the teeth and have a peculiarly offensive smell from the mouth.

Gums: Gingivitis (inflammation of the gums) may be due to the deposit of tartar on the teeth, deficiency of vitamin B, or an unknown cause.

Foreign bodies become lodged in the mouth and throat; rabbit and fish bones get wedged across the hard palate or at the back of the throat or sometimes in the oesophagus. Another foreign body often found is a needle, which has been swallowed when the cat (or more probably the kitten) has been playing with a piece of cotton which has a needle attached. This usually becomes embedded in the soft palate. Once in the mouth, a cat finds it almost impossible to get rid of anything undesirable because of the backward-pointing papillae on the surface of the tongue. If the foreign body is in the mouth, the cat will try to remove it with its forepaws at the same time moving backwards in an attempt to back away from the trouble. If it is in the throat or oesophagus, the cat sits in a dark secluded place, often with saliva hanging from its mouth, and the symptoms may be mistaken for those of cat "flu".

Gastritis: may be caused by bacteria; irritants which have been licked from the coat or feet; certain poisons; round worms in kittens. Vomiting is the principle sign of gastritis, sometimes bloodstained. Food and water should be withheld until the cat has been seen by a veterinary surgeon.

Long-haired cats accumulate fur in the stomach in the form of a "hair-ball" which may give rise to mild gastritis. The cat becomes languid, has a poor appetite, and usually will vomit the hair-ball; but the administration of liquid paraffin (mineral oil) or olive oil will speed the process. During the moulting season especially, long-haired cats should be groomed regularly to remove all dead hair. Liquid paraffin can be given once or twice weekly to lubricate the intestinal tract, or a bulk laxative mixed in the food. Sardines mashed up in plenty of olive oil will also help and will most likely be eaten by the cat, thus avoiding forcible administration.

Enteritis—Feline infectious enteritis or panleukopaenia: is really a viral disease and often does not cause enteritis at all. Affected cats always vomit but do not necessarily have diarrhoea or constipation. Kittens and young cats are particularly affected but cats of any age are susceptible, especially those who have not acquired natural immunity. The disease is highly contagious and may be rapidly fatal, especially in kittens, death occurring in a matter of hours from the onset of symptoms. The incubation period is normally 2-5 days, but may be longer. Vomiting, which may be prolonged and severe, is generally the first symptom; although the owner may notice that the animal was unusually quiet for a few hours before this takes place.

There may be diarrhoea, and combined with the vomiting, this produces rapid dehydration. The cat or kitten is very depressed and is unable or unwilling to take any interest in its surroundings. It sits hunched up, its eyes have a glassy stare, and often its tail is stretched out instead of being curled round the feet as is normal in cats. It will appear to crave for water, crouching over its water bowl or sitting in the kitchen sink, but will only take a lap or two. Finally, it lapses into unconsciousness and dies. In less acute and non-fatal cases, recovery is slow.

It is highly desirable that all kittens should be inoculated against F.I.E. and there are several efficient vaccines made by reputable drug firms, particularly the modern tissue-culture vaccines. Inoculation must be carried out by a veterinary surgeon and the choice of vaccine should be left to him.

Coccidiosis: (*see under* Parasites) causes enteritis in kittens, sometimes with permanent damage to the bowel wall. Enteritis may be bacterial in origin, and some of these bacteria, such as *salmonellae* and *pasteurellae*, are communicable to man, so strict attention should be paid to hygiene in nursing these cases.

Symptoms of enteritis are constant straining with the passage of small quantities of fluid faeces, sometimes bloodstained. There may also be some vomiting and discomfort when the abdomen is palpated.

Foreign bodies in the intestine: Unlike dogs, cats seldom swallow hard objects which lodge in the intestine. String is possibly the most common cause of the obstruction, probably from around the Sunday roast, so it is important to see that all such string is discarded out of the cat's reach. Sometimes plastic toys are chewed up and the pieces swallowed. Signs of a foreign body in the intestine are: vomiting, lack of bowel movements, depression, rapid pulse and reddening of the whites of the eyes. Help should be sought quickly, in case an operation is necessary.

Diarrhoea is largely caused by dietetic errors, whether on the part of the cat or the owner. The majority of cats have diarrhoea if given much fresh cow's milk. Many cannot take it at all. Worms in kittens cause persistent diarrhoea.

Constipation: Older cats tend to suffer from constipation, or more correctly stasis of the bowel, i.e. cessation of the peristaltic movements of the intestine. This is particularly the case in old Siamese. They should be given regularly a bulk laxative and, possibly also, liquid paraffin or mineral oil. In some cases an enema may be required, or even a surgical operation if all else fails.

Blood in the faeces occurs in bacterial diseases and also in warfarin poisoning.

The Liver may become affected in the course of viral and bacterial diseases, but unless there is massive damage to liver cells, its function is not seriously impaired. The most important causes of liver damage are various poisons, specifically coal-tar derivatives. The liver is also a common site for tumours which are nearly always malignant.

The Pancreas: Dysfunction of certain cells in the pancreas gives rise to diabetes mellitus, which occasionally affects cats. Symptoms are voracious appetite and excessive thirst accompanied by wasting of muscles and loss of subcutaneous fat. Treatment is by injections of insulin and the regulation of the diet to reduce the carbohydrate intake. Small feeds of high nutritive value should be given at frequent intervals. Long periods of fasting must be avoided.

Diseases of the Urinary System

The Kidneys: Acute nephritis is not common, but may be caused by some poisons. The cat is thirsty; only passes small quantities of concentrated urine; vomits periodically; is depressed and sits with its back arched and may show signs of pain when touched in the lumbar area.

Chronic nephritis is predominantly a disease of the aged cat. The cat drinks excessively, particularly water and will drink from rain puddles or water in flower vases; passes large quantities of pale urine; loses weight. Similar symptoms are seen in a cat suffering from diabetes, but analysis of the urine will differentiate between the two conditions. In the later stages, the cat becomes uraemic—in other words the kidneys are not filtering the waste products from the blood— and this is indicated by ulcers in the mouth and the strong odour of urine from the breath. The cat must be given a low-protein diet; avoid red meat, increase carbohydrates, and give thin barley water or glucose and water rather than plain water.

The Bladder: Cystitis may be simple (e.g. due to a chill or damage to the bladder in a road accident), bacterial (e.g. involved in infections of the genital tract in females), but most frequently, it is caused by calculi (stones) being formed in the bladder. Although the cat may manage to pass a certain amount of this material, the deposit will eventually block the exit from the bladder completely. The first signs are that the cat visits its sanitary tray repeatedly and squats in it straining, but only passes drops or small pools of urine which, in the later stages, will be bloodstained. Often the straining is accompanied by a cry of pain. If the abdomen is *gently* palpated and the bladder is felt as a hard round object, this means that the urinary retention is complete and veterinary attention is urgently required. On no account must the owner put any pressure on the bladder in an effort to empty it. At this stage, the bladder is easily ruptured. Paralysis of the bladder often accompanies damage to the pelvis in an accident, and this is usually permanent. It may result in complete retention of urine or in incontinence.

Diseases of the Genital System

Male: As most cats are castrated when kittens, disease of the genital organs is no problem, and in fact males in general seem to be remarkably free from genital diseases. The only trouble worthy of note is the occurrence of monorchidism or cryptorchidism. In the cryptorchid, both testicles are absent from the scrotum. They may be partially descended or, more likely, retained completely in the abdomen. The cryptorchid is not fertile because only in the scrotum are the testicles at the correct temperature to produce spermatozoa. The monorchid has one testicle in the scrotum, and therefore is capable of reproduction. He should not be used at stud as he is liable to sire monorchid or cryptorchid kittens. Both monorchids and cryptorchids pass urine with the typical male odour, and monorchids behave as entire males.

Female: Ovaries: Cysts occur in the ovaries and result in the queen constantly calling. If she mates she is most unlikely to produce kittens. Treatment is of little avail and the queen should be spayed.

Uterus: Pyometra (pus in the uterus) may occur after kittening due to a retained placenta; or a difficult labour with perhaps dead kittens; or simply an ascending bacteria infection. Symptoms are: a thick discharge of blood and pus from the vagina, rise of temperature, loss of appetite, and probably some vomiting. If treated in time, this condition responds well to antibiotic drugs.

Metritis may occur for no apparent reason and is not necessarily post-parturient. The uterus contains a secretion which may be quite free of bacteria. The secretion is a breakdown of the lining of the uterus. In this case, antibiotics will only control secondary bacterial invasion. Treatment may clear up the condition but it is almost certain to recur and, at present ovarhysterectomy is the most satisfactory remedy. It is though that this condition may be caused by allowing the queen to call too many times without mating.

Diseases of Muscles, Bones and Joints

Muscles: There are no specific muscular diseases in cats, but muscles may be involved in abscesses, the result of fights with other cats.

Bones—Rickets: which is caused by vitamin D deficiency, is seldom seen nowadays when most kittens receive an adequate diet. A kitten suffering from rickets has the typical "cowboy" appearance, i.e. the legs are bowed, and some joints may be misshapen and knobbly. Sometimes the "rickety rosary" can be felt—a line of hard knobs like beads along the ribs.

Osteogenesis imperfecta is a condition associated with a deficiency of calcium in the diet but there may also be some hereditary factor. The Siamese is by far the most commonly affected of all breeds, including the household pet. The bones are soft and fracture easily. The first sign the owner notices is that when the kitten jumps down from a height it shakes one or more paws after landing. This is due to pain in the limb. Varying degrees of lameness are seen and a kitten may easily fracture a bone just by jumping off a chair. An awkward fall may result in crush fracture of a vertebra. If given treatment in the early stages, many kittens recover. Exposure to ultra-violet light and injection of calcium can produce a spectacular recovery, but the owner must ensure that the kitten has plenty of calcium in its diet until adult.

Arthritis is not a great problem in cats; old cats are far more mobile than old dogs whose joints stiffen from arthritic changes in old age.

Fractures and dislocations: In the head region the most common fracture site is at the centre of the chin where the two mandibles join. The cat's mouth hangs loosely open, the jaw appears crooked, and there is a certain amount of bleeding where the soft tissues have been torn. If uncomplicated, this fracture is usually fairly easily repaired by a figure-of-eight wire around the lower canine teeth, which is left in position for some weeks. Fractures of the mandibles themselves are more complex.

Dislocation of the lower jaw can be differentiated from a fracture by the fact that the lower jaw is fixed in the open position. Simple dislocation can be reduced under a general anaesthetic.

Fractures of the hard palate are quite commonly seen, and while they may require surgical treatment, they mostly heal by themselves.

In spinal column injury, the force required to fracture a cat's vertebra usually results in such severe damage to the spinal chord that the cat becomes completely paralysed posterior to the site of the fracture.

Fracture of the long bones may be fairly obvious because of the distortion of the limb and swelling at the site of the fracture. The femur is the most common seat of injury. This is generally repaired by the insertion of a steel pin in the shaft of the bone. Cats recover their mobility amazingly quickly when treated in this way, and can usually use the limb within a few days of the operation, although naturally their freedom must be restricted until healing has taken place. Dislocation of the hip joint may be confused with a high fracture of the femur; an X-ray photograph will differentiate. After the reduction of the dislocation, the cat's movements must be confined for some time to prevent a recurrence.

Other bones can be repaired by fixing plates to unite the fractured ends. Some fractures may also be immobilized by plaster-of-Paris bandages. Fracture of the tail may heal well, but the tail may be permanently paralysed and drag on the ground. In such cases the tail must be amputated.

Fractures in young kittens: These may be caused by being accidently trodden on, shut in a door, or dropped by a child. In the writer's experience, in most of these cases, the best method of treatment is to confine the kitten in a pen so that its movements are restricted and so that it cannot rush around and jump on and off furniture until the fracture has healed.

Diseases of the Heart and Circulatory System

The heart of the cat is an exceptionally efficient organ, and rarely gives any trouble even in old age. A "hole in the heart" may occasionally be found in kittens, particularly Siamese.

Anaemia is mainly seen in the disease known as feline infectious anaemia, which is caused by a parasitic organism in the blood stream. The cat shows loss of weight, lassitude and pallidity of the mucous membranes. Veterinary diagnosis and treatment is required.

Leukaemia, sometimes called cancer of the blood, is a malignant disease affecting the white blood corpuscles, and is comparatively common in cats, especially older cats. As this is a disease of the blood, any organs may be affected, so that the symptoms vary enormously. The constant ones are loss of appetite, lassitude, progressive loss of weight and general debility.

Diseases of the Nervous System

There are many causes of nervous symptoms in the cat, but there are only three conditions found in the system itself which are of much significance.

1. *Epilepsy* is occasionally seen. It can be hereditary, and is evident for example in a colony of farm cats, where a great deal of in-breeding takes place.
Treatment: Fits can be controlled by the use of anti-convulsant drugs. Affected cats should not be used for breeding.
2. *Stroke.* This may be caused by haemorrhage or thrombosis of a blood vessel in the brain, and is a familiar occurrence in aged cats. It happens quite suddenly and without previous warning. The cat usually cries loudly and falls on its side. There may be some loss of consciousness. When it rises, it is seen to stagger and may walk in circles. Sometimes the head will be held on one side and a fairly constant symptom is nystagmus—rapid flicking of the eyes from side to side.
Treatment: The essential treatment is rest and mild sedation. Most cases recover, but as in man there can be recurrence at any time.
3. *Rabies*: This virus disease is not enountered in cats in the U.K., thanks to strict quarantine regulations. At present, cats entering Great Britain are placed in quarantine for six months. On entry, and before leaving quarantine, the cat must receive anti-rabies inoculations. Such regulations are lacking in the United States except for Hawaii, but the incidence of rabies is steadily declining. The incubation period of the disease may be lengthy, hence the long term of quarantine in Britain. Transmission is by the bite of an infected animal, the saliva being the infective agent.
Symptoms: There are two forms of the disease – furious rabies and dumb rabies, the former being more common in cats.

In furious rabies, there is firstly an alteration in the cat's behaviour. It becomes quiet and hides itself away, particularly in dark places. This may last for a few days when the cat will become intensely irritable and will attack anything that crosses its path, biting and clawing violently. This is succeeded by loss of muscular control of limbs, paralysis and death.

In dumb rabies, the excitable stage is omitted.
Treatment: There is no treatment once symptoms have appeared.

347

Diseases of the Skin

These can most conveniently be divided into parasitic and non-parasitic conditions.

Parasitic

Fleas cause considerable irritation to most cats and may be the bearers of diseases. They are found in greatest numbers around the head and neck and along the spine. When the hair is parted, the flea may be seen, but more likely its presence is indicated by black specks like coal dust. This is flea excretion and is mainly made up of dried blood. In a heavy infestation, flecks of blood will be seen in the milk which the cat is lapping. This is flea excretion which has fallen out of the coat and dissolved in the milk. Another indication of the presence of fleas is that when the flea bites, the cat is seen to turn its head quickly and lick a particular spot violently.

The licking and scratching consequent on flea infestation may cause a moist eczema to develop. The hair becomes broken and scanty, and the skin is reddened and moist.

Treatment consists of elimination of the flea and the application of a soothing lotion/powder to the skin. Fleas seldom lay their eggs on the cat; they may do so in the bedding, in cracks in a wooden floor, or any dry dusty place, so treatment must include these places. There are many suitable brands of insecticide powder on the market, those containing pybuthrin or derris are the least toxic to the cat. In the last two years or so, it seems as if a race of superfleas has appeared which is resistant to the action of present insecticides so that as well as powdering the cat it is advisable to use a small tooth comb to catch and destroy as many fleas as possible. Particularly in the U.S.A. flea collars are used, but although they are generally effective they are not suitable for long-hairs.

Lice: These are comparatively uncommon in the cat. Cat lice are tiny, and until observed closely look like scurf in the coat. Lice eggs (nits) can be seen attached to individual hairs. Treatment as for fleas.

Cheyletiella parasitivorax: This mite is normally found on rabbits, but has been seen on the cat. However, it is more likely to cause a skin rash on the owner than on the cat. Treatment as for fleas.

Ticks: Sheep or cattle ticks are sometimes found on cats. The tick climbs up a blade of grass and waits for a suitable host to pass by, to which it attaches itself. It burrows its head into the cat's skin and sucks blood until it is replete, when it drops off. It is a grey bead-shaped object varying in size depending on its state of repletion, and owners who have not seen one before may think it is a wart or tumour. Treatment is as for fleas, or the tick may be removed with tweezers, but great care must be taken not to leave the head embedded in the skin where it will cause a sore.

Harvest mites are seen in late summer, mainly on the head and ears or between the toes. They appear as small clumps of orange specks and they cause some irritation. Swabbing with any weak disinfectant solution will dispose of them.

Maggots: Blue-bottles will lay their eggs on cats which, for any reason such as illness or old age, are unable to clean themselves. The eggs are laid in neglected wounds where the fur has become matted with pus, or around the anus when the cat has had diarrhoea. The eggs hatch into maggots which then burrow into the skin, and unless they are removed quickly, the cat will die from toxins produced by the maggots. Treatment consists of clipping off all hair around the affected part, cleansing thoroughly with warm water and disinfectant and making sure all maggots are eliminated. Dust the area with talcum powder and inspect regularly for any maggots which may have hatched from unseen eggs.

Mange: Cat mange is caused by a mite, *notoedres cati*, and is usually confined to the head and ears. Small scars are formed, there is intense irritation, the hairs break off and disappear and the skin eventually becomes corrugated. Meanwhile, isolate the cat and use care when handling as the mites are communicable to man.

Ringworm: This appears as small, bare, often circular patches on the skin, which becomes scaly, and the hairs around the edge of the lesion are easily pulled out. There is some irritation, causing scratching and so the feet and claws become infected. Sometimes the skin is not affected and the only sign is profuse scurfiness. Again great care must be taken when handling an infected cat, particularly where children are concerned. Most adults have some degree of immunity to ringworm.

Non-parasitic conditions

"Fish" eczema: This is a miliary eczema often seen in cats which have been fed almost exclusively on fish. Small scabs appear on the lower spine and spread forwards. In severe cases almost the whole body surface can become involved. The skin becomes roughened and wrinkled and the hair is broken and sparse. The cat licks the area constantly. Treatment consists of changing the diet, and anti-inflammatory drugs, e.g. cortisone, may be given. Other dietetic errors produce similar symptoms, so stick to the time-honoured rule of "a good mixed diet".

Alopecia (loss of hair) is sometimes seen in neuter cats, both male and female. Hair loss usually occurs inside and at the back of the hind legs and on the abdomen.

Tumours occur on the skin, especially around the ears, nose and lips.

Diseases of the Ear

Otodectic mange, or ear canker, is caused by a mite which lives free in the ear canal. It causes great irritation with inflammation of the lining of the canal and the formation of a dark reddish brown exudate in the ear which may be hard and dry, or soft and semi-fluid. Secondary bacterial invaders cause the formation of pus. The cat will constantly shake its head and scratch the affected ear to such an extent that sores may be formed at the base of the ear. Treatment comprises daily cleansing with cotton wool buds to remove all discharge. If the discharge is hard and caked, it must first be softened by dropping in olive oil or liquid paraffin (mineral oil) and gently massaging the base of the ear to loosen it. Having cleaned out the ear, a proprietary lotion or powder may be used, taking care that it is described as suitable for cats. Better still, seek veterinary advice.

Otitis media (inflammation of the middle ear) is usually bacterial in origin. The infection may spread from the external ear or from the throat. The cat carries its head on one side, the affected ear downwards, and is unable to straighten it. Veterinary treatment only.

Deafness does not usually afflict cats, except in the case of blue- or green-eyed white cats, many of which have a built-in deafness factor. Occasionally, the old cat may become hard of hearing, but this is by no means as common as in old dogs.

Haematoma: this is a swelling containing blood which appears in the pinna or ear flap. It is caused by excessive shaking of the head as described under Ear Canker. A blood vessel in the flap ruptures, filling the flap with blood and producing a hot swelling which may involve the whole external ear. The discomfort of the swelling leads to more head shaking which aggravates the condition. A haematoma is a case for the veterinary surgeon. Depending on the extent of the swelling, an operation will probably be necessary. In the meantime, gently cleanse any discharge from the ear canal and try to prevent the cat from causing further damage. Talcum powder sprinkled in and around the ear has a soothing effect.

If untreated, or not treated in time, the condition will finally resolve into a crumpled or "cauliflower" ear. This is because of the damage done to the cartilage which keeps the pinna erect. If the haematoma has been extensive, some crumpling may result, even after the operation.

Papillomata: the cat's ear may be the seat of warty growths which can occlude the ear canal entirely. Surgical removal is the only satisfactory treatment.

Diseases of the Eye

Conjunctivitis (inflammation of the thin membrane covering the eyeball and lining of the eyelids): This occurs in viral respiratory diseases, giving the typical "red eye" appearance in such cases, or it may be due to irritant substances in the eye. A grass awn may become lodged under the third eyelid or haw. Pus-forming bacteria quickly produce a purulent discharge from the eyes following on conjunctivitis.

Keratitis (inflammation of the cornea, the transparent membrane covering the front of the eye): This appears as a blue opacity and can develop into a corneal ulcer. The cause is usually traumatic. Should the ulcer penetrate the cornea, the contents of the anterior chamber protrude through the opening and this is called a staphyloma.

The Haw also called the third eyelid or membrana nictitans, is well developed in the cat and gives added protection, also helping to clear debris from the eye. When cats are off-colour this membrane can remain partly over the eye. This is not a disease of the eye itself but rather a symptom of the condition of the cat, and is often apparent when the cat is harbouring tapeworms.

Glaucoma is a condition in which there is increased tension in the chambers of the eye. As the tension increases, the eyeball enlarges. The cause is usually an injury which has led to dislocation of the lens. Because of the complex nature of the eye and its importance as the organ of sight, all conditions affecting it should have veterinary treatment at an early stage.

Entropion (or inversion of the eyelid) when not caused by injury to

The haw, "third eyelid", or membrana nictitans. If the haw is visible this can be a sign of poor condition.

the lid is an hereditary condition and may be the result of breeding long-haired cats with ultra-short noses and flat faces. The eyelid rolls inwards causing irritation and excessive flow of tears down the face. Surgical correction is required. Affected cats should not be used for breeding.

Another result of breeding for type, and sometimes producing "over-type", is shortening and distortion of the lacrimal duct which drains the tears from the eye into the naso-lacrimal canal. The duct becomes occluded and tears overflow from the eye giving the familiar "weepy eye" seen in some cats.

A malignant type of tumour is occasionally seen in the iris.

Internal Parasites

Roundworm are harboured in the stomach and intestine of the cat. Adult cats show few ill-effects, but in kittens a heavy infestation can produce severe loss of condition. The stomach worms are vomited and immediately curl up into a corkscrew shape. The intestinal worms are passed in the faeces. They cause diarrhoea, loss of condition, pot-belly, lack of appetite and an "earthy" odour from the breath. Roundworms are easily eliminated by present day drugs which cause little if any discomfort to the cat.

Hookworms are extremely rare in cats in the British Isles. They are common in hot climates and are known in the southern U.S.A., but are not regarded as a serious health problem.

Tapeworms are found in the small intestine. The head remains attached to the bowel wall while ripe segments of the worm containing the eggs are passed in the faeces. It may be difficult to find the segment because of the cat's habit of covering up its faeces, but sometimes a segment may be seen either on the fur around the anus or on the ground where the cat has been sitting. The segment is creamy-white, soft and moist and, on exposure to air, it dries up and becomes brittle and straw-coloured. The affected cat eats voraciously, but loses some condition. The tapeworm eggs are ingested by and developed in an intermediate host such as the rabbit, mouse or flea which, in turn, is eaten by the cat. Treatment, which should be administered under veterinary supervision, is relatively simple nowadays, but attention must be paid to elimination of the intermediate host, particularly the flea.

Coccidiosis: Coccidia are parasites which burrow into the lining of the intestine. The condition is more common in kittens than is generally realised. Adult cats rarely show any symptoms, but may be carriers. In kittens, there is persistent diarrhoea, which does not yield to usual treatments. Sometimes there is vomiting of a milky fluid, especially first thing in the morning. The kitten loses condition and fails to grow at the normal rate. Diagnosis and treatment are matters for your veterinary surgeon. As the kittens can reinfect themselves from their faeces strict hygiene is essential. All faeces must be disposed of immediately, and sanitary trays scrubbed with water and ammonia.

Toxoplasmosis: This is caused by an organism found in the body cells, which is not always pathogenic. When it does cause illness, the lung is frequently involved, causing bronco-pneumonia with severe respiratory distress and a high persistent temperature. Other organs may be invaded giving rise to a variety of symptoms. In acute cases, death supervenes fairly rapidly. In other cases, the infection may become chronic.

Feline infectious peritonitis: This is thought to be a virus disease and has been seen in America for some years, but only recently in the U.K. It is mainly a disease of young cats. The symptoms are lassitude, lack of appetite and increasing swelling of the abdomen caused by dropsy. Jaundice may be seen before death supervenes.

Abscesses

As these account for a large proportion of feline cases presented in a veterinary surgery, they merit a heading to themselves. They are almost always caused by a bite or claw mark from another cat and the reason they are so common is that the cat's tooth or claw makes a deep punctured wound which heals quickly on the surface leaving any pus-forming bacteria which have gained entrance to get busy under the skin.

The formation of an abscess is seen as a hard swelling which increases in size. This becomes hot and painful and finally a soft spot is felt where the abscess bursts and the pus erupts. The cat may appear quite well until about forty-eight hours before the abscess bursts when it will be off-colour and have a rise in temperature. As soon as a swelling is seen hot fermentation or the application of a kaolin poultice will speed up the ripening of the abscess. If the wound is on a leg, the leg may be immersed in hand-hot water, otherwise bathe the part using a sponge or cotton wool. A poultice needs to be bandaged in place. The patient will also require antibiotic treatment. Some abscesses do not "point" satisfactorily and have to be lanced, probably under general anaesthesia, or again the abscess may erupt but not drain completely, and the wound has to be enlarged to allow satisfactory drainage. If the surface wound is allowed to heal too quickly, the underlying tissues become unhealthy leading to a chronic abscess and the formation of sinuses. The pus-forming organisms may burrow deeply into muscles and joints and become so firmly established that treatment is difficult or impossible.

In order to prevent abscesses, if your cat has been in a fight, search him carefully for any tiny wounds. A small tuft of damp matted hair may be the only clue to the location. Clip the hair from the site, bathe with warm water containing disinfectant and apply penicillin ointment, being sure to insert the nozzle of the tube into the wound.

Poisons: In recent years, many new substances are available in the garden as weedkillers and pesticides, and also insecticides for use on domestic pets. These have greatly increased the risk of poisoning in cats. The cat spends long periods every day grooming and licking its body, and this makes it particularly susceptible to poisons which contaminate its coat and feet; some poisons can be absorbed directly through the skin. The cat may nibble grass or plants which have been sprayed with a toxic substance, therefore it is important to keep cats away from any area recently sprayed until there has been a period of rain. Although the labels on containers may say that the product is harmless to pets, under certain conditions this is by no means the case and manufacturers do not seem to realise that while the cat will not actually eat the product, it will ingest it while cleaning contaminated fur. It is also possible for the cat to suffer a secondary type of poisoning by eating rats, mice, or flies which have been killed by poisons.

If the cat's coat has been contaminated with anything toxic, wash it off immediately with soap and water (not detergent, to which some cats are sensitive).

If the cat has just swallowed a poison and unless the mouth is burnt, make it sick. The simplest emetic is a crystal of washing soda, about the size of a pea pushed down the cat's throat. Failing that, give salt and water. Symptoms of poisoning are varied, and different poisons may give rise to similar symptoms. In general, in the cat the most constant symptoms comprise: sickness, and diarrhoea; abdominal pain; nervous twitching, fits, excitability, loss of consciousness and coma. Veterinary treatment is essential as soon as possible, and when available take the poison container with you.

Accidents

Because of its wandering habits, the cat is a likely victim of road accidents. In such a case the first thing to be done is to wrap the cat in a blanket. It is best to wear gloves while doing this, the cat will be frightened and possibly in pain, and is liable to bite anyone who moves it. The essential thing is to keep it warm; it will be suffering from shock at the very least. Having wrapped it in a blanket put it in a basket or box near a source of heat. It should be moved very gently in case there are any major fractures, and it is best to lift the blanket using it as a sort of a stretcher, rather than grasping the cat. Serious haemorrhage should be controlled by applying a tourniquet if possible or by firm bandaging. Meanwhile telephone your veterinary surgeon and arrange to take the cat to him straight away.

Cats suffer from gun-shot wounds, whether the shots are by intent or by an inexperienced person letting fly at anything that moves in the grass or in a hedge. The wounds are difficult to find in the case of shot. They are small with a clearly defined circular edge and their presence may be denoted by small tufts of fur matted with blood. In many cases the shot is best left in place; this is for your veterinary surgeon to decide.

Wounds of the skin should be bathed with warm water containing disinfectant, the hair clipped round about and penicillin ointment applied. Extensive wounds will require suturing.

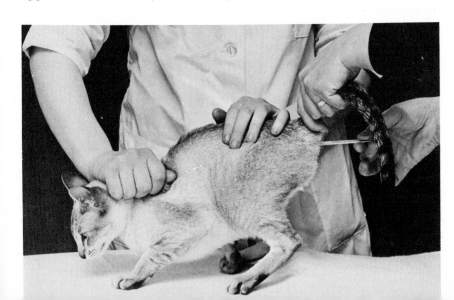

Taking the cat's temperature.

353

Evolution

Scientists, today, generally agree that the domestic cat belongs to the genus *Felis catus*, so designated in the year 1758, by Linnaeus. The name *Felis domestica* was chosen by Erlexen in 1771, and copied by Fischer, in 1788. Linnaeus's earlier name was subsequently rediscovered and, as the first-called name of any genus is permanently official, all scientists then had to discard *Felis domestica* in favour of *Felis catus*. *Felis catus* was already in general use for the European Wild Cat, which had to be renamed *Felis sylvestris* but, even so, some controversy remains to this very day. It is now generally accepted by zoologists all over the world that the cat as we know it today has its origin in the Eocene period, which also produced the very first primate ancestors of Man.

The ancestor of the cat, in common with the dog, weasel, hyena and other small mammals, was a small, vicious, weasel-like creature called Miacis, which prospered and developed through the next ten million or so years into two distinct groups known as *Dinictis* and *Hoplophoneus*.

Hoplophoneus was easily recognizable by the exaggerated upper and lower canine teeth, and the large flange on the lower jaw to cover and protect them. One species, the sabre-toothed tiger of our prehistory books, proved a formidable adversary of the huge, slow-moving beasts that roamed the plateaux and forest regions of his era. Known in zoological terms as *Smilodon*, the sabre-toothed tiger lived comfortably through the ages until he met his demise with the extinction of the big herbivores when, being unable to adapt his clumsy bulk and very specialized skull formation in order to catch the smaller and faster creatures, he also became extinct. Remains discovered in a Brazilian cave included the massive skull of *Smilodon* dating back to the Pleistocene, one and a half million years ago.

Descendants of *Dinictis*, on the other hand, developed specialized characteristics, which continued to stand them in good stead through the ages; one branch in particular was lynx-sized with retractable claws and a rather stream-lined appearance, thought to be the ancestors of the civet family, some of which survive unchanged to this day, and are very similar in several features to the domestic cat, but with longer body and head, and shorter tail. Members of the civet group, and therefore cousins of the domestic cat include the famous snake-killing mongoose, the palm-civet and the genet cat. This important subdivisioning of *Dinictis* occurred during the Miocene age. In all, *Dinictis* divided himself into some ninety sub-species, which are directly related to present-day cats and about thirty-five of which still actually exist in a similar and easily recognizable form.

Violent changes occurred all over the earth during the next few millions of years, and four great Ice-ages took their toll of life, allowing only the fittest and most adaptable creatures to survive, until, in the last million years of the Pleistocene, turbulent storms raged, mighty earthquakes heaved and changed the contours of the surface, the temperature increased over the land masses, and the last of the great ice fields retreated to the Poles. Man survived, and appeared at last in his recognizable form, intelligent and tenacious, and some forty species

Related in evolutionary terms to the domestic cat—above: the Spotted Genet; below: Malay Civet.

of the cat family, all highly-tuned for survival under the most rigorous conditions, came through unscathed.

It is reasonably safe to assume that the first tentative associations of cat and man occurred towards the end of the Stone Age, when the cat scavenged scraps of food from around human dwelling areas, and may also have been attracted in bad weather by the warmth of the wood fires.

Over many centuries, the cat generally assumed its place, along with other animals we now know as "domestic animals" as a natural adjunct to the human community and, by the time of the Egyptians, five thousand years ago, cat and man had established a very firm relationship; it is from the cats of this time that many of our present day breeds have evolved. Cats were trained for use in fishing, and hunting the wild marsh birds as well as to keep down the rats and mice in the huge grain stores along the Nile banks. The cat was considered a valuable family asset, and there were severe penalties for breaking the laws drawn up for its protection. Soon a cult developed for the worship of the cat, which was to last for more than two thousand years.

At first, the cat was considered sacred only to the goddess Isis; then gradually the great cat-goddess Bastet, sometimes known as Bast or Pasht, emerged. The earliest portrayal of Bastet as a cat-headed figure may be seen at the Cairo Museum, drawn on a papyrus of the twenty-first dynasty. Bastet took precedence over all other figures of worship, and a centre was built to her glory at Bubastis, east of the Nile delta—a huge square building of red granite. In the centre was a shrine with a great statue of Bastet. Feasts, holidays and pageants were held to her glory—the sacred statue was often brought forth from its shrine to be present at the festivities. The Egyptian word for cat is *mau*, literally "to see"—and legends abound in subsequent ages of links of the movements of sun and moon with the eye of the cat.

Images of the cat, Bastet's animal incarnation, were made in many forms and materials—gold, bronze, faience and common river clay. Amulet figures were worn by rich and poor alike. Cats, domestic and feral, were cared for lovingly. After death, the cat's body was rubbed with precious oils, and carefully wrapped in layers of cloth by specialists in embalming procedures, and if the owner was wealthy, the head would be encased in a papier maché cast, with the eyes indicated by circles of carefully painted linen. Thus preserved, the bodies were taken and laid out in special cemeteries, and the family would beat gongs and shave off their eyebrows as a sign of mourning.

One such cemetery, discovered at the turn of the twentieth century in central Egypt at Beni Hassan, contained over three hundred thousand mummified cats. The evidence of the past contained in this discovery was destroyed but, fortunately, other such finds were carefully examined by experts and provided much of our present knowledge of the early history of the cat. Of one hundred and ninety two skulls presented to the British Museum in 1907, the majority were found to be of the *Felis lybica* group, a form of small African bush-cat, which had a tabby body and a boldly ringed tail, and sported the distinctive "beetle" or sacred scarab mark between the ears. Sometimes called the Caffre or Kaffir cat, similar specimens can be seen today all over Africa.

Also a member of the civet group, the snake-killing mongoose.

Bronze statue from Egypt, made in the Saite Period, about 600 BC. It stands 6½ inches high.

355

This fowling scene comes from the tomb of an Egyptian, Nebamun, shown accompanied by his wife, who is standing behind him, and by his daughter, sitting at his feet. His hunting cat has caught a bird. From Thebes—about 1450 BC.

The remainder of the skulls were larger, and identified with the jungle cat, *Felis chaus*, but from other evidence it was thought that the latter was not truly domesticated, but merely foraged around human habitation for food scraps.

From Egypt, *Felis lybica* became well-established in China and India in a semi-wild state, and trade between Egypt and Rome brought the cat to Italy. At this time, cats with longer fur were known in Persia, and spread gradually into other areas; matings undoubtedly took place between the short-haired bush cats producing short-haired offspring, but when these eventually mated together, both short-haired and long-haired progeny would have resulted. Thicker coats would have evolved naturally in colder climates, and the cats nearer the equator would have kept their short, fine fur.

The Greeks acquired cats from the Egyptians; the Phoenicians carried cats with them at sea, and probably brought them to Britain when trading for Cornish tin; certainly the Roman legions brought cats with them to Britain, for the skeleton of a pet cat was found in the ruins of a Roman villa which had been destroyed by fire in the year 200 A.D.

A monetary value was put on cats in 936 A.D. by Hywel the Good, Prince of Wales, which put the cost of a kitten before its eyes opened at one penny, and once it could catch mice, at two pence. Laws were strictly enforced whereby anyone found guilty of killing a cat had to pay its worth in corn, measured by holding the dead animal by the tip of its tail so that the nose touched the ground, and pouring grain over the body until it was completely covered.

Wild and domestic cats could and did mate freely together thus

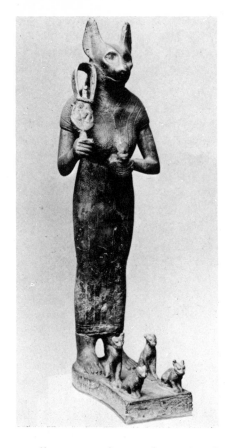

tending to moderate the pace of domestication of the species in the early stages, especially as it is the natural instinct of the mother cat to hide away the litter at birth; even fully domesticated cats' kittens are semi-wild if reared in this manner, and need a period of gentling.

No records exist of planned breeding of the domestic cat until the year 999 A.D., when it is written that on the "tenth day of the fifth moon" a female cat gave birth to a litter of five kittens in the Imperial Palace at Kyoto, Japan, and the Emperor was so delighted with this event that he ordered special treatment for the kittens, and decided to breed further generations. Cats at that time were used to control the mice that ate the silkworm cocoons, but following the Royal example, it soon became fashionable to keep cats confined for breeding purposes, and they were controlled and walked on leashes. The mice were quick to take advantage of this situation, and ran rife, until the silk industry reached the point of collapse, and the grain stores were overrun with vermin. The government eventually decreed that the cats be liberated in 1602, and imposed severe fines for anyone found buying or selling cats, and the rats and mice were soon brought under control once more.

Revered for centuries, the cat became the victim of sacrificial rites during the Middle Ages, a time which most cat lovers prefer to forget. In Germany, Christians reacted against a strange orgiastic cult named after Freya the Goddess of Love, in which the cat featured prominently, and they were put to death by the thousands. In 1484, Pope Innocent VIII denounced the cat and all who harboured it, and the innocent creatures were persecuted all over Europe. Many thousands of people, mainly women, were put to death in Germany alone for feeding, harbouring or protecting cats, and a vast number of executions

Above, left: Bastet—the cat-headed goddess.

Centre: An Egyptian mummified cat of the Roman period.

Right: The bronze Gayer-Anderson cat from Egypt. Probably Roman period, after 30 BC.

357

were performed in France. Hundreds of thousands of cats were destroyed in ceremonies presided over by priests.

These pagan ritual sacrifices spread even to the New World and more than two thousand trials for cat-sorcery were held in New England alone. Persecuted, tortured and destroyed, the cat, which had survived for fifty million years, was now in danger of extinction.

The black rat, which had returned with the Crusaders in their ships to the Low Countries and Britain, helped in the salvation of the cat. Multiplying by the thousand in the sewers, and carrying the dreaded plague, it became necessary ro reinstate the cat in order to control the rats, and gradually the numbers of cats increased.

Accepted once more as the family pet, the cat gained even more popularity when Louis Pasteur discovered the microbe in the middle of the nineteenth century. Dogs were suddenly considered unhygienic, but the fastidious cat was considered "safe" to have in the home, and it became fashionable to have the more exotic colours in cats, or cats from foreign countries, as house-pets. The French favoured the long-haired breeds, and pet cats were provided with silk cushions, and were groomed and cosseted. In Britain, many breeds were already known and visitors from abroad often brought frail-looking long-boned cats and kittens as gifts.

In the 1860's, the U.S. state of Maine held the New World's first cat show, for most homes in New England had at least one pet cat mated with the small wildcat which had become extinct around 1820. The resulting breed, named the Maine Coon because of the enormous bushy tail, striped like that of a racoon in the tabby varieties, is still bred today. It is a long-haired cat, which can be of any colour, but is not Persian in type, with ears and cheeks tufted with long hair, giving a very lynx-like expression, and it is a very popular house-pet.

England's first official cat show was held in 1871, at the Crystal Palace in London; many breeds were represented even then, and in the last hundred years, great strides have been made in the development and selective breeding of cats of many varieties all over the world.

Basically, today, two types of domestic cat exist, one type is long and elegant, very slim, with long legs and tail, a pointed marten face, large ears and oriental eyes; the second type is more heavily built, short and stocky, with a round head, small ears and round eyes set in front of the face. This second type is also found with long hair and is then designated "Long-hair" in Britain and "Persian" in the U.S.A. By selective breeding and importing cats with unusually mutated colouring or other "different" features, the many and varied breeds of today have been developed.

Logically, many more breeds or varieties are possible; for example, a long-haired Siamese-Manx would be feasible, but however man intervenes to control its breeding habits, the cat could revert to the wild in one or two generations, completely independent; even the most famous and pampered show champion would be able to provide for itself in the wild, and the genetic make-up of the cat is such that it would very soon revert to the type of the short-haired tabby of the African bush, if there were no human element involved in its selective breeding.

Genetics

A basic working knowledge of genetics enables the cat breeder to fix good points in his stock, to introduce desired features and colours, and to eliminate hereditary faults. Many top show cats bred without sound genetic knowledge are in great demand for stud services, and among the hundreds of kittens they ultimately sire, some may be excellent; however the breeder carefully and methodically following planned breeding programmes will produce stock of more constant quality. This article is a simple outline of the science of genetics as applied to the cat, so that standard reference works, which baffle so many with technical terms and symbols, may be read with greater understanding. Theoretical genetical knowledge may then be linked with the study of general breeding practice and results, the effects of in-breeding, line-breeding, and out-crossing, and the inheritance of particular characteristics.

Heredity was first conceived as an exact science by a nineteenth century monk, Gregor Johann Mendel, later Abbot of the monastery at Brno in Czechoslovakia. A keen gardener, he experimented in the monastery gardens by crossing varieties of garden peas, producing results acclaimed for their simplicity and accuracy. He published a paper in 1865, which faded into oblivion, to be rediscovered simultaneously by three scientists working quite independently in 1900. Mendel's importance was at last recognized; the definite hereditary units which he termed Mendelian factors are the *genes* of present-day terminology.

Let us consider first the *cells* of which all living organisms are made up, and those of their functions concerned with heredity. An individual cat's life starts with the union of the sperm and the ovum (known collectively as the *gametes*), which join to form one new cell, the *zygote*. Each cell is microscopic, consisting of a jelly-like mass called *cytoplasm*; in the centre of every cell, is a denser ovoid or spherical body called the *nucleus*, which plays a controlling part in the life of the cell, when two gametes join in sexual reproduction, the two nuclei fuse and become one. Each nucleus carries material transmitting characteristics from the parent; so the zygote inherits characteristics from both parents but is identical to neither. The zygote divides into two cells; they divide to become four and so on until the mature cat has about ten thousand million cells. This division process is called *mitosis*.

The first stage in cell division is division of the nucleus, within which are the *chromosomes*, the most important structures in the science of genetics. Each cell in the cat's body has nineteen pairs of chromosomes. For simplicity we will consider one set of chromosomes in one cell. The chromosomes differ from one another in size and shape, but with certain exceptions occur in identical pairs. Such a pair is said to be *homologous*.

Along each chromosome is arranged in fixed order a set of genes; each gene corresponds to its opposite number on the paired chromosome—such related genes are called *alleles* or *allelomorphs*. During mitosis each individual chromosome splits lengthways into identical halves (called *chromatids*); the halves travel to opposite ends of the cell and, acting now as full chromosomes, form two new nuclei. After mitosis, both new cells have chromosome sets identical to the parent, and thus the chromosome identity is maintained throughout all the cells of the body.

Ordinary cells with full chromosome complement have nineteen chromosome pairs; at fertilization each gamete contributes nineteen chromosomes, which pair up with their opposite numbers to produce nineteen pairs. Genes lie normally in allelic pairs; a gamete has only one of each allelic pair, and the members of these pairs, when they come opposite one another, may be either "dominant" or "recessive". Sometimes they can react to produce an intermediate result.

A kitten may receive a similar gene from both sire and dam for a particular feature—such a kitten is *homozygous* for that feature. On the other hand, it may receive a gene for a characteristic from the sire, say, but an alternative gene from the dam—the kitten is then *heterozygous* for that feature. If a cat is homozygous for a feature, that feature will show up in the cat irrespective of dominance or recessivity; if heterozygous, then whether the feature is expressed or not will depend on dominance or recessivity.

Mendel crossed a tall variety of pea with a dwarf variety; probably expecting intermediately high off-spring. But the off-spring were all tall, like one parent. Crossing the tall offspring, he produced 75 per cent tall, and 25 per cent dwarf plants. The short plants then bred true, while the tall were of two kinds; one third bred true (producing all tall offspring); two-thirds produced, like their parents, 75 per cent tall and 25 per cent dwarf plants. This can be explained. Assume that a pure-breeding tall plant receives from each parent a factor, or *gene*, for tallness—we can call this plant's genetic make-up, or *genotype*, TT. Similarly, a pure-breeding dwarf plant receives a dwarfness gene from each side; we can write its genotype as tt. The tall plants, which produced both tall and dwarf offspring, must have contained *both* genes (Tt). The tall genes (T) masked the effect of the dwarfness genes (t), and are therefore *dominant;* the dwarfness gene is *recessive.* These complementary genes are examples of allelomorphs. Gametes can carry only one of a pair—gametes from a TT plant will carry a T gene; gametes from a tt plant will carry a t. When the genotype of a plant is Tt, the gamete can carry T or t, but not both—half will carry T and half t; therefore the ovule from one plant stands an equal chance of being fertilized by a pollen grain carrying T or by one carrying t. If sufficient numbers are produced, we may expect in the first generation of offspring an approximation to Mendel's 1:2:1 ratio of $TT:Tt:tt$ according to the laws of chance.

Peas were again used in another experiment, which can also be applied to cat breeding. Peas with round seeds were found to be dominant to those with wrinkled seeds, just as tallness was dominant to dwarfness. Also, yellow seed colour was dominant to green. A plant with yellow round seeds was crossed with one with green wrinkled seeds; in the first generation all the offspring had yellow round seeds—both these characteristics are dominant. When these in turn were self-pollinated, four types of seeds were produced, in the ratio 9:3:3:1—yellow round, yellow wrinkled, green round and green wrinkled. Using the symbols Y (yellow), y (green), R (round), r (wrinkled), four types of gametes are possible: *YR*, *Yr*, *yR* and *yr*. A "Mendelian chequerboard" helps to show the possible offspring:

	YR	*Yr*	*yR*	*yr*
YR	*YR* *YR*	*Yr* *YR*	*yR* *YR*	*yr* *YR*
Yr	*YR* *Yr*	*Yr* *Yr*	*yR* *Yr*	*yr* *Yr*
yR	*YR* *yR*	*Yr* *yR*	*yR* *yR*	*yr* *yR*
yr	*YR* *yr*	*Yr* *yr*	*yR* *yr*	*yr* *yr*

In each square will be found the genotype of one individual resulting from the various combinations of parent gamete genes. Each individual showing *Y* will appear yellow, whether or not accompanied by *y*; every seed showing *R* will appear round, whether or not accompanied by *r*.

In this experiment the genes for the two characteristics, roundness/wrinkledness, and colour, behave quite independently as far as inheritance is concerned, as they are carried on different chromosomes. As explained already, an individual that breeds true for any particular character is called a homozygote for that character.

Sometimes hereditary characteristics are sex-linked, an example in the cat being the red factor, called yellow by geneticists, and symbolised as *O* for orange. Let us consider how the sex of a kitten is determined. The female cat has nineteen pairs of homologous, or identical, chromosomes. A male, however, has eighteen such pairs; the remaining pair does not match—the larger of the pair is known as the *X* chromosome, the smaller as the *Y*. (The female has two identical *X* chromosomes). All the ova therefore carry *X* chromosomes, while the sperm may carry *X* or *Y*, both produced in equal numbers. It is even chances whether an ovum will be fertilized by an *X* or a *Y*-bearing sperm. If by the former, a female, *XX*, will result; if the latter, a male, *XY*.

Now the red colour in the cat can only be carried on the *X* chromosome, never on the *Y*: as the male has one *X* only he can be either *O* (yellow) or *o* (non-yellow). The female however, has two *X* chromosomes, and can therefore be of three possible genotypes: *OO* (yellow), *Oo* (tortoiseshell) or *oo* (non-yellow). This heterozygous form is unique, as its coat shows the influence of both *O* and *o* genes in different parts of the animal at the same time. Some mating results may make this clearer:

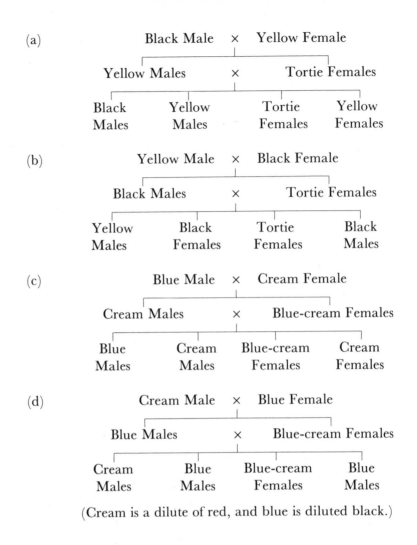

(a) Black Male × Yellow Female

Yellow Males × Tortie Females

Black Males | Yellow Males | Tortie Females | Yellow Females

(b) Yellow Male × Black Female

Black Males × Tortie Females

Yellow Males | Black Females | Tortie Females | Black Males

(c) Blue Male × Cream Female

Cream Males × Blue-cream Females

Blue Males | Cream Males | Blue-cream Females | Cream Females

(d) Cream Male × Blue Female

Blue Males × Blue-cream Females

Cream Males | Blue Males | Blue-cream Females | Blue Males

(Cream is a dilute of red, and blue is diluted black.)

As the red (yellow) colour can only be carried on the X chromosome, only when the sire and dam both show the red colour can a red female kitten be produced. These results obviously apply to any breed of cat carrying the red gene, be it Persian, Short-hair or Siamese in pattern.

Dominance of common characteristics in the cat are of great importance to the cat breeder, who will primarily be concerned with coat colour, coat length and pattern. Basically, it should be remembered that White is dominant to all colours; Black is dominant to Blue and Chocolate (and therefore Lilac); Short-hair is dominant to Long-hair; Self-colour is dominant to Siamese or Himalayan pattern; Tabby is dominant to non-tabby and Full coat is dominant to Rex coat. Since genes always occur in pairs, a gene can never be recessive on its own, only to some other characteristic.

A mating that puzzles some breeders is that between a homozygous (pure) Blue-point Siamese and a homozygous (pure) Chocolate-point Siamese because all the progeny are Seal-points! If, however the resultant progeny are mated together the kittens produced will be in the ratio of 9:3:3:1—nine Seal-points, three Blue-points, three Chocolate-points and one Lilac-point. The ratio of expected colour is as we have been led to expect from Mendel's Second Law of Heredity. The reason that the first cross produces all Seal-point kittens is that both Blue and Chocolate are modifications of Seal (Black), and the reason that we may expect one Lilac-point in sixteen kittens is due to the fact that Lilac is merely Chocolate carrying a double dose of Blue.

Tabby pattern in the cat is the original and wild type of coloration. There are four types of tabby, the mackerel striped, the pattern known as blotched, marbled, or classic, the Abyssinian or ticked, and the spotted. The Abyssinian is dominant to the other three types, the mackerel and the spotted are dominant to the blotched. The tabby effect can be produced in several colours, the most common being the brown tabby which is genetically black and equivalent to "normal" in the Abyssinian. Tabby is known as Agouti by geneticists and is symbolised as A, whereas Black, which is non-agouti is symbolised by a. A pure strain of tabby cats will produce only tabby kittens, and a pure strain of black cats will produce only black kittens. What happens if two such cats are crossed?

If a pure black is mated to a pure tabby, only tabby kittens will result; however, if the offspring are mated together, both tabby and black offspring will be produced in the ratio of 3:1. If the tabby offspring are mated back to the black however, the expected ratio of tabby to black would be 1:1. The pure tabby would have a genotype of AA and could have only tabby offspring, but the tabby produced from a mating between tabby and black would have a genotype of Aa. Both cats would look identical, that is they would have the same *phenotype*, however the Tabby Aa is capable of producing both tabby and black kittens. Tabby AA is therefore homozygous and Tabby Aa is heterozygous for tabby pattern.

Another interesting breeding experiment in the cat would be a mating between a Seal-point Siamese and a Blue Persian. The genes involved would be Siamese pattern (recessive to full colour), black colour (dominant to blue) and short-hair (dominant to long-hair) in the Siamese parent; and in the Persian parent, full colour (dominant to Siamese pattern) blue colour (recessive to Seal, which is genetically black) and long-hair (which is recessive to short-hair). All the kittens would be black in colour, and short-haired. If these short-haired blacks were mated together the second filial generation would be expected to produce self-black short-hairs, self-blue short-hairs, Seal-point Siamese, self-black long-hairs, self-blue long-hairs, Blue-point Siamese, Seal-point Colourpoint Persians, Blue-point Colour-point Persians, in the ratio of 27:9:9:9:3:3:3:1. The Siamese-patterned offspring then mated together would produce only Siamese patterned kittens.

Many other interesting crosses can be made, and can be worked out on paper, once the genotype of each parent is known, by means of the Mendelian chequerboard method as seen in the experiments with the pea plants.

The appearance of colour and coat pattern is not the sole concern of the cat breeder however, and it is not known how some characteristics, such as size of ears and tail length is carried, and whether these are dominant or recessive characteristics; therefore it is up to each breeder to draw up a "standard of perfection" for his own breed and to assess his potential breeding stock according to this. A scale of points should be drawn up, giving priority and highest score to the most desired features in the breed, and each kitten should be graded accordingly, and discarded if it does not measure up satisfactorily. In this way the overall quality of the breeding stock may be improved.

Controversy reigns as to whether the best method of cat breeding is in-breeding, line-breeding, out-crossing or a mixture of all three. These terms are often used in the wrong sense by uninformed breeders. In-breeding only refers to matings between father and daughter, mother and son or brother and sister. Line-breeding refers to the mating of members of the same family, daughter to grandfather and so on, and both these methods are often referred to loosely, as in-breeding. Out-crossing is the opposite to in-breeding, being the mating between two entirely unrelated cats. It has been seen already that all the characteristics inherited by the kittens are the result of the fusion of the genes of their parents at mating, so bearing this in mind, it is possible to assess the merits of in-breeding. The purpose of in-breeding is to fix as many points as possible in the resulting kittens, and to do this close relatives must be used because of the similarity of their genetic make-up. Sometimes the first and second generations in a programme of in-breeding are disappointing, with the desired results only coming to the fore in the third and subsequent generations. A programme using the in-breeding method can only be successful if the breeder has studied genetics, and starts with cats of a very high standard of both type and stamina. The breeder must also be very perceptive in the selection of kittens for succeeding generations and must ruthlessly cull those which do not reach his desired standard. (Culling, here, means disposing of cats as neutered pets, not, as with farm livestock, destroying them out of hand.)

The advantages of in-breeding are that type is fixed very quickly, and the breeder can achieve a distinct strain within the breed. Homozygosity is increased with the result that favourable characteristics are locked-in, and perhaps most important of all, any hidden faults are quickly brought to light and can therefore be eliminated, by selection. Disadvantages are that the faults in a strain are fixed as easily as the good points and therefore all foundation stock must be of the highest quality. In inexperienced hands in-breeding can lead to a rapid deterioration in the breed, so should not be attempted by the novice breeder unless with supervision from a specialist breed society.

Line-breeding is very similar to in-breeding and the same remarks apply in a somewhat modified form. It is a middle-of-the-road approach to cat breeding and can be a very successful one. Out-crossing when used in conjunction with line-breeding and in-breeding is valuable to bring in new genes to a line, but any programme based solely on out-crossing has no value whatsoever, and consists entirely of haphazard matings which may or may not produce quality kittens depending on chance alone.

It is suggested that having assimilated and learned the basic rules of genetics and the meaning of the simple terms, the progressive cat breeder should further his knowledge by specialized reading, applying the methods to his stock and carefully recording his results, when, with time and patience, he will achieve a line of healthy Champions.

Bibliography

A wide variety of books on cats are listed here – some of the older publications are difficult to obtain, but may be picked up from time to time in second-hand bookshops; the majority, however, should be available from local libraries or booksellers.

In addition to the books listed, the reader can gain much valuable information from stud books and from the specialist feline magazines published in many countries, and from the show rules, classifications, and show standards available from the various governing associations throughout the world.

Aberconway, C., Lady. *A Dictionary of Cat Lovers*, 1949.
Ashford, A. and Pond, G. *Rex, Abyssinian and Turkish Cats*, 1972.
Aymer, B. *The Personality of the Cat*, 1958.
Baker, Hettie Gray. *Your Siamese Cat*, 1952.
Beachcroft, T. *Just Cats*, 1936.
Blue Peter Book of Pets, 1969.
Boorer, M. *Wild Cats*, 1969.
Carr, W. H. A. *The Basic Book of the Cat*, 1963.
Chandoha, W. *The Complete Book of Cats*, 1957.
Clarke, F. *Of Cats and Men*, 1957.
Conger, J. *The Velvet Paw*, 1963.
Crew, F. *All These and Kittens Too*, 1959.
De Beer, J. H. *Cats*, 1955.
Dechambre, E. *The Pocket Encyclopaedia of Cats*, 1960.
Denham, S. and H. *The Complete Book of the Siamese Cat*, 1968.
Denis, A. *Cats of the World*, 1964.
Drew, E., and Joseph, M. *Puss in Books*, 1932.
Eddy, S. *Alexander and Some Other Cats*, 1929.
Eliot, T. S. *Old Possum's Book of Practical Cats*, 1939.
Eustace, M. *Mostly About Cats*, 1972.
Eustace, M. *The World of Show Cats*, 1970.
Eustace, M. and Towe, E. *Fifty Years of Pedigree Cats*, 1967.
Fairchild, L. and H. *Cats and All About Them*, 1949.
Gallico, P. *Jennie*, 1950.
Gates, G. S. *The Modern Cat*, 1928.
Gay, M. C. *How to Live with a Cat*, 1949.
Greer, M. J. *The Fabulous Feline*, 1961.
Herford, O. *The Rubaiyat of a Persian Kitten*, 1904.
Heriot, C. *Handbook for Cat People*, 1971.
Howey, M. Oldfield. *The Cat in the Mysteries of Religion and Magic*, 1931.
Ing, C. and Pond, G. *Champion Cats of the World*, 1972.
Jennings, J. *Domestic and Fancy Cats*, 1893.
Joseph, M. *Cat's Company*, 1930.
Joseph, M. *Charles*, 1943.
Lauder, P. *The Siamese Cat*, 1971.
Kirk, H. *The Cat's Medical Dictionary*, 1956.
Langton, N. and B. *The Cat in Ancient Egypt*, 1940.
Mackenzie, Sir Compton. *Cats' Company*, 1960.

Manning, O. *Extraordinary Cats*, 1967.

Manolson, F. *C. is for Cat*, 1965.

Marks, A. *The Cat in History, Legend and Art*, 1909.

Mason, J. and P. *The Cats in our Lives*, 1949.

Mellen, I. M. *A Practical Cat Book*, 1939.

Mellen, I. M. *The Science and Mystery of the Cat*, 1949.

Méry, F. *Just Cats*, 1957.

Mery, F. *The Cat*, 1966.

Metcalf, C. *Cats*, 1969.

Mivart, G. St. *The Cat*, 1881.

Montgomery, J. *The World of Cats*, 1967.

Newbery, C. T. *Drawing a Cat*, 1940.

Platt, C. *Things You Don't Know About Cats*, 1924.

Pond, G. *The Observer's Book of Cats*, 1959.

Pond, G. *Persian Cats*, 1963.

Pond, G. *Cats*, 1964.

Pond, G. *The Perfect Cat Owner*, 1966.

Pond, G. *Complete Cat Guide*, 1968.

Pond, G. *The Long-haired Cats*, 1968. American edition, 1970.

Pond, G. *The Batsford Book of Cats*, 1969.

Pond, G and Towe, E. *Cats*, 1970.

Repplier, A. *The Fireside Sphinx*, 1902.

Rice, B. *The Other End of the Leash*, 1968.

Ross, C. H. *The Book of Cats*, 1968.

Sillar and Meyler. *Cats, Ancient and Modern*, 1966.

Simmons, A. F. *Famous Cats*, 1958.

Simms, K. L. *They Walked Beside Me*, 1954.

Simpson, F. *The Book of the Cat*, 1903.

Smyth, Sir J. *Ming*, 1966.

Soame, E. B. H. *Cats Longhaired and Short*, 1933.

Soderberg, P. *Cat Breeding*, 1948.

Soderberg, P. *Pedigree Cats, Their Varieties Etc*, 1958.

Spies, J. R. *The Compleat Cat*, 1966.

Stables, G. *The Domestic Cat*, 1876.

Stuart, D. M. *A Book of Cats*, 1959.

Tangy, D. *A Cat in the Window*, 1962.

Tenent, R. *The Book of the Siamese Cat*, 1950.

Tenent, R. *Pedigree Cats*, 1955.

Tovey, D. *Cats in the Belfry*, 1957.

Tute and Fonteyn. *Cockney Cats*, 1953.

Uze, M. *The Cat in Nature, History and Art*.

Vechten, C. van. *The Tiger in the House*, 1920. British edition, 1921.

Wade, P. *The Siamese Cat*, 1934.

Weir, H. *Our Cats and All About Them*, 1889.

Whitney, L. F. *The Complete Book of Cat Care*, 1953.

Williams, K. *Siamese Cats*, 1960.

Wilson, K. *A to Z of Cats*, 1959.

Wilson, K. *Cats*, 1958.

Winslow, H. *Concerning Cats*, 1900.

Zanetti, A. B. *Journey from the Blue Nile* (Handbook on the Abyssinian Cat), 1966.

Contributors

In the following notes the salient details are given of the career and achievements in the cat world of the contributors of the articles, photographs and information of which this book is compiled. The contributors are well-known and respected throughout the world, particularly in Britain and the United States, where the names of their catteries (which appear as the prefixes or affixes to the names of the pedigree cats bred by them) can be found in many pedigrees today.

The notes are, of necessity, brief, and there are in most cases a great many more famous and champion cats produced by each cattery than we have space to mention.

Editor

Grace Pond, F.Z.S. – has spent most of her life with cats. She has owned long-haired cats since early childhood and has been a breeder for nearly thirty years. She is an international show judge in Europe and Britain, and has been for many years organizer of the National Cat Club Show held annually at Olympia, London, the largest cat show in the world. Mrs Pond is a delegate to the Governing Council of the Cat Fancy, the governing body for the whole of Britain, and a member of numerous committees; she is also a broadcaster on radio and television, and has written and contributed to many books about cats. Mrs Pond has also contributed to this Encyclopaedia the articles on the Blue Long-hair, the Tortoiseshell Long-hair, the Bi-coloured Short-hair and the White Short-hairs.

Associate Editors in America

Blanche V. Smith and Raymond D. Smith, a husband and wife team who have devoted much of their lives to cats. Blanche Smith began breeding Blue-eyed White Persians in the early fifties and in 1954 began her popular column, Tips to the Novice, in *Cats Magazine*; she is still a contributing editor of that magazine. Mrs Smith has been an approved All-breed judge in the Cat Fanciers' Association since 1959. Raymond Smith became publisher and editor of *Cats Magazine* in 1951 and, under his guidance, the magazine has become the most highly influential and widely read cat magazine in North America. Mrs Smith has also contributed to this Encyclopaedia the article on the Cat Fancy in the U.S.A., and the articles on Cat Shows in the U.S.A.

Special Photographs

Anne Cumbers – developed her present reputation as one of the world's leading animal photographers from a childhood love of animals. Her speciality is cats and dogs, and she has for many years been the official photographer at the National Cat Club Show in London. Over 400 of the photographs in this book have been taken by her specially to illustrate the best types in their breeds, and to illustrate the desirable points in each breed.

The Contributors

Angora, Balinese, Maine Coon, Peke-face, Shaded Silver, Blue Tabby, Cream Tabby (long-hairs); *American Short-hair, American Wirehair, Exotic Short-hair, Japanese Bobtail, Sphynx* (short-hairs); *Cat Fancy in Canada:* Edna Field, owner of the Chota-Li cattery, breeder of Abyssinians, international show judge in the C.F.A, and breeder of the internationally famous Abyssinian male, Gr Ch Chota-Li R.S.T., sire of many Grand Champions and Best-in-Show winners across North America.

Balinese: Mrs E. Field – *see* Angora, above.

Bi-coloured (long-hair): Rachel Knight, breeder of the Greenwood Persians, specialist in Tortoiseshell-and-Whites and Bi-colours. Her winners include the female red and whites Greenwood Trudie and Greenwood Goldilocks, while her best male was Ch Greenwood Harvestmoon, a Red Tabby Long-hair, a notable winner in 1970.

Birman: Elsie Fisher's interest in Birmans began with her first sight of one in Paris in 1965; before this she had specialized in Siamese, breeding at her Praha cattery, the Champion of Champions Ch Praha Poco Allergando, a Lilac-point, winner of over 200 awards. Mrs Fisher is a contributor to cat magazines in Britain and abroad, and is now fully committed to the breeding of Birmans.

Black (long-hair): Marjorie Bull, owner of the Deebank cattery in Cheshire, England, specializing in Black, White, Blue and Cream Long-hairs. Her most famous cat is Ch Deebank Mascot, a male, winner of five Best-in-Shows and sire of seventeen Champions and Premiers.

Blue (long-hair): Mrs G. Pond – *see* Editor, page 367.

Blue-cream (long-hair): Phyllis Fawell began breeding with Red Tabbies (bred the famous Ch Barwell Pedro, ten times Champion) and Tortoiseshells, graduating to Blue-creams and Blues, with the initial intention of improving the type of her Red Tabbies. Bred the highly successful Blue-cream Ch Barwell Athene, Best Long-hair at the British National in 1963. Her Barwell Helios, a Cream male, became Grand Champion in Australia.

Cameo: Mrs A. B. Britton, with her husband and her mother, breeds under two prefixes, Peachy and Mymmswood. The former name prefixes her Cameos and the latter her Tortoiseshells.

Chinchilla: Mollie Turney, owner of the Bonavia cattery, began breeding in 1947. She has been Chairman for the past eight years of the Chinchilla, Silver Tabby and Smoke Society in Britain, is a past delegate to the G.C.C.F. and in 1971 was elected to the International Committee of the C.F.A. in America. Mrs Turney's most famous cat, a male, is Ch Bonavia Contenta, three times Best-in-Show and sire of Champions in six countries.

Colourpoint, Any Other Colour (long-hair): Mrs S. M. Harding, a scientist and author, and one of the first women to be elected to the Royal Society, is one of the most successful breeders of Colourpoint Long-hairs (Himalayans). Her cats are exported from Britain to all parts of the world, and her Mingchiu cattery was the top scoring cattery in North America in 1968–69. Mrs Harding's most successful cat is Ch Mingchiu Mudoba, winner of ten successive open classes, three times Champion of Champions and twice Best in Show.

Cream, Blue-eyed White, Odd-eyed White (long-hairs): Effie G. Aitken, breeder at her Bourneside cattery of Black, White, Blue, Cream and Blue-cream Long-hairs. A delegate to the G.C.C.F., Mrs Aitken has served in many capacities on committees of cat societies in Britain. Her best known cat is the Black male, Ch Bourneside Black Diamond. Her current interest is in improving the type and eye colour of the Blue-eyed White Long-hairs.

Maine Coon: Mrs E. Field – *see* Angora, page 367.

Peke-face: Mrs E. Field – *see* Angora, page 367.

Red Self, Red Tabby (long-hair): Nancy Rosell and Lillie Shepard. Mrs Rosell owns the Bruton cattery, originally specializing in Abyssinians, but now concerned mainly with long-hairs. The name Bruton has been carried by eight British Champions, two International Champions and two Premiers to date. Mrs Shepard, at her Willow-glen cattery, is a specialist in Red Self and Tortoiseshell Long-hairs and, since 1969, pure Blacks. At the time of writing she has a stock of thirteen cats, all Champions.

Shaded Silver (long-hair): Mrs E. Field – *see* Angora, page 367.

Smoke (long-hair): Francesca A. Roden, breeder of twelve Champions since 1966 in Chinchillas, Smokes and Blacks – prefix Sonata. A judge and a past delegate to the G.C.C.F., she has published articles on grooming and show preparation.

Blue Tabby (long-hair): Mrs E. Field – *see* Angora, page 367.

Brown Tabby (long-hair): Frances Paddon, registered her prefix, Trelystan, in 1920 under her maiden name of Cathcart. Up to 1931 she bred many varieties of long-hairs but then began to concentrate on Brown Tabbies. One of the most famous Tabbies ever bred was her Ch Trelystan Garnet (1931), winner of twenty-three Challenge Certificates. Through the years she has had many successes, including Trelystan Fire Opal (1953), and in 1962, Trelystan Felspar, who was exported to Canada where he became International Champion. Mrs Paddon is an International Show Judge, President of the South Western Counties Cat Club and delegate of that club to the G.C.C.F.

Cream Tabby (long-hair): Mrs E. Field – *see* Angora, page 367.

Red Tabby (long-hair): Mrs N. Rosell – *see* Red Self, this page.

Silver Tabby (long-hair): Mrs M. Greenwood, a founder member and first President of the Tabby Cat Club in Britain, owns the Wilmar cattery; perhaps her most successful cats are the males, Ch Dorstan Darius, Ch Widdington Thistle and Ch Wilmar Wade. Mrs Greenwood is a judge of long-haired Silver Tabbies and British Short-hairs.

Tortoiseshell (long-hair): Mrs G. Pond—*see* Editor, page 367.

Tortoiseshell and White (long-hair): Norah Woodifield bred and showed cats since 1954, initially with Blues and Creams, graduating to Tortie and Whites. Her first Champion came in 1960 since when she has bred many others at her Pathfinders cattery. Miss Woodifield is a championship show judge in Britain, and the Pathfinders prefix is well-known in Britain and abroad for its Tortie and White, and Bi-coloured long-hairs and short-hairs.

Turkish: Laura Lushington brought her first Van cat to Britain in 1956 and has been largely instrumental in maintaining the present high standards of purity in the breed; she now has ten Turkish cats. Her most famous cat, and the first to enter Britain, Van Attala, died in 1970. Miss Lushington has contributed many articles to magazines about this unusual breed, and has appeared on television.

White—Blue Eyes (long-hair): Mrs E. G. Aitken—*see* Cream, page 368.

White—Odd Eyes (long-hair): Mrs E. G. Aitken—*see* Cream, page 368.

White—Orange Eyes (long-hair): Jean A. Hogan, owner of the Snowhite cattery, has a long career as a breeder of Persians. Her Ch Snowhite Giselle was the last cat to win the coveted Supreme Best-in-Show award at the British National before that title was dropped. Snowhite Persians have been awarded over 450 first prizes and have been exported to many parts of the world.

Any Other Colour (long-hair): Mrs S. M. Harding—*see* Colourpoint, page 368.

Bi-colour (British Short-hair): Mrs G. Pond—*see* Editor, page 367.

Black, Blue-cream, Cream (British Short-hairs): Joan Richards' lifelong devotion to cats crystallized into her present great interest in "British" breeds in 1951, when she acquired her first, a British Blue, Broughton Nimrod, later Champion. Since then she has established her Pensylva prefix, has bred many champions, a great many of which have become champions in many parts of the world. Mrs Richards is a judge of all British Short-hairs.

Blue-cream (British Short-hair): Mrs J. Richards—*see* Black, above.

British Blue (British Short-hair): Shirley Beever achieved fame in the breed with her Fendale Blue Imp, Fendale Mirage and Fendale Abigail, three of the many champions bred at her Fendale cattery. Mrs Beever is an international judge, has managed cat shows, is Secretary of the Short-haired Cat Society of Great Britain and Manx Club Incorporated, and a delegate to the G.C.C.F. She is a regular contributor to British cat magazines.

Cream (British Short-hair): Mrs J. Richards—*see* Black, above.

Spotted, Silver Tabby (British Short-hairs); *Manx;*

The Cat in the Home: Elizabeth Towe is an international show judge and a familiar figure at cat shows in Great Britain, Australia, New Zealand, Europe and Scandinavia. She is a well-known breeder of a number of varieties, numbering several champions among her show successes. Mrs Towe is a delegate to the G.C.C.F., has organized many championship shows, and is the author of a number of books and articles on cats.

Brown Tabby (British Short-hair): Patricia H. Absalom, although a comparative newcomer to breeding, is at present President of the Tabby Cat Club in Britain. Her prefix, Brynbuboo, is already famous in the cat world, with Ch Brynbuboo Brown Peter, and Ch Brynbuboo Easter Girl, a long-hair, being particularly well-known.

Red Tabby (British Short-hair): Grace Hardman founded her Killinghall line of Red Tabbies with the female Ch Barwell Cherry, acquired from Mrs P. Fawell in 1951 (*see* Blue-cream Long-hair, page 368); since then she has produced twelve champions, nine of them Red Tabbies. Miss Hardman is a judge in Britain of Short-hair kittens.

Silver Tabby (British Short-hair): Mrs E. Towe—*see* Spotted, above.

Tortoiseshell (British Short-hair): Gladys A. Genty has been breeding under the Donnymeaux prefix since 1955 and, in fact bred Siamese before that, in 1953. She is a judge for all British Short-hairs and many other breeds of cat.

Tortoiseshell and White (British Short-hair): Mr H. V. Biswell has been showing under his Prospero prefix since 1966, with notable success. Tortie and White has always been his favourite colour.

White (British Short-hair): Mrs G. Pond—*see* Editor, page 367.

Siamese, Blue-point: Elizabeth Biggie has owned and bred Siamese since 1941, specializing in Blue-points in 1955, when she registered her prefix, Linton. Her most successful cat, both at shows and as a stud, was Ch Linton Ajax. Mrs Biggie is a judge of Siamese in Britain, has served on committees of the Siamese Cat Club, and is a delegate to the G.C.C.F.

Siamese, Chocolate-point: Dora Clarke is an international show judge, registered with the G.C.C.F. and F.I.F.E., and is either President or Chairman of a number of British cat clubs. As a breeder, under the Craigiehilloch prefix, she has produced such champions as Ch Craigiehilloch Chozaro (Chocolate-point) in Britain, Ch Craigiehilloch

Chojuliette (Chocolate-point) (Triple champion in America) and International Ch Leonora (Lilac-point) in France.

Siamese, Lilac-point: Judith Burlton has been concerned with Siamese since 1937. Under her Bru-Bur prefix she has produced many notable Siamese cats, including Bru-Bur Leon, a distinguished sire, among whose progeny, Ch Ona Lopez, Ch Bru-Bur Yogi and Premier Bru-Bur Poitou became worthy champions.

Siamese, Red-point and Tortie-point, Siamese, Any Other Colour; Egyptian Mau, Foreign Lilac, Foreign White, Havana; Boarding, Evolution, Genetics: Angela Sayer began showing at the highest level in Britain, the G.C.C.F. Golden Jubilee Show in 1959, where her Lilac-point kitten won five awards, including a first. As a breeder, under the Solitaire prefix (registered with the G.C.C.F. in Britain and A.C.F.A. and C.F.A. in America), she has produced such champions as Ch Solitaire Apache (Chocolate-point Siamese) and, more recently, Ch Solitaire Maneki Neko. Mrs Sayer is the only person ever to have taken her cats to America, where her Red-pointed Siamese Solitaire Fireopal (female) and Solitaire Cinnabar (male), shown at the A.C.F.A. show at Willamette, won all four rings and became American Champions. These cats are now in new homes in Denver.

Siamese, Seal-point: Mary Dunnill, under her prefix, Sumfun, breeds Seal-point Siamese, Havana, and Foreign White Short-hairs, and her stock is exported to many parts of the world. Mrs Dunnill is Honorary Secretary of the Siamese Cat Club in Britain and a delegate to the G.C.C.F.

Siamese, Tabby-point: Nancy Hardy's Senty-Twix cattery has produced both Siamese and Cornish Rex; she began breeding with her first Siamese in 1954, and her first success came in 1957, with the Seal-point Senty-Twix Xenia. Mrs Hardy is a show judge in Siamese and Cornish Rex and an active member and office holder in two Siamese cat clubs.

Siamese, Any Other Colour: Mrs A. Sayer—*see* Siamese, Red-point and Tortie-point, above.

Abyssinian: Edith Menezes, under the Taishun prefix, following a period of breeding Siamese, began her present interest in Abyssinians in 1948. She is a committee member of the Abyssinian Cat Club in Britain, and a delegate to the G.C.C.F. Mrs Menezes has for many years been a judge of the breed, and of Short-hairs. Among her many

successful cats is Ch Taishun Leo, a notable champion and sire of champions, and Ch Taishun Sabina, now in Colorado.

Red Abyssinian: Doris Threadingham, owner of the Bernina cattery, has been breeding pedigree cats since 1948, limiting her interest to Abyssinians and Burmese in 1960, and expanding her speciality to Red Abyssinians in 1964. In 1966 she produced two special females, Ch Bernina Princess and Ch Bernina Naomi. There followed numerous champions.

American Short-hair: Mrs E. Field—*see* Angora, page 367.

American Wire-hair: Mrs E. Field—*see* Angora, page 367.

Blue Burmese: Mr V. Watson under the prefix Sealcoat has bred many noteworthy Burmese cats. He first became interested in breeding pedigree cats in 1949, associated at that time with the Milori Siamese, and adopted the Burmese in 1953. Mr Watson founded the Burmese Cat Club in Britain (he is still Chairman), is a judge in the breed and has published many articles on the genetics and breeding of Burmese. His most famous Burmese is Sealcoat Blue Surprise, the first Blue Burmese.

Brown Burmese: Mr V. Watson—*see* Blue Burmese, above.

Burmese, Other Colours: Mrs R. M. Pocock owns the Pussinboots cattery. She began breeding Siamese, graduated to Burmese, and helped to pioneer Cream and Blue-cream Burmese. Mrs Pocock is owner of Ch Sable-silk Mouse (Brown), Ch Lamont Blue Burma-boy (Blue) and, currently, Ch Buskins Blue Sunya, a champion and sire of champions. She is Assistant Secretary and News Editor of the Burmese Cat Club in England.

Egyptian Mau: Mrs A. Sayer—*see* Siamese, Red and Tortie-point, this page.

Exotic Short-hair: Mrs E. Field—*see* Angora, page 367.

Foreign Lilac: Mrs A. Sayer—*see* Siamese, Red and Tortie-point, this page.

Foreign White: Mrs A. Sayer—*see* Siamese, Red and Tortie-point, this page.

Havana: Mrs A. Sayer—*see* Siamese, Red and Tortie-point, this page.

Japanese Bobtail: Mrs E. Field—*see* Angora, page 367.

Korat: Daphne Negus was born in England and is now a distinguished figure in the American cat world, as breeder and as active member and officer of many cat associations. Starting with Siamese in 1961 her interest in cats spread to include Burmese and, since 1964, Korats; she has been to Thailand to obtain further specimens from their native land and to meet Thai breeders. Mrs Negus is owner of the famous Grand and Triple Champion Ma Laid's Doklao Noi of Si Sawat, bred in Bangkok, and breeder of Grand Champion and Champion Si Sawat's Sunan.

Manx: Mrs E. Towe—*see* Spotted, page 369.

Cornish Rex: Ann Codrington is an outstanding authority on Siamese, White Short-hair and Rex cats; her Watermill prefix has been borne by champions in Britain, Canada and Australia. She is an international judge of Siamese, British Short-hairs and Rex, and has judged in America, Canada, Australia and Holland. Miss Codrington entered the cat world from a distinguished career on the stage, cinema and radio.

Devon Rex: Alison Ashford began breeding Siamese cats in 1958, in which year she registered her cattery name, Annelida, since become famous throughout the world. She acquired her first Rex, a Cornish Rex, in 1961 and soon was breeding kittens of both Cornish and Devon Rex genotypes. Her experimental breeding in 1964 produced the first "Si-Rex", from out-crosses using Siamese. Mrs Ashford later imported a Canadian Cornish Rex, Riovista Kismet and, using a British White Short-hair as an out-cross, she bred the first pure white Cornish Rex in Britain (Kismet was owned by Miss Codrington, *see* Cornish Rex, above).

Russian Blue: Florence Laugher, prefix Jennymay, first owned a Russian Blue, of the old Blue Foreign type, in 1948. She did not begin breeding, however, until 1960, with Archon Titania, from whom all her present breeding stock is descended. Miss Laugher exported Jennymay Astrii to Miss O'Boyle in America in 1961, and has supplied Jennymay cats to Denmark, Sweden, Holland and America where, currently, Jennymay Lucinda is a champion.

Sphynx: Mrs E. Field—*see* Angora, page 367.

Any Other Variety (short-hairs): Mrs G. Pond—*see* Editor, page 367.

Pet Cats (Non-pedigree): Elizabeth Wood founded a cat sanctuary in 1950, where stray and abandoned cats were cared for. She is a breeder of Siamese under the prefix Merrybrooke and is a judge in the Household Pet sections at shows. Her household of cats includes not only the pedigree Siamese of which she is so knowledgeable, but also many cats of more doubtful parentage, of which she is no less caring.

Anatomy, Vetting-in (Cat Shows in Britain), *Nutrition, Diseases:* Muriel Calder acquired her first pedigree cat, a Chinchilla, in 1941, and started breeding and showing after the Second World War—Chinchillas, Long-hair Blacks and Whites, Smokes and Blue Long-hairs. She is a judge of a number of Long-hair breeds, in Britain and abroad, and a judge of British Short-hairs. Mrs Calder has recently retired from veterinary practice after thirty-four years.

Boarding: Mrs A. Sayer—*see* Siamese, Red-point and Tortie-point, page 370.

Breeding: Mrs M. Brunton started breeding in 1923; Meadowsweet of Dunesk and her kitten won Best Cat and Best Kitten at her first show at Lanark in 1924. Mrs Brunton has since then bred many champions and Best-in-Show cats and kittens, including her world-famous Dunesk Blue Persians, and her cats have been exported all over the world. She is an international judge, Chairman of the National Cat Club and Blue Persian Cat Society, and Vice-Chairman for some years of the G.C.C.F.

The Governing Council of the Cat Fancy (Great Britain); *The Cat Fancy in Europe:* Dr Ivor Raleigh is the present Chairman of the G.C.C.F. A consulting engineer by profession, he joined the Cat Fancy just after the Second World War, breeding Blue Persians and Siamese for many years and serving as an international judge. A prolific author on feline topics, he has devoted much of his time to re-organizing the Cat Fancy, and its institutions, and to the creation of a higher regard for the cat in the public mind. Dr Raleigh is also Chairman of the Rex Cat Club and the Seal-point Siamese Cat Club.

The Work of the Registrars (The Cat Fancy in Great Britain): Miss P. Saunders began breeding with Siamese in 1961 and her two most famous cats were Ch Timbers Blue Jakko and Timbers Lilac Jonny, both winners of numerous awards— Timbers is her prefix. Miss Saunders participated in the compilation of the G.C.C.F. Stud Book from 1963 to 1968 and is G.C.C.F. Registrar for Long-hair and Short-hair breeds.

The Cat Fancy in the U.S.A.: Blanche Smith—*see* Associate Editors in America, page 367.

The Cat Fancy in Canada: Mrs E. Field—*see* Angora, page 367.

The Cat Fancy in Europe: Dr Ivor Raleigh—*see* The

Governing Council of the Cat Fancy, page 371.

The Cat Fancy in Australia and New Zealand: Mary Batten is a prominent figure in the Antipodean cat world, as breeder of Siamese cats, as a specialist Short-hair and All-breeds judge, as foundation member of the Queensland Society of Cat Genetics, and author of three books, and a judges' training manual. Mrs Batten is today Queensland's Chief and Examining Judge.

The Cat Fancy in South Africa: Linda Emery has been a breeder since about 1945, breeding Siamese, Burmese, Abyssinians (she bred the first Red Abyssinian in South Africa), Long-hairs, Russian Blues and Korats. Mrs Emery has been Registrar for the South African Cat Register since 1964; is Chairman of the Rand Cat Club, Secretary of the Governing Council of the Associated Cat Clubs of South Africa, and an All-breeds judge.

Organization of Cat Shows (Great Britain): Mary Wilson shares with her husband the Amberley cattery, specializing in Siamese, Blue Persians, Chinchillas, Silver Tabbies and Brown Burmese. In 1957 she founded the Three Counties Cat Society in Britain and, later, began to manage shows. In 1965 she was granted a championship show licence and in 1967 was appointed a delegate to the G.C.C.F. She serves also on the Council's Executive Committee and, since 1969, has managed the Siamese section of the British National Cat Club Show.

Judging, Becoming a Judge, Stewarding (Cat Shows in Great Britain), *Judging in Europe:* Doris Brice-Webb is a well-known international show judge, a familiar figure at shows in Europe. Under her Ronada prefix, she has bred many champions and international champions in Blue, Cream and Blue-cream Long-hairs. Mrs Brice-Webb is a member and officer of two cat clubs and a delegate to the G.C.C.F. and member of the Council's Executive Committee. Among her distinguished cats are Ch Donnachaidh Kirsty, a Cream now in her sixteenth year, and a beautiful Blue Persian, Ch Borrowdale Playgirl.

Vetting-in at Cat Shows in Britain: Mrs M. Calder—*see* Anatomy, page 371.

Cat Shows in America (incl. *Judging*): Mrs B. Smith—*see* Associate Editors in America, page 367.

Judging in Europe: Mrs Brice-Webb—*see* Judging, above.

The Cat in the Home: Mrs E. Towe—*see* Spotted, page 369.

Nutrition: Mrs M. Calder—*see* Anatomy, page 371.

Diseases: Mrs M. Calder—*see* Anatomy, page 371.

Evolution and History: Mrs A. Sayer—*see* Siamese, Red-point and Tortie-point, page 370.

Genetics: Mrs A. Sayer—*see* Siamese, Red-point and Tortie-point, page 370.

Glossary of Terms

A.C.A: American Cat Association.

A.C.F.A: American Cat Fanciers' Association.

A.O.C.: Any other colour.

A.O.V.: Any other variety.

Affiliation: Term applied to clubs attached to a larger body such as, in Britain, the G.C.C.F., and abiding by their rules.

Agouti: Coat pattern with banded hairs of brown, black and yellow, as found in wild feline species, also in the Abyssinian cat.

Ailurophile: A lover of cats.

Albino: An animal (or human) with a congenital lack of colouring pigment, the hair or fur being white and the eyes usually pink.

Almond-shaped: Shape of the eyes found in the "foreign" short-haired varieties.

Alter: Term used in America for castrated or spayed cat, known as "neuter" in Britain.

Anal gland: Gland sited at the anus.

Angora: One of the original varieties of long-coated cat found in Turkey.

Back-cross: The mating of a cat heterozygous for a character back to a cat homozygous for the same character.

Balanced: Symmetrically proportioned as a whole, usually used when referring to a cat's head.

Barring: Form of tabby marking which is considered a fault in a self-coloured cat.

Bat-eared: Having very large ears, as in the Rex.

Bite: Position of the upper and lower teeth when the mouth is closed.

Blaze: A distinctive contrasting marking running down from the cat's forehead to the nose.

Brindling: Having hairs of incorrect colouring interspersed with those of the correct shade.

British: The British Short-hairs, in all their recognised colour varieties, are the descendants of the short-haired cats native to the British Isles. The term "British" is also used more generally to describe "type" similar to that of the British Short-hairs – i.e. broad, round head and cobby body with short, sturdy legs; this is in contrast to the more slender build of the "foreign" breeds, e.g. Siamese.

Brush: The short, full tail of a long-haired cat.

Butterfly: The shape of the pattern of markings required on the shoulders of Tabby cats.

C.A.C: Certificat d'Aptitude de Championnat.

C.A.C.I.B: Certificat d'Aptitude de Championnat International de Beauté.

C.C.A: Canadian Cat Association.

C.C.F.F: Crown Cat Fanciers Federation (America).

C.F.A: Cat Fanciers Association (America).

C.F.F: Cat Fanciers Federation (America).

Calico: American term for a Tortoiseshell and White.

Calling: Cry made by a female cat when in season.

Canker: Inflammatory condition affecting the insides of the cat's ears, often caused by ear mites.

Castration: Neutering or altering of males.

Challenge Certificate: Award given in Britain to the winner of an open breed class reaching a certain standard – three such certificates awarded by three judges at three shows entitle a cat to become a Champion.

Champion: Winner of three challenge certificates under given conditions.

Champion of Champions: Class at British shows for full champions. Cat has to win three champion titles to be eligible for entry. Points are awarded according to number of cats in class.

Championship show: A show where challenge certificates are awarded to cats of a certain standard winning the open breed classes.

Chromosome: Thread-like structure in the nucleus of animal cells carrying genetic material.

Classic: Name given in America to the most usual pattern of tabby markings, known in Britain as "marbled".

Cleft palate: Congenital fissure in the roof of the mouth; this may happen in kittens which are in-bred.

Club class: Class at show put on by clubs specifically for their members.

Coarse: Term used when the cat's fur tends to be harsh rather than soft.

Cobby: Having a low-lying body on short legs in proportion.

Condition: General state of health and fitness.

Cross-bred: Resulting from the mating of one purebred variety with another.

Cryptorchid: A male cat having both testicles absent from the scrotum and hence useless for breeding.

Cull: To weed out from litters the weak and undesirable kittens.

Dam: Mother cat.

Digitigrade: Walking on the toes without touching the ground with the soles.

Dilution: Variation in colour producing a weaker hue.

Doctoring: Neutering, or altering.

Dominant: Main characteristic appearing in the first generation of breeding inherited from one only of the parents.

Double coat: Having a thick, soft undercoat with another, top, thick coat of long hairs, as required in the Manx.

Eumelanin: Brown or black pigment.

Exemption show: A small show where no challenge certificates are given and the rules are not so stringent.

Experimental: Often describes matings carried out for the possible production of a new variety.

F.I.E: Feline Infectious Enteritis.

F.I.F.E: Fédération Internationale Féline de l'Europe.

Fancier: One especially interested in cats.

Feral: Wild.

Foreign: The Foreign Short-hairs are, in general, those with "type" generally similar to that of the Siamese, i.e. with long, narrow, svelte head and body structure, as distinct from the more cobby build of, for example, the British or American Short-hairs.

Frill: Ruff; the fine hairs around the head, forming a frame to the face.

Furball: Fur swallowed by a cat when washing the coat forming a sausage-like body in the stomach and bowels, which may necessitate veterinary attention.

G.C.C.F: Governing Council of the Cat Fancy (Great Britain).

Gait: Manner of walking.

Gene: The units in body cells responsible for passing hereditary characteristics from one generation to the next. Each gene is responsible for one attribute.

Genetics: The study of heredity.

Genotype: The genetic make-up of an individual in respect of one character.

Gestation: Pregnancy. The period of time between mating and the birth of the kittens, usually about 64–66 days, but this may vary by a day or two (*see page* 280).

Ghost markings: Faint tabby markings which may be seen on many kittens when first born, but which disappear with growth.

Gloves: White feet, as seen in the Birmans.

Grand Champion: Cat that has gained three best champion titles under three different judges and in addition in America, has also been awarded 100 grand points, according to number of champions competing.

Haw: The third eyelid, known as the nictitating membrane. If visible, may mean poor condition or the start of an illness.

Heat: A term used when the female cat is in season; the oestrum.

Heterozygous: A condition in which any given genetic factor has been derived from only one of the two generating gametes.

Homozygous: Designating that condition in a cat in which any given genetic factor has been derived from both generating gametes.

Hot: A term used when referring to the coat colour, particularly on the back of a Cream, when too red.

Hybrid: A cross between two breeds.

I.C.F: Independent Cat Federation (America).

In-breeding: Breeding from closely related cats.

Infertile: Unable to breed.

Inocculation: In the feline world, usually refers to vaccination against feline infectious enteritis.

Jaw pinch: Indentation of the muzzle giving a pinched effect.

Jowls: Well-developed cheeks usually seen in an older male cat.

Kink: A bend or twist in the tail caused by a malformation, thickening or break of two vertebra. Once liked in the Siamese, but not now encouraged.

Kitten: A cat up to the age of nine months in Britain and ten months in North America.

Lactation: The secretion of milk by a female.

Level bite: Teeth meeting evenly – edge to edge.

Line breeding: The mating of members of the same family, such as the grandmother by the son, usually in the hope of perpetuating a particular feature.

Litter: The number of kittens born to a female cat at the same time.

Mackerel: A pattern of tabby markings resembling that of the mackerel fish, with rings as narrow and numerous as possible.

Malocclusion: Faulty closure of the upper and lower teeth.

Marbled: The usual pattern of tabby markings, known as classic in North America.

Mask: The darker colouring of the face seen in cats with contrasting points, as in the Siamese.

Micturition: The action of passing water.

Mongrel: Cat of mixed unknown parentage.

Monorchid: A male cat with only one testicle visible. Such a cat may not be exhibited in Britain.

Mutation: Genetic variation in the structure.

Muzzle: The projecting jaws and nose of the cat.

N.C.F.A: National Cat Fanciers Association (America).

Neuter: A castrated male or spayed female cat – often known as "alter" in America.

Nictitating membrane: The third eyelid or haw.

Nose leather: The skin of the nose; the colour may vary, e.g. brick-red in the Chinchillas.

Odd-eyed: Having one eye blue and the other orange.

Oriental: The eye shape of the "foreign" varieties.

Out of coat: Lacking quality and quantity of coat; the coat during moulting.

Pads: The cushions on the soles of the paws.

Parasite: An organism living upon another, host, organism.

Parti-colour: Having a coat of two clear distinct colours, as in the Bi-Colours.

Parturition: The act of giving birth to kittens.

Patching: Clearly defined patches of colouring, as seen in the coats of Tortoiseshell and Whites.

Pedigree: Genealogical table showing the ancestors of a cat.

Pencilling: The light markings seen on the faces of tabbies.

Persians: Cat with long fur said to have originated in Persia. These cats are now officially designated "Long-hairs" in Great Britain, although the term "Persian" is still widely used and is still the official term in many other countries, including America.

Phaeomelanin: Yellow or red pigment.

Phenotype: A strain of organism distinguishable from others by some character.

Points: The dark colouring on the head, ears, legs and tail, as in the Siamese.

Polydactyl: Having six toes or more on the front feet, and five or more on the back.

Premier: A neuter equivalent of a champion.

Pricked: Ears, standing high.

Progeny: Offspring.

Pure-bred: Produced from cats of the same variety.

Prefix: A registered cattery name that may only be used by the breeder in front of a cat's personal name.

Quarantine: Period of isolation imposed on all cats entering the British Isles (at the moment, six months) and some other countries.

Queen: A female cat used for breeding.

Recessive: Inheritable feature passed on to the progeny which may not show in the first generation.

Recognition: Acceptance of the standard for a new variety by the appropriate governing body.

Registration: The registering of a cat's name, date of birth, parentage and breeder with the appropriate registering body.

Ringed: Showing bands of colour in rings running evenly all the way down the tail or legs.

Ruff: Frill; the long hair around the neck.

Rumpy: True Manx with no sign of a tail, and with a well-rounded rump.

Sanction show: A show in Britain run on similar lines to that of a Championship show, but no challenge certificates are given.

Schedule: Booklet issued by the club organising a show, giving details of the various classes, the judges, the rules and regulations.

Scissor bite: Having the top teeth just overlapping the lower.

Self: The same colour all over, e.g., the Red Self, known in America as the Solid Red.

Si-Rex: Cornish or Devon Rex with Siamese colouring, i.e., light body and dark points.

Sire: The male parent.

Solid: See Self.

Spaying: Neutering of a female cat.

Spraying: A male cat's habit of micturating all over the place, leaving a most pungent smell around.

Squint: Placement of the eyes so that they look in different directions or look towards the nose. Not now permitted in show Siamese. Also known as Strabismus.

Standard of Points: The characteristics required for a recognised variety, and by which cats are judged.

Stop: A break between the nose and the skull.

Striations: Stripes.

Stripes: Markings as in tabby cats.

Stud: Male cat used for breeding.

Stud book: A record of breeding.

Stumpy: Having a stump of a tail, and frequently found in litters of true Manx.

Svelte: Long and lithe in the body, as in the Siamese.

Tabby: The name given to a cat with definite markings. Said to have been derived from a similarly marked material first made in the Attabiy quarter in old Baghdad.

Tapered: A long slim tail coming to a point, as in the "foreign" varieties.

Telegony: The supposed influence that a previous mating or mismating of a queen can have on the subsequent progeny. This is quite untrue.

Thumb mark: The marking on the ears of the Tabby-point Siamese.

Ticking: The two or three bands of colour seen on each hair of the Abyssinians.

Tipping: Contrasting colouring at the ends of the hairs, as in the Chinchillas.

Transfer: On change of ownership a registered cat must be transferred officially by application, and payment of a small fee, to the appropriate registering body.

Tri-colour: Having three distinct colours in the coat.

Type: The essential characteristics distinguishing a breed. Also used to describe the particular facial bone structure of a breed, e.g., the long nose, and muzzle of the Siamese, and the short nose and broad muzzle of the "Persian" long-hairs.

U.C.F: United Cat Fanciers (America).

Undercoat: The soft hair lying below the hair of cats with double coats.

Undershot jaw: A lower jaw protruding further than the upper.

Vaccination: Inocculation, usually against feline infectious enteritis.

Virus: Minute organism which may cause disease.

Wedge-shaped: The head shape required in some varieties, such as the Siamese.

Whip tail: A long thin tapering tail.

Wrinkle: Loosely folded skin, for example on the face of Peke-face Red cats.

Whiskers: Long thick bristles protruding from the face of the cat.

Zoonoses: Diseases that can affect both humans and cats, such as tuberculosis and ringworm; these are very few in number.

Index

The index does not contain breed references in photograph captions, which come generally within the relevant article. Colour plates are listed at the front of the book. Where a page number refers to a whole article, it is given in italics.